SECURING THE PAST

We all have a stake in the past and in its tangible preservation, and we trust professionals to preserve our cultural heritage for the future. However, the concept and practice of restoration in all its forms are entangled in many contemporary theoretical debates and problems. This book is the first concerted effort to examine together the linked philosophies of the different arts of preserving and uncovering the past: the restoration of buildings, conservation of works of art, and editing of literary works to retrieve their original or intended texts. By investigating a series of recent crises in each of these areas, *Securing the Past* shows how their underlying justifications relate closely to one another. Paul Eggert demonstrates that they have been philosophically undermined by postmodern theories, and finally points the way to a new future for the past.

PAUL EGGERT is Professor of English at the University of New South Wales at ADFA. He has published a number of books and articles on English literature and textual studies, and has edited scholarly editions of D. H. Lawrence and Rolf Boldrewood.

SECURING THE PAST

Conservation in Art, Architecture and Literature

PAUL EGGERT

CAMBRIDGE
UNIVERSITY PRESS

CAMBRIDGE UNIVERSITY PRESS

Cambridge, New York, Melbourne, Madrid, Cape Town, Singapore, São Paulo, Delhi

Cambridge University Press
The Edinburgh Building, Cambridge, CB2 8RU, UK

Published in the United States of America by Cambridge University Press, New York

www.cambridge.org
Information on this title: www.cambridge.org/9780521725910

First published 2009

Printed in the United Kingdom at the University Press, Cambridge

A catalogue record for this publication is available from the British Library

Library of Congress Cataloguing in Publication data
Eggert, Paul.
Securing the past : conservation in art, architecture, and literature / Paul Eggert.
p.   cm.
Includes bibliographical references and index.
ISBN 978-0-521-89808-9 (hardback) – ISBN 978-0-521-72591-0 (pbk.)
1. Arts and history.   2. Historic preservation.   3. Authenticity (Philosophy)   I. Title.
NX180.H57E38   2008
363.6'9 – dc22   2008035216

ISBN 978-0-521-89808-9 hardback
ISBN 978-0-521-72591-0 paperback

Contents

List of illustrations

Preface

This book has been brewing, and periodically bubbling, in my mind for quite some time. I first gave a talk in 1992 comparing the restoration of paintings to the scholarly editing of classic literary works. That was the beginning of an alertness to the problems, in both practice and theory, of what is involved when professional practitioners try to secure the past, whether in tangible three-dimensional form in museums, art galleries and historic houses or in the recovery by scholarly editors of the corrupted texts of literary works and historical documents from the past.

For many years, my main field as an academic has been scholarly editing. But I have frequently found myself looking over my shoulder, wondering whether or how the methods and ideas that I found to be second nature mapped to the other restoration arts. Could they all be understood in terms of one another? Posing that question was the genesis of this book.

I had some success in bringing representatives of the various areas together to discuss some of the issues they had in common at a conference at the Humanities Research Centre in Canberra in 1994. That occasion resulted in a collection of essays called *The Editorial Gaze* (1998). Naturally enough, the contributors tended not to stray too far from their specialist areas. So, although the volume contains some excellent essays, I still felt that my question had not been sufficiently answered.

Crises and the odd disaster in restoration energise this book. Less spectacularly, conservators and editors have repeatedly found their approach to their work being subtly undermined by paradigm shifts in wider cultural thinking as they laboured at their very long-term projects. Witnessing this happen during the 1990s and having occasion, in 2000 as a visiting professor at the University of Washington in Seattle, to give public lectures on the topic, I finally realised that I *had* to write this book.

I could not have done it alone. An important stimulus for my thinking about art and its presentation has been the conversations on these matters that I have been having with my artist-wife Anna Eggert for nearly twenty years now. I have many other people to thank as well, including: Michael Bogle, Curator, Hyde Park Barracks, Sydney; James Broadbent, formerly Senior Curator, Historic Houses Trust of New South Wales; Lynn Collins, Curator, Hyde Park Barracks; Scott Carlin, Curator, Elizabeth Bay House, Sydney; David Evans, Property Manager at Uppark, Petersfield, Hampshire; Bob Griffin, History Curator, Royal British Columbia Museum; and Megan Martin, Librarian, Historic Houses Trust of New South Wales, 'Lyndhurst', Glebe.

I am grateful to those friends of mine who read and commented on the evolving parts of this book or who in other ways have contributed to its ideas, especially Trevor Howard-Hill, John Jowett and the two anonymous readers of the manuscript for Cambridge, and also Virginia Blain, Andrew Brown, David Greetham, Colin Hearfield, †Harold Love, Roger Osborne, Philip Pettit, Peter Shillingsburg, Chris Tiffin, Elizabeth Webby, Thérèse Weber and James L. W. West, III.

My postgraduate and honours students at my home institution in Canberra have, over the years, sharpened my appreciation of the ideas presented here. I thank them. I also thank the graduate students in the Textual Theory class at the University of Washington in 2000, and my colleagues there, especially, Raimonda Modiano, Fritz Levy, Leroy Searle, and Sandra Kroupa at the Allen Library. The Centre for Textual Studies at De Montfort University in Leicester, where I had visiting appointments in 2006 and 2007, provided a welcoming environment to the thinking in this book. I thank its director at the time, Peter Shillingsburg, for his hospitality; and I wish to recognise publicly his intellectual generosity and unflagging enthusiasm for the common endeavour, qualities that have helped and sustained many scholars in the field, including me. And lastly I have learnt from the various editorial projects (and friendships) that I have been involved in since the 1980s: I thank those many collaborators who have stimulated my thinking in ways, perhaps, of which they have not been aware. They may see some of the fruits of the encounter in the final chapters here.

In Canberra, I would like to thank my academic colleagues for their encouragement and support, and Tessa Wooldridge and Susan Cowan for research assistance. At Cambridge University Press, Linda Bree championed the project, Maartje Scheltens and Joanna Breeze shepherded it through production, and my copy-editor Frances Brown eliminated a range of tiny errors and inconsistencies: I thank all four. I also gratefully acknowledge the financial support for the project provided by the Australian Research Council and the periods of study leave extended to me by the University of New South Wales, without which this book could not have been written.

Only Chapter 10 has appeared previously in much the same form: in a special issue of *Library Trends* in 2007 on preservation and conservation, although it is expanded here. In other places in the book, material has been adapted from other of my essays, listed in the Bibliography. I thank the editors of the various publications. Every effort has been made to seek permission from the appropriate parties to reproduce the illustrations in this book. In a few cases efforts to identify or contact them have failed; such owners are invited to contact the Press.

CHAPTER I

Introduction

[T]he past is where we come from . . . Yet we can no more slip back to the past than leap forward to the future. Save in imaginative reconstruction, yesterday is forever barred to us; we have only attenuated memories and fragmentary chronicles of prior experience and can only dream of escaping the confines of the present. But in recent years, such nostalgic dreams have become almost habitual, if not epidemic.

(David Lowenthal, 1985)[1]

World-withdrawal and world-decay can never be undone. The works are no longer the same as they once were. It is they themselves, to be sure, that we encounter there, but they themselves are gone by.

(Martin Heidegger, mid-1930s)[2]

Everyone is interested in the past, or at least everyone old enough to have begun to reflect on their own past. The interest may take almost any form. We can all fill in different details of the scenario. Here are mine. I have a friend in his mid-fifties, a keen surfer when he was younger, who collects surfboards, some going back decades to pre-fibreglass days and made of wood. He has developed a way of mounting them on the walls of his garage. They are gradually infiltrating the house. He can talk knowledgeably about the changes in their technology over the years. And he has ridden all of them.

Everyone knows someone, a friend or uncle, who restores old machinery, steam trains perhaps or vintage cars, or who deliberately drives a restored sedan such as he or she drove when younger, despite having to double-clutch when changing gears. *Or*, who would like to do so but has chosen instead to buy a so-called *retro* vehicle, a new Mini Cooper or Volkswagen Beetle perhaps, that picks up the design style of the earlier (and therefore authentic) vehicle from the 1950s or 1960s but has all the latest gadgetry in the engine compartment. The authentic starts yesterday, it seems, and only improves as it works backwards in time. The past must have some pastness about it. But, failing that, an alluring aesthetic of the past may serve as well.

But whatever our vehicle, we will probably have found ourselves driving through villages or country towns and being surprised to discover that some nondescript, otherwise unremarkable place has established a museum for itself, recording and celebrating its own history. Its contents will probably be miscellaneous and will have been contributed by the townsfolk. There has, in all likelihood, as yet been no professional curatorship applied to the collection. But there is perhaps a grant application going in soon to some ministry of heritage and culture. Private pasts are one thing, but the past that is held in common must, the townsfolk generally feel, be looked after, be secured.

No matter how far away or how desperate the job might be, the conservation must be done. In November 2006 the *Canberra Times* reported that a 'team of carpenters and conservators planning to restore the historic Mawson's Huts in Antarctica has reached Cape Denison in winds over 100 km/h, a temperature of minus 20 and visibility of just 30 m'. And why? 'Mawson's Huts are the only physical connection back to the period of pioneering Australian Antarctic exploration during the Heroic Era, that is 1911 to 1914.'[3] Recognition of the past brings anxiety with it: to let the physical connection go and to rely only on historical accounts of it is unthinkable to many people (to the Australian Government's Antarctic Division and the Mawson's Huts Foundation, in this case). A memorable past, tangibly preserved, increases the density of the present and proposes a long and somehow more real future, a satisfying continuity. Because we live in bodies, because we are not digital objects, this desire for a physical reassurance of the past is understandable.

Conservation has a similar rationale in the semi-desert. Driving back recently overland the thousand kilometres from Adelaide on the coast in South Australia to Canberra in the mountains south of Sydney, I passed through the now desperately barren Mallee district in northern Victoria. Farming by Europeans has been carried on there since the mid-nineteenth century, but it has always been a risky affair. The soil is generally poor and the rains unreliable. Very big farms were just viable. After World War I large extents of the Mallee were made available for returning soldier-settlers to take up, but generally in allotments that proved too small. The settlements at first grew into small townships. But when most of these new farms gradually failed the townships dwindled; some disappeared entirely; and the remainder have been struggling for some decades. Some are virtually ghost towns now. There has been a drought in this region for several years,

Figure 1.1 Sofala, old gold-mining town, New South Wales, 2007.

and farmers are said to be just walking off the valueless land. The landscape is all shades of brown, and the prevailing winds sweep the surface soils away.

Travellers like me mostly hurry through this massive area aiming to get somewhere else as fast as possible. The roads are straight and flat, and the scenery monotonous. The only things left to attract or divert the traveller are the spring flowers and the history of the place. Brochures have been prepared and are liberally distributed in cafés and petrol stations. They trumpet early, local innovations in various kinds of farming and irrigating machinery. And, of course, the old buildings. At Torrita on the Mallee Highway there is a 'small, corrugated iron hall [that] is National Trust listed', as the brochure says. That is all there is worth looking at in Torrita, a tiny settlement. I only glanced at it as I drove by. I did not stop: I have seen any number of corrugated iron buildings in the smaller country towns, where, often lacking money for new investments that would reshape the town, preservation comes for free. What has been built is not removed unless it falls down, and sometimes not even then. (See Figure 1.1.) Underbool has a 'Pioneer Memorial, a Mallee Roller

Figure 1.2 Kow Plains Station, Cowangie, Victoria, 2006.

and the replica of the train once used to cart salt from the Pink Lakes. The cemetery gates are a real point of interest.' One's heart sinks. But I did stop at Cowangie: its Kow Plains Station, a farm first leased from the Crown in 1859, has been the subject of a recent restoration. (See Figure 1.2.)

One does not pay to go in at a turnstile, for there is no-one to pay. The property is not locked. There is no-one there. It is utterly windswept. One struggles to orient oneself to the non-existent aesthetic of the place. The buildings are of a drop-log construction: cypress pine logs have been dropped into slots formed from pairs of sturdy vertical beams rammed at intervals into the earth. The homestead is said to be one of the few remaining ones in this rough pioneering style still standing on its original site. Victorian government Public Heritage Grants in 2001 and 2002 paid for the building to be reroofed and the exterior and interior walls to be restored, as well as the collapsed cookhouse to be rebuilt, mainly from original materials (see Figure 1.3). There is, as yet, almost nothing *in* the buildings and without full-time custodians there cannot be. The buildings have no ceilings, nor are the interior timber walls lined with plaster or packed with mud. Such as it is and preserved for the future,

Figure 1.3 Kow Plains Station outbuilding: cookhouse interior. Kow Plains Station, Cowangie, Victoria, 2006.

Kow Plains Station simply stands – that is all – silent testimony to a long, ultimately failed effort to sustain a farming life in a hostile Mallee landscape.

Living history

Let us change continents: the scale changes with it, there are some thousands of people present, and the past has become what is called living history.[4] The scene is Colonial Williamsburg in Virginia. The tourist infrastructure here is extensive and well oiled. One pays to go in. On offer is a series of little dramatic re-enactments by actors in period costume in rooms of buildings mostly recreated in the 1930s. Little tricks of language supplement those of dress to encourage visitors to 'see' the scene in 1774, scored by the history lessons of the guides, so that the reality of the buildings as a 1930s recreation (which is what the precinct *is*) is left behind. Patriotic piety hangs heavy, and the day comes to a stirring end with fifes, drums and cannon, heavily saluting America's presidents, one by one.

There is very little emphasis, as one tours the precinct, on whether a recreated building is original: that would, if dwelt upon, interfere with or complicate the 'historical' playlet on offer, in which the visitor, despite modern clothing, is occasionally an actor. It is not that an attempt is made to hide the unoriginality, but that it gradually comes not to matter.

In the Bruton parish church (established in 1715 and continuously in use since then) a wigged and costumed actor plays preacher, giving a Bible reading from the King James version – a complex bit of prose from 2 Corinthians on the day I attended. Then he reads an authentic eighteenth-century sermon whose balanced and often periodic sentences defeat parts of the congregation with their unfamiliar orotundity. Prior to the reading, another actor with a good voice sings each line of an old hymn and pauses for the response – a repetition of the line by the congregation. Later, heads drop among the congregation (if that is what we are) as prayers are intoned: there is devoutness here.

And yet it is not a real church service. Everyone present knows it is an act, a playlet: but yet some or many of us are willing participants. Nobody gets up and walks out during the long sermon. Is this a religious experience in an unfamiliar idiom from the past? Or is it make-believe? Or worse, an elaborate joke?

Down the street from the church is the Governor's Palace, built in 1934. It is a painstaking recreation of the original one, which was built on the same spot in the early eighteenth century. An actor is doing a very fair job of impersonating 'Mr' Jefferson (as he is invariably called), giving a political speech, revealing 'his' opinions, and then bravely answering questions from the audience in an antique parlance. The audience restricts its questions to things he could have known about or had opinions on in 1774: this they do without being told, although they cannot affect the same speech patterns.

Another kind of impersonation has been carried on at Colonial Williamsburg in its brief past in some book and pamphlet publications. In 1941, after the decade or so of recreating Colonial Williamsburg was mainly finished, a history of the place appeared. But which place? Colonial Williamsburg of the 1930s or colonial Williamsburg of the eighteenth century in the period leading up to the Revolution of 1776? The prose runs the two together. In physical appearance and in diction, the book gives a strong impression of having been written and printed in the eighteenth century.[5] (See Figures 1.4 and 1.5.) The Caslon font, the orthography (note the capitalised nouns and the use of the long *s*), the meandering periodic sentences and the elaborate courtesies of address indicate that a knowing pretence

A

BRIEF & TRUE REPORT

CONCERNING

Williamſburg

in VIRGINIA:

Being an Account of the moſt important
Occurrences in that Place from its
firſt Beginning to the preſent Time.

TO which is added an Appendix compoſed
of Records and Works from which this
Account is drawn; with Copies of the
Acts for building the Capitol and the
City of *Williamſburg*, and its Charter.

By *RUTHERFOORD GOODWIN*,
An Inhabitant *of the* Place.

A third Edition reviſ'd & enlarg'd by the Author.
Reiſſued now with ſome ſmall Alterations.

WILLIAMSBURG:
Printed for the *Colonial Williamſburg* Founda-
tion, by *Auguſt* and *Charles Dietz* on their Preſs in
Cary Street at *Richmond, Virginia.* MCM, LXXII.

Figure 1.4 Frontispiece and title-page, Rutherfoord Goodwin, *A Brief and True Report Concerning Williamsburg in Virginia* (3rd edn, 1972).

of authenticity based on imitation has been executed with extraordinary diligence. It is a game, yes, but one the author is in love with, one that is half-believed to be real. 'Mr' Jefferson's speechmaking at the Governor's Palace and the church service have bibliographic forebears in capital C Colonial Williamsburg.

The illustrations reproduced here come from a revised printing of 1972; even the copyright page has been antiqued but legal requirements apparently required some concessions in font. This 1972 production is therefore not a fake: it is a would-be facsimile of a fake that simultaneously confesses what it is up to. As a bibliographical object, it is a strange fish. Both object and text raise questions about the ways in which the past may be legitimately addressed, legitimately presented in public: this, in general terms, is the subject matter of the present book. It is not about the *writing* of history but about its retrieval through one form of restoration or another. In particular it is about the forms of it that we trust trained professionals to carry out on our behalf: the restoration of buildings and paintings, and the editing of works of classic literature.

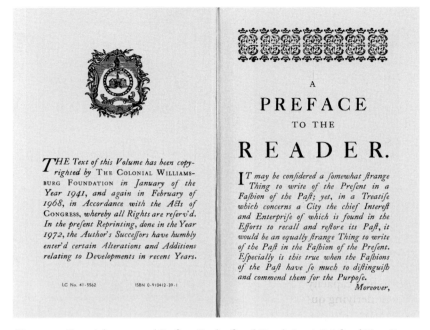

THE Text of this Volume has been copy-righted by THE COLONIAL WILLIAMS-BURG FOUNDATION *in January of the Year 1941, and again in February of 1968, in Accordance with the Acts of* CONGRESS, *whereby all Rights are reserv'd. In the present Reprinting, done in the Year 1972, the Author's Successors have humbly enter'd certain Alterations and Additions relating to Developments in recent Years.*

LC No. 41-5562   ISBN 0-910412-39-1

A

PREFACE

TO THE

READER.

IT may be considered a somewhat strange Thing to write of the Present in a Fashion of the Past; yet, in a Treatise which concerns a City the chief Interest and Enterprise of which is found in the Efforts to recall and restore its Past, it would be an equally strange Thing to write of the Past in the Fashion of the Present. Especially is this true when the Fashions of the Past have so much to distinguish and commend them for the Purpose.

Moreover,

Figure 1.5 Copyright page and Preface, Rutherfoord Goodwin, *A Brief and True Report Concerning Williamsburg in Virginia* (3rd edn, 1972).

The authenticity of these undertakings, of the pasts they present, is a complex and curious matter. This book deals with the question of what authenticity is, as well as with the associated questions of what forgery and fakery are: how they may be distinguished from the real thing. And the question of authorship, a highly contested one in recent decades, raises its head. The roles of agency and time loom large in the answers this book has to offer. But its central subject is the kind of history that restorers offer us. This book is about how we might better understand it and about how the restorers might better understand the philosophies behind what they do.

The revival of the past

I have presented the examples above of preservation and restoration in the form of anecdotes for a good reason. In the 1980s and 1990s a number of remarkable studies appeared that took the past, and contemporary fasci-nation with it, as their subject. David Lowenthal's *The Past Is a Foreign Country* (1985), Raphael Samuels's *Theatres of Memory* (1994) and Tom

Griffiths's *Hunters and Collectors: The Antiquarian Imagination in Australia* (1996) were among the most notable.[6] In one way or another, implicitly or explicitly, each rejected J. H. Plumb's famous thesis from the late 1960s: *The Death of the Past*. Partly these studies were made possible by the broadening of the kinds of documentary evidence that historians had gradually come to see as legitimate (including photographs, oral histories, films, even historic villages). Partly, post-1968 literary and cultural theory had questioned the very existence of historical fact as a securely objective thing standing over and apart from the historian. It was being seen instead as created by or implicated in the historian's framing discourses.[7] This had the effect of putting popular and professional forms of interest in the past on an equal footing – as being themselves, proper objects of historical enquiry. Suddenly, the whole world – in looking back at its past, both now and in previous ages – was the historian's oyster.

Lowenthal's and Samuels's marvellous panoramas of past-directed activity opened up a fertile field. Lowenthal's sources are eclectic, and he is tolerant of what he sees. But his failure to adjudicate the adequacy or truth-telling capacity of the historical endeavours and positions he surveys leaves underlying questions naggingly unanswered. The present book takes its cue from this absence.

Fascination with the past is both popular and professional. I happen to live in both camps, which makes it difficult to find a reliable position outside what Lowenthal shows to be a general scramble to secure the past. The past is all around us: so anecdote is unavoidable. But it is not enough, though for a long while it has been made to seem so. And I am not expert in all the areas this book has to cover. Inevitably I must stray outside my field if I am to address the subject at all as one held in common. I believe the risk is worth it.

This is the first book to bring the arts of restoration together to examine their linked, underlying philosophies.[8] Some practitioners would deny the existence of a philosophy underlying what they do at all, thinking it better to keep their head down and simply get on with the job of restoration in hand, preferring to solve the technical difficulties by reference to the traditions of their professional practice. But even when the professional pursuits are considered reflectively and critically, they are normally considered from within their own narrow cells. This book proposes to end that insularity, to open up some communicating corridors.[9]

To that end, it brings right out into the open a continuing paradox that is normally shuffled under the carpet: the mutual incompatibility of, on the one hand, traditional methodologies of restoration and, on the other, postmodern theories of culture. Awareness of the mediated nature of knowledge, including knowledge of the past, was one of the great breakthroughs of the post-'68 theory movement. It helped to clarify how we *make* sense of things. It helped us see how knowledge is implicated in the making, and vice versa. The allied fact of the cultural relativity of knowledge was brought home by the emergence of multicultural societies during the 1990s in most Western countries. However, the thoroughgoing scepticism about the objectivity of knowledge – about the possibility of it – which results from taking these related awarenesses to heart can disable the taking of action, can render helpless those charged with the professional presentation of the past.

Accordingly, this book works through a commentary on examples of restoration in the three fields where accepted methodologies have been challenged by a crisis of one kind or another. Failures in and contradictions between the fundamental positions about the nature of the thing being restored emerge. Tracking down the nature of the problem at the level of theory leads me, in the final chapter, back to the source. I propose there a solution: a revival through adaptation of the concept of the work that was displaced, post-'68, in favour of *text* and *discourse*. Incorporating the dimensions of agency and time into the concept via the negative dialectics of Theodor Adorno and the semiotics of C. S. Peirce provides the basis of the approach. It will, I believe, afford a clarifying grounding for practices of restoration that profess to tell the truth about – to present – the past.

This book is interested, then, in historical witness, especially that offered by physical objects from the past, about which precise questions can be fairly asked. It starts with broader fields of historical endeavour – the conservation and curation of historic churches and houses – whose witness is often intensely felt by visitors but is quite generalised. It is important to analyse it at the practical and also at the philosophical level so that the authenticity that visitors yearn for, and the options of conservators and curators, can be better understood. The book then moves to the more finely honed – the conservation and attribution of paintings and, finally, to the scholarly editing of literary and historical documents – where knowledge of the past is highly focussed by concepts of authorship, authenticity and textual authority. None of these concepts is simple or uncontested. Crises, scandals and shifts in paradigm have dogged each of them since the 1980s. Reviewing these intellectual flashpoints comparatively, in the light of one another rather than exclusively from within their own areas of study, reconfigures the representing of the past, acknowledges the tinge of anxiety that *securing* it always has.

STALEMATE: EDITING THE PAST

That, in summary outline, is where this book is going. In order to establish rather than only sketch its rationale another circling of the allied sets of problems found in the restoration disciplines needs now to take place. But this time it is a more focussed one.

Consider the dilemma of the scholarly editor. It is one I have faced myself on several occasions. Typically, editors have to establish reading texts of literary, philosophical, biblical or other works. The works chosen for this treatment are generally those held to be culturally important enough to be worth the considerable effort that the initial identification, comparison and analysis of their variant forms requires. But to stand between the reader and the often confusing evidence of multiple or incomplete versions of works can be like vertigo. You know you are about to save one form of a particular line or phrase for the continuing attention of readers, but by doing so you will consign the alternative forms to the outer darkness. Yet you also know that, from a point of view other than your own, the alternative readings may be richer, or more revealing, or they may respect the author's right to control his or her own meanings when you have, on very good grounds, decided to respect instead the textual forms that generations of readers have encountered. Or, of course, as is more usually the case, you may have adopted the opposite approach. But you have to go one way or the other.

The design of your edition will force you to sacrifice many variant readings to retrieve the few. You can, at best, grant some percentage of the sacrificed ones a half-life of recognition by recording them in tables and other apparatus, which some dedicated readers will consult. As you do this, you ask yourself, for instance, whether you are *sure* that it is one poem – one literary work – that you are dealing with here, not two that share similar, reworked lines of verse. Or, if it is a nineteenth-century novel that you are editing whose corrected proofs are lost, you ask yourself: *Who* wrote this weak phrase that appears in the first edition but is not in the manuscript? Was it an in-house editor, the compositor typesetting the expected rather than the actual phrase, or was it indeed the author who was revising, but on a bad day? In such situations, making decisions on the run – editing by the seat of your pants, as it is sometimes called – soon becomes an uncomfortable experience.

Recovering in detail the history of the writing, revision and production of the work being edited radically limits any temptation to whimsicality. But it does not answer the underlying, more philosophical questions that lie insidiously in wait as you try to make sense of your editorial methods.

Appeal to the criterion of final authorial intention has, in Anglo-American editing, traditionally provided an idealist solution for editorial anxiety. But all editors experience the fluidity of the textual evidence to which they are usually obliged to give a static form. Lifting their heads from the textual microscopy of their laborious work, editors find that, meanwhile, cultural theory has moved on, calling into question their whole empirical effort. Explaining textual genesis by reference to the social discourses that the text exposes, rather than in terms of the capacities and motivations of gifted or inspired individuals, has been the prevailing one since the 1980s. So does it matter any longer whether we can tell who wrote the phrase, whose variant forms one is, as an editor, tussling with? By extension, does it matter any longer whether we can tell who wrote the whole work? And what is the meaning, anyway, of this category, *the work*? What are its boundaries?

In trying to answer these questions I begin by recognising the categorical difference between editing and restoration. Scholarly editors do not physically alter the original documents that witness the work's texts. In comparison, conservators of historic houses, paintings and sculptures make changes to the physical objects themselves. The editorial surgery can range from the gentle to the heroic. The standard according to which the restoration or conservation is performed needs to be cogently argued. That is where the trouble normally starts. The preceding research may be (and nowadays often is) breathtakingly comprehensive. But that will not stop the argumentation from oscillating, as it characteristically does, between a respect for the aesthetic functioning of the object on the one hand as against its function as historical witness on the other.

Walter Pater put his finger on this a long time ago:

there are two legitimate views or motives in the restoration of ancient sculpture, the antiquarian and the aesthetic . . . the former limiting itself to the bare presentation of what actually remains of the ancient work, braving all shock to living eyes from the mutilated nose or chin; while the latter, the aesthetic method, requires that, with the least possible addition or interference, by the most skilful living hand procurable, the object shall be made to please, or at least content the living eye seeking enjoyment and not a bare fact of science, in the spectacle of ancient art.

As an example of the aesthetic approach, he refers to 'the visitor to Munich [who] actually sees the marbles of Aegina, as restored after a model by the tasteful hand of Thorwaldsen'.[10]

What was 'actual' in Bertel Thorwaldsen's restoration for the Munich Glyptotek is a pretty point. (King Ludwig I of Bavaria had bought the ruin in 1811 during a visit to the Greek island and carried it off as a cultural treasure.) But even if, by great good luck, Thorwaldsen had got his restoration of the stones exactly right, he would not have reproduced the original. As Heidegger remarked in the mid-1930s (see the epigraph to this chapter), works do not stand still. For one thing, the world changes around them, and for another they are not *only* physical objects. What they originally disclosed is gradually lost sight of. The later act of conceptualising them as, say, religious or artistic objects co-opts them into frames of reference or into discourses that change what, in an important sense, they are.

Nevertheless, the professional question remains: *how*, if they are not to be put into storage and ignored, are the objects to be presented? Our postmodern scepticism, which in some important ways derives from Heidegger, does not help us to answer this question. Granting Heidegger's case, how do we respect their past-ness even if their meaning *has* changed? Does modern museology offer an answer? What view of knowledge do museums' practices imply? What is *their* history?

Museums, history and Kant

The nineteenth was a historicising century. Antiquarianism gave way to archaeology, philology and Humboldtian science. The modern discipline of history grew up in response to Leopold von Ranke's call for document-based analysis of the past. And museums learned the explanatory value of chronology. In 1806, Alexandre Lenoir articulated the principles of the modern museum for his Museum of French Monuments in Paris. He displayed the materials in chronological order, century by century, so that the museum would both educate and also serve as a sort of three-dimensional encyclopaedia, thus extending the Enlightenment tradition.

Recent commentators, influenced by the writings of Michel Foucault, Jacques Lacan and others, have not been slow to point out the effects on the viewer of how museums present historical, archaeological and ethnographic specimens and objects. Their placement in the museum wraps them up in a relationship to the intended viewer.

They have traditionally been (and to some extent still are) offered as prologues or evolutionary forebears of the viewer in the enlightened European present. This now old-fashioned mode objectifies them as primitive or exotic things, on which we viewers exercise our privileged gaze.[11] Looking at them as objects positions us as coherent subjects. Therefore the museum, according to Donald Preziosi, can be seen as 'an optical instrument' that presents the past as something 'the present needs to legitimize, naturalize and sustain itself'.[12] The Western natural museum's geographical 'other' – the animals, plants, landscapes and peoples of Asia and Africa – has been appropriated in a subtle complicity that, since the 1980s, has become the subject of trenchant postcolonialist criticism.[13]

The *art* museum comes out nearly as badly in this critique. The art object, with its chronological label, plays its part in the art-historical account of artists' progressive solution of the technical problems of visually representing the world. But this account has had its effects in naturalising one kind of vision. We cannot now look at a scene without seeing it perspectivally. (Byzantine painters, in contrast, sometimes used an inverse perspective.) The Renaissance rediscovery of perspectival illusion positioned the viewer in front of the painting, able to take in the whole scene in one perfectly ordered, god-like gaze. Thus the viewer-as-subject was confirmed in his or her coherence by the act of looking.

This argument is an extension of Kant's enormously influential philosophy of the 1780s and 1790s. For Kant, the make-up of our minds drives us to see design in nature, and mankind inevitably at the centre of that design. Therefore the act of looking at paintings exercised our aesthetic faculty, improving us morally as it gave us pleasure. The idealist extension – that aesthetic appreciation helped to confirm us as unique individuals, as organic wholes (like the artworks themselves) – would saturate thinking about art and literature in the nineteenth century. The authenticating source of the artwork (the original artist, workshop or primitive culture) was necessarily elsewhere. The work's existence was, then, partly ideal. It was sustained by the art-historical narrative of its own coming into being.

For Kant, the physical frame of a painting was merely secondary: by virtue of its 'charm' it could 'enliven the representation . . . thereby awakening and sustaining attention to the object itself' – the work of art.[14] In his essay 'Parergon' (1987 in English), Jacques Derrida deconstructed the claim,[15] and others have taken his lead in generalising the so-called rhetoric of the frame: 'If', Wolfgang Ernst comments, 'the work of art comes into existence only by being re-presented, exhibited, it is inextricably bound to its frames of reference.'[16]

Far from acting as a neutral frame for the works, then, the museum participates in their meaning. The narrative coherence that was imposed upon the fragmentary and scattered stones from Aegina, and again for the Phygalian and the Elgin Marbles in the British Museum, reflected the contemporary taste for aesthetic unity. Missing parts of the Elgin Marbles were fabricated from plaster casts made from pieces from other collections, and then incorporated.[17] But the rejection by modernist artists of the high level of finish and assumed coherence of nineteenth-century academic painting, and their visual dismantling of the represented object or scene, helped create the conditions for curators, by the 1960s, to take a different approach. Thorvaldsen's restoration (rearranged by Adolf Furtwängler in the 1900s) was overturned and his additions were removed. Fragments could now be presented in the absence of the (fabricated) narrative.

The most recent restoration of Leonardo's *Last Supper* shows this. It was commenced in the 1970s and not finished until 1999. All previous restorations were removed. They had made good the depleted areas so that the fresco could continue to be read as a history painting. Removing them revealed the fragmentary remains of the work as it left Leonardo's hand. They have been joined here and there by transparent and removable watercolour. The fresco was intended to become, after centuries of botched restorations, definitely and only a Leonardo. The purity of this commitment to the absent authenticating source – Leonardo – positions the restoration as a final, if unintended, end-of-century protest against the loss of faith in the author-function (as Foucault had defined the discourse[18]). That shift had been gathering strength during the very decades in which the restoration was taking place.

Except, of course, that there is no evading the clutches of Foucauldian discursivity. The restoration could not, as a neutral editorial practice, *reveal* the ideal presence since it had inevitably participated in advance – as a reading practice – in the very definition of what it means to be 'a Leonardo'. The world into which the fresco first came into being is irretrievably in the past, as Heidegger teaches us. What it means to be 'a Leonardo' has moved on, and on. So here we return to the position reached above, armed but simultaneously disabled by postmodern scepticism. Since the conservator must prevent the painting from crumbling off the wall, what paths are defensible?

The answer this book puts forward comes from keeping the parallels between editing and restoration in mind. In fact, scholarly editing found itself in much the same predicament as these restorations, and at much the same time.

Editing and restoration

This should not be surprising. Both professional fields offer to present – that is, to make present, not just represent – crucial moments of high achievement from the past. Both developed remarkably in methodology in the twentieth century. Both reflect assumptions about knowledge and scientific method that come down from the nineteenth.

As noted above, in editorial practice it is normally seen as essential, as far as possible, that the editor identify the parties responsible for the changes between versions so that informed decisions between competing readings can be made. The techniques of physical bibliography help the editor to reconstruct the history of the production of the work in printed form. In a somewhat parallel way restorers seek evidence of *pentimenti* (revisions) or earlier versions beneath the painted surface, and analyse the build-up of the layers of paint from the so-called ground coat outwards. Attribution is then more soundly based, and catalogues raisonnés, delimiting the boundaries of the artist's *œuvre*, become possible. These parallel the descriptive bibliographies employed by editors. If curators and conservators are archaeologists of the image – if they can make the surface articulate the painting's history – then editors are archaeologists of the printed or written word, of its history of writing and production.

In both areas, it has traditionally been felt that the primary upshot of this considerable effort is to bring forth to the viewing or reading public a restored painting or a reading text of the literary work – the real thing, or as close to it as we can get. Just as, it is believed, accumulations of dirt and varnish should be removed to reveal the painting as it left the artist's hand, so ought editors to aim at recovering the text that the author intended. Through the glass darkly, we can – with conservators' and editors' help – espy the thing itself: the work of literary or painterly art.

Well, *yes*, but then one's scepticism comes into play. This conclusion cannot be true if the cultural-theory argument that I sketched above is correct. There is a stalemate. And we ought to recognise that we have been in it for some time. It impinges on anyone and everyone who is interested in retaining a tangible connection to the past. That is why, in this book, I look for moments of cultural crisis in the restoration arts. From the explosive tension of these moments, I try to grasp and develop the suddenly disclosed fundamentals.

The persistence of the empirical

The empirical pursuits of restoration and scholarly editing, which had formerly operated under the protective umbrella of the Enlightenment subject–object relation, have felt the chill wind of exposure in recent years. But their rigorous standards have maintained for them a certain respect. So, for instance, editorial collations and analysis of variant versions of a work give results that are no less reliable than before. (Indeed they are probably more so, ever since the introduction of the computer.) So, also, does the library catalogue continue its remorseless functioning, though based on the outmoded assumption that authors are authors and that works are works. Scientists continue to report on the way aspects of the 'real' world – on displaced traces of which they gaze in ever more sophisticated ways – function. And computer operating systems continue to rely on hierarchical logics for file-management and in programming, even though such forms of thinking have been diagnosed as at the heart of the Enlightenment problem.

At another level, authors continue to be interviewed and biographies of them written and read in increasing numbers. Readers continue to want guidance from literary critics about what works are best to read and why they are worth reading. (This requires the assumption at least of some commonality as between critic and 'general' reader: the very world that has supposedly been lost.) And, as we have seen, the heritage movement came to its popular peak in the 1980s and remains in healthy shape, offering to put visitors in relation to a living history. New museums (often local ones) and historical re-enactments proliferated in the same period in which the presentation of the past was being cast in cultural theory as irremediably problematic.

Doubtless, cultures have always had internal contradictions but have managed to get by for quite a while in the face of them. Some sort of continuity as between theory and practice is probably desirable nevertheless. A reconfiguring of the ways in which our (formerly positivistic) knowledge-machines *make* (rather than reveal) sense seems to me to be preferable to the stalemate we have.

This book operates, then, within the orbit of this larger problem. It pushes me – as a practitioner – to investigate those fields not normally considered to be relevant to mine but which are philosophically stranded on different parts of the same shore. Crises that each have faced in recent years have exposed the fault-lines of their practice. Their contradictions deserve to be exposed and need to be searchingly examined and compared. But empirical practice will not be patronised in this book, as so often it has been, as a mere reflection of the Enlightenment subject–object relation. The late twentieth-century critique of it is granted from the start. The challenge lies in Hans-Georg Gadamer's observation that the 'one thing common to all contemporary criticism of historical objectivism or positivism' is 'the insight that the so-called subject of knowledge has the same mode of being as the object'.[19] In the arts of restoration that would secure the past, *what* can be built upon this apparently non-existent foundation?

Contradictions between assumed theory and actual practice offer fertile ground, not just for those familiar, sadder-but-wiser exposures of our epistemological illusions, but for redefinitions and new directions. If some ground is to be found for our dealings with a past not seen as entirely of our own discursive invention, then the *work*, I will be arguing, has to be detached from its traditionally idealist moorings. An understanding of its semiotic life must be refined. I am not the first to call for this. But the attentiveness to empirical detail that conservators, curators and scholarly editors bring to their pursuits seems to me a promising place to try to find a new kind of enlightenment – one that reports different conclusions from those afforded by the fast-moving theory movement of recent decades. That enlightenment is what this book seeks. It is a search for a new way of understanding curatorial, conservatorial and editorial dealings with works from the past. Emphasis falls upon the agencies of their production within what I call the production–consumption spectrum of the life of the work. And balancing this emphasis on agency is a concern to conceptualise, in twenty-first-century professional practice, what John Ruskin unforgettably called the 'golden stain of time'.[20]

CHAPTER 2

The witness of historic buildings and the restoration of the churches

[S]he passed down the gallery whose floor was laid with oak trees sawn across. Rows of chairs with all their velvets faded stood ranged against the wall holding their arms out for Elizabeth, for James, for Shakespeare it might be, for Cecil, who never came. The sight made her gloomy. She unhooked the rope that fenced them off. She sat on the Queen's chair; she opened a manuscript book lying on Lady Betty's table; she stirred her fingers in the aged rose leaves; she brushed her short hair with King James' silver brushes; she bounced up and down upon his bed (but no King would ever sleep there again, for all Louise's new sheets) and pressed her cheek against the worn silver counterpane that lay upon it. But everywhere were little lavender bags to keep the moth out and printed notices, 'Please do not touch,' which, though she had put them there herself, seemed to rebuke her. The house was no longer hers entirely, she sighed. It belonged to time now; to history; was past the touch and control of the living . . . The great wings of silence beat up and down the empty house.

(Virginia Woolf, 1928)[1]

[T]he word *restoration* . . . means the most total destruction which a building can suffer . . . a destruction accompanied with false description of the thing destroyed . . . it is *impossible*, as impossible as to raise the dead, to restore anything that has ever been great or beautiful in architecture . . . that spirit which is given only by the hand and eye of the workman can never be recalled . . . Do not then let us talk of restoration. The thing is a Lie from beginning to end.

(John Ruskin, 1849)[2]

Scholarly editions deal with versions of literary works, both original and revised. Artists sketch their composition right onto the canvas but may later change their minds, as X-radiography often shows. Architects draw and then revise their plans according to the response their early ideas receive from their clients. None of this is surprising. But, as Stewart Brand observes in *How Buildings Learn* (1994), we ought to get into the habit of thinking that buildings get revised after they are built and that, indeed, revision is their normal state of affairs. If buildings are very long-lived (most are not), they mature at the hands of attentive owners. Owners co-evolve with their buildings: 'We shape our buildings around our routines, loving the fit when it becomes intimate and sure.'³ In a sense, as we shall see in later chapters, this agency of inhabitants within buildings parallels the agency of restorers of and (despite themselves) *in* paintings, and of editors of and in editions.

As owners gradually sort out what aspects of the building's dynamics might be made more efficient and pleasing, changes are made. What does not work is eliminated. There are constraints: the site is not generally changeable, the structure is the most expensive element to revise and might survive fifty years without demolition or major change (though Brand says thirty years is the average). The outer skin of the building, on the other hand, may be changed every twenty years. (For example, commercial buildings have to be updated – especially their façade – if they are to maintain parity with the changing appearance of the rest of the street, thus supporting the building's rental value.) The services will need replacing every fifteen to twenty years because of breakdown and changes in technology, and the space plan within the building will on average be altered every five to seven years. And then furniture is shifted at will. All is in a slower or faster state of change. If adaptability fails because it has become too expensive, and if repurposing (such as warehouses being altered to become apartments) is not practical, then the building will be demolished, whether sooner or later. Buildings that survive are those that go on working for their inhabitants.

Vernacular buildings constructed without formal plans tend, functionally and structurally, to embrace what has already proven itself, usually with some adaptation. They are in this sense folkloric,⁴ whereas buildings that materialise a documented architectural intention ask to be read within the domain of aesthetics. Such buildings, which usually aim to solve a design problem with some measure of originality, are *works*. But *works* and what in fact works over time are two different things. So Brand calls for a 'transition from image architecture to process architecture . . . from the certainties of controllable things in space to the self-organizing complexities of an endlessly raveling and unraveling skein of relationships over time. Buildings have lives of their own.'⁵

Brand advocates the study of before-and-after photographs of buildings, both internally and externally, so that architects may learn to design for anticipated change over the lifetime of a building – to think of the

building diachronically – rather than contenting themselves with the aesthetics of the frozen present. Architectural history is a derivative of art
history, Brand argues. It focuses on style. Building history, if it were systematically pursued, would focus on use over time. The dichotomy shapes
the discussion in this chapter where a more sympathetic attitude will be
entertained towards our instinct for connectedness with the past than is
possible with museum villages such as Colonial Williamsburg, even though,
in truth, both are two sides of the one coin. The name of the coin is the
material object.

The final use for a tiny percentage of buildings is as historic-house museums. In them, change seems to stop. In Dickens's *Great Expectations* (1861),
Miss Havisham's Satis House is their avatar; and the great house in Virginia
Woolf's *Orlando* (see epigraph) is an early registration of a house, open to
the public, from which life has fled. The implications of accepting the
metaphor 'life' for a house are discussed below; but in the two novels an
artificial stoppage of that life is brought about. The house is maintained at
a particular point in time, forever looking backwards into the time when
it was 'alive'. In this sense historic-house museums are ghosts, *revenants*.
We should never have too many of them. But their having been there
for so long – in a three-dimensional materiality – *is* important for they
potentially give our embodied lives a sense of chronological amplitude,
of connectedness with a continuous history of domestic, civic or grander
living than our own.

I use the term *embodied* life deliberately. Place is fundamental to it. If we
are fortunate as we grow up, our childhood and adolescence roots us in a
place, that is, in a variety of locales that we never forget, for our young lives
are intertwined in them. Place connects us, by this means, with the other
people there. Bonds are forged. We are scarcely aware that the process is
happening. In this way, place operates as a close cousin of the moral sense,
which it helps awaken in us. Return to those earlier locales as an adult can
be something of a pilgrimage, a regathering of faded memories – of the
core (we may think) of a subsequently dispersed self. Being there again, in
or at the place, is for most people a far more powerful stimulant of memory
and imagination than just thinking about it.

Everyone has an individual past. The small but real imaginative leap
from interest in *it* to an interest in a shared, social and cultural one is a
transition that very many of us make. So people get involved in campaigns
to support local heritage and conservation initiatives. There is a new one
in the paper nearly every week. A predictable scenario – the lobby group of

concerned citizens squares off against commercial development interests –
plays itself out repeatedly. If and when such places are established as historic
sites, they become the destination points of secular pilgrimage. We go along
because we have, in advance, an intuitive sense that they will expand our
life by pointing to (and to a limited extent will embody) an elongated past.
In its difference from our own modern ones the historic building will, we
think, stimulate our imagination into a satisfying enlargement and thus,
by contrast, into a new sense of the present.

The crucial matter (if I am right about the importance of place) is
that a different, grander, finer, more dramatic or heroic, or a humbler life
was actually lived there. We need to know that *that* life was rooted in
this place and that a professional conservation and curation are presenting
the place to us. We tend to be generous, overlooking the inevitable gaps,
losses and curatorial failures. But we do expect what we visit to be authentic,
even if partial, even if ruined. This is a serious matter, since (I think) we
automatically read our rootedness in place across to that of the house's
earlier inhabitants. Our imaginations shuttle back and forth between what
we find familiar in the house and what is outside our experience. In other
words, what authenticity is, how it may be judged – and, more generally,
what the nature of historic witness is – are questions in which we most of
us come to have a genuine stake.

Replicas and reconstructions lack this historical witness in some essential
way. The Nashville Parthenon (1922–32) is not the Parthenon even though
it recreates it and improves on it by making good its missing elements.
Salisbury House in Des Moines, Iowa is not the same thing as the building
that once stood in Salisbury in Wiltshire, even though it is a stone-by-
stone reconstruction of it. (It was sold to an American manufacturer,
dismantled and transported.) London Bridge, reconstructed in Arizona, is
now cleaner thanks to the scarifying effect of the desert air: but it is no
longer *London* Bridge. What constitutes identity is a tough, philosophical
problem that historical buildings that remain on their original site usually
avoid having to face, for they maintain a mute continuity of historical
witness, and time leaves its marks on them. As we move on to consider,
in this chapter, buildings and structures that claim a more precise and
powerful historical witness than that of museum displays and heritage
villages, pressing questions emerge. How historical need the re-presentation
be? What, for historic buildings, is history's authenticating source?

Thinking in terms of origin – of the moment of production as the sole
legitimating one – does not get us far enough with buildings, since, as we
have seen, their fate, if they survive, is to undergo continuous change. Only

adaptive reuse will have put very old buildings in a position to be proposed for professional conservation and curation in the present. As I will argue, that is not the end of the story of adaptation. The hand of the curator (and heritage architect, and builder) is inevitably *in* the fabric, not merely (as the curatorial term 'interpretation' implies) something that is lightly added and can readily be taken away. 'Reversibility' is the catchphrase of conservatorial and curatorial work, and to some extent it applies. The fake convict hammocks slung across the space on the top floor of the restored Hyde Park Barracks in Sydney (1819) could be removed should school groups lose their appetite for convict-style sleep-overs. But whether the turned bricks on the exterior of this stern but harmonious Georgian building designed by convict architect Francis Greenway (1777–1837), discussed further below, will ever be turned again to reveal their decayed face (now oriented inward during the building's restoration) is doubtful. How little or much ought to be done to old buildings – whether to preserve them as they are, or restore them to some aesthetic standard or historical moment – has been the crux of an argument that has been proceeding now for more than a century and a half.

Restoration of the churches

The Victorian restorers in Britain believed they knew how to treat old churches. All around them, the familiar past was receding, the effect first of the French Revolution and the Napoleonic Wars, and then, from the 1840s, of the railways, steamships and the telegraph. There was a new appetite for the past. While many, including the Utilitarians, were not in love with it, nearly everyone read Sir Walter Scott's historical novels. Byron's *Childe Harold* had piqued the existing taste for classical ruins, and much public statuary reflected a passion for the certainties of Roman culture. Architects despaired of being able to nominate a new, distinctive style of their own as they copied and adapted a variety of styles from the past, 'often beset by a sense of belatedness and inferiority'.[6] The Gothic Revival would in fact ultimately be seen as their triumphant signature style, yet they themselves could not quite believe it. The architect George Edmund Street (1824–81) declared defiantly: 'We *are* medievalists and rejoice in the name, wishing to do our work in the same simple but strong spirit which made the man of the thirteenth century so noble a creature.'[7]

Their visual transformations of medieval churches were profound. In 1818 the Church Building Act was passed, granting one million pounds for church construction, and in the same year the Church Building Society was established. There was great enthusiasm for restoration in the 1820s and 1830s. Crucially in 1833 came the launch of *Tracts for the Times* from the Tractarian or Oxford Movement, revitalising the Anglican Church as an independent spiritual institution (as opposed to an Established one) and looking to medieval and seventeenth-century church traditions for a renewed purity of worship. Led by John Henry Newman and R. H. Froude, the Tractarian Movement was receiving a hostile reaction by the 1840s – a measure of its effectiveness – but the church building movement went on gathering momentum. The leading architects were George Gilbert Scott (1811–78), William Butterfield (1814–1900) and Street. In 1834, the Royal Institute of British Architects was established, and, from the 1840s, numerous societies and associations sprang up, pursuing archaeological, architectural or antiquarian agendas. Between 1840 and 1873, 7,144 churches in England were restored – about half of the existing medieval ones. Today, the untutored eye can find it difficult to tell whether an apparently medieval church is a Victorian restoration or is original.

Interest in Gothic architecture had started late in the previous century as a Romantic interest in the medieval (as at Horace Walpole's Strawberry Hill); but the nature of the interest then deepened. Augustus W. N. Pugin (1812–52) was the chief theorist of the Gothic Revival, especially in his *Contrasts: Or, a Parallel between the Noble Edifices of the Fourteenth and Fifteenth Centuries and Similar Buildings of the Present Day, Shewing the Present Decay of Taste* (1836) and *An Apology for the Revival of Christian Architecture in England* (1843). For him the matter was a deeply religious question, but the wealth of new archaeological-architectural knowledge that he and others introduced was used by architects to justify their practice. The first issue of the *Ecclesiologist*, the journal of the Camden Society (established by Cambridge undergraduates in 1839), explained that 'To restore is to recover the original appearance which has been lost by decay, accident or ill-judged alteration.'[8] The architectural activity of restoration made a ready metaphor for the spiritual revival: for both purposes, the source of authenticity was the original font of purity. A unified style – often (as in Scott's case) reflecting the early Perpendicular – would typically be imposed on the church, replacing the decorative and other evidences of the centuries.

Here is a description from the *Builder* of 1871 of the typical manner of proceeding:

The restoration of an old Gothic church would seem to be, to a certain extent, a straightforward sort of work, and to consist simply of undoing all that the last century did in it. Galleries are pulled down, all the closed pews are condemned; the walls and roof are well scraped, and white-wash and yellow-wash got rid of, and the bare wall-surface is made visible; the old pulpit, reading-desk and clerk's desk come down; the quaint communion-table makes way for a more imposing piece of church furniture; and, in short, by the time all is done, no one going into the building could possibly know it for the same structure; it all looks so new and dainty! This is called 'restoration', *i.e.* the church is restored to what it may be supposed to have looked like four or five centuries ago.[9]

The newness of appearance and homogeneity of style in vaulting, walls, flooring and furnishing betrayed the church to critical Victorian eyes as being more like a showroom than a historical building.[10] The perfected unity of style began to be seen as fake. The reaction against restoration started in the late 1840s while the restoration of churches was still in its infancy. Scott – usually seen as the prime villain, but curiously inconsistent as between what he professed and what he practised – had called it 'destruction' as early as 1841.[11] He had witnessed frescoes and fifteenth-century paintings being chiselled off, medieval glass thrown out and fourteenth-century ceilings removed. Ruskin branded the movement 'a Lie' in 1849 and denounced the 'restoration mania' in 1854.[12] But it was a long time before the reaction gathered strength.

It was finally galvanised by William Morris in his establishment in 1877 of the Society for the Protection of Ancient Buildings. He called the movement 'Anti-Scrape' in reference to the treatment routinely dealt to medieval churches in preparation for their 'restoration'. In 1878 he famously helped to prevent the restoration of part of St Mark's in Venice. A French counterpart organisation sprang up around a journal, *L'ami des monuments* (published 1887–1910); and in 1892 Paul Planat declared: 'If we should start *to rebuild in the style*, the original building would eventually be nothing more than a veritable "harlequin" without any authentic value.'[13]

Alois Riegl, writing in 1903 as part of a legislative proposal for the protection of monuments in the Austro-Hungarian empire, extended the idea implicit in Ruskin's thinking that buildings have a 'life'. Their ageing should not be artificially impeded by restoration, he argued, since 'their evanescence was the best testimony to the whole cycle of organic existence'.[14] The nineteenth-century cult of monuments, on the other hand, had a distorting effect: 'Restorative gestures', Riegl claimed, 'typically conjure up a past that never was and compel the present to acts of homage before a vacant throne.'[15] For Ruskin, imperfection necessarily attended the finer pursuits: restoring a church to an aesthetic criterion (while pretending it was also a historical one) allowed a unified perfection of line and function to be achieved. But modern technology slid effort-lessly over the difficulties that the original workmen had had to solve, and thus the restored or new building misrepresented the nature of their achievement.

Despite what must have been a great temptation to ground an idealist conception of the churches in the skills of the workmen who built it, linked in a common spiritual purpose, Ruskin went the other way. He articulated an alternative conception, startlingly modern in a high-Victorian writer: *'We have no right whatever to touch them.* [The buildings] are not ours. They belong partly to those who built them, and partly to all the generations of mankind who are to follow us. The dead have still their right in them.'[16] The walls 'that have long been washed by the passing waves of humanity' only gradually acquire their living value, 'their lasting witness against men'.[17]

Buildings and their witness

Many terms were used in the debate about the identity (or integrity or authenticity) of the ancient church because the philosophical ground of its identity was no longer clear once the idealist appeal to origins – its moment of production – was overthrown by Ruskin and Morris. The restorers' appeal to history had in the event only condoned their stronger yearning to impose a unified style at whatever cost to the fabric of the building as it had evolved over the centuries. Despite Ruskin's strong advocacy of an anti-restoration position, his own was not quite as anti-idealist as at first it seems. Although the identity of the building was constantly recreated (or accreted) as it moved through time, continuously intersecting with the lives of men and being changed by them, this position itself had an idealist underlay. This was his notion of a 'living nation' which found expression in architecture. In his day, this ideal was fed by 'the religion of home': 'Our God is a household God, as well as a heavenly one.' New building therefore needed to be worthy of respect: domestic architecture should be a reflection of 'contented manhood' – as well as being its ongoing witness. Architecture stood as a record of continuity between the ages. Its walls recorded 'that golden stain of time'.[18] The grounding of the work's identity lay, then, in a pseudo-religious abstraction: the nearly sacred, historical witness that the building as physical fabric manifested.

The notions of divine witness – being a witness to Christ – and, more widely, witness as attestation or testimony are first cited by the *Oxford English Dictionary* as Middle English. They were adapted within the new discipline of philology in the nineteenth century to explain the relation between a physical document (a medieval manuscript, say) and the text of the literary or sacred work that it transmitted – often badly, because of scribal error. (*OED* gives 1853 as the first citation of *witness* in this sense.) The problem became either to identify the manuscript that appeared to witness best the text of the work; or, if a work was witnessed by a great number of manuscripts, to recreate the textual tree on which to plot that witness's place in a history of copying, in relation to all other witnesses. In this way its ancestors and descendants could be discriminated, and thus ultimately the original source or the manuscript closest to it could be identified. On the basis of such reconstruction, the unique readings of the manuscript in hand might be assessed. The activity was backward-directed.

The witness of a building was necessarily different. Ruskin's proposal that its identity existed in its ongoing life was a reaction to the destructive consequences of the restorers' appeal to the historical-religious moment of the medieval churches' construction. Restoration of the original was 'impossible', Ruskin argued, since 'the life of the whole, that spirit which is given only by the hand and eye of the workman[,] can never be recalled'.[19] The line of thought is logical once the (counter-intuitive) pill of refigured identity as a process over time is swallowed. Ruskin did not ignore the importance of the moment of original production. But since it was irrecoverable, one had to deal with the philosophical and practical consequences.

Nevertheless, a problem remained. If preservation was the only defensible reaction to decay – if the idea of the 'life' of a building sanctified all past dealings with it, without privileging any particular stage of its existence – then it left no philosophical ground to support the later rejection or replacement of any part of the fabric. Ruskin's idea afforded a position of historical oversight, but not one that would justify taking action. Worse still, ill-advised action, if it were perpetrated, must subsequently be condoned. The architectural historian Nikolaus Pevsner pointed out the logical trap in the 1970s. If we remove the George Gilbert Scott window from a restored church, 'replacing it with a copy we should make the Victorian mistake once again. Yet if we can sanction the Victorian mistake, [would] not our grandchildren find it equally easy to sanction our copy?'[20]

The passage of time will, in other words, tend to redeem the fake as it gradually attracts to itself sentiments formed in ignorance of the initial moment of its production or installation. So for instance in Britain, the new building code of 1774 led to the chaste style of Georgian architecture and decoration that the Victorians found unutterably monotonous. But it has been admired ever since. Stucco and (artificial) Coade stone were invented to imitate real stone, which was too expensive in London. Yet 'both, in a sense, fake materials' have since come to feel like a comforting guarantee of the presence of the past.[21] There is a philosophical quandary here that has been played out many times in recent restoration work and has attracted attention by Marxist critics (see Chapter 4) and more recently by postmodernist commentators, as we will see next.

THE FAKE AND THE REAL

Anxiety about authenticity and forgeries has taken different postmodern forms since the 1980s. Sometimes this is inflected by Jean Baudrillard's ideas from the early 1980s about simulacra in modern living. Artificial environments such as shopping malls pre-package and channel our experience. Virtual online environments supplant their real-life equivalents. Outdoors, signage in national parks that is intended to direct our attention as we walk towards the wonders of nature unavoidably appropriates them for a discourse (usually about preservation of the environment). This line of thinking reveals as an illusion the assumption that we have direct or pure access to the real thing, whether it be nature, human achievement from the past (historic buildings, paintings) or even historical facts. (Post-structuralist doctrines of textuality readily deny facts this objective status, as we saw in Chapter 1.)

From this point of view authenticity can never be grasped because the real thing is always at one remove, always mediated by a history of reception, cultural interpretation or cultural translation. Authenticity is therefore all the more anxiously grasped *for* by followers of the Green movement, heritage conservationists and others. Tourists who visit cathedrals hanker after it too. It is something that seems so palpably real as they (we) walk through the nave. The ancient building seems to testify to it, going back in an unbroken line to the medieval period. This temporal extension of our lives can put the clamorous and self-important claims of the present into a sobering perspective.

The trouble is, as Stephanie Trigg argues in her essay 'Walking through Cathedrals' (2005), such churches do not have a seamless continuity with the medieval. *That* claim to authenticity is not available as there has been a series of disruptions of that supposed continuity: the shift from medieval Catholic to post-Reformation Anglican ritual in English cathedrals, the countless changes in the internal decorations over the centuries as fashions shifted, the cathedrals' having been subject to 'scrape' and Gothic renewal in the nineteenth century and (some of them) to the clearing out of visual obstacles in the 1960s. The medieval is so overlain by the effects of use and adaptation, it seems, that it is not directly apprehensible.

Tourists visiting cathedrals also find the evidence of current religious practice inserting itself into their experience of the past in distracting ways and insisting on its own privileged interpretation of that past. As they walk through the still-functioning cathedral, they find themselves funnelled down preordained paths to assist in traffic flow. They are prompted by guides or guidebooks to interpret what they see in accepted ways: they are never free or uninfluenced. They have no direct connection to what they fancy they have come to see. Trigg concludes: 'Whether we like it or not, there is no "pure" medieval; there is only medievalism.'[22]

How does this position about our access to the past change things? It makes us sceptical, granted; but does it clarify, say, the responsibilities of the keepers, the curators or the parish in whose charge these ancient buildings repose? To think about these questions we need tools. We need to be able to distinguish between the witness of Canterbury Cathedral and, say, the cloisters of various French churches that were reconstructed in Fort Tryon Park in Upper Manhattan after they were collected by George Grey Barnard by 1913 and acquired by John D. Rockefeller, Jr., in 1925. This is Trigg's other example. She believes that the latter's artificiality enables us 'to challenge the privilege customarily accorded to the link between authenticity and place, or continuous use'.[23] But surely the reverse is true, as my examples above (Salisbury House, London Bridge) suggested. Artificiality does not challenge the link; rather, it reinforces it.

Fort Tryon opened in 1938. The collecting had only been possible because of the availability of fragments from the ruins of four cloisters from monasteries and abbeys that had been partially destroyed during the sixteenth-century Wars of Religion and the French Revolution. The vandalised fragments had by the end of the nineteenth century mostly been adapted into Gothic decorations in private gardens. Barnard bought them and shipped them to New York in late 1913, immediately before the French government passed a law to impede the export of historical monuments.

The museum was not intended just to collect and display these architectural fragments in the ordinary way. Rather, as the official guidebook tells us, it was to present them so that 'the galleries reflected the original functions of the architectural fragments they incorporated'. More than this, a 'contemplative atmosphere [was] originally envisaged for the Museum . . . [with a] serene ambience . . . [and] a respectful setting'. When an apse from the partially ruined Spanish church of San Martín at Fuentidueña became available in 1958 the 'installation of the apse required that the original Special Exhibition Room be reconfigured as a churchlike gallery space'. It is 'known today' – states the guidebook, as if hundreds of years had intervened – as 'the Fuentidueña Chapel'.[24]

This building on the island of Manhattan has its fair share of authentic medieval basilisks and griffins on display, but the most (unintentionally) significant cross-species creation is the Museum itself. Incorporating authentic fragments into the fabric of a functioning modern building that we walk through has resulted in a chronological and architectural *bizarrerie*. The cloisters both are *and* are not medieval cloisters. They are certainly cleaner than any other cloisters I have walked through. One of them is half the size of the original (forgivable as a reconstruction?); another is on the ground floor of the museum when the original was probably one storey up (also forgivable?).

When one stands in the reconstructed Cuxa Cloister (from the Benedictine monastery of Saint-Michel-de-Cuxa near Perpignan), the visitor may notice, as I did, a discreetly placed diagram of it, which shows shaded areas indicating those areas of stone that are original. The remaining columns, bases and lintels were cut (surprisingly) from the *same* twelfth-century quarry. This literalising, bearing in mind the 'respectful' atmosphere aimed at, bespeaks the same anxiety to recreate an integral historical environment as Colonial Williamsburg manifests. And the source of most of the money was the same: John D. Rockefeller, Jr. He bought Barnard's collection in 1925, gave it to the Metropolitan Museum and gifted the land as well. Additionally, he provided 700 acres on the opposite side of the Hudson River (the imposing bluffs called the Palisades) so that the would-be monastic environment at Fort Tryon would not be aesthetically infringed by evidence of modern life.

The obvious distinction that begs to be drawn between the contrasting medieval testimony of Canterbury Cathedral and Fort Tryon (but that is resolutely not drawn by Trigg) shows that the scepticism of her postmodernist position is disabling. This is unconsciously exposed twice: once, when she objects to an egregious misquotation from Chaucer's *Canterbury Tales* in a brochure at the Canterbury Tales Visitor Attraction not far from the Cathedral; and later, when she defiantly states:

Many medievalists – and I count myself amongst them – still wish to make a meaningful theoretical and practical distinction between the original and the facsimile, between, say, the Ellesmere manuscript [of *The Canterbury Tales*] in the Huntingdon Library and its recent facsimile edition.[25]

How can a quotation be a misquotation if all evidence of past intention and achievement is inevitably mediated by its own history of reception? And what ground does Trigg's distinction between original and facsimile stand on if simulacra of the medieval (medievalism) are unavoidable? Answering that question is what the final theoretical chapter of this book is about. It proposes that we return to the 1960s idea of the *work*, which was supposedly superseded by post-structuralist and postmodern thinkers, but in order to reconfigure it, adapt it, in light of the lessons learnt from the various kinds of restoration discussed in the intervening chapters.

To idealise the origin, whether in order to embrace it (as the Victorian church restorers did) or to reject it (as Trigg does) is not the only option. To think instead in terms of a production–consumption spectrum allows us, as I have begun to suggest, to model the identity of historic buildings without trivialising either end of the spectrum. Time and agency seem to be crucial factors here, and the traditional distinction between the historical and the aesthetic to be in close attendance. Clarifying these things is the business of the rest of this book, as successive restorations and crises are explored.

The positivist claims of physical bibliography to be able to recon-struct the history of the making of individual books, and thus the ver-sions of texts they contain, were discredited during the post-structuralist moment. Twentieth-century New Bibliography went down the same drain that nineteenth-century philology did. Trigg's protest about the facsimile (which bibliography's descriptive and analytical working methods deal with readily) suggests that we have thrown away too much. It has evidently left us helpless. Indeed, worse than that: for think about the rest – most? – of the medievalists whom Trigg is holding out against and who, she implies, would *not* want to make the distinction between original and facsimile? Postmodern scepticism that places experience of the past at a mediated remove, and then throws up its hands in helpless deference to that fact, is a luxury we can no longer afford.

HISTORIC BUILDINGS: THE HYDE PARK BARRACKS

The remainder of this chapter and the next discuss some historic-building conservations of the 1980s and 1990s. The ghostly voices of Ruskin and Morris are usually to be heard somewhere behind the professional jargon of the management plans or inflecting the smoother prose of the published booklets and brochures, whether in justifying preservation of the building or, in the case of reconstructions, as spectres to be warded off. The issues

Figure 2.1 Joseph Lycett, *Convict Barrack, Sydney N. S. Wales 1819–20*. Watercolour.

surrounding the policies adopted are still very much alive. Confusion or ducking of the philosophic issues is common, as are premature appeals to what 'common sense' would dictate. As such appeals are little more than intellectual conversation-stoppers, some unpicking of them is needed.

One way forward is to note, as I have been doing, parallels and contrasts with the terms used by scholarly editors in dealing with literary works from the past. The building fabric is like the editor's source document (manuscript or printed book). Viewers look at buildings and readers read editions. The (textual) authority of the author that editors often invoke is akin to that of the architect or original builders. And there is the alternative source of authority deriving from the continuity of the building's occupation, which is like the reception of a book: a composite, say, of the Revised Version of the King James Bible as well as of the earlier Authorised Version. If reception is the key, then both are equally important. Neither displaces the other.

Again, the jumbled nature of the historical witness embodied in the fabric of a building is like a manuscript tradition that, confusingly, kept throwing off new versions in related but separate traditions of copying. Architects feel the pull of aesthetic criteria and stylistic unification in restoring the building. Eighteenth-century editors felt the need to emend the text of Shakespeare's Folio to what it *should* have said, since genius cannot have intended stylistic imperfection. (This was judged, of course, by eighteenth-century standards.) But a significant difference from editing emerges in the very conscious way that many curators of historic buildings see the semiotics of what they call their 'interpretation' of the building's fabric. For them (as will emerge in commentary below), interpretation necessarily incorporates the visitor.

The Hyde Park Barracks in Sydney (see Figure 2.1) was constructed during 1817–19 for the purpose of housing convicts who were, by day, out on work assignments. From 1848, after the transportation of convicts to New South Wales ceased, the building served as the Female Immigration Depot (until 1886) for newly arrived women seeking employment, usually as servants. Since then its walls have housed offices serving a multitude of changing legal and coronial functions. There have been fifty occupant-groups since the Barracks's construction. The Master in Lunacy held court there from 1887 to 1951; the Necessary Commodities Control Commission went about its business there during World War I; as did the Profiteering Prevention Court in the early 1920s. Many occupants required adaptations of parts of

Figure 2.2 Aerial view of the Hyde Park Barracks, 1960s.

the fabric of the building and, as the years went by, adaptations of adaptations occurred. (See Figure 2.2, from the 1960s.) By the 1970s, when the building was finally recognised officially as of historic value in documenting the history of New South Wales and was funded for conservation, the conservators found that they were dealing with a confusing palimpsest of physical evidence – multiple texts, as it were, but all inscribed on the same physical document.

Or, rather, conservators *would* have found this had they been involved at that stage. In fact, the profession of conservator-curator scarcely existed locally. The first historic-building curator was not appointed in New South Wales until 1978,[26] and the Historic Houses Trust came into existence soon after; so that the Public Works Board was the obvious body to take control of the site. During 1975–80, it proceeded to demolish most of the additional structures that the original Barracks had acquired over the decades to fulfil the various functions it had been allotted. The ruling assumption seems to have been that only the original buildings, especially the central one, were worth saving. It was seen aesthetically as a Francis Greenway building and as one of the triumphs of the reforming Lachlan Macquarie's governorship. The building was a material performance of Greenway's (lost) plans and a testimony to the famous Governor's vision. These were the sources – to pursue the editorial parallel – of its textual authority.

Decaying walls were made good, doorways were repaired or replaced, and a museum space was created from 1979, now guided by conservation

Figure 2.3 Western aspect, Hyde Park Barracks Museum, 1991.

architects and town planners. Thereafter, when a dig was done, archaeologists and museologist-curators were added to the team. Physical evidence of by-then disguised former functions of the building was researched, and a stratigraphy of the soil was performed. The building opened as a museum in 1984, but not until it was transferred to the Historic Houses Trust of New South Wales in 1990 could a full curatorial interpretation of the site commence. Inevitably, it was carried out in respect of a now much-depleted structure. Ruskin's metaphor of a natural life-cycle for a building no longer held for this one: the evidence, or much of it, was gone. The Hyde Park Barracks had, like many a medieval church, been 'scraped'. (See Figure 2.3.) A curatorial choice had to be made: 'How to make *sense* of the remnant clutter', as the Barracks's management plan puts it.[27] Which of the building's many stories might be better told in printed form as a history; which would be best told in a three-dimensional way?

Architects and curator-conservators do not always see eye to eye in this. The architect tends to be more concerned with the function and aesthetics of each aspect of the structure, the curator with maintaining the historical record. The one would replace the worn stone with a perfectly square replica; the other would prefer the inconvenience of the old one because of its humble recording of a history of being worn down. A gradual shift in decision-making power from architects to conservator-curators is suggested by the change in terminology from restoration (architectural restoration of original function) to preservation and interpretation. For the Ruskinian curator, restoration of an artefact can easily diminish its value as historical witness, but it can never make artefacts more significant. Intervention can only be justified as interpretation that mediates between the object and the viewer; but it does not change the value of the object itself. Replicas (even if unavoidable) fake history, no matter how closely they are modelled on the original. For the less Ruskinian curator, the requirements of interpretation can outweigh the requirement to respect the existing fabric, especially when, as at Hyde Park Barracks, choices had to be made about what was to be revealed and what concealed.

The curatorial urge (of the less Ruskinian kind) now got to work at Hyde Park Barracks, tempered by the usual constraints of observing public safety and fire regulations, and the necessity to provide facilities for visitors. Curators, literally and not just semiotically, have to incorporate their visitors into their presentation of the building. Yet the ramps that allow visitors to walk over and inspect digs beneath vulnerable parts of the flooring are supposed, like the proscenium arch in a theatre, to be invisible; they are there to direct the visitor's attention, as is the Barracks's signage – done in a discreet, consistent way (achieved via a house style-sheet), throughout the building. And the motif of bevelled glass in replaced windows is picked up everywhere to give some stylistic continuity and a sense of age (although it is in fact not known what kind of glass was originally there). Where there is information, though, it prevails. Where information is entirely lacking for important elements, it has been replaced by an obviously contemporary interpretative element. So the demolished central staircase (a victim of the adaptations) was replaced by a ghost staircase in steel that picks out the line of the handrail and has no treads to walk on. It is meant to display the absence of the original staircase.[28]

Much of what little evidence remained of the convict-dormitory period had been preserved (in a fashion) by the indefatigable efforts of early generations of rats. Rats were one of Europe's unwelcomed gifts to Australia. These ones, however, stole small or broken objects and then secreted them in the under-floor areas of the Barracks. Embodying a self-conscious curatorial determination to draw attention to the business of interpretation, a display on the second floor shows in cabinets some hundreds of convict-made clay pipes, buttons, bits of crockery, bones and tangles of rough material, most of which the rats had preserved. Each shelf in the cabinets is divided into a wide grid made of thin strips of cotton that place each item within a small frame, named and identified in good, scientific, 1960s fashion. A computer and archive boxes that document and hold the thousands of other pieces stand at the end of the room behind a glass wall. The archaeological study is itself on display, not only the objects. Accordingly, the Historic Houses Trust of New South Wales lists itself merely as the latest occupant of the building, not as its final, scientific overseer and chronicler. This is a clever, early 1990s postmodern display.[29]

Other users of the building are also documented or acknowledged by what accidentally remains of their doorways and signage and by what has been revealed by paint-scrapes and digs. The top floor contains, as already mentioned, a speculative recreation of the convicts' sleeping quarters. Nearby, factual descriptions of individual convicts from prison records are inscribed on wooden two-dimensional cut-outs of slouching human figures. This is done in good Foucauldian fashion: his ideas about the effects of surveillance and punishment in individuating and controlling people are embodied here as an act of obviously curatorial interpretation. It stands in for what cannot be present: the rigid, often brutal discipline of convict life in the colonies. This is a story that the building itself struggles to tell.

The shortfall suggests that the conceptual model of the historic building as inhabiting a production–consumption spectrum (sketched above and further developed in Chapter 3) needs to differentiate its historical witness from the meanings that attach to it in present readings of it, including those by its curators. In other words, we need to differentiate the building's temporal continuity as physical 'document' from the 'textual' meanings it acquires and their reorganisation by curators. This literary-editorial metaphor only fails insofar as curatorial readings of buildings invariably leave physical traces. The interpretations *require* adaptations. The scholarly editor, too, will almost certainly change the text of the basic document that serves as copy-text, and by definition the edition will be a new book. But the originating documents from which the edition derives will be physically unaffected.

History versus aesthetics again, and some conclusions

If the three-dimensional social history evidenced in historic houses is inevitably subject to the interpretative strategies of curators, then the importance of history's relics and leftovers increases, for they are its only physical objects available for first-hand interpretation. In response to them, the unifying aesthetic of the interpretation may range from the 1960s-fragmentary to the self-consciously quotational and multi-voiced postmodern. But the tension between this aesthetic and the historical witness of the unmediated fabric is and will be played out as long as people are interested in buildings from the past.

So it is that, from time to time, museum attendants at the Barracks bring to the curator bits of mortar that have fallen out, even the odd brick, in the belief that they are relics to be preserved. He throws them out, because from his point of view they have no meaning-bearing potential that is not already there aplenty. Similarly, he told me he would like to throw out the wooden shingles that were taken from the roof and replaced with new ones made from the same native timber as was originally used, casuarina. The new shingles are golden-orange when first cut, but weather to a grey-brown, just as they always have. There may be meaning in the discarded bricks and shingles. Chemical analysis *might* reveal different sites for the burning of the lime and the digging of the sand or clay from those used today. Modern splitting tools *may* leave different marks from those used in the early nineteenth century. But any one shingle would reveal this, any piece of mortar or single brick. Three-dimensional evidence needs to earn its continuing passage through time: in this case, it needs to do it better than a textual record of an architect or archaeologist. It needs to assist in the 'best' story the Hyde Park Barracks can tell. But given that curators' sense of *that* will change with intellectual fashions and cultural tastes, it is perhaps wise, after all, not to throw those shingles out . . .

Three conclusions emerge from this account of the Barracks's restoration. The first is that the visitor – and what can be done to reveal the building's history to the visitor – is being factored-in to decisions about the physical fabric, not just to its interpretation. The second is that, despite references in the Museum Plan to the Barracks as a 'work' of Francis Greenway,[30] it is difficult to think of any stable or complete form of it by which we could judge the conservation. The elimination of the ad hoc additions to the central building eliminated at a stroke its completeness (that is, if completeness be considered accretive). The act of refining down to the original building effectively framed it, purified it, rendered it aesthetic at the cost of removing most of its history. The hoary old Barracks suddenly acquired a false virginity.

The building is elsewhere referred to in the Plan as 'an integral whole' – which is to grant the synchronic co-existence and perhaps complementarity of all its features. This term comes from an archaeologist's report[31] that implements the philosophy and practice of the Burra Charter (1979, revised 1981 and 1988) – the official adaptation for Australian purposes of the Venice Charter of the International Council on Monuments and Sites (ICOMOS: 1964 and 1978).[32] Unfortunately the term does not acknowledge the diachronic confusion of the fabric and does not allow for the fact that some of the building's historical uses could only be revealed by removing, occluding, even partially destroying subsequent ones.

Historic-house conservation loses its parallelism to the scholarly editing of *literary* works at this point: normally, such conservation can only offer a selection of the work, not the whole thing. It is closer to the editing of a series of linked historical documents that possess no aesthetic unity, the link between them here deriving, one could say, from their shared geographic location over time. The curators had to work out what they believed the 'best' story was and then to help the fabric to tell it, while simultaneously allowing the fragmentary evidence of other stories to remain half in view – to allow the variant readings to be visible at the foot of the reading page, as it were – but requiring some astute attention of the viewer.

This lack of exact parallel between the historic building and the literary work points to a third conclusion about the status of the building. A historic house, say, being always in a process involving conscious alteration, accidental change and natural decay, does not and cannot have a stable constitution. It never did. Given the loss of furnishings, the limitations of contemporary catalogues of furniture and decorations by which the deficiency might be made good, the usually radical changes in the surrounding gardens (the effect of natural growth and changes in style of gardening) and loss of land through subdivision and sale; given also the common absence of original plans and (depending on the age of the building) of photographic documentation of it, and the limited helpfulness of early watercolour and other sketches – given all of these factors – a historic house *cannot* be reliably returned in every detail to its original condition, even if this were desirable.

Although the process of change is itself witnessed historically by the physical evidence it leaves behind, one cannot imagine the existence of an ideal physical form of the house, specified in every detail, behind its faulty presentation, as one can – in theory at least – in the case of literary works. The conservator-curator cannot achieve a consistency and precision of the kind that scholarly editors require for a policy of emendation of their chosen copy-text. Emendation is thorough: it is considered by the editor for every word and every mark of punctuation. The curator's interpretation, on the other hand, performs something of the function of a (rather intrusive) form of explanatory annotation, telling the reader-viewer what to look for in the fabric and how to read its historical testimony. At the same time the selective activity of repair (preservation) of the physical fabric is supposed to extend its life while altering it as little as possible.

The Hyde Park Barracks shows the difficulty of separating conservation and interpretation in practice – although their conceptual separation is assumed by the various national ICOMOS charters (such as the Burra Charter) in order to elaborate the practical decision-making within the contexts and constraints that are usually faced.[33] Moreover, as we shall see in the next chapter, at moments of crisis the two activities – conservation and interpretation – are deeply and most problematically intertwined. The guidelines ultimately fall down, I will be arguing, because of their conceptual impoverishment.

CHAPTER 3

The new Ruskinians and the new aesthetes

It is better to preserve than to repair, better to repair than to restore,
better to restore than to reconstruct.

(A. N. Didrion, 1839)[1]

The hardest lesson to learn, the bitterest pill to swallow, for those
bred to aesthetics, (particularly architects and gentlemen of taste),
who would play the conservation game, is to accept, and believe
in, the integrity of the artefact and its history. Not its superficial
appearance but its inherent qualities of age and associations.

(James Broadbent, 1986)[2]

The Ruskinian stress on history over aesthetics recognises the 'life' of a
building as inhabiting the lives of its occupants – as well as their occupying
it – but it affords, as I remarked in Chapter 2, no justification for intervention beyond repair. It is building-oriented in its philosophic appeal,
whereas curatorship is by nature Janus-like in having to look also towards
the requirements of visitors, incorporating them into the semiotic act of
curation at every point.

This can become quite literally the case. The interpretation at Elizabeth
Farm, Parramatta (home of John and Elizabeth Macarthur, successful early
New South Wales colonists) is self-consciously a theatrical set using fake
rather than antique furniture on which the visitors are invited to sit, thus
'performing' the meaning of the house. (The family descendants still retain
the original furniture.) Dundullimal, an 1840s wooden-slab homestead
near Dubbo, had only a few pieces of original furniture left when acquired
by the New South Wales Historic Houses Trust. Simple substitutes were
made and painted an editorial grey so that the house could be explained to
visitors while leaving them in no doubt as to what was original and what
was fake. The same approach was used during the 1990s for Government
House at Waitangi in New Zealand, the site of the British Crown's founding

treaty with the Maori. But the grey furniture has since been replaced with conventionally tasteful pieces.

Aesthetics are never far away. While denouncing this imperative in general, modern rehearsals of the Ruskinian approach can be criticised for covertly slipping in an aesthetic of their own under the banner of historical witness. This is the style of pleasing decay or 'shabby chic', which had its fashionable moment in the 1980s in English country houses. There is probably some degree of truth in this criticism, and we will see an example of it below. But whether or no, curatorial 'framing' of one kind or another is unavoidable for the Ruskinian preserver, no less than for the Victorian church restorer. The building fabric re-enters the realm of meaning – the semiotic order – through the act of curation. It is simultaneously an act of reception and of production, which necessarily mediates the larger production–consumption spectrum over time. Only the continuing existence of the fabric as fabric allows this mediated access to the past to be performed at all, both now and through later enframings. The successive curations become later acts in that history.

BRODSWORTH AND THE RUSKINIAN APPROACH

The Ruskinian approach seems to work best when there has been a continuous ownership of a house for many generations, and when a tradition of respect for the building and its history has stayed the hand of the occupants from attempting significant adaptation. English Heritage has followed this preservational approach with its property Brodsworth Hall in Derbyshire. (See Figure 3.1.) It is said to be the most complete surviving example of a Victorian country house: over 17,000 items were catalogued after the house was given to English Heritage in 1990. It was built during 1861–63 and furnished, mainly by a single firm Lapworths, out of an extraordinary fortune suddenly acquired. Nothing is known of the designer-architect, an Italian named Casentini. So the house is not readily amenable to an aesthetic reading – as a master 'work' by an acclaimed architect. Rather than being restored to its original condition, stripping away the changes of later occupants, the house is presented more or less as found – a 'Victorian core', with additions. It opened to the public in 1995, and interpretation and research is ongoing.

At Brodsworth, explains Caroline Carr-Whitworth:

people see wallpaper damaged by rising damp where missing elements have not been reproduced, silk upholstery and wallcoverings held in place by netting, and

Figure 3.1 Brodsworth Hall, 1995.

losses in the painted marbling simply toned in but not remarbled. There are plumbed 1960s washbasins alongside Victorian mahogany washstands. Rooms abandoned by the most recent inhabitants are shown as such – the old kitchen metalwork has been conserved but not brightly polished as if still in use . . . and in one bedroom steel tacks previously used to hold up peeling wallpaper have been retained, since they are still effective.[3]

In this room, the floorboards are bare. An impressive, boat-shaped bed survives (see Figure 3.2) and makes the room read like an example of decayed splendour – or, rather, like a painting of it – with negligently disposed lace coverlet and rich, olive-green, formal bedspread thrown over a box, and with pillows bearing the supposed imprint of recent habitation: the bedroom was never used after 1919. 'These rooms', comments Carr-Whitworth, 'perhaps because of their apparently romantic decay, are among the most popular in the house.'[4] Preservation turns out to have an aesthetic of its own. The policy is not simply an act of historical piety.

It 'seemed right for this house at this time', Carr-Whitworth concludes.[5] Editors of scholarly editions often say much the same thing about their

Figure 3.2 French boat-shaped bed, before conservation, Brodsworth Hall.

policy of emendation when they do not want to challenge precedents or their conceptual underlay. The editor's analysis of existing and new archival information aims at a reconstruction of the circumstances of the production of the literary work. It is often an extraordinary and original achievement. The announcement of the editorial policy, coming after, has sometimes, in comparison, a merely rhetorical force. This tacitly admits that the policy-making was vulnerable to the influences of the day (it 'seemed right') because it failed to conceptualise them.[6] The present case is much the same. The very persuasiveness of the objection to the alternative approach ('sanitising properties – often very quickly and on the grounds of taste – of later accretions') helps to instal a new ground of appeal without a proper scrutiny of it. A reference to 'standard practice of museum conservation (e.g. minimum intervention and reversibility)' is not enough.[7] These – on the face of it – sensible practices are in fact, as we shall see, not standard, even though they are often put forward as ideal criteria.

A fuller conceptual model seems to be required. I have already shown that such a model would need to incorporate the function of the visitor. Carr-Whitworth observes that the audience's needs (safety, circulation, information and refreshment) influenced the conservation of even the most lightly touched rooms. So, for instance, a replica of the carpet in the inner hall was produced and was still, in 2006 when I visited, looking much newer and plusher than the one it replaced. This was done because otherwise visitors would soon have worn the old one to shreds. In other words, the interpretation of the fabric for the audience could not remain conceptually separate from the fabric on display. One is simply pretending to be the other, without loss. Yet this distinction (fabric versus interpretation), prescribed in the Venice Charter and the policy statements that derive from it, is often appealed to in order to defend the fakery that 'interpretation' for the sake of the audience involves. That is, provided the existing fabric is not damaged beyond what is necessary to preserve it, then anything and everything else is allowable. In this case, which is a common-enough one, we are right on the edge of the guidelines validating fakery.

It is difficult to believe that this was the intention of the Charter. Preservation, as usually defined, involves stabilisation and repair. Restoration 'is limited to the reassembling of displaced components or removal of accretions' (usually the latter); and reconstruction involves 'the completion of a depleted entity' by incorporating new material into the original, with the new work to be 'identifiable on close inspection as being new work'.[8] (Speculative recreation of buildings without original material falls outside official international guidelines altogether.) In practice, all conservatorial intervention involves alteration, however minimal, to the existing physical fabric. Whether restoration to the 1860s had been the aim at Brodsworth instead of small-scale alteration, the fact would have remained that the ongoing life of the building is dependent upon the intrusive late twentieth-century technologies that were applied to it. New services were necessary, as was the reinstatement of stone affected by acid rain, the correction of subsidence that had led to failures of guttering and downpipes, and the prevention of further rising damp. It seems that the historic house – any historic house – once opened to the public, no longer exists as a physical object independent of the requirements of its presentation. Presentation alters the fabric to lesser or greater degrees. The distinction between fabric and interpretation is, then, not as robust a philosophic grounding for conservation and curation as at first it seems to be, even when, as at Brodsworth, a policy of minimal intervention is feasible. Nor, it seems, can the two curatorial allegiances – the historical and the aesthetic – be fully distinguished.

The Brodsworth Hall approach has since been carried out with greater rigour for the homestead Rouse Hill (1813), near Windsor in New South Wales (opened 1999). Its interpretation is conceptualised by its curators as a diary, collage or palimpsest of the possessions of six generations, framed by the only slowly changing, early colonial house of a prosperous settler. The evidence of each generation sits next to or overlays that of the others. No attempt has been made to unify or improve the taste of the furnishings of the owners. The family members were great hoarders, so that virtually everything on display has provenance to them. The shabby is left as it is – though of course the act of selection and placement of the possessions is inevitably part of the semiotics of presentation.

The fragility of the historical record at Rouse Hill is a continual reminder of its importance. The passing of the past is palpable here. Strange to say, it is enliveningly sad. Whether this approach will attract visitors over the longer term remains to be seen, although in fact the house could not tolerate large numbers.

This is even truer of Susannah Place at The Rocks, near the Sydney Harbour Bridge. Dating from the 1840s, this building, now a museum, consists of three terrace-houses in an area that, until recent times, was a down-at-heel, working-class district. In terms of their furnishing the rooms are interpreted to evoke, variously, the 1840s, the 1920s and the 1950s–60s. The walls and ceilings are in varying states of decrepitude. Peeling paint is allowed to peel. Exposed underlayers of wallpaper can be seen behind rough chicken-wired frames. Only essential repairs have been carried out and, where restoration has been required, as much of the existing fabric as possible has been incorporated into the repair. The outdoor WC, added in the late 1850s upon the introduction of sewerage, is still there, together with the crude, outdoor, corrugated-iron bathhouse from the 1910s. The distinct air of decay gives a strong sense of the lostness of the past, while many knick-knacks are there to be handled and the furniture to be sat on. Recorded recollections of the people who lived there come on automatically as the visitor walks through. The visitor 'completes' the display by this (perhaps gimmicky) participation.

The touch of the dimly remembered familiar is nevertheless very close. Some visitors are said to be quite overwhelmed by this house: and that of course is due to what they bring to it rather than what, as a physical thing, it contains in and of itself. Released from the subject–object binary of presentation behind a glass case, the little objects are the site of an unrolling semiotic. None of them has provenance to the family and any could be found in a second-hand shop, so damage or loss is not an expensive consideration.

UPPARK RECONSTRUCTED

On this note about Rouse Hill and Susannah Place – both 1990s conservations – this chapter might have found a quietly confident ending in keeping with Ruskin's metaphor of the life of buildings. The chapter *could* have ended thus were it not for the unignorable case of another, distinctly grander, family archive. Uppark (*c.* 1690) in Sussex was on the verge of being reopened by the National Trust in 1989 when it burned down. (See Figures 3.3 and 3.4 and also the cover image, a photograph taken in the early stages of the fire.) This disaster opened up a can of worms: a policy of 'minimum intervention' and 'reversibility' would not be an option. Philosophies of restoration would be subjected to public pressure, but clarification of them was not, as we shall see, one of the outcomes.

The original architect of Uppark was probably William Talman (1650–1719), but little is known of him. The substantial, two-storey house with basement and attic that he designed had a classical, well-proportioned simplicity. It was built for Ford Grey, later 1st Earl of Tankerville, who sold it in 1747 to Sir Matthew Fetherstonhaugh (1714–74). On his grand tour a few years later, Sir Matthew assiduously collected paintings and fine furniture. Upon his return, he redecorated and embellished parts of the house, including commissioning some excellent rococo plasterwork on walls and ceilings in some of the principal rooms, probably the design of James Paine (1717–89). There were significant, neoclassical alterations after 1770, and in 1810 Humphrey Repton designed a new entrance and portico, and part of his design was built. About 1865, tiles on the outer roof slopes were replaced with slates, but from 1874 hardly anything was changed. Sir Matthew's son Sir Harry Fetherstonhaugh had not married till he was over 70, and after his death in 1846 his young wife, a former dairy-maid, kept the house as it was, a tradition that continued to be respected in the next century.

At the time of the fire in 1989,

Uppark remained largely as it had been in the nineteenth century, even preserving its old paint, gilding and wallpapers . . . As early as 1910, *Country Life* pronounced that Uppark had 'escaped alteration in a wonderful degree' and, in 1941, the architectural historian Christopher Hussey in the same magazine described its antiquarian atmosphere, 'as delicate and fragrant as the bloom on a grape . . . It

Figure 3.3 Uppark: the Dining Room (facing south) following the fire of
30 August 1989, cleared of rubble.

is the kind of house where you feel you might look through the window into the life of another age.'[9]

The easiest, best and obvious curatorial solution – preservation and presentation of the historical record of this 'ideal English house'[10] – went up in smoke with so much else in the 1989 fire. The question became: what

Figure 3.4 Uppark: the south-west aspect of the House at Uppark, fully restored
after the disastrous fire.

to do with the smouldering remains from which only the contents had
been saved. The roof, the top floor and the main staircase were entirely
destroyed; the ground floor was heavily damaged by fire, smoke and water,
and its ceilings had collapsed. Only the servants' quarters below-stairs
escaped significant damage.

Doubtless, those charged with making the decision would have had
some of Ruskin's pronouncements ringing in their ears. If 'life' for a physical object implied chronological progression and change, there could, for
Ruskin, be no going backwards in time. If repair was no longer possible,
his advice would have been unequivocal: 'pull the building down . . . do it
honestly, and do not set up a Lie in [its] place.'[11] In his essay on the opening of the Crystal Palace exhibition halls in 1854, he had asked why the
supposedly civilised progress that its collection of reproductions signified
was everywhere 'prefac[ed] . . . with obliteration':

We shall wander through our palaces of crystal, gazing sadly on copies of pictures
torn by cannon-shot, and on casts of sculpture dashed to pieces long ago. We

shall gradually learn to distinguish originality and sincerity from the decrepitudes of imitation and the palsies of repetition; but it will only be in hopelessness to recognize the truth, that architecture and painting can be 'restored' when the dead can be raised, – and not till then . . . [T]he power neither of emperors, nor queens, nor kingdoms, can ever print again upon the sands of time the effaced footsteps of departed generations, or gather together from the dust the stones which have been stamped with the spirit of our ancestors.[12]

Pace Ruskin, the decision taken was to reconstruct Uppark. The insurance would be paid only on this basis; and there was the consideration that much of the contents had been saved. A part-restored, part-reconstructed replica of the building for which they had been collected would, it was felt, be likely to provide the most sympathetic setting for them. The decision caused some spirited protest in the newspapers, including objections from William Morris's Society for the Protection of Ancient Buildings (SPAB), which was (and is) still in existence. In 1996 the Trust published a 200-page book by Christopher Rowell and John Martin Robinson on the reconstruction, providing a history of the house, surveying the dispute, defending the Trust's decision and describing the processes of repair, conservation, restoration and reconstruction that were undertaken. *Uppark Restored*, despite its technically inaccurate title,[13] is a careful, authoritative work, akin in spirit and procedure to the historical and textual introductions to the scholarly editions of literary works. It has a history to tell, a case to argue and a decision to justify. Despite appearances – it is beautifully designed and illustrated – this is no mere brochure for the general public.

Meanwhile, the house had reopened in 1995. The visitor goes first through a large Nissen hut. Its displays (which were due to close in October 2007) retell vividly the story of the fire, the heroic response by staff on the day it broke out, and the subsequent renaissance of lost craft- and trade-skills brought about by the decision to restore the house to the condition it was in the day before the fire. Not as much had been destroyed as at first thought. But the damage was still *very* substantial. Those involved in the stirring rescue soon convinced themselves that reconstruction would be possible. Understandably, they were seized by the ambition of reconstructing what, on the day of the fire, had seemed irredeemably and so suddenly lost. Many of these people had just finished a substantial preservation program and seen it go up in smoke before their eyes. Initial despair evidently gave way to determination not to allow themselves to be cheated by Fate in this way.

One can only sympathise; but this cannot have been the best situation or time for making a clear-headed decision. There was simply no preparedness to allow this house to become a controlled ruin:

Many recall the excitement and spirit of endeavour in the early stages: it was, as Trevor Proudfoot put it, something to 'go for'. As confidence grew, it was mixed with a sense of surprise at the sheer gall of trying to reproduce work of such quality and beauty, and on such a scale.[14]

One commentator echoed Ruskin in referring to the '20th century's inability to accept the consequences of catastrophe';[15] this objection is brushed aside in *Uppark Restored*. An alternative – the construction of obviously modern rooms within the shell of the still-standing walls – would not have been, it was argued by Andor Gomme, the setting for which the contents had been collected. This is undoubtedly true – although the fact of the historical importance of the collecting itself only underlines the far less certainly historical nature of the reconstructed rooms. The many precedents cited by Rowell and Robinson for the reconstruction of private houses after fire – 'carried out so unobtrusively that many people do not realise what has happened' – cannot be persuasive in a decision to reconstruct what is still claimed to be a 'historic' house.[16] In what sense is it still historic? In what senses is it not?

Detailed notes and computer drawings are available to visitors in every ground-floor room of Uppark, detailing the exact division between what is original and what has been reconstructed. (They function like a textual apparatus recording editorial emendations of a literary text.) This self-consciousness of intervention is an extension of the display in the Nissen hut, as are the poignant reminders of the fire left unobtrusively here and there, such as the fire-scarrings on the original ground-floor timbers. Working counter to these historical footnotes, however, is the need for each room to read aesthetically, to reflect (in the words of the Trust's Statement of Significance for Uppark) its spirit of place. Hence the meldings of old and new, the fadings-in and conjoinings, and the careful composition of the furnishings in each room.[17]

'Each part of Uppark contributed to a greater whole':[18] this appeal by Rowell and Robinson to the traditional Romantic, distinctly post-1690s criterion of the organic or integral whole conceives of the house as a work functioning aesthetically in the present. We have already noted, with the Hyde Park Barracks and more generally, the trouble that this defence typically encounters. So it was that at Uppark the destroyed staircase posed a particular problem. Its recreation focussed the dispute between the Trust and SPAB, which wanted a newly designed, obviously modern structure.[19] Wanting to preserve the 'unity and sequence of the ground floor rooms', the Trust decided upon a reproduction based partly on extant photographs of the staircase. Rowell and Robinson admit that the result is unsatisfactory:

'the patina and texture [of the original] proved impossible to match. The new polished wood has something of the appearance of Edwardian luxury neo-Georgian joinery.'[20]

Since the authors recognise that a house, unlike a painting, is the result of many hands and is always evolving, the organic nature of it (if it has one) can only be located in the eye of the observer. This belief elevates the intended effect of the house on the visitor over the historical nature of its production, adaptation and (latterly) reconstruction as a physical object. The installation of the aesthetic as a category ultimately of superior importance to the historical is a precarious ground upon which to justify the philosophy of so substantial and thorough a work of historical reconstruction as Uppark. The two criteria seem to me to be working against one another: this reconstruction wants to eat its cake but still have it.

What is true of the house 'as a greater whole' is also, we learn, true of individual rooms. Thus Rowell and Robinson agree with Gervase Jackson-Stops that:

'. . . we should not slavishly follow some scheme just because it is well documented. There may be very good reasons why it would not work today. The contents of the room may be different; the pictures and textiles may have darkened, altering the whole balance; even the original documents (samples of paintwork, wallpapers or damasks) may have gone through a chemical change over the centuries, radically altering their appearance.' Most important is, in Pope's words, 'to consult the genius of the place in all'. Within a room it is vital to maintain or create a coherent and consistent effect; this was the intention of the original designers, in most cases, at least from the seventeenth century onwards.[21]

Appeal to original intention within an argument dependent on the semiotic of presentation (and an argument that has just recognised the effects on the house of the passage of time) only muddies the waters. To invoke the 'genius of the place' is to try to install a new idealism that is above history: there is a conceptual lacuna here.

When the authors of *Uppark Restored* move from their survey of the rejected alternatives to the decision to reconstruct there is in fact no argument. The opinion of the Trust's director-general is given instead of one.[22] This is intellectually unacceptable. We learn that it was a committee decision, taken less than six weeks after the fire: 'The main rooms were capable of skilful repair and this would not, in the Trust's view, be pastiche. If philosophical quibbles were put aside and common sense allowed to prevail, all the problems presented by reinstatement could be resolved.'[23] There is a cost in rendering the philosophy underlying acts of historic-house

restoration as only quibbles and counterposing to them the practical realities of 'common sense'. In some situations, *un*common sense is a higher
virtue. One that clarified the (philosophic) confusion surrounding the competing claims of the aesthetic and the historical would have been preferable.
The catastrophe that Uppark suffered demanded it, but the house did not
receive it.

Viollet-le-Duc and Uppark

The overhang of influence of Ruskin's near-contemporary Eugène-
Emmanuel Viollet-le-Duc (1814–79) is perhaps the root cause. He was the
leading figure in the Gothic Revival in France; his major writings, which
come just after Ruskin's, sustained the Gothic movement there. Whereas
'Ruskin was a speaker and writer', as Nikolaus Pevsner put it, 'Viollet was a
doer – architect, restorer, Inspecteur Général des Edifices Diocésans from
1853 onwards, and much else.'[24] His encyclopaedic *Dictionnaire raisonné
de l'architecture française du XIe au XVIe siècle* appeared in ten volumes
during 1854–68. He stressed rational building techniques: what a later generation of modernist architects would, in another idiom, translate as the
need for form to follow function. This was preferable, when designing a
building, to allowing the decoration or preconceived image of the façade
to take precedence over the interior functioning. Viollet's position was a
reaction against the then-dominant classical tradition of architecture in
France.

Amazingly, he discovered his central principle in medieval church buildings. Rather than interpreting, as Ruskin had, the beauty of the light-filled
spaces, the decorative fluting of the columns and delicate carving of the
pointed arches and tracery as testimony to the moral force of the hand
of the workman and therefore of his period, Viollet concentrated on the
underlying and very rational structural solutions bodied forth in the construction of the cathedrals. For instance, he demonstrated that the problem
of supporting the enormous weight of the ceiling vault in a building likely
to undergo some movement over time had been resolved by the medieval
cathedral- and church-builders by communicating the lateral and down-
ward forces, through a series of precisely placed columns, arches and coping
stones, to the fixed and flying buttresses. Viollet pinpointed the solution,
stone by stone, in his innovative drawings and entries in his *Dictionnaire
raisonné*: 'The entire system', he explained, 'consists of a framework that
maintains itself, not by its mass, but by the combination of oblique forces
neutralizing each other.'[25] Style, unity and ornament – much-discussed

issues of the day – would all but take care of themselves if the determining structural principle were respected.

When it came to restoration Viollet had, of course, to admit into his habit of systematic thinking the actual history of the building. Respecting the historical testimony of the building's fabric was, in a historicising age, crucial. But so also was its ongoing utility – as a church, for instance. So the issues were not clear-cut. In some cases, the restoration of the original form of the building would mean the destruction of later alterations that themselves might be historically important (and even structurally required for the ongoing physical existence of the building). Therefore, no 'absolute principles' could be invoked that would determine the decision, which could go either way.[26] Instead Viollet declared allegiance to an ideal that rose above the building's mixed history – the intentions of the builders – which he took it upon himself to interpret. 'To restore a building', he declared, 'is not to preserve it, to repair, or rebuild it; it is to reinstate it in a condition of completeness that could never have existed at any given time.'[27] This was the obverse of Ruskin's approach, described in Chapter 2.

Underwriting the idealist appeal was an aesthetic–moral belief in the unity, wholeness and integrity of medieval buildings: 'planned with deliberate skill; their organism is delicate. We find in them nothing more than is required, nothing useless in their composition; if you change one of the conditions of the organism, you alter all the rest.'[28] The introduction of this Romantic defence induces a characteristic swivel in argument between history (or archaeology) and aesthetics. Viollet's examples where he defends the absence of an absolute principle move backwards and forwards between the two appeals. Invoking first one, then the other, puts the interpreting restorer in the box seat. Similarly, he had no hesitation in reconstructing buildings partly in ruins. (His best known are Pierrefonds and Carcassonne.) The only proviso was that the architect 'should as far as possible replace [reuse] these old remains even if injured: this will furnish a guarantee for the sincerity and exactitude of his investigations'.[29] This statement might have been custom-made for the restorers of Uppark, as indeed are his idealist appeals to a (fancied) organic wholeness and to the intentions of the builders. The ideas that Viollet expressed have lingered, even as his interventionist practices have been widely criticised – a criticism that Rowell and Robinson acknowledge.[30]

In 1843 Viollet had argued for the 'total abnegation of all personal opinion' on the part of the restoring architect so that the historical witness of the evolving building's consecutive phases would be respected. But within half a page a slogan that he offers confuses the issue at once: restoration, he declares, is 'first for the sake of history and above all for the sake of art'.[31] Since the building (in this case Notre-Dame de Paris) should work as an aesthetic whole, he proposed to replace all the destroyed statues of kings and the saints. This was 'because everything is related in this ensemble of statues and reliefs and one cannot leave incomplete so admirable a text without risking making it unintelligible'.[32] When he then goes on to propose 'to harmonize all the accessory objects with the design of the edifice . . . [to] replace the convoluted grills and the bad taste of the galleries with grills more in sympathy with the architecture they accompany', it becomes clear how extensive the compromise of the historical witness of the building's fabric was that Viollet's idealising editorial aesthetic could tolerate.[33]

In the history of scholarly editing the comparable form of aesthetically based decision-making has had a chequered career. It was decisively replaced in the early twentieth century by the New Bibliographers. That Viollet should have been tempted down this architectural counterpart of an aesthetic form of editing that pretends to be historical is not surprising. Like every other thinker he was influenced by the assumptions of his day, to some extent consciously and to some extent not. That the justification of Uppark's restoration should be philosophically aligned with, if not exactly resting on, this wobbling, now-slender reed, is only a measure of how little the professional disciplines that aim to secure the past have been in communication with one another in recent times. Yet all editings of the past bear, in their different ways, on related problems.

What Uppark actually is

Close bibliographical analyses during the 1950s and 1960s of the extant copies of Shakespeare's First Folio revealed the different habits of spelling and layout of various compositors. This helped editors to identify and correct for some of the features of the lost manuscripts from which the plays were partially set – the editorial Holy Grail being the recovery of Shakespeare's hand. In the case of Uppark, much new knowledge about the original building and later adaptations of the house came to light because of the decision to reconstruct. 'Bodges and fudges [in the original fabric] were detected and it was possible to identify the hands of different craftsmen, including at least three who moulded the original ceilings.'[34] So expert did the new workers become in reviving the lost craft of working, and carving *in situ*, the slow-drying lime plaster (instead of the fast-drying gypsum plaster that is used for ceilings today), that it became 'impossible to tell which parts of the ceilings were modelled in the mid-eighteenth century and which in the 1990s'.[35] Moreover, '[n]one of the restoration woodwork is an approximation; it is exact in every detail'.[36] This is a great tribute to the skills of the people involved: personal inspection confirmed the claim. But in a *historic* house, it is an equivocal benefit not to be able to tell the difference between the old and the new. The reconstruction is undoubtedly a triumph, but of a simulacrum. Uppark has been Williamsburgered, but (thankfully so far) minus the costumed playlets.

The restoration techniques pioneered at Uppark are a late twentieth-century achievement, and many modern techniques, tools and materials were utilised or incorporated. As the years go by, the 1990s context for the house will become plainer.[37] How long the guides will remain able to pretend that Uppark is still a fine example of a late seventeenth-century country house with neoclassical alterations is anyone's guess. But, although postponed, 'Its evil day', as Ruskin remarked of the fate of all buildings, 'must come at last; but let it come declaredly and openly, and let no dishonouring and false substitute deprive it of the funeral offices of memory.'[38] Memory of fine work done in the 1990s, that is: for, after all, would those responsible for the house think it worth reconstructing again if there were another such fire?

Perhaps the twenty-second-century viewer will see a grace in Uppark that I cannot presently see. Stewart Brand maintains that every building that reaches one hundred years is seen as beautiful. Barring further ill-fortune, Uppark (*c.* 1990) will reach its century. We no longer look at the depradations of the Victorian church restorers through the eyes of architectural historians of the 1950s when the reaction against the Victorians was in full swing. We see (and, nowadays, openly admire) a style that the Victorian architects were themselves reluctant to claim as their own. The former Midland Hotel (1867–74) at St Pancras Station in London, designed by George Gilbert Scott, is one exuberant example. The fabric of most English cathedrals exhibits a series of styles evident as one looks from one end to the other, reflecting their building, extension and interior alteration over some centuries. Can we now see the Victorian – even the west wall of St Albans: 'Lord Grimthorpe's private massacre', as John Harvey described it in the 1950s[39] – as simply *one* of those styles? Are we far enough removed now from the Victorians to see their restorations as part of the continuing life of the buildings rather than as a final and definitive (because irreversible) architectural editing?

That way were tempting, and I, for one, cannot resist the answer 'yes'. But it is a troubled affirmative. Our interest in an architectural style and historical moment is surely different in quality if that style is itself consciously historicising. Seeking to recapture a valued moment from its past is not the same as expressing unselfconsciously its own period. When we look back to the Victorian we cannot treat it as merely another style, one of many along a chronological line. We look back at the Victorian Gothic only to find it looking further back to the real Gothic. The life of a building in Ruskin's sense, when people lived in it and around its walls, is especially in danger of being resigned for a death-in-life when, as Heidegger realised, a building becomes the object of a historicising architectural science. This is the moment of embalming. Uppark (*c.* 1990) is in that tradition, but the churches narrowly escaped it.

OLD ST PAUL'S, KATHERINE MANSFIELD'S HOUSE AND RØROS

Two New Zealand restorations and one in Norway might, through comparison, sharpen the nature of this misgiving. Old St Paul's in Wellington, New Zealand, is a timber church built in 1866 in early English Gothic Revival style. It received a satisfying restoration, even though it was carried out in the 1960s when raising money for such things was a difficult matter. If this helps explain the lightness of touch with which the work was done we can only be grateful: new foundations, fumigation, replacing most of the timbers in the north transept that had become rotten, and oiling the rest of them, were the main tasks. When I visited in 2001 and again in 2005 evidence of the continuity of the building's function and of the continuous rather than catastrophic change in its fabric was all around me. Although no longer a consecrated church, it is still used for weddings, funerals and other community occasions in need of special notice.

The burnishing of the wall brasses continues to erupt the wood stain of the contiguous timbers on the walls. The now very abraded modern cork tiles are still saving the worn or damaged timbers beneath. The restraint of not lining the walls but leaving the native timbers exposed, and the localisation of worship implied in the use of New Zealand timbers, have been left to tell their own story. These things lend a satisfying sense of integrity of fabric, and continuity of human presence and function, to this building. Ruskin would surely have approved.

He might equally have also given the nod to the related approach adopted during the conservation and restoration of the town of Røros in Norway. Copper mining and smelting were carried out there continuously from 1644 until 1977. Town farming in smallholdings over the centuries influenced the buildings and landscape, but the original layout and structure of the town remains basically unchanged. As farming was gradually abandoned during the twentieth century the maintenance of the wooden outbuildings fell away and their gradual decay was the inevitable result. In 1994 the *Uthusprosjekt* took as its aim the repair of some 400 such outbuildings 'according to [ICOMOS] preservation principles, using traditional materials and techniques'.[40]

One of the questions the project faced was whether the 'repairs should be made to copy exactly the authentic materials'.[41] This begged the question of what they were: the original materials used in construction or those used over the centuries for repair? The position on authenticity arrived at by the conservators does not privilege a return to the original moment of construction. Rather, the tradition of repairing the wooden buildings, and the changing methods used over time, is itself defined as the source of the authentic:

'So long as a tradition continues, construction may be maintained, repaired, rebuilt, repainted or redecorated respecting traditional form[s] and rituals; authenticity could be identified – if it is [at] all possible – not so much in the originality of material or form, but rather in the process.' . . . Concerning the outbuildings in Røros Bergstad it is reasonable to claim that such tradition was broken little by little when urban agriculture came to an end during the 20th Century.[42]

The break placed the restorers at one remove. They have therefore taken their responsibility as being to the tradition – the 'process' – rather than to the original construction. Thus earlier repairs receive conservation and documentation equally with the original materials at this UNESCO World Heritage Site.

Again in New Zealand, the Wellington birthplace museum (1996) of the modernist short-story writer Katherine Mansfield is, in contrast both to Old St Paul's and Røros, a very different affair. It self-consciously idealises a moment in time – a moment when, we are to suppose, her Beauchamp family have popped out and we happen to have dropped in for a visit. The kind of research usual for buildings of this kind has been generously exceeded. Three archaeological digs were carried out. Paint scrapes were done. The refabricated wallpapers in the house are based on scraps discovered lurking behind later alterations. A baluster found under the house was painstakingly repaired and incorporated into the staircase. The removal of all post-1890 alterations to the fabric of the building has been carefully done, and a discriminating collection of period furniture and decorations has been put together.

Does any of this recreate a lost past in our present? Katherine Mansfield and the Beauchamps lived there from 1888 to 1893. They are all dead. The house as it was is gone. What exists now – what we walk into – is an elaborate, loving and professional act of homage enacted in three dimensions. It is a series of props pointing us, guiding our imaginations, towards that lost past. The three-dimensional explanatory notes which constitute this house – most of them, preciously, *from* that past – are excellent, and one is grateful for them: but there is no text. As Heidegger says: 'World-withdrawal and world-decay can never be undone.'

This, perhaps, is the root of the problem with historic-house restoration. We value it, we *want* the connection, because in some significant sense it makes the past present. It gives us a genuine connection, we feel, with a physically experienced, three-dimensional past. But it pulls up short of a fully lived history. We have to create *that* historic text in our own imaginations, prompted by the mostly annotational work of the curators. In some historic houses desperate curators have allowed themselves, as part of their interpretation, the mournful satisfaction of dressing-up shop-window dummies in replica 'period' clothes. They are supposed to evoke the life that was lived in the house. In genuinely historical surroundings they remain, all too clearly, what they are. Which begs the question: why are they there at all? Their presence only underlines the dilemma that Virginia Woolf named in *Orlando*: that the historic house is one from which life has fled.

The professionalising of our desire for authentic contact with a three-dimensional past has called forth curatorial working distinctions between fabric and interpretation, the one gesturing backwards to the past, the other towards the needs of visitors. Williamsburg-style curation brings down its emphasis on the latter in a literalistic way. Uppark's curators had wanted to bring it down on the former till disaster struck and a conflation of past and present set in. The examples considered in this chapter suggest that a conceptual clarity has yet to arise from the pragmatic shuttle, typical of most restorations, between statements of cultural significance and empirical decision-making, and between history and aesthetics. A more open acknowledgement of the semiotics of presentation, of the way in which historical buildings 'work', of the nature of their parallel to artistic and literary works, may be the solution. The idea of the production–consumption spectrum, discussed above and in Chapter 2, may offer the means for this clarification of aims for the conservation and curation of historical buildings.

But before this conception can be proposed meaningfully (as it will be in the final chapter), it is necessary to gather into the discussion more focussed notions of authorship: of agency (considered quite generally) at the production end of the spectrum. So the following chapters concentrate on moments of crisis in other kinds of professionalised dealings with artworks and literary works from the past. Restoration of damaged paintings and connoisseurship are the subject of Chapters 5 and 6. Chapter 4 raises in advance the question of forgery and authorship. Chapter 7 returns to it, thus extending the discussion of authenticity from historic villages and houses to literary works via a discussion of copyright, and then to Shakespeare. Authenticity, it transpires, is an elusive quality for which we seem to have retained a steady appetite, despite the blandishments that postmodernist theory so seductively put in our way.

From the heat of dispute comes also, potentially, much light. This outcome may be especially welcome now, in the early twenty-first century, as the already old-fashioned cultural-theory movement of the 1980s and 1990s begins to be ushered towards a new intellectual dispensation.

CHAPTER 4

Forgery and authenticity: historical documents, literary works and paintings

> [B]e not soon shaken in mind . . . by letter as from us . . . Let no man deceive you by any means.
>
> (2 Thessalonians ii.2–3)

There has been in recent decades a widely shared desire to maintain connections with a past that would remain palpably present in our lives. We have wanted to be able to be present in the body in reconstructed or restored historical environments. We have gone to historic buildings in the hope that they will, to some degree, reliably re-*present* the past, not just represent it at one remove, as history books and documentary films do. As we saw in the preceding chapters, the question of what is fake and what authentic in historic buildings and villages can be difficult to adjudicate, even when extreme lengths have been gone to in order to establish the likely shape, character and contents of the houses and environments. We know, for sure, that the social life and environment for which the original buildings were a locus cannot be recovered in the same way. Even in those aspects of the past that they do bring back into the present, well-researched conservation and curation cannot entirely evade the ordinary questions raised by representation: both activities involve interpretation, which itself is affected by its time and place and by its likely audience. Anxiety about the authenticity of this historical work leads curators and conservators to grasp whatever conceptual straws can bear the most weight (such as the distinction between fabric and interpretation), however unsatisfactory they may be in themselves, as we saw in Chapter 3. With paintings from past eras, however, we seem to enter different territory. Paintings *can* gain from hanging in their early surroundings, testifying in this way to the taste or connoisseurship of the original or later collector.[1] But more often our commerce with paintings is in the art museum. And *there*, we are likely to think, the painting, though also a historical artefact, functions more importantly as an aesthetic object that brings its past into the present, that makes the

Renaissance (say) alive here and now and in the most focussed way. With paintings, questions of authenticity, restoration and fakery, accordingly, take on an added importance.

In this chapter, I treat aspects of the problem one by one, building up from examples, and drawing connections with the range of activities that we may think of, loosely, as 'editings' of the past. Before turning to paintings I first look at the expert fakery of supposedly authentic historical documents to try to define what the nature of their offence consists in: what it is that they are forging. I then move on to the question of the forgery of paintings. Recent scandals to do with the authorship of Aboriginal paintings extend the line of thinking.

The underlying notion of the *work*, in its traditional formulation at least, does not emerge as a secure category. Associated with the hand (whether God's or man's) since late medieval times, it embraces the material and the immaterial aspects of communicated meaning, whether in art works or in literary works. Historically, *the work* consorts with authorship. But this relationship becomes fraught the moment any pressure is applied to it. All of the examples I discuss apply such pressure. Once the malleability of the work's sources of authenticity is recognised, one becomes tempted to resign the concept altogether and to explain works purely in terms of socially circulating discourses. Whether the pragmatic requirement for focussed explanation should prevent this slide is one of the larger questions that this book is pursuing. There are of course wider theoretical matters here: they are treated more directly in the final chapters, and especially in the last.

FORGING HISTORICAL AND LITERARY DOCUMENTS

Sceptical analyses of the once-prevailing attachment to the idea of authenticity in artworks and literary works are not hard to find. In a study of forgery published in 1987, Ian Haywood pointed out that the earliest meaning of *forgery* is of something made, as on the blacksmith's forge. The first recorded use of the term in its modern sense is given in the *Oxford English Dictionary* as sixteenth century. Haywood argues that 'A forgery is still a making: its condemnation is [therefore] a matter of interpretation and law.'[2] After a wide-ranging survey and discussion of forgery over the last few centuries, he concludes that the concepts of authenticity, authority and the author have operated as a kind of superstition. He ridicules the idea that holograph manuscripts, for instance, have a 'self-evidencing light'.[3] He claims that there has prevailed a 'totemic worship of the original act of authorial creation' and that the law has participated in the cult by locating literary and artistic property in the original creator of the work of art.[4] He implies that art, in being thus defined, has served as a disguised buttress of the capitalist system. He is scathing about the complicity of the art trade in fostering the cult, feeding – as it does – so directly into auctioneers' own purses. Forgery is therefore, according to Haywood, something that is ideologically implicated and not intrinsic to the aesthetic object. From this point of view, the very notion of forgery is exposed as a swindle.

How true is this? For a start, as I argue in later chapters, it clarifies things if we distinguish between authorship, understood as a cult, and personal agency in a work, taken as a basis for further analysis. Second, although the verb *to forge* only gained its derogatory and illegal meaning in English in the sixteenth century, the activity must be age-old, since St Paul's second epistle to the Thessalonians is an attempt to warn the recipients of his letter that others may seek to deceive them by writing in his name (see this chapter's epigraph).[5] Nevertheless, the history of literary forgery – of what it has meant in ordinary practice and in law – almost certainly corresponds to shifts over time in understandings of authorship. Roland Barthes's doctrine of the death of the author and Michel Foucault's call for a shift from historical explanation centred in individuals to one decentred into the discourses of the period began to have their effect in anglophone countries in the 1970s and became dominant in the 1980s and 1990s. Authorship could no longer be treated as an unproblematic eternal verity. It began to be cast as a cultural creation coincident with the history of English copyright, especially from the eighteenth century. In literary criticism the notion of the author as originator came under pressure. And in the editorial area methods of textual analysis and historical explanation that relied upon the textual intentions of individual authors seemed suddenly less secure.

Authorship and copyright

In fact, ideas of authorship of one kind or another go back a very long way.[6] In the thirteenth century, St Bonaventure repeated classical distinctions between scribe or copyist, compiler of the writings of others, commentator, and finally author (or *auctor*) who 'writes both his own words and other's, but with his own in prime place, and other's added only for purposes of clarification'.[7] In the fourteenth century, as Roger Chartier has shown, manuscript miscellanies of works chosen on an authorial principle increased substantially in number.[8] But, as *auctor* implied 'authority', St Bonaventure had probably not been envisaging the modern sense of author as originating mind. Artists and craftsmen in the Middle Ages routinely copied other works without any notion that there was something reprehensible in this. In the literary field what we would today call plagiarism went on happily under the respectable banner of imitation throughout the sixteenth century.

The period after the Norman Conquest in Britain gave encouragement to forgery because legal title of every kind was suddenly in doubt.[9] Nevertheless, the legal definition of forgery was slow to develop. Well into the Tudor period, the crime of forgery was limited to imitation of the King's seal (signatures being then only a southern European custom). In the late fourteenth century, in the absence of adequate legislation, a self-regulating London Scriveners' Company emerged, able to punish members who forged legal documents or financial instruments. Not until 1563, however, did any effective protection against such forgery become available in common law.[10] Not long before, in 1557, the members of the Stationers' Company had been given the (nearly exclusive) right to print books.[11] The books were to be licensed by entry in the Stationers' register, the aim being not so much to protect the rights of authors as, by the regulation of publishing, to reduce the dissemination of seditious and heretical writings. By the early seventeenth century in England the claim of Shakespeare's Folio to contain his 'true and originall copies', and Ben Jonson's close attention to the scholarly apparatus and appearance of his Folio, suggest a new interest in the status and dignity of authorship in a recognisably modern sense. But it was not until the Statute of Anne in 1709 and a further one in 1730 that authors' rights over their own copy – that is, copyright – was officially recognised. Prior to that, authors had sold their manuscript (and thus the opportunity to publish it) to printers, who usually gained a perpetual copyright in the work thereby. The two Statutes had been necessitated by a breakdown in the earlier system.

The institution of a true copyright is part of Haywood's argument about the cultural construction of authorship. However, he goes too far in asserting that 'Copyright relied on the essentially mystical link between the text and the author: one is parented by the other, and exists as an offspring . . . The creative act is inimitable; that is why it deserves to be enshrined in law.'[12] Haywood's satire may hold true for French *droit d'auteur*, or author's right. Under this regime, according to David Saunders and Ian Hunter, 'the work is conceived of as an embodiment of the writer's authorial personality'; the 'elements of author's moral right are by legal definition perpetual, unassignable, and inalienable'.[13] Under English law on the other hand, copyright was, until the introduction of an additional category of *moral* copyright in 1988, a completely alienable right. People other than authors could possess it if it were sold to them or if they inherited it. It was therefore not 'mystical' at all. Indeed Defoe, in an account of the book trade in 1725, dryly referred to authors as merely 'Operators' or workmen employed by booksellers.[14]

In 1769, in the British case of *Millar v. Taylor*, Mr Justice Yates stated:

Property is founded upon occupancy. But how is possession to be taken, or any act of occupancy to be asserted, on mere intellectual ideas? All writers agree, that no act of occupancy can be asserted on a bare idea of the mind. Some act of appropriation must be exerted to take the thing out of the state of being common, to denote the accession of a proprietor.[15]

Thus was the notion of the idea as against the expression of it enshrined in law. Expression of an idea was deemed to be a form of occupancy: 'being there' in the idea, witnessed by a written form of it, would justify a claim of ownership. The other key legal distinction was between the work and its physical manifestation in paper and print. Property rights existed in both, but ownership of the manuscript or of a particular typesetting or plates was no longer the same as ownership of copyright in the *work*.

Nevertheless conceptions of authorship were changing, and the literary work came to be viewed as an individualised rather than composite or collaborative product. There were various factors at work. The eighteenth century was the age of a new literary form, the novel, frequently bearing claims of the literal truth of fantastic voyages or tall tales, and sometimes concealing the identity of the author. Readers felt the burden of sorting fiction from history writing. The age was also the first one of the professional writer. And it was heavily studded with forgeries, piracies and anxieties about authenticity and authorship.

In 1742 'correspondence between Brutus and Cicero, which had been read and cited by generations since its discovery in the Italian Renaissance' was declared a forgery.[16] Conyers Middleton had recently published a biography of Cicero that depended on the letters. The ensuing dispute had, of course, a context. In 1697, Dr Richard Bentley, the great scholar and editor, had disproved the authenticity of letters of Phalaris. He had demonstrated 'the extent and abundance of classical forgeries' often carried out by the Sophists writing some time after the original authors and in their supposed style.[17] Whether the Sophists' writings would, in their own time, have been considered forgeries, or merely a legitimate form of historiography or practice in rhetoric, is unclear. But they were most definitely considered forgeries after Bentley's exposé – which was a painstaking analysis of anachronisms and inconsistencies of language, fact and chronology.[18]

The authenticity of the Brutus–Cicero correspondence on which Middleton relied was also impugned on stylistic grounds. He rebutted the charge as being inherently based on taste and judgement from whose conclusions he differed, arguing that Cicero did not have always to write as one would have expected him to. Rather, he was 'a practical politician addressing different correspondents under the pressure of events'.[19] The quarrel went on, with various writers and scholars entering the fray. Joseph Levine, from whose study I take this information, remarks appositely:

Publishers and readers in the 18th century seem to have had an extraordinary appetite for scholarly controversies of an abstruse and technical kind . . . The fact is that the appetite for the classics was insatiable in a neo-classical age, and something important seemed to be at stake. As Tunstall [Middleton's original antagonist in the Cicero controversy] put it, no doubt thinking of Bentley, 'The distinguishing of what is genuine and what is spurious, in the several writings which have come down to us under antient and celebrated names, is justly allowed the first place in the province of Criticism . . .'[20]

Finally a young Cambridge student, John Ross, wrote a disguised satire pretending to believe that the great ancient authors 'could produce nothing but what was perfect in kind'. This was the test, he mischievously argued, by which the spurious could infallibly be distinguished from the authentic. Although his intention was satirical, his contribution was taken seriously in some quarters.[21]

This new pressure was being applied to the notions of authorship and authenticity in the very period when a close form of textual criticism, and painstaking early forms of scholarly editing, were being developed. It was no coincidence. But there were also other factors constituting the pressure in the eighteenth century: frustrations at adequate copyright protection (most notably in Alexander Pope's fight against the pirate Edmund Curll); the general proliferation of piracies despite the new copyright laws; William Lauder's wilful attempt to prove Milton a plagiarist by first inserting translations from *Paradise Lost* into works of seventeenth-century poets writing in Latin; William Henry Ireland's unblushing fabrication of Shakespeare manuscripts (including a supposedly lost tragedy, *Vortigern and Rowena*), to which James Boswell knelt; James Macpherson's creation of the writings of the supposed fourth-century Scottish bard, Ossian; Thomas Percy's 'improved' *Reliques of Ancient English Poetry*; Thomas Chatterton's invention of a medieval poet, Thomas Rowley; and the exposure of the ticklish question of Pope's use of assistants in 'his' translations of the *Iliad* and the *Odyssey*.

All of these acted as ingredients in a cultural brew that would give Edward Young, in his *Conjectures on Original Composition* of 1759, the heart to celebrate originality over imitation. An original, he wrote, '*grows*, it is not *made*'. He encouraged writers to 'resemble' rather than 'copy' the Ancients, to 'dive deep into thy bosom; learn the depth, extent, bias, and full sort of thy mind'.[22] Thus was the groundwork for English Romantic notions of authorship laid in the eighteenth century. Samuel Taylor Coleridge's imagining in his poem 'Kubla Khan' of the 'caverns measureless to man' and the sacred spring which issues from them was, courtesy of German philosophy, just around the corner. D. H. Lawrence's 'not I, but the wind that blows through me' would continue the Romantic notion into the early twentieth century; but he was perhaps the last English Romantic.[23]

Haywood's especial target, as it was for many post-structuralist critics in the 1980s, is the Romantic notion of the author's original and originating creativity, and its giving rise to a supposedly organic literary work. As Haywood portrays it, the cultural brew soon became a dangerous intoxication. For example, John Payne Collier's textual criticism of Shakespeare, published in the 1850s, was based on Collier's spurious claim to possess a Folio with 1,100 emendations inscribed by a contemporary of Shakespeare. Haywood's interest is in Collier's desperation 'to achieve this authentic [Shakespearean] reading, and striving to give his version relic-status'. For Haywood, Collier's desperation was merely a symptom of a general cultural superstition about authenticity. But when Haywood concludes that 'The quartos and folios [of the seventeenth century] are the closest we can get to Shakespeare',[24] he reveals a blindness or forgetfulness of the documentary grounding of textuality. That grounding can yield insights. Haywood ignores what the last several generations of Shakespearean editors and bibliographers have uncovered by getting in behind the early printings (as described in Chapters 3 and 7). This forgetfulness is very widespread. The problem lies partly, I believe, in the critics' lack of a bibliographic vocabulary that would answer to the theoretical and critical need.

The forgeries of letters of Keats, Shelley and Byron by Major George Gordon Byron (who claimed to be Byron's illegitimate son by a Spanish countess) illustrate the situation. In the 1840s, Major Byron 'was selling letters and also collecting them for an edition of his "father's" works and a biography . . . When he had a genuine letter in his possession he would copy it. The counterfeit would then be kept, the original given back to its owner, and the counterfeit sold on the market . . . The forged letters', Haywood concludes, 'are another example of the tenuous nature of authorial identity in a text: if it can be harnessed by another, to what extent is it unique?'[25]

This rhetorical question is a needless mystification. Although the Major had to read the original letter, and therefore to raise its textual meaning into his mind before recommitting it to ink on paper, there is a distinct difference between his textual work and that of the writer of the original letter. Haywood's verb 'harnessed' confuses matters by running together the Major's creation of the second document with the textual origination recorded in the first. There are two documents in this situation which, even if they 'say' the same thing, are intersected by different historical and personal contexts and motives. Haywood is failing to distinguish between document and text. This is the distinction that is preliminary to all scholarly editing, except it rarely takes this form.

It is true that the pressures of the literary marketplace have, in the past, ballooned the significance of the originating context and the link of the document with the author's mind and hand. Nevertheless, it remains just as true that there will have been an originating document or documents and they will have each had both an agent and a moment of composition. This is so whether the documents are extant or not and regardless of the complexities of the inscription and transmission. At this documentary level a clarifying notion of authorship can be sustained, a notion at least on the level of St Bonaventure's *auctor*, even if not the Romantic 'author'. Haywood does well to question the commercial and cultural motives for the ballooning of authorship. But when he surveys the field from his sceptical distance all he sees is an undifferentiated continuum of textuality in which the contingencies of its documentary embodiment do not raise a bump. This scepticism is a disabling, not an enabling, one: it gives no practical help at all.

Forgeries: separating the dimensions of 'document' and 'text'

The good Major, to add to his sins, not only copied existing letters, but created new ones by weaving together material he found in magazines and books. He acted as 'a compiler and sub-editor', as Haywood says. Haywood concludes of these fakes that the 'extent to which [their] "mixed" texts are authentic and inauthentic is somewhat dizzying'.[26] This may be so, if one has no vocabulary to deal with it. But some is available in the bibliographic field. There is material in the forged letters we might identify as, say, Keatsian – that is, having characteristics we associate with Keats. (This is our attribution, and it would reflect our methods and knowledge.) There is the document that contains this material – the ink on paper from which we have raised the text. If Keats had been responsible for the physical inscription, or if the inscription were an accurate copy of what he wrote, then we can rely on this document in our creation of 'Keatsian' text. In the case where a forger copies accurately, he has acted essentially as a scribe or copyist would have done, but in order to turn an exorbitant profit. What he misrepresents are the circumstances of production of the copy. They will be different from those of the original inscription. Where material has been strung together from disparate sources, there is again no need to get dizzy: the forger is showing textual originality in the act of compilation. Were he to acknowledge his sources, there would be nothing wrong with it. But its commitment to a documentary form, which is represented as having had an agent and moment of composition that it did not have, turns it into a forgery.

A celebrated French example of forgery demonstrates these distinctions nicely. It began in 1861 when Vrain-Denis Lucas began selling letters to a credulous French Academician, Michel Chasles. In the end, Lucas worked long and hard in libraries to create over 27,000 documents mainly of the sixteenth and seventeenth centuries but also including three purporting to be by Mary Magdalene, six by Sappho, ten by Plato and twenty-eight by Pliny. Presumably Chasles understood that these were later copies since they were written in French. But he, a celebrated mathematician, used and published some by scientific figures including Galileo to 'prove' that Pascal rather than Newton had discovered the laws of gravity and that Galileo rather than the Dutchman Christiaan Huygens had discovered the first moon of Saturn. Chasles presented some of the letters to the French Academy of Sciences.

Each time an objection to some factual detail in the so-far presented letters was raised, a new discovery was tabled that dealt with it. Vigorous protests began appearing in the British press, but the forgeries were not finally exposed until 1869 when Chasles suggested that Italian authorities decide on the authenticity of his Galileo letters by comparing them with autograph letters in Florence. Chasles seems to have been the dupe in all of this, believing that one man alone could not have forged all the letters, in view of the extreme breadth of their subject matter and their level of detail. The *Penn Monthly* drew the moral in May 1870: 'No keenest insight into the circumstances and events of any age can suffice to render historical fiction perfect in its ver[i]similitude. Some point will be missed; some Achilles' heel will always be vulnerable.'[27]

The cases of Major Byron and Lucas show that if we separate what I have called *document* from the reader's raising of text, then there is no need to invoke a mystical link between author and work, even if the cultural marketplace encourages us to do so. Bearing this in mind, Haywood's later difficulties with facsimiles and the faked books of Thomas James Wise are readily dealt with. (In fact, they are now believed to have been a collaborative creation with his partner-in-crime, H. Buxton Forman.) Haywood asks: 'Would a photographic reproduction of a manuscript fetch as high a price as the original, or be as highly regarded by dealers and scholars? The answer is obvious. Yet one would have access to the same words in the same form.'[28] He seems to think that facsimiles somehow undermine the notion of authenticity. (As we saw in Chapter 2, this has since troubled postmodern medievalists.) It is a basic confusion of the dimensions of text and document. A reader with the original, and a facsimile of it, might well raise the same verbal text from each. But clearly the two documents would have different histories and tell different stories about the cultures in which they were produced. For those who believe in magic, the original might well be thought to contain 'that "magical value" of the presence of the author' as Haywood puts it.[29] But a calmer assessment leads to less spectacular conclusions. Haywood's disabling scepticism is not the only alternative to idealising the origin.

Let us now reconsider Rutherfoord Goodwin's history of Colonial Williamsburg discussed briefly in Chapter 1: see Figures 1.4 and 1.5. Glancing at its title-page one thinks at first it is a piece of particularly fine eighteenth-century printing. The elaborately rhetorical language of 'A Preface to the Reader' reinforces this first impression. The library copy of the book that I inspected had buff-coloured paper with chain lines. As I picked it up I noticed that it was in surprisingly good condition. The binding was tight and the boards marbled. This did not tell against it since it could be a nineteenth-century or later *re*binding. I found the catchword at the foot of the page reassuring, but its 32-page sections (which are typical of twentieth-century printing), together with the lack of signature numbering and pressmarks, were a concern, a counter-indication. A now-careful reading of the title-page down to the last line declared what in fact the book is, a production of 1972. The verso of this leaf (Figure 1.5, left-hand page) is more forthcoming, stating that the first edition appeared 'in January of the Year 1941, and again in February of 1968', and the ISBN number is given.

The author, 'Rutherfoord Goodwin, An Inhabitant of the Place', was the son of the clergyman who first put the idea for restoring Colonial Williamsburg into John D. Rockefeller, Jr.'s head and who also had restored the Bruton Parish Church in 1905–7, well before Rockefeller came on the scene. Goodwin the author plays an elaborate game throughout this history, fabricating a pseudo-eighteenth-century style with some aplomb and introducing as many of the orthographic and typographic oddities of that period as one could hope for. Nevertheless, the fact that twentieth-century technology needed describing ultimately proved a problem:

Seeking to create Conditions favourable to Understanding through Exhibits and a new motion Picture – "*Williamsburg:* The Story of a Patriot" – *Colonial Williamsburg* opened in 1957 a new, $12,000,000 *Information Center* featuring twin 250-Seat Theatres utilizing the latest and most advanced audio-visual Techniques.[30]

This must have been an addition after the first edition carried out by 'the Author's Successors', and although I have not reproduced the *st* ligature or the long *s* in this passage, the eighteenth-century flavour is nevertheless much diluted. But what to conclude? The production could be accused of being a bibliographic equivalent of the Victorian restoration of the churches (i.e. Goodwin reproduces the eighteenth century of his imagination), except that no existing book is defaced by his activities. The book is, I consider, a harmless *hommage* to the restoration. If a man wants to spend his time doing this, and has the resources to give it to the world without falsifying its origins, let him do so.

Of Wise and Forman's production of first editions of nineteenth-century poets, which were exposed as fakes only in 1934, very different conclusions are appropriate. Haywood comments:

The line between forgery and reproduction is a thin one . . . the text remained unchanged in every way. Those who bought a Wise pamphlet may have been deceived by its date of origin by a few years, but the text was the same as in the genuine first edition. The literary status of the text was not damaged or transformed . . . The extent to which they are inauthentic is very tenuous.[31]

I take issue with Haywood's conclusion. Once again, in the phrase 'the literary status of the text', there is a conflation of the dimensions of document and text. The circumstances of publication of the pamphlets were not as they posed as being; in particular their date was some years or decades out. Wise included some of the fake first editions in his bibliographies. Bibliographies serve as the basis of most scholarly work; in this way forgeries can seriously mislead and falsify. Properly understood, *that* is their 'inauthenticity', and it is not tenuous at all.

FORGERY IN THE 1980S

In the rare-book trade, the question of forgery is taken very seriously indeed. The trade in Americana had been prospering since the 1960s with the libraries in new campuses across the USA creating competition for rare printed documents. The problem for dealers had been not so much to sell it as to find it. The demand finally induced a forged supply. When this was recognised a conference was called in 1989 to deal with the widespread sense of betrayal in the trade, and a Committee of Questioned Imprints was set up by the Antiquarian Booksellers Association of America. A list of suspected imprints was drawn up and distributed. It emerged that an underlying problem was (and is) that booksellers frequently lack the expert bibliographic or forensic skills that would allow them to assess the authenticity of historical items that are offered to them for sale. They normally have to fall back on trying to establish the provenance of the material instead.

An alternative approach was provided at the same conference by Nicolas Barker of the British Library. He described how he established as a forgery what would have been a unique copy of 'The Oath of a Freeman', a broadside of 1639. It was the first printed matter from North America, previously known only through a later printing of 1647 and a manuscript of 1634. The Library of Congress had failed to detect the forgery (see Figure 4.1), declining to buy the document only because they were not satisfied as to title. This is what Barker was up against:

[The forger had] produced the original by photographing the pages of the *Bay Psalm Book* [1640] using the excellent 1956 Meriden facsimile. He enlarged these photographs and cut them up, letter by letter, sometimes using groups of conveniently adjacent letters, but very rarely whole words, creating the entire text of *The Oath of a Freeman*. He then reduced it down to the right size again and made a process line block. Hofmann knew that one can distinguish process block facsimiles from genuine type impressions because the height of the type is different, so he took a small industrial drill and ground down the height of letters individually on the block so that it would produce a slightly irregular impression. He made his own ink out of beeswax, carbon and linseed oil, making his carbon by burning seventeenth century paper because he was afraid that carbon dating might catch him out. Finally, he printed it by laying a sheet of genuine seventeenth century paper (a blank endleaf from a contemporary English book) on the surface of the inked block and pressed it down, using an ordinary clamp and a padded board and moving the clamp along to produce a convincingly irregular impression.[32]

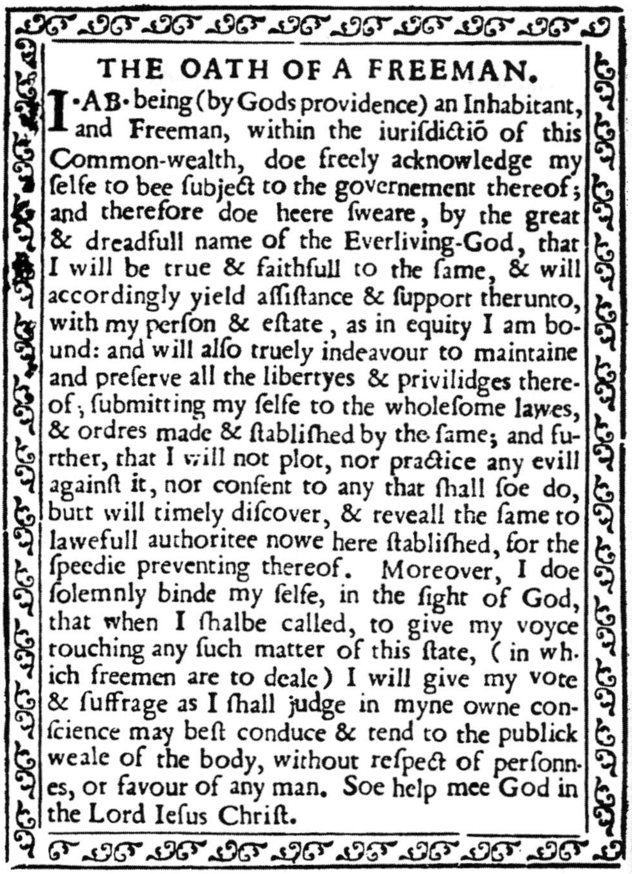

THE OATH OF A FREEMAN.

I·A·B· being (by Gods providence) an Inhabitant, and Freeman, within the iurisdictiō of this Common-wealth, doe freely acknowledge my selfe to bee subiect to the governement thereof; and therefore doe heere sweare, by the great & dreadfull name of the Everliving-God, that I will be true & faithfull to the same, & will accordingly yield assistance & support therunto, with my person & estate, as in equity I am bound: and will also truely indeavour to maintaine and preserve all the libertyes & privilidges thereof, submitting my selfe to the wholesome lawes, & ordres made & stablished by the same; and further, that I will not plot, nor practice any evill against it, nor consent to any that shall soe do, butt will timely discover, & reveall the same to lawefull authoritee nowe here stablished, for the speedie preventing thereof. Moreover, I doe solemnly binde my selfe, in the sight of God, that when I shalbe called, to give my voyce touching any such matter of this state, (in which freemen are to deale) I will give my vote & suffrage as I shall judge in myne owne conscience may best conduce & tend to the publick weale of the body, without respect of personnes, or favour of any man. Soe help mee God in the Lord Iesus Christ.

Figure 4.1 'The Oath of a Freeman', forgery done by Mark Hofmann.

Barker's account of how he painstakingly prised apart, in the one document, the technologies of the seventeenth and twentieth centuries demonstrates his basic proposition that 'a forgery must be related to time':

Within this time continuum, huge human upheavals – war, vast expansions in economic demand for some commodity – will lead to changes which leave their mark on the way people make things. These marks are not charted, nor will they be recognized by a potential forger, unless he is very clever indeed.[33]

As it turned out, Mark Hofmann (b. 1954), the forger in question, was not quite clever enough. He did not grasp that an initial drop-capital should align with the top of the x-height on the first line and the bottom of the x-height on the line below: his capital is slightly out. He correctly used a suspension bar over the second last letter of a word to replace the letter n. But not recognising that a compositor would only have done so where there was a need to save space, Hofmann used his bar in a line with quite generous spacing. And so Barker's list of Hofmann's *kitsch* authentications goes on.

Locating authenticity

Thus was the *in*authentic exposed. But is the opposite possible? Can one establish authenticity positively? Postmodernist doctrines of textuality – the textual mediation of all knowledge – have had the effect of undermining belief in positive knowledge in all its forms. One is increasingly wary of referring, say, to 'the' text of a document, as if the text were an uncontested site of meaning. Readers and viewers, under the postmodern dispensation, are said to participate in the things they know; they cannot know anything objectively. Judgements of authenticity must, accordingly, be locked into changing climates of belief and desire, or reflect negotiated agreements.

Thus it becomes hard to maintain that the notion of forgery in Ancient Rome and in the Middle Ages meant exactly what we mean by it. The idea that 'authenticity' is a culture-specific rather than objective quality is reinforced if we think of a text as a communication. For any particular text, we are always deprived of some of the contexts of communication presupposed by the writer and printer of the document, especially so if it was produced in the distant past. Whatever we decide the text 'is saying' must be partly fictional, something we (provisionally) project to cover the gaps in the communication. How, therefore, can we be so confident of our reception of the communication as to allow us to guarantee its authenticity absolutely? This is the problem that Haywood is circling around in his book. Must we then abandon the notion of authenticity, or can we distinguish the dimensions of text and document, as I suggested above, and confine authenticity to the latter?

This distinction that I am making is not the traditional one. The one that scholarly editors make is that between the text of a document and the text of the work. Editors must be sceptical of the bona fides of the text of any particular document if they are to discover what the text of the work was originally meant to be. Their distinction is unnecessary for the art connoisseur for whom, normally, the material object and the work are the same thing. For most purposes indeed, they can be assumed to be identical. Editors rarely need to go to the opposite extreme and entertain a complete conceptual distinction between text and document. They say, as we saw in Chapter 2, that documents 'witness' a text. In practice, however, editors frequently have to suspend judgement about what a particular ink squiggle in a holograph manuscript 'says' if at first they cannot read it. Once they decipher it, its material status as ink squiggle is immediately resigned for one of text. Within the one manuscript or imprint, editors do not distinguish for long, then, between the level of document (paper, ink, typography) and that of text. Sometimes editors want to expand the boundaries of what they mean by text to include illustrations and, rarely, some aspects of typography. But these occasional practices do not disturb the operating convention.

It is clear that textual meanings shift because the communities that recreate the meanings keep changing. But documents do not. Their graphic inscriptions remain unchanged, subject only to the very slow disintegration of time. This temporal distinction can be widened if the importance to the bookseller of provenance is considered. Provenance, if established, allows the artefact to be tracked back to a period when no-one would have had a reason to commit the forgery. Under this criterion, the text is not the important thing so much as when its documentary stability was originally achieved – a period when the relationship between text and document had not yet been skewed by forgery (or, indeed, by facsimile). This relationship is a crucial issue.

Forgery of books, pamphlets, broadsides and manuscripts differs from the forgery of banknotes and the like in that the former kind has the insidious capacity to mislead us in our attempts to understand the past. The real crime of 'this branch of human wickedness', as Nicolas Barker calls it,[34] is only incidentally monetary or political or religious. It is only temporarily its tendency to make buffoons of the people who are deceived. The real crime is the spurious conjunction of text and document from different periods as if the intervening time had never existed.

History and herstory are both stories, and are both perpetually retold (though the latter, until the 1970s, got into print very much less often). But the documents that our cultural storytellers interpret and reinterpret remain stable. Deprive us of them or of confidence in them, and dialogue with the past retreats to the second-hand. Understanding of writings from the past can always be assisted by, can even depend on, the early physical documents and the histories they focus. How a document came to survive, why it was felt worthy of collection, its physical form, layout, hand or typography are factors that tell us about the expectations of the initial audience and the conventions of its manuscript or print culture. The reproductions it spawned and the readings of its successive audiences also become relevant.

The collector will have some sense of this, and will feel the satisfaction of ownership. The scholar will get a different kind of stimulus, whether dealing with the newly unearthed manuscript, the scarcest of imprints, or the document that has been the object of a history of readings. Although the scholar's reading can never escape its own present, at least the scholar is face to face with traces of the past. The experience will be unmediated by the technologies of photographic-facsimile platemaking or of resetting, with the inevitable, usually considerable, textual and physical changes that new typesettings bring with them. Both technologies obtrude their meaning and signals on the reading experience: but at least, unlike the forgery, they make no secret of it.

TEXT AS READER RECEPTION: THE CONSEQUENCES FOR FORGERY

A theoretical digression will take this discussion of forgery further. In the late 1970s and 1980s, Wolfgang Iser, Robert Scholes, Stanley Fish and others began to point, in their various ways, to the role of the reader in 'creating' the literary text – that is, bringing it into temporary existence (once again) in the act of reading. Iser refers to the reader's 'entanglement' in the text. Having read only some of the text the reader projects a consistency that the remainder undermines: 'We look forward, we look back, we decide, we change our decisions, we form expectations, we are shocked by their non-fulfilment, we question, we muse, we accept, we reject; this is the dynamic process of recreation.' On the one hand Iser says that our 'formulation is carried out on terms set by someone else, whose thoughts are the theme of our reading' (thus accepting the book as the transparent vehicle of them and preserving authorial meaning intact). On the other hand the fundamental fact is that, 'in reading, the reader becomes the subject that does the thinking.'[35]

As an aesthetic theory of text, reader-response theory amounted to a shift in interest from production to reception, from origination to consumption. On the face of it, this was an encouragingly inclusive move, egalitarian rather than idealist. But it does not necessarily simplify matters. The eye, after all, is not a camera. There are always unconscious factors at work, usually unacknowledged, in how we see and what we see. As psychoanalytic theorists point out, desire and fantasy enter into commerce with knowledge at every point. 'Consumption' can be a matter of much distortion as meanings assigned by the consumer are indulged or entertained. Additionally, proponents of consumption models tend to turn a blind eye to the empirical aspects of textual production, in particular to the documentary site of the reader's performance of textual meaning. There is advance, but at a cost.

Normally we speak of *text* as meaning a particular sequence of words and punctuation. I am proposing that we go behind this concept of text and distinguish the constituent levels of its actualisation in practice: the level of physical inscription (the documentary dimension) as against its reception (the textual). Only in the interaction between the documentary and textual levels does it become meaningful to talk in the traditional way of *particular* texts. The interaction of the levels is what happens when we read. Agreement, for so long as it holds up, about the results of this interaction (what the text 'says') depends upon our highly socialised training as readers – upon our willingness to negotiate and stand by linguistic and epistemological bargains. Editors' interest in documents witnessing texts starts at this moment, except, as I have remarked, when the text is uncertain. Then editors must anxiously linger in the less differentiated documentary domain, proposing readings for the ink squiggles, assessing and reassessing them in order to advance the job-in-hand.

I deal with the theoretical aspects of this document–text distinction in the final chapter, but what is relevant here is its clarification of claims, such as Haywood's, that forgery as a cultural notion has no real existence and is therefore a kind of swindle. Under the definition I am proposing, the question of forgery cannot arise at the level of text. If readers' participation in textual meaning is an essential constitutive factor of text and if each instance of text is therefore a new one, it is not possible to forge it. A forgery of *text*, if there could be one, would simply be another instance of it. This corresponds to a notion that became widespread among cultural theorists in the 1980s and 1990s that, because all readers constitute texts differently, the text must be an empty site available for constitution. I contend that this latter belief is fundamentally mistaken because it ignores the level of document, which is where forgery takes place. This contention is generalisable but requires demonstration. My case study (in Chapter 3) of Uppark, where extensive parts of the building's 'documentary' fabric were simulated, has already suggested as much. But the forgery of paintings provides clear examples, even though, as already noted, the changed medium entails different adjustments.

FORGERY OF PAINTINGS

Vermeer by Han van Meegeren

Take the case of the forged Vermeer paintings done by Han van Meegeren in the 1930s. A Dutch painter of considerable technical ability, he had studied the literature about Vermeer. Very little was known about this seventeenth-century Dutch painter. There was hardly any contemporary documentation, and his paintings had not been identified as an *œuvre* until an article of 1866, but then more authoritatively by the connoisseur Hofstede de Groot in his *Catalogue Raisonné of the Dutch Painters* in 1911.[36] The number of Vermeers was reduced to only thirty-three. Their unusual variability of technique, size and subject matter made Vermeer an enticing enigma. By 1940, twenty books on Vermeer had appeared, including three in 1939. There were scholarly disputes about the dating of many of the paintings, including the *Supper at Emmaus* discovered in 1937. Thomas Bodkin, writing in 1940, noted that '[the connoisseur Abraham] Bredius concludes that the "Supper at Emmaus" was painted about 1653: but de Vries, with more plausibility, places it some ten years later.'[37] Bodkin describes the painting as 'superb'.[38] In fact it was painted in 1937 by Han van Meegeren. (See Figure 4.2.)

To our eye today his paintings look very dissimilar to genuine Vermeers. If one compares Vermeer's *Christ in the House of Mary and Martha* with van Meegeren's *Supper at Emmaus*, it is hard to understand how experts were taken in by van Meegeren.[39] But they were. Van Meegeren may have been applying a contemporary observation that Vermeer's early work showed the influence of Caravaggio.[40] But more importantly, he was appealing to what the 1930s eye was unable to see: the naturalised tastes and unconscious assumptions of its own era. A Greta Garbo look in Christ's face in van Meegeren's *The Washing of the Feet* (1941) looks painfully dated sixty years on, but was grounds for esteeming Vermeer's modernity at the time.[41] (See Figure 4.3.)

Forgery can, then, be seen as a translation of the original or supposed original paintings into the cultural vocabulary of the forger's period. From this point of view, forgery is merely a contemporary reading of the paintings (or painted documents) of an earlier period. This would be perfectly acceptable except that the forgery poses as one of those documents. Were it not for this, van Meegeren's efforts could be defended as an essay in paint exploring his conception of what Vermeer's early style could have been like.

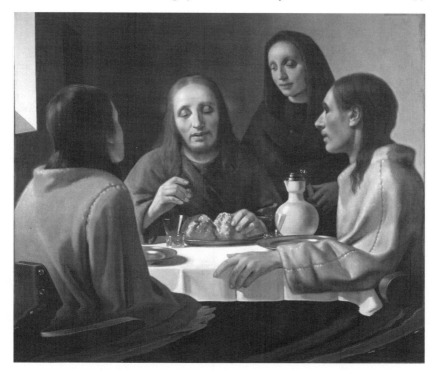

Figure 4.2 Han van Meegeren, [fake Vermeer's] *Supper at Emmaus*
[*De Emmaüsgangers*] (1937).

The forgeries were exposed only because he had made the mistake of allowing one of his forged Vermeers, a supposed national treasure, to be sold to Goering during World War II and was subsequently accused of collaboration. To defend himself he proved that he had sold Goering only a forgery by painting another 'Vermeer' for the court.[42]

Unpacking the 'aesthetic object'

The case raises the question of what aspect of the existence of a work of art is amenable to forgery. Van Meegeren's *Supper at Emmaus*, said to be his best, was considered to be a Vermeer one day and a next-to-worthless forgery the next. And yet the physical object had not changed. In viewers' minds, however, paintings do not exist only as aesthetic *objects* for they depend for their meaning or impact or beauty upon perception – the

Figure 4.3 Han van Meegeren, [fake Vermeer's] *The Washing of the Feet*
[*De Voetwassing*], 1941.

artist's originally, and later the viewers'. As Denis Dutton remarked in a
1960s study of forgery, an artwork 'provides us with an . . . experience'
that takes place in the present. But also it 'is an object with a history.'[43] A
changed attribution does not change the painting – that is, the documentary object hanging in the gallery – but it certainly changes its meaning for
viewers.

To accept the idea of 'pure aesthetics' as some philosophers have done,[44] or of the 'aesthetic object' as most people still habitually do, is to conflate the levels of document and meaning for viewers. Clive Bell, for instance, once remarked that if a work of art 'were an absolutely exact copy, clearly it would be as moving as the original'.[45] However, in its concentration on the object, Bell's statement leaves out any and all particular viewers, defers any and all viewings. His formulation ignores the fact that what we bring to a painting is crucial.

Exact copying is impossible in any case. To the expert eye, artefacts will, as we have seen, sooner or later betray their period and method of production. As in the case of historical documents, changes in technology inevitably 'leave their mark on the way people make things'.[46] The forger cannot make all the appropriate allowances. Like the literary document, the painted one begs for an explanation of both its moment and its agent of production. The situation with Rembrandt workshop copies, for instance, is far from straightforward. But this does not mean they cannot be differentiated from Rembrandt's. Because Rembrandt typically sorted out the shade and lights towards the end of preparing any one painting, the lead white, used to achieve highlights, tended to be added late in the process. Only producing highlights, it does not show up much when subjected to X-radiography. But copyists who laid the lead white down early and liberally in the process, and allowed the colour to come through the subsequently painted overlayers, have their imitation revealed when the copies are X-rayed. In the photograph, the underlying lead white suddenly dominates the painting. (Rembrandt's authorship is discussed further, at some length, in Chapter 6.)

Generally speaking, we may state that the painted object itself records the artist's activity. It could have been mere doodling. It could have been a struggle in paint with artistic convention and contemporary expectations. That struggle, and the risks involved in it, are an important part of our understanding of the painting's achievement. Our understanding of it takes place at the same site but is a different process. Forgeries, it is said, may be able to reproduce the painting but they cannot duplicate its achievement.[47] Yet to talk about 'the painting's achievement' in this traditional way endows it with an aesthetic objectivity, a notion that is readily deconstructed when a supposed masterpiece is exposed as a forgery and yet is physically unchanged.

My proposal, which I develop at more length in Chapter 7, is this. If we distinguish the act, circumstances and residue of physical inscription – what

I call the documentary dimension – from the artist's and viewers' creation of what I call the textual or meaningful, then we clear a space within which to define forgery and to differentiate it from authorial activity. We also jettison the unworkable notion of aesthetic objectivity and the supposed totemic link between author and work – what I believe is Haywood's straw man. The distinction I am making is, it must be emphasised, a conceptual and general one. In practice – when, say, we are reading a poem or a novel – the textual and documentary dimensions are never fully distinct. The meaning we take from a reading derives in some part (sometimes large, usually small, never negligible) from the physical qualities of the document. It is only when we reach a point of crisis – and forgery is such a case – that the two dimensions need disentangling, so that the activity of meaning-creation can be tracked back to its stimuli and sources.

CODA: FAKING ETHNICITY AND ABORIGINALITY IN AUSTRALIA

There is a tradition of literary and artistic hoaxing in Australia, going back to 1944. It began with the creation of a modernist poet, Ern Malley, by two traditionalist poets, James McCauley and Harold Stewart. Concerned at 'the gradual decay of meaning and craftsmanship in poetry', they fooled the editor of the Autumn 1944 issue of *Angry Penguins*, Max Harris, who was a champion of avant-garde poetry, into publishing sixteen poems by the (supposedly) recently deceased Ern Malley. The poems had been concocted in an afternoon by drawing from reference books at random.[48] In 1980, giving the tradition a new twist, Paul Radley won the Vogel literary prize given for a first novel by a person under thirty (*Jack Rivers and Me*); in fact his uncle had written it. The fact evidently weighed heavily over the years, but the publicity surrounding a new, less savoury hoax in 1994 allowed the pair to ease their consciences publicly.

Helen Demidenko's *The Hand That Signed the Paper*, published in 1994, went on to win the country's top literary prize. But then it was revealed that the author's Ukrainian ethnicity, upon which she had relied for this anti-Semitic novel of testimony about World War II death camps, was an assumed one. Her real name is Helen Darville and her background is mainstream Anglo-Celtic. In this period of official multiculturalism all hell broke loose in the popular media during 1995 and 1996. Two books and a collection of documents were published on the affair.[49]

Then, in March 1997 it was revealed that the Aboriginal artist Eddie Burrup was in fact a nom de plume of the elderly West Australian artist Elizabeth Durack. She concocted a transcription of taped interviews with

Eddie Burrup to legitimate the paintings, and an extensive web page of fabricated materials supposedly by and about Burrup appeared on the internet in about 1996.[50] Her falsification of authorship was a case at first of catering to an anticipated reading practice: the demand and appreciation, both in Australia and overseas, for Aboriginal artwork.[51] The false persona would have coloured the reception of the paintings without altering their status as physical objects. If Haywood and Clive Bell were to be consistent in their conflation of the levels of document and text in the aesthetic object, they would have to defend Durack's faking of Aboriginality or at least be neutral in the face of it. Yet this situation clearly called for their disentangling.

Later in 1997 another, sadder story of deception emerged. The well-known Aboriginal artist Kathleen Petyarre had been showing and selling dot-paintings some of which were actually painted, in large part, by her former de facto husband, an English-born man, Ray Beamish. They had separated, and he had exposed the fact. This exposé, on which the newspapers were quick to moralise, needs to be seen in historical context.

Aboriginal painting of the kinds now widely sought after by collectors and art museums is a recent phenomenon. Traditionally, only some tribal groups developed rock painting. Body-painting, designs in the sand made during ceremonies and the decoration of the inside of bark-huts were more usual forms. Paintings were not intended to be kept. Since the culture was semi-nomadic, visual archives of a Western kind were out of the question, and what is now called art existed only for its ceremonial function. The transience is best appreciated in the shimmering of sand in ceremonies under moonlight as it was dropped to form patterns relating to Creation or other myths. The well-known Western Desert dot-paintings are a recent adaptation of this for a non-Aboriginal audience. The production of bark paintings as commodities to be sold or traded began in the 1930s. The use of coloured crayons on drawing paper began in 1946 and then of oils and acrylics on bark and canvas. This occurred when the materials were introduced by well-meaning white Australians as ways of allowing the tribal peoples to record their ancestral narratives for others.

The recording media and the market into which the artworks were sold affected the mode of production right from the start. Mounting pressure began to be put by dealers and relatives upon successful artists to produce more and more.[52] By the end of the 1990s, the scandalous situation was reached in the region around Alice Springs in the Northern Territory that unscrupulous art dealers were using the poverty and alcohol-dependency of some recognised indigenous artists to sign canvases that were being painted by others and sold as authentic. In 1999 police, with the assistance of one of the artists who identified his own work, took action in Sydney against dealers who were selling fake paintings.[53]

The issue at stake, once again, was authenticity. A Western history of authorship underwrites it, but does not match Aboriginal understandings. Art production employing other workers, especially family members, is normal, at least in the areas near Alice Springs. Yet modern law has difficulty with such conditions of workshop production, despite the fact that they were common at least until Rembrandt's time in the seventeenth century. Nor, traditionally at least, does the indigenous artist create an aesthetic commodity so much as activate a belief-system in the performance of the painting.

Aboriginal art and curation

The first large-scale exhibition of Aboriginal art to demonstrate the development of a tradition of bark painting was held at the National Gallery of Australia in Canberra in 1997. It was based upon the Yolngu legend of the Wagilag Sisters (a Creation Dreaming). According to one of the curators:

For the Yolngu, the Western convention of seeing – that is, to see a painting from the past as if it effects some historic closure – has little meaning insofar as all art exists simultaneously in the present and in the past . . . The presence of a bark painting from the past is no more than a confirmation that things have always been so.[54]

More than one clan can have the right to paint the same Dreaming. But the performance of the painting is the prerogative of the person with the inherited authority to carry it out.[55] The painting itself enacts that authority as it depicts the story; but the painting appears to have relatively little inherent importance as an object. The motifs are given in advance, but each artist gives the depiction an individualising stamp, thus reaffirming the vitality of the tradition.

The exhibition showed this plainly, by documenting the development of the Wagilag Sisters story in paintings from 1937 to 1997, by tracing individual signature styles and by tracing the genealogy of the artist-authorities. The creation of the paintings for sale was an attempt to set the terms of trading relations with the outside world, as well as being a form of communication with it. Unlike the situation for Aboriginal artists around Alice Springs, this relatively happy outcome for clans in Arnhem Land, east of Darwin in the Northern Territory, has meshed well enough with Western structures of belief about authorship, as ideas have shifted from seeing the works as primitive artefacts (not requiring the authenticating stamp of individual authorship) to works of art, which do.

Both kinds of explanation (ethnographic, art-historical) tell the story of the work's production within contexts deemed to be relevant; but the art-historical tries to be finer grained than the ethnographic. I saw a good illustration of this distinction in Vancouver, also in 1997. The Vancouver Art Gallery held a retrospective exhibition of the works of Robertson Davies, an artist trained in Western traditions but originally from the Haida tribal group. His works were curated within the normal art-historical narrative of the development of an individual *œuvre*. Only a few miles away, the anthropological museum at the University of British Columbia had, on permanent display, its older works from various tribal groups of the Northwest Coast, including the Haida from the Queen Charlotte Islands. These were curated in ethnographic terms of tribal affiliation, place and date (when known).

Document and text, artwork as physical object and as meaning-laden, can beg different sets of questions. The two reading practices (ethnographic, art-historical) answer them differently. They both produce sense and value, but differently. When fakes are exposed, the authenticity about which journalists want quick answers is, then, not a natural or inherent quality that can be known positively. So far, so good. But we cannot allow ourselves to be content to see the relativity of discourses and reading practices used as a screen when distinctions about the source of an artwork need to be made. The burden of my argument is that the production end of the production–consumption spectrum must not be occluded by discursivity. Nor, as I have shown, does the older-fashioned view – that the artwork is an independent aesthetic object resting upon its (undifferentiated) authorship – get us far enough when tough questions about its agents of production need to be clarified.

The shock of faked ethnicity or Aboriginality has demonstrated the need for a renovation of thinking about the concept of the work. The crises have exposed our normally unspoken but very real dependence on a reliable account of the work's production. The wider postmodern cultural debate had shot off elsewhere; but then the chickens came home to roost. This dismaying situation points to a larger subject. Even if it lacks the tang of fraud, it is the more significant question: authorship and the work. The next two chapters probe the question in different ways. Once again, relevant disputes provide the refining salts.

CHAPTER 5

Conservators and agency: their role in the work

[L]et us now see in what manner time operates on the colours themselves; in order to discover if any changes in them can give a picture
more union and harmony than has been in the power of a skilful
master, with all his rules of art, to do. When colours change at all,
it must be somewhat in the manner following, for as they are made
some of metal, some of earth, some of stone, and others of more
perishable materials, time cannot operate on them otherwise than
as by daily experience we find it doth, which is, that one changes
darker, another lighter, one quite to a different colour, whilst another,
as ultramarine, will keep its natural brightness . . . Therefore how is
it possible that such different materials, ever variously changing . . .
should accidentally coincide with the artist's intention.

(William Hogarth, 1753)[1]

[T]he more one retouches paintings on the pretext of preserving them,
the more they are destroyed, and even the original artists, if they were
alive, now could not retouch them perfectly because of the aged tone
given the colours by time who is also a painter according to the maxim
and observation of the learned.

(Francisco Goya y Lucientes, 1801)[2]

Chapters 2 and 3 looked at the disputed business of restoring historic
buildings. Because physical fabric from the past that is of cultural significance must be preserved and probably conserved if it is not to decay or
collapse, and also must usually be interpreted by curators for the benefit
of the public, the agency of the conservator-curator is incorporated, as
we saw, into the building fabric on display. The discussion of artistic and
documentary forgeries in Chapter 4 showed that agency and its contexts
at the initiating end of the spectrum from production to consumption
are ignored at our peril. Concentration on the consumption end of the
spectrum in recent decades has been a reaction against the 1960s notion of
the self-contained aesthetic object. Professional literary critics have come,
since then, conventionally to discuss literary works as free-floating texts, as

86

carriers of discourses that are in turn constituted by their readers. This view captures part of the truth that the notion of aesthetic objectivity suppressed; but by itself it involves, I will argue, a dangerous ignorance. My argument will be that works, literary and artistic, have material or documentary embodiments and textual lives, and that we must acknowledge all the implications of these twin facts.

A primary implication, to be dealt with in the present chapter, is that famous artistic works are nowadays, increasingly, available to us only through the mediation of others. I refer not to the art-historical and other ideological discourse that in a sense pre-packages our experience of them. (Who comes – who *could* come? – to the *Mona Lisa* truly afresh any more?) I refer, rather, to their physical presentation. The agency of the restorers of paintings is discussed. Despite the standard defences of their professional practice, conservators' role in the paintings they restore emerges as authorial in nature.

The objectivity of paintings, frescoes and sculptures seems at first to be scarcely in question. Yet the existence of mediation has been driven home during recent, celebrated but also intensely disputed, restorations of some of the supreme works of the Western artistic tradition. The restorations of Michelangelo's ceiling of the Sistine Chapel in Rome and then of his *Last Judgement* on the altar wall of the Chapel, of Leonardo's *Last Supper* in Milan and Massacio's Brancacci Chapel in Florence were financed in significant part by large corporations and heralded as triumphs of scientific method and conservatorial skill by the media of the world. Few people with access to television or weekend newspapers can have escaped exposure to this ongoing work during the 1980s and 1990s. We were repeatedly told that the disfiguring veils of the past were being lifted. The accumulated dirt and candlewax, the chemical deposits and the cracked glazings and discoloured varnishes, once removed, were revealing the original beauty of the works. In national and other wealthy galleries many other treasures have also been subjected to full-scale cleaning, sometimes in preparation for their being loaned for touring or special exhibitions. Brilliant colours have emerged from behind the veils, and they have found an admiring audience in this age of digitally enhanced colour. Time's golden stain has received an unexpected heightening, a new lustre.

This triumphant narrative has brought forth new Pugins from the conservation departments of the major art museums and also at least one new Ruskin from the universities. Disputes have raged, and they have once again drawn to the surface underlying assumptions about our access to the past, in this case to art treasures and to the intentions of their creators.

There is opportunity here to find a clarification about the functioning of works, to understand our part in them and also the mediations of restorers and editors.

RECOVERING THE PAST IN THE NINETEENTH CENTURY

The desire to recover this lost immediacy with the past began to function with new vigour in the nineteenth century. The restoration of the medieval churches discussed in Chapter 2 only reflected a wider movement. The emerging science of archaeology was affording a new knowledge of ancient cultures. Restoration of paintings in the National Gallery, London went ahead confidently and had begun to be controversial as early as 1846.[3] And there occurred the flowering, especially in Germany, of philology. The new science of languages found ways of plotting the relationship of dead and living languages to one another. Hierarchical forms of thinking in philology in turn sharpened editors' understanding of the familial relationships of manuscripts of ancient and medieval works to one another. The belief that scientific endeavour would permit of a new era of knowledge about the world extended gradually through all fields of enquiry, reinforced by the Comtean doctrine of positivism. It took myriad forms (and comes up again in Chapter 6 in relation to the Rembrandt Research Project).

In Henry Kingsley's three-decker novel of 1859 *The Recollections of Geoffry Hamlyn*, Dr Mulhaus, an amateur botanist, zoologist, phrenologist and geologist, is constantly attempting to recover lost pasts. He uses the fragmentary evidence he has to hand: visible geological strata, the odd shape of the villain George Hawker's head (he has a gypsy ancestry), and links between the sea creatures he finds in rockpools in Australia and England. He is the very type of the Humboldtian scientist who seeks to plot the relationships that will unlock knowledge of how the natural world has developed into its present form.[4] Dr Mulhaus also has a passion for taxidermy. It is his form of zoological 'editing', and his audience is normally fascinated or admiring:

drawing from his coat pocket a cardboard box, [he] exhibited to the delighted eyes of the vicar that beautiful little brown-mottled snipe, which now bears the name of Colonel Sabine, and having lit his pipe, set to work with a tiny penknife, and a pot of arsenical soap, all of which were disinterred from the vast coat-pocket before mentioned, to reduce the plump little bird to a loose mass of skin and feathers, fit to begin again his new life in death in a glass-case in some collector's museum . . . 'Some idiots,' said the Doctor, 'take the wing bones out first. Now, my method of beginning at the legs and working forward, is infinitely superior . . .'[5]

These are the accents of editorial pride. The result, in this case, is a perfectedness of suspended animation; it captures a past life on the wing for permanent display and study. As such, it links to the hopes for the intellectual discipline of archaeology. The term *Renaissance* was first used in English in 1840 to mean the revival and renewal of classical forms of culture. By 1872 it had been extended to mean any revival in art or architecture.[6] Breathing life back into the fragmentary remains of Etruria and other ancient sites was a favourite metaphor of the new humane science.[7] *Restoration* was the term by which the activity was known. Meanwhile, philologists aimed at putting texts of, say, biblical books and Shakespeare back into a more intimate and direct relationship with the source of their divine or human inspiration. To restore was to restore life, or at least the simulacrum of it – including the appearance of organic unity or, at least as in the case of the Sabine snipe, the feathery outline of an integral identity that remembered its former living function. For literary works, the source of life was usually seen as the author. The restoration of authorial intention and the elimination of corruption by others was seen as the editorial aim.

Although Humboldtian science developed into laboratory science, and although philology and archaeology refined their working methods, this general corpus of assumptions was passed down into the twentieth century – finally, with effects on museums such as I described in Chapter 1. Nevertheless, in the popular press, the old ideas still chimed familiarly. The excited announcement of the discovery in 1995 in Germany of a death mask that was claimed to be Shakespeare's makes this clear. Its rather grisly triumph is that it contains, stuck to its inner side, some eyebrow hairs – possibly the Bard's. Here was unmediated connection to the author at last! And who was to say what future biotechnology would not be able to do with the genetic code that is, perhaps, still resident in those hairs? In a similar vein, another newspaper article reported that members of the Caodaist cult in Vietnam, which had recently been given some freedom by the government to practise again, 'routinely talk to famous dead writers and thinkers' including Shakespeare and Victor Hugo. They had been denied the right to practise, according to the report, for fear they would claim to connect with the ghost of Ho Chi Minh and thereby acquire an authority potentially in competition with that of the Politburo.[8]

In this 1980s and 1990s atmosphere, that journalists would uncritically acclaim the scientific renewal of life in great artistic masterpieces is therefore not to be wondered at. But of course, the situation with these restorations was not so simple.

THE RESTORATION OF THE SISTINE CHAPEL

The Sistine Chapel was built in the Vatican in Rome in the 1480s, and Michelangelo painted his magnificent frescoes on the ceiling during 1508–12 and the *Last Judgement* on the end wall during 1536–41. The ceiling's restoration occupied the decade of the 1980s, and the restoration of the *Last Judgement* was completed in 1994. I had seen the Chapel in the late 1970s and been struck, like so many people before me, by the confidence and power of the design, and by the triumphant humanism of its religious theme. A great deal of cultural capital would be invested in the restoration.

In order to make decisions about methods of restoration, the restorers had to reconstruct how Michelangelo went about his work. The surface of the frescoes and the subsurface had to be investigated thoroughly. Very little evidence of co-workers was found; the ceiling was not therefore a workshop production. Michelangelo painted up to eighteen square feet per day, having transferred his preparatory drawings to the surface first. He required only about 450 stints, each of up to a day in length, to complete the ceiling. Painting *a buon fresco*, he had to work while the surface plaster was still damp. The lime that is the setting agent finally carbonises the plaster, incorporating the pigment that has been applied, into a very hard surface chemically identical to marble. Only mineral pigments could have withstood the effects of the lime but, once the plaster was dry and chemically inert, it would have been possible to paint *a secco* to retone or correct as necessary, using animal glues as the medium with organic or other pigments.

The total cleaning of the ceiling was a revelation. (See Figure 5.1.) Michelangelo had been revered by his contemporaries for his modelling and drawing, and he himself had believed sculpture to be the supreme art. No contemporary or near-contemporary is known to have praised his abilities as a colourist (as they did those of Raphael). Yet here were glowing colours, diaphanous clothing, emerging from the 'opaque and vitreous screen': 'the heavy, dark blanket of foreign matter such as glues and soots' that had built up naturally over the centuries and as the result of earlier cleanings and restorations.[9] Having occasion in 1992 to write a paper that tried to bring restoration and editing under the same purview, I relied on before-and-after reproductions that had been produced as the restoration had proceeded, on newspaper reports and a television documentary, as well as on a lecture with slides given by the Senior Restorer Gianluigi Colalucci in 1992. I found myself writing with enthusiasm:

Figure 5.1 Michelangelo, *Sistine Chapel Ceiling* (1508–12), during restoration. Detail of *God Separating Light from Darkness*.

Time has wreaked remarkably little havoc since the fifteenth century. Ceiling leaks, candle smoke, and the wine, animal glue, arabic resin and other substances used in the many earlier restorations dating from the sixteenth century are nearly all being removed. The dark and gloomy surface which suffocated the range of Michelangelo's tonality and fed the nineteenth-century myth of his being a black and melancholy artist is being stripped away. Dott. Colalucci, the Senior

Restorer, has argued the 'necessity to recover all full chromatic effects intended by Michelangelo . . . without which [the fresco] would appear flat and without modelling'.[10]

For me as an editor, the belief that, in any historically oriented editorial endeavour, the original moment of creation could be recalled or reconstructed had been ebbing during the latter half of the 1980s as the editorial-theory movement had got into full flight. But here, confounding this direction of thought, the pure authorial presence seemed to be available, uncorrupted. The veil of a disfiguring history had been stripped away. The justification for the restoration of the Sistine Chapel was therefore uncannily like the ideal put forward by the leader of the postwar Anglo-American editorial movement, Fredson Bowers. For him, the business of the editor faced with competing but corrupted printed versions of a literary or historic work was to 'strip away . . . the veil of print' so as to reveal the text as its author intended it.[11]

Almost miraculously, then, the Sistine ceiling seemed to offer the limiting case: underneath the veil of time, now removed, was the lost authorial manuscript, the actual work of the author's hand. The crucial piece of evidence was the discovery, during the restoration, of a piece of the original fresco which in 1565 or 1566 was used to fill a crack that had already developed in the ceiling. The colours of this fragment, which had suffered only a relatively short period of exposure, are extremely close to the colours that emerged from the restoration process. It had no discolouring glue or *a secco* work on it. This, for me, clinched the argument – until, a few years later, I read the 1996 edition of James Beck's polemic, *Art Restoration: The Culture, the Business and the Scandal*.

It is written for a popular audience: Beck argues tendentiously, passionately and often with a suspicious air. The first chapter concerns some Italian court cases in which Beck was charged with impugning the reputation of a restorer who had cleaned Jacopo della Quercia's *Ilaria* tomb in Pisa. This account provides the book with a narrative thrust where Beck is both victim and art detective, wresting the truth from a semi-corrupt establishment of scholars and restorers. Nevertheless, the facts and argument put forward cannot be ignored, even if (as is possible) Beck has made some mistakes that more intimate acquaintance with the figuration and chemistry of Michelangelo's fresco might have prevented.

Beck argues in essence that the disfiguring veil that was stripped away probably contained Michelangelo's *a secco* finishing of the ceiling, what is called *l'ultima mano* or the final autograph revision in which he applied more shadows and chiaroscuro. The cleaning therefore should not have been attempted. For Beck, the darkening of the colours that restoration has removed was intentional: for Michelangelo's art was tonal, not chromatic. He argues that thinking of Michelangelo as a colourist, as the new state of the ceiling forces us to do, negates the whole history of recorded readings of it, and that therefore the toning down should have been assumed to be his until proved otherwise. He cites various responses,[12] including the close observations of a well-informed painter Charles Heath Wilson in 1876 that the glue layer was an *a secco* finishing, not (as Colalucci has it) a varnishing applied during a previous restoration or cleaning to heighten the colours of the fresco.[13] Beck concludes:

We are looking at a unique art historical phenomenon: on the basis of a single cleaning, with an experimental solvent, of a single work by probably the most studied artist in the history of art, much of the art-historical establishment has been prepared to change its view fundamentally. Would it not have been more sensible to judge this cleaning by the historical record rather than vice versa?[14]

Colalucci denies that, with the exception of the *Last Judgement*, Michelangelo did any *a secco* work.

Part of the difficulty is the scarcity of records of earlier cleanings and restorations.[15] There is apparently no documentary proof that the glue applied to the ceiling was done during the only known major cleaning programme (of 1710–13).[16] This opens up space for Beck to argue his general case that the restoration of masterpieces is driven by corporate donations, the economics of travelling exhibitions and the fame of the work, rather than, as it ought to be, by the need for restoration. This criterion should apply whatever the status of the work and only after proof that the cleaning agent and the level of intervention can be guaranteed to be safe. Beck and his collaborator Michael Daley are also suspicious of the influence being wielded behind the scenes in art museums by scientific conservators, and of their now habitual but self-serving criticism of previous restorations, which, because they lacked the full range of modern information, were necessarily botched. The evidence of the crucial fragment used to fill a crack may be explained, they argue, by its original organic glue-size having been burned off by the lime during the application of new plaster in the mid-1560s. The original glue's temporary effect as a barrier may explain why the fragment emerged as a discrete entity at all.[17]

Beck is a new Ruskinite: he inveighs against intervention except where it is unavoidable. He believes that the present generation of restorations are having potentially destructive effects on the works, which will shorten their life-spans. In general, he mistrusts the scientifically based confidence that says that, because the total cleaning could be done with newly developed agents after a battery of tests and inspections have been done upon the surface, it *ought* to be done, regardless of the need and the danger. For me, his most worrying speculation about the Sistine ceiling restoration is that its real motivation derived from an experimental cleaning of part of a lunette done in 1979. The restorers were amazed at the colours they revealed with the new solvent they were using (which had been devised for cleaning marble). Probably aware of the revolutionary effect their work would have on readings of Michelangelo, they could not, Beck contends, restrain their enthusiasm to continue with the whole ceiling.[18] The parallel with the decision to restore the fire-ravaged Uppark (because it *could* be done, regardless of the historical cross-breed that would result) is unsettling (see Chapter 3). In the arrogance of its new knowledge of materials-science and its skills, this generation of restorers has, according to Beck, been systematically destroying what it professes to preserve – just as the church restorers did in Victorian England.

Beck is an art historian, as are curators. Colalucci (now deceased) was a restorer and conservator. A series of conferences was held around the world from 1989 to 1992 to promote dialogue between the two camps.[19] But Beck, a professor of art history at Columbia University, has gone his own way: he writes from the outside as the gadfly of the art-conservation establishment. According to a recent conservator's report that he cites, the ceiling's new chromatic brilliance (which has, as is normal with total cleanings, already faded) may be the result of migration of the pigment in the surface of the fresco under the stress of the strong cleaning agent used. The effect 'is to lighten the pictorial surface';[20] Beck believes the brilliant colours to be 'a chemical deceit'.[21]

Time will tell.

THE ART OBJECT AND READING PRACTICES

Were it not for this last consideration, I would have observed that, even if Beck were right, the restoration had at least revealed Michelangelo's first creative burst (done *a fresco*), although at the expense of removing his second thoughts (done *a secco*). Even if Beck is entirely wrong and the restoration has indeed revealed the fresco more or less as it left Michelangelo's hand, the case of the Sistine Chapel has its refractory aspects. On the face of it, the restoration might have been custom-made to illustrate the traditional view of the work as an object quite independent of the editor-restorer's ministrations. So minor retouchings from a previous restoration have been removed: Colalucci refers to them as 'unartistic'.[22] But some additions done in 1565 as a result of the Council of Trent's objections to the nudity in the *Last Judgement* have been retained, despite the fact that their removal would have been a simple matter. Daniele da Volterra painted some small pieces of clothing over the offending portions. Figure 5.2 shows John the Baptist after restoration, still with covered genitals. A pre-1565 copy in Naples shows how the painting originally looked in this respect; in it, John is uncovered.

The decision, in the case of the Sistine Chapel, to retain what editors might think of as the Council of Trent's bowdlerisation was done on the grounds of their historical value, despite the fact that the justification of the entire restoration was based on appeals either to Michelangelo's intention or to the recovery of the original state of the frescoes. This does not seem a consistent application of a principle, if the principle is authorial. If the principle is historical, then it is running together two historical moments within a third: the moment of late twentieth-century restoration. Although Colalucci envisaged the need for successors, the rationale of his team's activities was backward-directed. Yet clearly their restoration, which was an intervention of the most radical kind, has eliminated the primary evidence on which generations of viewings and interpretations of the ceiling have been based.

Essentially, the conservator's rationale refuses to acknowledge the role of the viewer or of time in the work of art. Instead, its authenticity as an act of painterly editing derives, or claims to derive, from Michelangelo – mostly, but with a little bit from the Council of Trent. The shuffle acknowledges a *contemporary* synthesis – an appeal to conventions in the present – while the rhetoric of the justification is an appeal to the past and to authorship. In other words, the painting in the Sistine Chapel is an *ongoing* work that continued in the activities of Dott. Colalucci and will resume in those of his successors. The artwork and the physical object are, we can say with confidence in this case, not identical. Put in literary terms, the work's textual dimension – the meanings attributed to it – was considered dispensable. The restorer-editors decided they had to alter the documentary, material basis of those readings: heroically or foolhardily. Which will it prove to be?

Figure 5.2 Michelangelo, *Last Judgement* (1536–41), Sistine Chapel. Detail of the figure
traditionally identified as John the Baptist, after restoration.

Leonardo's Last Supper

The conclusion that the Sistine Chapel painting is an ongoing work may be felt provocative – or, at best, teasingly paradoxical. We normally prefer to think of the work and the conservation (or editing) as two separate things. The work is the quarry which, in all its details, the conservator-editor seeks out. The Kantian subject–object binary seems to hold. Indeed, works may even be thought to possess rights. In the Bill of Rights for works of art that Beck and Daley startlingly propose, they refer to 'the integrity of the artists' and the need to respect 'the intention of the artist'. Then, by a sort of moral transfer, the works themselves are deemed to have 'the inalienable right to an honourable and dignified existence'.[23] I doubt that many restorers would disagree: all would expect that the object needs to be treated with the greatest respect for the talent of the artist that it manifests.

Leonardo's *Last Supper* (1498) at the church of Santa Maria delle Grazie in Milan is an interesting example in this respect. Given the reverence in which the painting has been held since its earliest days, the location of the artwork in the physical object would seem to be axiomatic and to be confirmed by its history of restoration. The most recent one began in 1979 and was completed in 1999. At fairly regular periods the weekend press provided readers around the world with progress reports. The authorship of these articles varies but their narrative trajectory – from despair to triumph – was constant. They told the story of the painting's commissioning by the Duke of Milan in 1495 on a refectory wall subject to extreme damp; Leonardo's using a dry rather than a fresco technique allowing him to ponder it at will during its protracted execution but rendering it vulnerable to the absorption of water; its decay being noted as early as 1517; primitive early attempts to restore it including a repainting of its entire surface; Napoleon's troops' use of the refectory as a stables; the bombing of the chapel in 1943 followed by the first modern attempt to restore it from 1947; and the final and triumphant use of modern, scientific technology, on the part of Dr Pinin Brambilla Barcilon. She was to diagnose the chemical causes of decay and carry out the needful cure. Following the taking of thousands of infrared, ultraviolet and other photographs and the undertaking of intensive chemical analyses, Barcilon decided to remove entirely the overpainting of earlier restoration attempts and to clean and stabilise the surface. She would thus reveal the remaining fragments of Leonardo's work, filling in the gaps in the composition opened up by this process with neutral, removable, undetailed watercolour.[24]

A newspaper account in 1997 reported her saying in reply to the question of whether it took her a long time to understand Leonardo: 'Quite a long time, because so much of his painting was concealed. But little by little I fell in love with the work. The process of understanding him was like a courtship. I had to contemplate him, encircle him and win him over.'[25] Such conceptual marriages are jealous ones for they exile all other viewers from any essential participation in the work. We viewers are displaced by the conservator who heroically stands in for us to make the nailbiting physical changes to the painting that are necessary if she is to reveal what remains of it, as close as possible to the condition in which it left the artist's hand. Assisted, in this case, by study of Leonardo's intentions and working methods revealed by his voluminous notes and by her own exhaustive scientific analysis, Barcilon participated in the painting-as-object until such time as its remaining authorial evidence was revealed. In 1999 she withdrew, merely, like the rest of us, able to look *at* it. With the veil of its disfiguring history stripped away, the real work, or what is left of it, is on the wall. The work now re-entered the world of representation. The journalists were surely right to celebrate the triumph of science and loving understanding. (See Figures 5.3a and 5.3b for a revealing detail of the painting, before and after restoration.)

Or were they mistaken? Martin Kemp argued at a conference in 1990 that, far from being the natural and inevitable response, Barcilon's method of restoration, like all restorations, involved critical interpretation:

I am not someone who believes that the artist's intentions are either imponderable or irrelevant to the historian who wishes to understand the work and, by extension, to any spectator who wishes to enrich the potential of their viewing. In Leonardo's case we are fortunate in possessing a large body of notes to help us identify his 'intentions' – in the most obvious sense of this term . . . [But any] artist's intentions, and most especially during the deeply pondered and protracted execution of a work like the 'Last Supper', will be a complex and shifting compound of conscious and unconscious aspirations, adjustments, re-definitions, acts of chance and evasions. It is unlikely that there was ever a stable set of transparently accessible intentions . . . Any programme of restoration of a badly damaged and extensively repaired artefact which aims to reinstate some measure of the original experience has to make an implicit choice as to which of the artist's intentions or groups of intentions and which of the various spectators' criteria are to be satisfied.[26]

Kemp went on to argue that what may have seemed the natural choice in 1979 probably reflected reading practices already established in view-ers' minds by the advent of blown-up photographs of minute details of paintings as used in exhibitions and artbooks in recent times, and from the absorbed gaze upon details encouraged by the movie camera panning slowly over the cherished object. This mode of reading was quite foreign to earlier generations of viewers and restorers, many of whom looked at the fresco as a history painting and all of whom, according to Kemp, looked for the overall effect rather than to the fragment. The unspoken link between the available technology, late 1970s reading practice and the conservatorial method adopted operates at a different level from that of the conscious justification. For Barcilon, the authenticity of the work of the artist's hand must prevail over that of lesser mortals who, in earlier restoration efforts, had tried to reinstate the painting's historical storytelling effect. But, as Kemp points out, they were participating in reading practices whose day has passed. Respect for the scientific highground upon which Barcilon stands may also pass in its turn, as may our preoccupation with 'the seductive fragment'. Our 'conception of what is essential in a work of art', Kemp concludes, 'determines what demands we make on visual images'.[27]

Although Barcilon's position is a very defensible one, it cannot give us access to what does not exist: the true or real Leonardo as an essence outside of a reading practice (in Kemp's terms), or without benefit of the conservator's agency in it. Once acknowledge either context, and the neoplatonic idealism that undergirds Barcilon's enterprise becomes hard to sustain. The conserved painting does not, then, exist unproblematically on the wall. In an important sense, it is completed by its readership both during conservation (via the agency of the conservator) and after.

The case of the Leonardo painting raises the question of how far the search for authorial traces should go. In the collection of the New South Wales State Library there is a painting of an important colonial figure, Elizabeth Macarthur, by an anonymous journeyman painter. (This is the same Elizabeth Macarthur whose now historic house is mentioned in Chapter 2.) Dating from about 1840, the portrait was partially overpainted, possibly in the Victorian period, to conceal the subject's lace-up bodice. Conservators of the painting argued that 'The guiding principle behind the[ir] project was that it is more important to display what remains of a work rather than a restorer's interpretation of it.'[28] Even this stance, however, is interpretative. They removed the overpainting, thereby revealing a Regency-style bust but destroying a piece of later censorship. Given that this painting is in a documentary and historical collection rather than a fine-art museum, that its aesthetic achievement is modest and its authorship unknown, the question of restoration to the original is a debatable matter. There must be examples of this kind in many museums around the world.

Figure 5.3 (a) Leonardo da Vinci, *Last Supper* (1498), detail of Thaddeus before restoration (with adjoining figure, Simon, during cleaning).

Figure 5.3 (b) after restoration, Santa Maria delle Grazie, Milan.

THE AGENCY OF TIME, AND OF THE CONSERVATOR

The Michelangelo and Leonardo cases were total cleanings carried out in the belief that it would be possible to restore either all or what remained of the artist's work. What was revealed would, it was believed, be authentic. More usually, however, the restorer cannot be so sanguine. Compare the epigraph of Hogarth at the beginning of this chapter with a comment of John Brealey made in 1981:

You must be aware, for instance, that the contrast between the lights and the darks has often been parodied by time because the darks have darkened but the lights have not changed to the same extent and so the distance between them has become a grotesque caricature of their original relationship. The half tones where all the subtlety of expression lies, have become closer to the lights than to the shadows . . . If you are going to do the right thing by the artist, you have to consider how, through the removal of oxidised layers of varnish, it is possible to bring back some semblance of the picture's original cohesion.[29]

Both Hogarth and Brealey defer to the artist's intention, yet both recognise that its complete recuperation is likely to be impossible, although one may get some way towards it.

The unavoidable conclusion is that total cleaning of a painting, even when it is completely intact, usually cannot restore the painting as it left the artist's hands. All it can do is reveal the *present* state of the paint beneath the grime. Thus rightly to appreciate as viewers what we see in front of us on the walls of the art museum, we have to recognise the agency of time in the life of artistic works and to appreciate the limitations that its passage imposes on the 'editing' of paintings.

As a consequence, we need to recognise the agency of conservators *in* paintings. We need to know whether the painting has been totally cleaned, partially cleaned (this is where 'the surface of the original paint is not revealed, but remains covered by a thin layer of varnish') or, thirdly, nuance-cleaned (where differential amounts of cleaning are done in order to 'restore the relationship of values that, it is believed, would have existed in the original'). Obviously, both partial cleaning and nuance-cleaning involve critical and aesthetic choices. They flow from an interpretation of the document. Partial cleaning seeks to maintain the harmonising function of the first thin yellow layer of varnish and acknowledges its cultural function as a signifier of 'the age, the antique character' of the artefact.[30] Nuance-cleaning stresses the recovery – although it is, unavoidably, the renewed creation – of balance and unity in the painting.

Gerry Hedley, whose paper I have been quoting, stresses that, where the original painting has undergone significant change (and scarcely any painting survives a century without physical damage), the artist's intention will not be recoverable in full. The best that can be done by the conservator, he argues, is the institution of 'new found relativities to that intention and to time'.[31] The artist's agency was indispensable; but, as far as the work is concerned, that is not the end of the matter. The 'mortal body' of the painting, as another conservator calls it,[32] is always in a state of physical change. At crucial moments in its history it is, as it were, partially rewritten – republished in a revised form – by its editor-conservators. Whatever approach is adopted the fundamental artefact, the documentary-material foundation, is changed, taking on new meanings.

Artists as conservators

If artists are still alive when their work deteriorates then they may act as their own conservators. Their assuming this role creates new twists in the definition of the artistic work. These are akin to those created for the literary work by the writer's returning for revision when, some years after first publication, a second edition is called for. Take the case of Liz Magor, a well-known artist-sculptor in Toronto. For her and many other artists in the 1970s inspired by Walter Benjamin, the phenomenon of mechanical reproducibility tended to undermine commitment to the individual creation of the unique art-object in favour of transformation of pre-existing cultural artefacts. Hence her description of one of her works, *Time and Mrs Tiber* (1976), which the National Gallery of Canada purchased in 1977 (see Figure 5.4):

When *Time and Mrs Tiber* was purchased, we all knew – the curator, the conservators and myself – that it was unstable and subject to slow deterioration. In fact, death, decay, and entropy constitute both the physical and intellectual content of the work – the form being several dozen canning jars filled with various vegetable substances [placed in an old-fashioned kitchen dresser]. These provisions had been put up by a West Coast homesteader in the late 1940s and early 1950s, and it was my intention to honour and preserve the evidence of Mrs. Tiber's rescue of the crop of 1948.[33]

Magor says she thinks of 'the life of a work as correlated to my own'.[34] But the gallery had longer-term ideas. So when in 1987 three jars were found to contain botulism she suggested that she simply replace them, and she was fortified by the fact that the three had not been among those put up by

Figure 5.4 Liz Magor, *Time and Mrs Tiber* (1976).

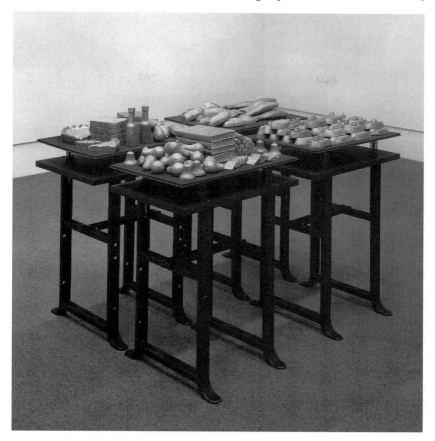

Figure 5.5 Liz Magor, *Dorothy: A Resemblance* (1980–81).

Mrs Tiber but ones that she had originally prepared herself so that the dresser's shelves would be completely filled. This time she sought assistance from an experienced hand at preserves, Mrs Coburn. The anxiety and the irony of preserving preserves illuminate a crossover in attitude to art on the one hand (where the artist has presumed authority) and to historical artefacts on the other (where time is ceded higher authority). The original moment could only be simulated, not retrieved: neither in 1976 nor in 1987.

Another of Magor's works *Dorothy: A Resemblance* (1980–81: see Figure 5.5), in the same gallery, consists of four tables, each covered with small objects cast in lead: bottles, pears, slices of bread, books and small loaves. Each object had been cast in moulds that Magor had made herself, but in rather primitive circumstances: the pears had been produced from one mould, the loaves from another, and so on. Trouble started when light fingers made off with some of the temptingly pocket-sized items on the tables. The gallery contracted another artist to make new moulds from remaining examples on the tables and so to cast replacements. However, the replacements turned out to be not exactly the same as the objects the moulds were made from because of the superior equipment and technique that the contractor made use of. Magor's disappointment is evident: 'In spite of the fact that it is a piece made up of many parts, it was [originally] forged as a whole, and any replacement is unable to be part of that moment.'[35]

Magor's problem is the problem of all conservation, just as the problem of the author's revision is the problem of all editing. The later activity (assuming its presence is established) is unable to be part of the original moment, whether or not undertaken by the same person. Hershel Parker has demonstrated the problems for scholarly editors who would attempt to conjoin in a single reading text the results of radically separate acts of composition or revision.[36] And many readers must have questioned the wisdom, even as they marvelled at the execution, of editions such as the Clarendon edition of Thomas Hardy's *Tess of the D'Urbervilles*, which incorporates into the manuscript base-text some revisions made by Hardy more than twenty years after his original writing.[37]

This raises the question of textual authority: the right of the author to go on controlling the work's meanings by making changes to its underlying documentary condition. Editors, as we will see in Chapter 8, have traditionally respected the author's right to do that. And the National Gallery of Canada, in consulting Liz Magor about conservation, was doing much the same thing. But in both cases we are likely to confuse documentary ownership with textual authority. Having sold her pieces – her physical documents, as one may say – Magor no longer owned them. That is uncontentious, but one can go further: although she thinks of the life of her work as correlated to her own, its life goes on predominantly in the viewing and thinking of other people, including the gallery's conservators. Over these readings – this 'textual' consumption – she has little control and no authority. Magor's statements of her intentions and the contexts of those intentions in her life and other work will and should influence others' textual activities: but only as part of viewers' efforts to understand, contextualise and conserve. Whether she should have the right to reconfigure or replace aspects of the physical artefacts is moot. She acts as a conservator rather than an artist when she does so.

The original moment *cannot* be recalled, as Claes Oldenburg also found when he replaced the pickle on top of his 1.4 metre *Giant Hamburger* of 1962. The piece is made of sailcloth, foam rubber and newspaper. The original pickle had been destroyed, but Oldenburg had offered to replace it for exhibition in 1967 in Ottawa. He made it in New York and flew up with it to Ottawa, using it as a comfortable headrest on the way. When it was inspected at the Gallery, the paintwork was found to be significantly different from the original, more characteristic of his recent 1967 work than his earlier technique.[38] Both examples show that the personal and historical locatedness of a work is unavoidable and unique. This is true, even for works that, in their apparent mechanical reproducibility, embody their creator's rejection of the notion of the unique and inspired work of art.

Conservators, rather like editors, do not occupy a neutral, ideologically innocent position that is legitimised by their scientific techniques. As we saw in Chapters 1 and 2, post-structuralist theory made it a commonplace that we participate in what we know and that power inheres in the ways that we know. The application of this position is clear. Editors and conservators are not simply engaged in other-directed action. And the artistic work is not an object that of itself necessitates certain criteria in the restorative activity. One such criterion, authorial intention, is, according to Martin Kemp, too slippery a notion to be of use. It needs redefinition to become applicable. But the redefinition will deprive it of its capacity to encompass the wholeness or integrity of the work.

Nevertheless, underneath all of this, the object itself still persists. And in its persistence it points. It begs questions of us. Thus it seems clear that, understood only as a form of initiating agency, authorship still has practical work to do and questions to answer. Another curator acknowledges as much when she writes: a work of art is 'something that records itself in the making: that was made with intentions, yes, but without full knowledge of the end product'.[39] Agency, and process over time, seem to be the key. Thus where, in some passages of a painting, distinctions can be made between traces that are probably authorial and overpainting that is not, there *can* be a justification for removal: the claims of the competing agencies have to be balanced. And, it should not be forgotten, at a popular level authorial agency remains of prime interest to most viewers and readers.

This justification for a revived interest in authorship can be best understood, I believe, as pragmatic rather than idealist. The examples of restoration discussed in this chapter point to the conclusion that conservators,

like editors, are interventionists, go-betweens, rather than scientifically dis-
interested technicians. In and through their activities, literary and artistic
works continue to function – and function differently than before. Editors
and conservators broker workable solutions between documents and new
readers, between artefact and new generations of viewers, on the basis of
criteria that enjoy a currency and persuasive power in their day. Where this
leaves the traditional notion of the work (whether literary or artistic) is a
significant question. New definitions have been rendered necessary by the
theoretical shift of the 1980s and 1990s that has upset the old one but seen
no necessity to replace it. In Chapters 7–9, I deal with the counterpart
of the present discussion in the literary area, particularly the need that
editors were experiencing at the time to find and respect more flexible
understandings of authorship.

Chapter 4 was aimed at sharpening this debate by re-examining the
grossest form of its appropriation, forgery. Chapter 6 examines the sub-
tlest, connoisseurship; the case-study is Rembrandt. Authorial agency and
the much slower agency of time are crucial components, I believe, of any
explanation of the work that can withstand the scepticism of postmodern
theory. Reconfigured, the work can potentially serve as an enabling theoretical base for curatorial interpretation and conservatorial intervention.
In order to understand what we viewers are looking at in the art gallery we
need to appreciate where we place ourselves on the work's production–
consumption spectrum. And, to avoid philosophical confusions, we
need, at least sometimes, to be able to invoke the distinction (as argued in
Chapter 4) between the documentary-material and textual dimensions of
works.

The common notion of the work, I have shown, must be reconfigured. It
is not best understood as an aesthetic object, a pictorial or verbal icon whose
status is underwritten by an undifferentiated notion of authorship. As the
examples discussed in this chapter have shown, the work is, unavoidably,
always in process across time, and agents of production take their decisive
roles in it. The final chapter of this book gathers up these and other threads
into a proposal for a new definition of it.

CHAPTER 6

Subtilising authorship: Rembrandt, scientific evidence and modern connoisseurship

The Cunning-sures & the aim-at-yours . . .
(William Blake, 1808–11)[1]

I leave to learned fingers, and wise hands,
The artist and his ape, to teach and tell
How well his connoisseurship understands
The graceful bend, and the voluptuous swell:
Let these describe the undescribable:
I would not their vile breath should crisp the stream
Wherein that image shall for ever dwell;
The unruffled mirror of the loveliest dream
That ever left the sky on the deep soul to beam.
(Lord Byron, 1818)[2]

In the fields of artistic endeavour discussed in this and the previous chapters, a subtler understanding of the nature of authorship is called for if it is to survive as an explanatory tool rather than as a merely rhetorical, sometimes bludgeoning device. Understanding agency at the front end of the production–consumption spectrum, as well as their own participation in it, is no less important for conservators of paintings than for conservators of historic buildings. For the latter however, as we saw in Chapters 2 and 3, the agency of time is typically an even more important one.

However it is defined, we cannot ignore authorship. The author's voice and the artist's hand are traditionally linked to the notion of authenticity. But the voice is not univocal and the hand is not a single one. I will argue that the strands of agency that weave in and around the work need, at the production end, a more subtilised understanding than they are conventionally accorded. The need for this is all around us, and yet we do not normally appreciate it. And even that most sensitively attuned form of art appreciation – connoisseurship – has its eyes still partly averted from the problem of agency, as I will argue in this chapter.

The question of the ambiguous authorship of works of art is often raised at a more popular level than the connoisseurial. Perhaps the most obvious examples are the sculptures of the ubiquitous Henry Moore. They are such a familiar sight around the world partly because Moore was long-lived, a shrewd businessman not incapable of sharp practice, and well organised as a producer. His assistants in his studios at Hoglands in Kent produced enlarged plaster copies of his small maquettes – the originals he made. Next, craftsmen in Berlin and Italy produced the versions in marble taken from the plaster copies, and often also produced and even finished the casts in bronze. The extent of his supervision varied from his completely finishing off a plaster enlargement an assistant had brought to within two inches of where the surface would finally be, to making only a subtle adjustment in the angle of the head in a bronze casting prior to welding. This was in his mature years. In his old age he did less and less. The degree to which Henry Moore sculptures were actually the work of the artist is a nice question.

Certainly he was adamant that all castings and copies were his property to dispose of. On one occasion an artisan in Italy employed to make large copies in marble of two of Moore's sculptures took it into his head to make an extra one of each for himself. The authorised two were to be sold in the usual way as sculptures by Henry Moore. The other two were literally from the same artisan's hand. Nevertheless, Moore must have considered them to be unauthorised fakes for, according to his biographer Roger Berthoud, he stormed down to Rome when he heard they were for sale and took to one of them with a hammer.[3]

Philologists who assess variant readings of a written work with a complicated textual transmission distinguish between the authorial purity or scribal corruption of the readings. The assumption is that the author is the source of textual authority and that only the author has the right to change the text (or to delegate this right). In either case, textual authority and textual ownership are assumed to be in close alliance, if not actually identical. In this context, to maintain that the artisan's first two copies were Henry Moore sculptures and the next two were not can only underline how unholy the alliance is. The situation also points to a strain of sentimentality – a willed optimism – in the traditional notion of creative genius as an autonomous thing working through individual artists and manifested in their works of art. Distinctions between the terms artist and artisan, art and craft begin to blur as we allow our attention to stray past the finished work of art to encompass the actual facts of production, as we have to with Henry Moore.

When Moore died, all work on enlargements then in progress at Hoglands ceased, as he had stipulated they should. Berthoud comments:

[This] gave the rather misleading impression that he had exercised some super-vision in [the previous three years, following an operation]. It is true that from time to time an assistant would bring a working-model-sized piece into the sitting room and stand it on a table for him to see; and on occasion a large polystyrene model was trundled to the window for his inspection. But Moore was in no state to suggest or make any changes. 'Very good my boy,' he might say, pleased to know that the good work was going on.[4]

The anecdote reveals an assumption underlying a lifetime's practice; doubt-less, many artists' workshops have shared it.

Berthoud's reiterated defence of this is that it does not matter much by which methods the end product is achieved provided it emerges as intended. But this ignores by a naive act of faith the production histories Berthoud has, in his biography, disturbingly cited. The defence identifies the essence of the sculpture with the artist's intention, putting to one side the indisputably collaborative processes by which it came into being. The phrase *the work of his hand* is a potent metaphor related to the editorial term, *autograph manuscript*; unfortunately it generates expectations that Moore's case often did not substantiate.

Where did the belief come from? Leonardo da Vinci was one of the first moderns to claim special privileges for the artist. In his notebooks he was a propagandist for a contemporary change in social status for craftsmen-artists. He claimed that the occupation of painting – 'which is the sole imitator of all visible works of nature' – is that of a gentleman, whereas sculpting, a strenuous and dirty manual skill, is that of a tradesman.[5] In his book *Mona Lisa: The Picture and the Myth* (1975), Roy McMullen observes that, at the beginning of the sixteenth century, 'Religious pictures were still being produced under contracts that specified the traditional details and colors that were wanted, and allegories were often painted according to programs that were supplied by the patrons.'[6]

But change was in the air. A demand grew for paintings and statues that allowed artists to demonstrate their talents or *virtu*, and in *c.* 1490 Lorenzo de' Medici 'erected a monument – with a portrait – to the painter Fra Filippo Lippi (*c.* 1406–69) in the cathedral at Spoleto. By the fifteenth century it was no longer unusual to find artists' self-portraits incorpo-rated into compositions.'[7] McMullen speculates that Leonardo's deliber-ately enigmatic rendering of the *Mona Lisa* was an attempt at a purely personal creation, teasingly untied to established iconographic traditions.

In this situation the only way of understanding the painting, he argues, would be to investigate its tangled history of intertextual relationships with other paintings. One would compare it with copies and adaptations taken from it by painters visiting Leonardo's studio while it was in its probably very long period of gestation, and with further and later developments of those copies. This proposal of studying the *ongoing* life of the painting, rather than assuming that that life was confined to the object itself, was novel in 1975 when McMullen was writing. '[W]orks of art', he observes, 'like people, often look enigmatic merely because they are marked by past lives – and discarded accessories – of which we know nothing.'[8] While we know nothing, the 'myth' can stay in place. But that leaves the relationship of the artist and the work wrapped in a mystery that rendered both vulnerable to post-structuralist dismantling and the helplessness, when it comes to practical restorative action, that went with it.

Chapter 5 argued that the role of conservators needs reconceptualising. Traditionally conservators come after, to repair damage. But, if the life of a work of art does extend beyond its original moment of production as McMullen presciently observed, then conservators must be seen as a competing or complementary authorial (or editorial) agency, occupying a place *in* the work. This has effects on how we view the concept of the work, and how we understand each individual one.

The present chapter and the next take up the question of whether authorship can and should be thought of in a more subtle form – whether, as such, it deserves to survive as part of the explanation of the production process. Connoisseurship in relation to the Rembrandt Research Project (from 1968) is my case-study. Its conclusions parallel those in my critique of the so-called Materialist Shakespeare in Chapter 7. And the Rembrandt case looks forward to the subtilising of authorship in Hans Walter Gabler's edition of James Joyce's *Ulysses*, in the D. H. Lawrence Letters and Works project and in German postwar editing, considered in Chapters 8 and 9.

REMBRANDT CONNOISSEURSHIP

Knowing too little of the processes of production of artistic works is nothing like the problem it used to be in the case of Rembrandt, but the question of authenticity nevertheless remains. One might have innocently expected that the problem of determining what is or is not 'a Rembrandt' would be a mere matter of counting, had not the successive compilers of inventories and catalogues raisonnés of the artist's works disagreed markedly. The counts of his *œuvre* have increased since 1883 from 377 to 452, to 595, to

630; till a retreat set in, so that by 1969 the most authoritative count was 420.[9] It is still falling. Blake's 'Cunning-sures' (see this chapter's epigraph) seem to have got it badly wrong, repeatedly. Connoisseurship seems to cultivate crises.

Such extreme variation in attribution questions the efficacy of the whole connoisseurial endeavour. Yet it must be conceded that there is and always has been a logistical problem: the need for cataloguers to view *all* the paintings in order to make the required judgements, or failing that, to have access to reliable photographs of them. Cornelis Hofstede de Groot's catalogue of 1915 (which was based on that of John Smith of 1836) benefited from the enormous collection of photographs of seventeenth-century Dutch paintings that he had amassed. The impossibility of seeing doubtful paintings hanging side-by-side with supposed authentic ones compounded (and still compounds) the problem. And there is also the complication that the demand in the late nineteenth century from newly established museums in the United States finally 'created' a supply and so tended to corrupt the connoisseurship. However, most importantly for our purposes here, the problem is, I believe, one of underlying concept and method of argument.

There is, for a start, an inherent circularity in the appeal to authentic Rembrandts to judge those in doubt. Should any of the authentic ones subsequently turn out to be themselves doubtful, then any argument based on their status collapses. Art-historical interpretation is similarly vulnerable to this dilemma. The year 1650 has often been claimed to be the turning point in Rembrandt's career. Yet no painting from that year is now unchallenged as to its authenticity.[10] Since the 1950s a great deal of work has been done in identifying the pupils in Rembrandt's studio and the other artists associated with him. Study of the successive states of his etchings has also revealed the subtleties of his progressive alteration of his works on paper; and in recent years scientific techniques have revealed some of the history of revision of each painting. The Italian term used is *pentimenti* – literally, the repented (i.e. superseded) aspects of the painting that become visible as the overlayering becomes gradually transparent with the passage of time. It was introduced into English by Roger Fry in the early twentieth century and is now extended to include the evidence of alteration revealed by X-radiographs and infrared photography. They also reveal otherwise invisible underlayers of paint and drawing. Auto-radiographs – carried out in atomic reactors but employed very sparingly – have also been used for the Metropolitan Museum's Rembrandts in New York. In addition, dendrochronology can identify whether the timber in the panels of two

paintings came from the same tree. The technique can give a reliable esti-
mation of the year-range in which it was felled. If the final ring of timber,
just under the bark, is present the exact year can be established. Study of the
threads in the canvases can show that two paintings came from the same
roll. Scanning electro-microscopic analysis of tiny paint chips, suddenly
energised by X-rays or a laser beam, can reveal a cross-section of the layers of
paint and the constituents of the pigments from the so-called ground layer
outwards to the presently visible surface. Forensic handwriting expertise
can also be brought to bear on paintings' signatures.

Not all of these techniques were available in 1968 when the Rembrandt
Research Project (hereafter, RRP) commenced work. Nevertheless, its aim,
at least as seen in the press, was to identify the boundaries of the artist's
œuvre once and for all. This was an era of great scientific advance and
confidence in its capacities to develop new techniques that would reveal
previously hidden physical facts. Art confronted by science would surely
surrender its secrets.

X-radiography was a longstanding technique that revealed the subsurface of the painting. It had been carried out on a great many Rembrandts. The X-ray results needed to be gathered by the RRP and analysed.
First, there was learning how to read them. Second, a careful physical
description – and not only the traditional stylistic one – of every painting
would be carried out. Every part of each painting's physical condition, and
every passage in it, needed to be described along with its micro-stylistic
features. This was done by pairs of RRP team members. The pairings were
often swapped so as to minimise subjective habits unconsciously predis-
posing the teams only to see, and therefore describe, what they were used
to seeing. Forcing themselves to describe physically and minutely was part
of the same regime. The idea was to assemble data that might or might
not later be used for the interpretation and comparisons to other works
when the team got down in earnest to discussing the authenticity of each
painting.[11]

The parallel between this *wissenschaftlich* approach (if not exactly, in
the English sense, *scientific*) and the descriptive and analytical routines of
the earlier New Bibliography, at the peak of its influence in the 1960s, is
striking. Physical and analytical bibliographers attempted to uncover the
production history of pre-nineteenth-century books. Very close inspection
was required. Signatures (individual sewn sections of the volume, usually
being made up of a folded sheet or half sheet) were collated into a descriptive
formula. Any peculiarities that the bibliographer's knowledge of printshop
practices would not have led him or her to anticipate had to be explained.

Then came the optical (machine) comparison of other copies of the work so as to establish the existence of corrections or revisions made while any individual sheet was actually being run through the press. Versions (called *states*) of each sheet could thus be differentiated. An ideal (not necessarily an actual) copy of the work would be one that contained the final corrected state of each sheet. Quasi-facsimile description of title-pages, together with the descriptive (collational) formulae and textual variants sheet by sheet, allowed users to know precisely what the copy in hand actually was. Its production history could be established, in relation to all other existing copies that had been similarly inspected and described. All this provided the informed basis upon which scholarly editing could proceed. Editors would bring their critical prowess into play when adjudging the competing claims to textual authority of variant readings between states of the same edition and between the original and later editions. This usually involved an interpretation of the author's changing intentions.

The positivistic spirit of the bibliographic enterprise is now very striking. Although editors themselves rarely made the claim, others made it for them: that such well-based editions would be definitive and would never need to be done again. Chapter 8 deals with the inevitable theoretical reaction in the 1980s and 1990s when belief in this positivist spirit broke down. As we shall see, the RRP would, in the end although not at the beginning, respond to much the same changed climate.

The first three volumes of RRP findings appeared in 1982, 1986 and 1989. There were three categories: (A) Rembrandts, (B) inconclusive attributions and (C) non-Rembrandts.[12] (This is known as the ABC system.) A great many paintings that Gerson had believed to be genuine autographs were re-attributed to Rembrandt's studio. Controversially, *The Polish Rider* – which the renowned connoisseur Abraham Bredius had discovered and which was acquired for the Frick Collection in New York in 1910 – was questioned, as was a favourite of the German public, *The Man in the Golden Helmet* in Berlin.[13]

A series of exhibitions with scholarly catalogues and associated con-ferences was mounted in the 1980s and 1990s, largely to digest the new information as it emerged and to gauge the extent to which it challenged the conclusions and methods of traditional connoisseurship. The first of these was the exhibition at the National Gallery, London during 1988–89: 'Art in the Making: Rembrandt' was said to be the most well attended exhi-bition the Gallery had ever had. The results of the new battery of scientific testing were on display. People could see for themselves the previously hid-den history of well-known and much-loved paintings. In some cases, they

Figure 6.1 Rembrandt, *The Lamentation over the Dead Christ*.

could see where Rembrandt's hand stopped and where a student's or later hand took over.

The exhibition's scientific and art-historical analysis of the gallery's *The Lamentation over the Dead Christ* was particularly striking (see Figure 6.1). The evidence that David Bomford, Ashok Roy and Christopher Brown marshalled – quite ingeniously – leads to the conclusion that Rembrandt originally intended it to serve as a design for transfer to a plate for etching but that he had trouble elaborating the deposition idea. Another drawing by him of the same subject shows that he moved backwards and forwards

Figure 6.2 X-ray mosaic, Rembrandt, *The Lamentation over the Dead Christ*.

between the drawing and the monochrome design, trying out ideas. He must have become dissatisfied with the latter for he cut away parts of it (it was originally paper). Then, probably realising it would no longer be strong enough to survive the incising required by the transfer to the etching plate, Rembrandt attached the paper to a piece of canvas that was lying around in his studio. (See Figure 6.2: the X-ray. Weave-study shows which of his paintings have identical canvas.) He then painted the surface, among other things disguising the joins (see Figure 6.3: the diagram of the stages).

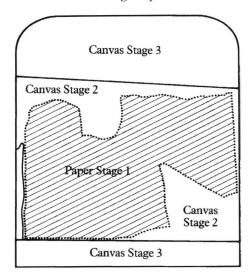

Figure 6.3 Diagram of stages of production of Rembrandt, *The Lamentation over the Dead Christ.*

Next, the painting was mounted on an oak panel. Since 'the handling of paint' at top and bottom 'bears no resemblance at all to that on the central part', these areas must have been done later, possibly by a later collector or restorer who also 'added small touches to Rembrandt's own figures'.[14] The painting must have existed in the intervening time with the top and bottom sections painted only with a ground layer, as microscopic cross-sections show what appears to be a layer of varnish between the ground and the paint. This layer of varnish would have covered the entire painting before the overpainting was added.

The power of this kind of analysis lies in its capacity to clarify the painting's production history. It allows the disentangling of the various agencies that contributed to the present surface – the thing that we, as viewers, take to be offering us the work of art. Normally we are quite unconcerned with the canvas, panel and supports, for the good reason, as Arthur Danto put it, that they have not yet been 'thematized' as being part of the work.[15] What the Rembrandt exhibitions have been eloquently arguing, however, is that this traditional assumption is no longer a safe one. The paintings in this particular exhibition were being offered not only as finished or static aesthetic objects but also as the products of an extended process that was itself on display.

Exhibitions followed in Amsterdam, Berlin and London in 1991–92, in New York in 1995–96, in Melbourne and Canberra in 1997–98 and again in London in 1999. Celebrations in Holland in 2006 to celebrate the four hundredth anniversary of Rembrandt's birth continued the trend. (The exhibition in the Mauritshuis in The Hague is discussed in Chapter 10.) In the New York exhibition catalogue (*Rembrandt/Not Rembrandt*), the curator and the conservator, Walter Liedtke and Hubert von Sonnenburg, argued their (sometimes contrary) opinions about the authenticity of the forty or so Rembrandts acquired by the Metropolitan Museum since its establishment in 1889.[16] Viewers were invited to make up their own minds. The Melbourne exhibition showed twenty-eight Rembrandt paintings, some recently rejected ones and a large number of his drawings and etchings. This was in the context of a display of the works of the best of the painters who had been affected by Rembrandt as pupils. They gradually grew away from him as they took on (as he never did) the newer, carefully planned Italianate style that would, in terms of changing fashion, eclipse his so-called rough manner. In a variety of ways, then, the meaning of the term *Rembrandt* was being distended by the new, invasive means of technical examination, queried on connoisseurial grounds through disagreements in attribution, and to some extent unravelled into the newly understood continuities of historical and workshop contexts.

Meanwhile there had been a falling out amongst the members of the RRP. Its business had been to resolve the embarrassment, by eliminating the confusions, of a history of connoisseurial mistakes. But in 1993 the four older members (born around 1925) of the five-man research team announced that the project was to be completed by the youngest member, Ernst van der Wetering (born in 1938), because they could not support his determination to abandon the three categories of attribution.[17] Given the immense prestige of the connoisseurial tradition and the availability of scientific forms of examination of the physical object, this generational shift was remarkable. It amounted to an acknowledgement that positive knowledge in the matter of attribution was, strictly speaking, unachievable. The second RRP team under van der Wetering has continued its work but concentrates now on marshalling the evidence and arguments for and against a particular painting's attribution rather than putting all the stress on the final decision.[18] Nevertheless, the work of the project continues to be carried out, and judgements made, under the authorial sign *Rembrandt* – but with some notable qualifications, discussed below.

The sixteen-year wait for Volume 4, published in 2005 after the publication of Volume 3 in 1989, allowed some resistance to the RRP's initial phase to build. One of the paintings shown in the Melbourne exhibition as a Rembrandt, now called *Study for the Lost Baptism of the Eunuch* (*c.* 1630), had been rejected in 1982 in the first volume of the RRP's *Corpus of Rembrandt Paintings* because 'the manner of painting exhibits a coarseness in the modelling and a lack of cohesion in the background that one cannot accept as possible with Rembrandt'.[19] Since then, however, analysis and dating of the paper of some impressions of an etching of 1634 by Johannes van Vliet (who was working with Rembrandt), which itself copies the painting and attributes the invention to Rembrandt, have shown fairly conclusively that it is authentic after all.

Another rejection, *The Departure of the Shunamite Woman* (?1640), had previously been regarded 'as a first-rate Rembrandt' but its quality was queried in the *Corpus*:

It says of the man, for instance, that the 'highlights are scattered in rather indeterminate fashion' and that his 'head and hands are poorly characterized'. It also faults the 'row of almost pedantically done catchlights on the chain running across his turban', while the illuminated parts of the woman's figure are said to be 'singularly lacking in articulation' and consequently of a 'somewhat syrupy appearance'.[20]

I take this from Albert Blankert's essay in the Melbourne exhibition catalogue. He clearly has a quarrel with what he sees as the narrowness of the range of achievement of which Rembrandt is deemed to have been capable, and with the dangerous potential for circular argument. But he does not have an argument with the activity of connoisseurship per se:

Recognizing the author of a work of art is not a matter of applying a formula. It is knowledge that simply comes to a connoisseur of the painter, in the same way that one recognizes one's mother or neighbour, regardless of light conditions, viewpoint, clothing or facial expression . . . In Rembrandt's case such efforts are fraught with extra difficulties, as others sought to be exactly like him, while he dedicated himself to teaching them how.[21]

How we perceive things *is* a mysterious matter. For Byron (see his epigraph to this chapter), art was 'The unruffled mirror of the loveliest dream/That ever left the sky on the deep soul to beam'. Like a pure stream reflecting the image eternally, art was directly and naturally apprehensible to us. But it was a stream that the critic's or connoisseur's 'vile breath' might 'crisp'. The ideal of unfallen representation is quintessentially Romantic. But reception is never uncrisped. It is always already affected by contexts and history. Thus connoisseurship, if taken as a formalist reading practice, is no more immune to the postmodernist exposures described in Chapter 1 than is any other.[22] Whichever circle of Hell the Utilitarian Jeremy Bentham would have consigned Blankert's appeal to this specialised form of intuition to, there is probably some truth, nevertheless, in what he claims. Certainly the connoisseurial act of judgement is a strenuous and very real one to its practitioners, who often bring decades of experience to it. Nevertheless, we have to ask what conceptions of authorship such a naturalising appeal as Blankert's may be shielding from the light.

The connoisseurial argument that Rembrandt could not have painted a disputed work because some aspects of it are inferior resembles the arguments proposed by Shakespearean editors in the eighteenth century. They knew that his works had been transmitted through printings of dubious authority. For them, this man for all seasons could not have written lines with faulty scansion such as they encountered in the available editions. It was a simple matter, then, to emend the syllabification or wording so that the lines did scan. And many other improvements became permissible once the standard of perfection was admitted. The criterion adopted was aesthetic – it reflected the editor's taste. The transcendent sign *Shakespeare* under which the editing operated was taken to be stable. Drawing the text of a play eclectically from more than one printed source also became defensible on the same grounds. The New Bibliography of the first half of the twentieth century developed by Alfred Pollard, R. B. McKerrow and Sir Walter Greg rejected the aesthetic approach of their eighteenth- and nineteenth-century forebears. They preferred instead to rely on empirically observable data, other data that could be inferred from it, and knowledge of printshop working practices. This methodology created by the 1950s a site of appeal for editors having to settle questions of variant readings. In this way, the typical criterion – the author's final intentions for the text – was taken out of the realm of taste and aesthetic preference.

Or at least it was believed to be. In the 1980s and 1990s, as we will see in later chapters, this instinct was continuously challenged by editorial and other theorists. A related instinct seems to have underlain the pre-1993 work of the RRP. In his essay quoted above, Blankert is reacting against the Project's severe defining of the boundaries of Rembrandt's *œuvre*. He is therefore, implicitly though not explicitly, questioning the thinking that essentialises the capacities of this 'author'. The name of the Melbourne exhibition and conference nominalised 'genius' as the source of interest (doubtless a concession to the publicists). But Rembrandt scholarship has been progressively moving towards a recognition of the instability and less than fully integrated nature of the expressions of genius. On the biographical front, fervent admirers of Rembrandt are still struggling to digest the disturbing discovery of his seemingly heartless dealings with his de facto wife Geertje Dix after their separation, and his cynical treatment of his creditors before and during his bankruptcy.[23] Rembrandt may well lose his heroic status as truth-telling, cavalier but essentially honourable, bohemian artist.

'Rembrandt' is not, then, the man who lived and painted. *He* cannot be reconstructed: that were impious. The term *Rembrandt* lives in its usages. Other than its iconic status in the public mind, it has become an art-critical and curatorial abduction.[24] It is an umbrella term that gestures at a lost reality. Our conversation goes on under that umbrella. Without its nominalising force we could not profitably discuss the phenomenon. In effect, it functions as an explanatory regime that holds together the complex and refractory array of information that has been assembled by the increasingly sophisticated area of Rembrandt scholarship. In its simpler forms, it always threatens to run away with the show. Auctioneers need it for their encomiums; indeed, they have been using it since the eighteenth century. It holds things together by its reference – factually, gesturally, wilfully – to the man who lived. The underlying appeal is to an integralness that reflects that of Rembrandt's own body.[25]

Connoisseurs expect a continuity and interrelatedness throughout Rembrandt's *œuvre*, even as he came under different influences, suffered various reverses, was affected by his own earlier reception, and grew older. Fortified by external documentary facts that support and subtilise this growing web of abduction, the various registers of the style that is called Rembrandt's are gradually recognised and their relationship to one another better understood. But, because of its very size and concentration, Rembrandt scholarship is beginning to face a similar problem to the one faced by the editors of some modern writers. For such English writers as Charles Dickens, D. H. Lawrence and Joseph Conrad a superfluity of evidence is now available. In each case there are thousands of contemporaneous letters to and from the author. And there is a great abundance of autograph and scribal manuscripts, typescripts and even corrected proofs. So much is known, the abductive field is so criss-crossed with so many and sometimes conflicting trip-wires of data – some robustly connective, some teasingly untied – that a simple essentialising of the authorship cannot be maintained any longer.

In these circumstances, authorship is more accurately understood as a productive explanatory tool. In connoisseurship, it permits the generation of the finest distinctions: it helps to reveal what is hidden to untrained perception. The fear of losing this necessary ground is presumably what has kept post-'68 French theory at bay amongst the connoisseurs. I can testify that no post-structuralist or postmodernist theorist was mentioned at the 1997 Melbourne conference I attended. And even the gadfly of Rembrandt connoisseurship Gary Schwartz, who objects to what he called its 'crumbling categories' of attribution, does not wish to go the way of deconstruction.[26] Authorship appeals to the connoisseurs as a highly productive way of explaining the original creation of the works, but it is going to have to be flexibly reconfigured. To reverse Shakespeare's account of unwavering love in Sonnet 116, it is going to have to alter, as it alteration finds.

This process has already begun. The new battery of scientific information that has allowed study of Rembrandt's *pentimenti* has been tailored by David Bomford into a narrative, for each such work, of evolution or improvement or refining: Rembrandt's changes, according to Bomford, were nearly always for the better.[27] Sooner or later, however, this interpretative move will come up against the same obstacle that it did for scholarly editors. Until the 1980s, editors working in the Anglo-American tradition routinely accepted that an author's revisions (or final intentions) were part of a gradual perfecting of the text. Therefore, once identified, these revisions ought to be incorporated into the chosen copy-text, which may well have been the earliest complete form of the text, often a manuscript. It was gradually realised that the revisions might have multiple motivations. The author may well have been fashioning the text for different audiences or have been aware in advance of the publisher's requirements or predilections. Or the author may simply have been unable to make up his mind. A single, evolutionary line of development in many cases misrepresents how authors saw their work. Many authors have been shown (as we shall see in Chapter 9) to be perfectly content to have different versions of the same work in circulation at the same time.

Paintings are in this respect, of course, limited by the physical object: one state painted over the top of the other necessarily replaces it. But in fact, today, when artists talk of the 'body of work' on which they are presently engaged it is usually the case that each individual painting is in a loose, conceptual sense a 'version' of the one just completed. Both are attempts to embody the idea that the artist is developing. The idea itself does not stand still because of the feedback loop from each successive attempt to express it. Though shape-shifting in time, the idea gives some sort of unity to the works of this 'body'. The later ones in the series are not necessarily better conceived or more finely expressed than the earlier. Accordingly, all we can be certain of in Rembrandt's case is that an overpainting is a different painting, the subject of slightly different contextual pressures, including his response to what underlies it. To see him as a restless genius (as Bomford does) is, though, a distinct advance on the earlier, tighter connoisseurial shaping of 'Rembrandt' because it allows (among other things) for the variation that the new scholarship has uncovered.

THE REMBRANDT RESEARCH PROJECT: VISIONS AND REVISIONS

The Preface to Volume 4 of the *Corpus* (2005) is particularly interesting in this regard. Given the original team's breakup in 1993, the first and surprising thing that one notices is Volume 4's continuity with, rather than its radical departure from, the thinking in the earlier volumes. The Preface to Volume 1 had commented:

the scientist arrives at his interpretation from relatively fragmentary and, of itself, unstructured information relating to the physical make-up of the work of art, while the art historian is concerned mainly with the stylistic interpretation of the picture and its execution . . . [T]he craft that governed artistic practice . . . is not taken sufficiently to heart in either field. As a result a coherent idea of the artist's working process is often lacking.[28]

Volumes 1–4 and the forthcoming (and apparently final) Volume 5 make good that deficiency.

Volume 1 was open about the potential for distortion inherent in the RRP methodology. Its Preface admits the likelihood that the team members' previous assumptions, brought to the task of detailed description, would determine what was seen and commented on and what was overlooked. There is thus a self-conscious awareness of the fallibility of the ensuing interpretation and the judgements on authenticity offered. The authors mention, for instance, 'the painful process' of being forced to accept that some of their stylistic attributions of doubtful paintings to later centuries turned out, on scientific grounds, to be seventeenth century after all (but still not Rembrandt's).[29] At the very end of the Preface they properly acknowledge the unavoidable subjectivity of their work:

The primary aim of our work was thus to delimit Rembrandt's painted *œuvre*, by reconsidering the authenticity of the paintings generally attributed to him . . . [against] a conception of his style and working methods formed over the years [of

RRP collaboration] . . . testing observations and data against a conception that is just as open to discussion as any scholarly hypothesis.[30]

The search for objective criteria (in the tradition of Morelli and Berenson) that would hem this subjectivity into tolerable limits was the ruling aim of the RRP initially, but one that, they admit, did not and could not materialise fully. However, the scientific and technical evidence could at least provide stimuli for, and limitations on, interpretation and judgement in the team's 'quest for authenticity'.[31]

The authors presuppose that 'the evolution of an artist must be thought of as logical' so that 'dated works that do not meet our expectations about his stylistic development may be either rejected or given another date'. Their defence of this abductive procedure is purely pragmatic: 'The preconception of a logical evolution is obviously such an indispensable aid to finding one's way in an *œuvre* that it is hard to do without.' Alert to the danger inherent in this, however, the authors warn: 'But these preconceptions may pave the way for misinterpretations as they tend to stretch reality along the ruler of causality.'[32] The need to engage in 'the "reconstruction" of an individual'[33] is, however, redeemed as a methodology by having to expose it time and again to experience of the actual paintings (and to team discussion of them).

The shift in emphasis in Volume 4 is really an extended, subtle but important quibble over the importance of the term *individual*. In the Preface to Volume 4, Ernst van der Wetering's history of the RRP retrieves its prehistory as a way of accounting for his own shift away from positivist authentication. He does not refer to one of the causes sometimes cited: the exhibition in Amsterdam in 1956 (the 350th anniversary of Rembrandt's birth), which recognised the danger inherent in the fact that there were a number of artists called Rembrandt working in the same period. Rather, and more interestingly, van der Wetering cites the van Meegeren affair (described in Chapter 4, above) as formative:

in 1945–7 . . . [it] traumatised both the art-historical and the museum worlds . . . [and] engendered veritable paranoia regarding possible forgeries . . . [the role of the] Institut Royal du Patrimoine Artistique in Brussels (one of the few laboratories specializing in this area at the time) demonstrated that the painter Han van Meegeren's claim to be the author of the most admired of the Vermeer forgeries, the *Supper at Emmaus* in the Boymans Museum in Rotterdam . . . was in fact true. Nor should one overlook the impact of the Van Meegeren debacle on the RRP in its initial period.[34]

Bredius had 'discovered' the Vermeer and announced it in 1937. Bob Haak, the instigator of the RRP, worked from 1950 with the dealer who had acted as intermediary in the sale of the painting to the Boymans. In this climate, the news that the RRP would make use of scientific and technical investigation 'was enthusiastically received'.[35]

But only a year after its formation, in 1968, the team concluded, with some disappointment, that scientific and technical information alone would not be decisive: 'Whilst in theory it may sometimes be possible to prove that a painting is *not* by Rembrandt by means of technical investigation, the converse – using the same methods to prove conclusively that a painting *is* certainly by Rembrandt – is never possible.'[36] This did not mean scientific evidence was useless. On the contrary. According to van der Wetering:

dendrochronology, research on grounds, and X-radiography (with the latter's potential for investigating the canvas) came to play the most important roles in the project . . . Once it had become apparent [on these grounds] . . . that paintings previously doubted on stylistic grounds could not be later imitations or forgeries, the project participants were forced to accept their reliance on a form of evaluation largely consistent with traditional connoisseurship . . . [But we] continued our intensive use of scientific research . . . primarily to gain insight into the genesis and into aspects of the painting technique and the material history of the paintings under investigation. The painting as 'object', therefore, received greater attention than previously.[37]

The shift in the RRP's balance of interests from a central one in the aesthetic object and its authenticity, to its condition and history as material object, has involved a conceptual readjustment and thus a methodological one. Van der Wetering effectively corroborates Blankert's criticisms of the RRP but goes much further himself. Referring to the project's previous phase, he comments:

Stylistic characteristics discerned in clusters of related paintings from a relatively brief period [1625–42] were extrapolated to the subsequent brief period. In the process, deviations from the period norm could either lead to disattribution or be 'tolerated' if they could be explained, whether on the basis of stylistic and technical developments or because the painting in question was assumed to have a particular function, for example, when it was unusually sketchy. At this point, since the results of technical investigation carried hardly any weight in attribution and disattribution, this strictly inductive stylistic approach was the only way forward. The need to underpin our views with thorough and solid arguments often led to rationalisations of these views that were as useful as they were dangerous.[38]

This realisation had to produce changes in aim and method for Volumes 4 and 5. No longer would the RRP's *raison d'être* be positivist attribution or disattribution. Instead, Volume 4 assembles the evidence for and against attribution, and makes a probabilistic judgement that reflects the convergence of evidence from the various technical, physical and stylistic reports. But this is done in the awareness that 'new information . . . can revise the probabilities and shift the balance of the entire structure of convergent argument such that the earlier conclusion . . . now has to give way to a different solution'.[39]

Van der Wetering's defence of the shift is disturbing. In the following quotation, he is not far off saying that the scholarship of Volumes 1–3 was recruited by other agendas:

The principal reason for relinquishing this [ABC] system was that in many cases no indisputable answer can be given to the question of authenticity. In Volumes I–III the B-category [inconclusive attributions] should perhaps have been the largest rather than the smallest . . . The inclination to keep the B-category as small as possible was . . . an unconscious response to the social need for the greatest possible clarity relating to the art-historical, museological or financial value of a work of art.[40]

Connoisseurship was being hedged into a tighter and tighter circle in Volumes 1–3, exempted from what van der Wetering now sees as the real action: the contexts of production.

Accordingly, Volume 4 dislodges the assumption that individual genius is all-important:

Relinquishing the ABC system also means that the paintings we believe to be workshop variants on Rembrandt's works [formerly C's] . . . can now be considered together with Rembrandt's presumed prototypes . . . [A]long with authenticity the broader question of the production of Rembrandt's workshop has been given high priority. These changes, however, do not mean . . . that we have renounced the RRP's original intention of making the question of authenticity its central concern . . . [But] we are convinced that certain patterns in the workshop production as a whole will become visible and comprehensible only if we persevere in the attempt to isolate Rembrandt's own work from the large body of Rembrandtesque paintings.[41]

In other words, individual genius may not be everything, but it is still worth identifying whenever possible. This is because authorial agency, once apprehended, allows distinctions to be made. That is its power. But it must be understood within its proper contexts. Thus, observes van der Wetering, 'We are not primarily interested in connecting the

names of pupils to non-Rembrandt paintings, but rather in discover-
ing the conventions of seventeenth-century training- and workshop practices.' This reflects 'a growing interest in the *raison d'être* of the putative
non-Rembrandts'.[42]

Despite these notable concessions and this reorientation, the power of
the RRP's empirical methodology – still in 2005 relatively untroubled
by cultural theory – remains demonstrable. Precisely when in 1632–33
Rembrandt changed the orthography of his signature from 'Rembrant' to
'Rembrandt' became a crucial matter for authenticating *Rembrandt, Self-
Portrait, 1632* after dendrochronological results in 1995 helped convince
the RRP it was authentic. The team realised that the panel of another
painting, an authentic one in much the same style, was from the same
sawn-up tree trunk and the date made it too early for imitation to be at
all likely. They had first seen the painting in 1977. Restoration in 2005
has since confirmed their argument written prior to the restoration that
the awkwardly placed hand and the broadening and shifted tilt of the hat
(as in Figure 6.4) must be later overpaintings: this stage of revision was
removed in 2005.[43] This triumph may be compared to the helplessness of
the postmodern position discussed in Chapter 3. Though undertheorised,
the RRP has acknowledged the practical results of connoisseurial mediation – in particular the 1960s mindset that so valorised the artworks as
expressions of individual genius that they were effectively lifted out of their
actual contexts of production. And the RRP has gone on to adjust for
them.

Rembrandt scholarship is no longer a matter of connoisseur–subject facing the aesthetic object in a reading practice underwritten by an unproblematic idea of author–genius. Connoisseurship as a formalist reading practice
seems to have been more ready and able to absorb the material facts of the
physical production of paintings than has art history in its theoretically
inflected forms. The area of study is far more sophisticated now. More
historically sensitised understandings of the functioning of authorship are
starting to be accommodated, as is, more surely, evidence of the inherent
instability of works. But to achieve this fully the connoisseurs will need to
go further than they have so far gone. Another conceptual leap remains
to be taken. The Rembrandt scholars need, I believe, to detach themselves decisively and consciously from the Romantic idealism that Byron
expressed in *Childe Harold*. They need finally to allow their 'breath' (now
not so 'vile' after all?) to 'crisp the stream' of artistic creation rather than
forever seeking – and by seeking, reinforcing – the stylistic integrity of

Figure 6.4 Rembrandt, *Rembrandt, Self-Portrait, 1632*, before restoration.

their essentialised Rembrandt. To accept instead the pragmatic ground I have mentioned for the connoisseurial appeal to authorship would mean completely unlocking Rembrandt scholarship from servitude to the genius that it has in some measure created. The RRP's Volume 4 has set off down that track, but there is further to go.

More generally, this pursuit would maintain into our third millennium a defensible continuity with the curiosity of art lovers near the start of the first. In AD 77, Pliny the Elder recorded the 'very unusual and memorable fact that the last works of artists and their unfinished paintings . . . are more admired than those which they finished, because in them are seen the preliminary drawings left visible and the artists' actual thoughts'.[44]

CHAPTER 7

Materialist, performance or literary Shakespeare?

> So long as men can breathe or eyes can see,
> So long lives this, and this gives life to thee.
> (William Shakespeare, 1609)[1]

This chapter offers a literary counterpart to the previous one on Rembrandt connoisseurship. Here the question has to do with editorial presentations of Shakespeare's works. As Rembrandt and Shakespeare have become equally canonical in their different arts, and as the question of authorship is therefore equally significant to both, it will be no surprise to learn that it has not been a straightforward matter to sort out. The stakes being high, editors and critics have disagreed trenchantly and at times bitterly over how to edit the Bard's works. The disagreements are very longstanding. Eighteenth-century and early twentieth-century editing styles have been briefly described in earlier chapters. The emphasis here is on proposals that emerged during the 1980s and 1990s and that were responding, directly or indirectly, to the then-dominant post-structuralist ways of thinking.

Editors, looking up from their labours, found that authorship was now, suddenly, a dirty word: but what other principle did they have around which to build their editions? Editors need to have one. They must nominate a source of textual authority. Otherwise they have no consistent basis upon which to emend their chosen copy-text whenever it lets them down. What to do if the text has a word or a whole passage obviously missing? What if it makes little or no sense as it stands? Should the emendation come from one of the other early printings, and if so, which one? What if the other printings of it have different readings and they seem more correct, or aesthetically more pleasing, or if, on bibliographical grounds, they can be shown to be later and are therefore potential authorial revisions?

There are shifting sands here. If readers are to appreciate what it is that they are reading, they need to be able to follow the editor's line of thinking as he or she goes about establishing the reading text. This observation runs parallel to my argument in Chapter 5 that we need to understand the status of the Old Master painting in the art museum: if it has been partially cleaned, nuance-cleaned or totally restored. The agency of its passages needs to be made clear to us. The curation is irresponsible otherwise.

CHANGES IN THE AIR

Like other dramatists, Shakespeare wrote plays that found their dramatic realisation and social reception upon the stage. This traditional way of distinguishing the functioning of plays and performed musical scores from, say, novels, which seem to be nicely contained within the covers of a book, seems like plain common sense at first. But the neat distinction has been questioned by a succession of theorists. As early as 1970 Barbara Herrnstein Smith, in a debate with the aesthetic philosopher Nelson Goodman in the *Journal of Philosophy*, argued tellingly that all silent readers actualise and therefore in a sense perform the text they are reading in their heads.[2] They may do it skilfully or not. But they are definitely part of a communicative exchange in which their participation is a crucial element. The textual work does not end at the printed book. There is still work to do, and the reader does it.

As noted in Chapter 4, Wolfgang Iser and the reception theorists in the 1970s and 1980s took the performance idea very much further. Steven Mailloux's idea of negotiated protocols of reading gave the idea a cultural or social extension. And it historicised the moment of reading, since the protocols in operation change over time. Stanley Fish was not slow to point this out.[3] On the face of it, then, why was the idea of a Shakespeare for reading, as proposed in Lukas Erne's book *Shakespeare as Literary Dramatist* (2003), seen by some scholars as a corrective and breakthrough in studies of Shakespeare?[4]

The answer to the question, naturally enough, has a lot to do with the recent history of Shakespeare criticism, editing and bibliography. The debates and groundwork that led up to the Oxford Shakespeare in 1986 rang the crucial change. Until then, the practice of conflating the variant texts of early printings of the plays (which in some cases are of wildly different lengths) was done to ensure that nothing of Shakespeare's was left out. Manuscript copies, it was reasoned, would have been shortened for one or more stagings, but they are no longer extant. Some printings, it was speculated, may have been prepared by actors who remembered their own parts well and could cobble together the rest from memory so as to produce a manuscript they could then sell to a publisher. (This is called memorial reconstruction.)

There was no formal law of copyright to protect the script, but common law extended some protection to the play company's right of production by virtue of possession and control of the playscript. It took about a full-time week, T. H. Howard-Hill has calculated, to copy a playscript. The alternative of engaging the services of a professional scribe was expensive. Copying only the individual parts for players to memorise (and then only the longer ones, as the minor ones could be learned in rehearsal) was economical and minimised the chance of competitors getting hold of the whole script.[5]

So what copy, then, did each of the early printings emerge from? Was it Shakespeare's rough first draft (usually called the foul papers), a fair copy made for the censor to read, the prompt copy used in stage production, a memorial reconstruction created by actors, or, in the case of the later Folio of 1623, any one or some combination of these possibilities together with an earlier quarto printing?[6] This, in summary, is the dilemma that editors of Shakespeare's works have faced over the decades. Most of the possible scenarios that I have outlined were clarified during the course of the twentieth century. Erne's book subjects them all, as we shall see, to a stringent analysis.

Given these circumstances, and given the resultant difficulties of understanding the transmission of the text of each play, the approach usually adopted from the 1960s for literary works of the nineteenth and twentieth centuries could not be straightforwardly embraced. This approach, usually called copy-text editing (and also, more recently, 'Anglo-American editing'), in fact emerged from the editing of seventeenth-century works during the 1950s. It was proposed by Sir Walter Greg in 1949 and was taken up enthusiastically and extended remarkably by Fredson Bowers for the next thirty years, in his own editing and general editing, and through his forty-year editorship of *Studies in Bibliography* – where Greg's essay had first appeared.[7]

The approach may be understood this way. A simple scenario occurs if only two editions of, let us say, a seventeenth-century work were published in the author's lifetime and the original manuscript, used as setting copy for the first edition, is lost. Detailed comparison ('collation') of the texts of the two printed editions showed some different wordings in the second edition that, on critical grounds, the editor believed were authorial and not just accidents of new typesetting. In this situation it made sense to treat the second edition as a revised version. But since its so-called accidentals (spelling, capitalisation, punctuation and word-division) would have been affected by the second typesetter's habits, they would thus be at one further remove from the (lost) manuscript than was the first edition, which was set directly from it.

Since the manuscript would have recorded the author's own inscriptions it made sense to choose as copy-text the edition closest to it: the first edition. The editor would emend it by incorporating into its text the revisions in the second edition judged to be authorial, and then make any other corrections deemed necessary for sense. While the purview was historical and bibliographical, the aim was ultimately aesthetic in its respect for recovering the text of final authorial intention. This became the reading text. The relegated readings not incorporated would be recorded in tables of variants ('textual apparatus') at the back of the book. The partially subjective methodology was frankly acknowledged by the term usually employed, *critical* edition. But, more importantly perhaps, its unavoidable subjectivity was hedged in at every point by thorough bibliographic and historical investigation.

There is a striking parallel here with the early phase of the Rembrandt Research Project, once its team members realised in 1969 that positive scientific proof of a painting's authenticity could not be achieved. Objective criteria were searched for, but ultimately scientific evidence and technical data could provide only prods and barriers. Paintings were judged for their authenticity against 'a conception of [Rembrandt's] style and working methods' that the Project team had gradually formed over years of study. But they readily admitted, as we saw in Chapter 6, that their conception 'is just as open to discussion as any scholarly hypothesis'.[8] '[T]he inevitability of subjectivity in the quest for authenticity' was frankly acknowledged in the Preface to the first volume of the *Corpus of Rembrandt's Paintings* in 1982.[9]

The Oxford Shakespeare

The decision in the Oxford Shakespeare in 1986 was to treat the crucial case, *King Lear*, effectively as two works. This arose from interpreting the different texts of the play in the Folio and Quarto as the result primarily of deliberate authorial revision (rather than both being simply incomplete), and therefore resistant to the traditional approach of conflation. This decision was to some extent influenced by a changed environment of the new editorial theory of the 1980s.[10] (This is discussed in the next chapter.) In that decade the postwar consensus about the methodology of final-intentions critical editions was broken. This was largely because consensus about what a literary work *is* evaporated, or nearly did. An emerging understanding of the role of the reader in the work, described above, was one factor. More crucially, the consensus changed because of the new and, by then, widely accepted post-structuralist modes of thinking. Editorial theory was, although liberated by the new freedoms, not essentially post-structuralist. It always kept at least one foot planted in the realm of the empirical, which remained very influential in editorial circles. The result was that, by the early 1990s, works came to be seen as always in a process of change that could, in principle at least, be documented. Thus the traditional editorial goal of capturing a final version could, even if successful, be no more than a partial representation of the work.

In Shakespeare studies, this insight got a somewhat different twist and led to some extraordinary lines of thinking. The exposure of the instability of the text of so canonical a work as *King Lear* led to a tough-minded and sceptical reassessment of some of the underlying conceptions of Shakespearean editors since the eighteenth century. The ideal of attempting to recapture or recover the manuscript behind the First Folio's 'veil of print' in 1623, as Fredson Bowers famously called it, by means of rigorous study of the original compositors' work habits was criticised not so much on technical as on theoretical grounds. This kind of analytical bibliography was suddenly old hat. To seek to base textual authenticity on authorship was now routinely cast as the pursuit of a chimera. A new orthodoxy in Shakespeare criticism emerged that saw textual authenticity as deriving from the practices of Elizabethan and Jacobean stage performance.[11] Basically, the Shakespearean work was something for the stage. *That* was Shakespeare's business, and it was the stage that he wrote for. So the Oxford general editors declare: 'in this edition we have devoted our efforts to recovering and presenting texts of Shakespeare's plays as they were acted in the London playhouses which stood at the centre of his professional life'.[12]

Take for instance the first Quarto version of *Hamlet*. Until recently it was called, after Alfred Pollard (the most influential of the early twentieth-century New Bibliographers), the 'bad' Quarto. He meant *bad* in the sense of being radically imperfect. It is only half as long as the version in the second Quarto, which is itself somewhat longer than the Folio and is generally agreed to be closest to the author's manuscript. The first Quarto version can be successfully staged and probably represents – well or badly, but probably the latter – a version or versions played in Shakespeare's lifetime. This is argued by some to give it a textual status worthy of respect, and by others a pre-eminent status, despite the material from the play, familiar to us all, that it lacks. Any editorial conflation of the versions (usually of the second Quarto and the Folio) might aim to correspond to an ideal – the text Shakespeare intended – but such a conflation will never have been acted in Shakespeare's period nor will it duplicate exactly the text of any version printed then.

Resisting conflation as the Oxford editors decided to do, and instead basing their text on the Folio, affords clarity and was a bold move. But the primary justification they invoke in the case of this play is not the authority of performance (as we might have expected from their general statement) but that of the author: they argue that the Folio text represents Shakespeare's revision of the second Quarto. Despite this shuffle, the new reliance on the idea of performance by other editors as well as critics seemed to supersede the old idealist one because it claimed to be more firmly historical. 'The primacy of performance', Thomas Clayton could write by 1992, is 'so firmly entrenched at present that there is scarcely a black sheep's bleat to be heard in dissent.'[13]

However, in an article published in 1994 in *Shakespeare Quarterly*, Janette Dillon sounded a sceptical note, objecting to the new orthodoxy as witnessed in a recent edition in a series called *Shakespearean Originals: First Editions*, edited by Graham Holderness and Bryan Loughrey (1992). She objected that the editorial rationale proceeds by demonising authorship and relying instead on 'an abstract and unitary conception of performance as a characteristic of text'.[14] This, she observed, is merely to replace one piece of idealising (authorial intention) with another (performance), when all that we have to go on in either case are the printed texts. Indeed, the *only* thing of which we can be sure about the transmission of the variant versions of *Hamlet* as they moved from manuscript to stage to print and back is that they were all subject to the exigencies of printing and probably of (underlying) scribal copy as well. But if, as believed, the first Quarto and Folio of *Hamlet* both relate more directly to stage versions than does the second Quarto, then their competing claims to our attention translate into appeals to an authority based on performance rather than authorial intention.

Adjudicating these claims still requires reconstructing the likely line of transmission that would explain their extreme variation. Thus analytical bibliography has turned out not to be dispensable after all.[15] In other words, if performance is to be the new source of historical authenticity in Shakespeare editions then the problem remains of how to distinguish the input of the workers in the printing-house from that of the actors on stage, since the actual performance or performances will be related in some way to the printed versions. Thus the question of individual responsibility for details of the text – i.e. textual agency – remains, even if the Bardic author is removed from the editorial equation.[16]

That was the early 1990s. Casting authorship as only a species of textual agency, rather than as capital A Author origination, was a crucial shift in editorial theory of the time. It did not get imported into Shakespeare studies instantly however. Nor did its expanded notions of the work as a continuum, rather than a crystallised aesthetic object, carry across in their ordinary forms. Instead what we saw in Shakespeare studies was the evolution of a rather exotic plant, the outgrowth of what I could only imagine as a hothouse of literary theory and criticism. This was the so-called materialist Shakespeare.

THE MATERIALIST SHAKESPEARE

The argument started promisingly. In 1993, in their article in *Shakespearean Quarterly*, which would provoke a number of responses, Margreta de Grazia and Peter Stallybrass effectively reintroduced bibliographic attentiveness into the discussion.[17] This pointed to a surprising absence in scholarly editing, which, after all, prized itself on the firmness of its foundation in bibliography. In comparison, the German editorial tradition for modern works has been more manuscript-based. This was not possible with Shakespeare and some of his contemporaries where, in the main, the primary evidence was in printed books.

In 1996 Hugh Amory articulated the experience of many editors when he pointed out that scholarly editing effaces much bibliographical evidence simply by deeming it irrelevant. To 'strip away the veil of print' as Bowers advised, from works whose manuscripts were not extant, was effectively to 'shr[i]nk . . . bibliography'[18] in the minds of its practitioners. Excluded from the editor's purview were those features that literary holographs lack but which printed texts contain: typeface and variations in typeface, page-design, publisher's information, ornaments, binding, illustrations, running heads and so on. So editors traditionally concerned themselves with establishing the text of the work, and with documenting its rejected forms. It was assumed that the text, taken as a sequence of letterforms and punctuation, could be isolated from its physical presentations.[19]

Refreshingly, in their article de Grazia and Stallybrass try to reverse this situation. The implications of their move are not just editorial, they are literary critical as well. The post-structuralist groundwork had in some

ways been prepared by others in the 1980s when the anti-Bardolatry movement got under way. Studies of the editorial tradition, particularly that of
the eighteenth century, had uncovered some disturbing illusions and allegiances (described below). Now de Grazia and Stallybrass found themselves
proposing a new form of Shakespeare studies – but without Shakespeare.

In their essay, they turn our attention instead to the paper and typography of the early printings. They remind us that plays in Shakespeare's
quartos and Folio show diversity of titles and names of the same character,
and that the quartos of Shakespeare's plays and most of the Folio fail to
provide lists of dramatis personae. Thus they lacked the clear differentiation between characters, and the unity *of* character, that such lists would
come to imply when finally provided at the beginning of each play in
Rowe's edition of 1709. And the authors remind us of the variability of
orthography, with the lexical fields that variant spellings can invoke, but
which are silenced by regularisation and emendation.

For them, the proposal of a revising Shakespeare was only the first stage
of the new response to the larger and unrecognised scope of variability.[20]
The recent appearance of, for instance, multi-texted *Lear*s and *Hamlet*s[21]
had only broadened the sustaining category of authorship while leaving it
essentially in place. This has been a catastrophe, they argue, for the study
of Shakespearean texts. They trace its source to the eighteenth century.
In deference to a newly felt concern for modernisation and regularisation,
eighteenth-century Shakespearean editors gradually removed the potentially rich variability in presentation of the early printings. They venerated
Shakespeare as the Bard who had access to the eternal truths of human
nature. As a result, the plays came to be regarded as expressive of his genius.
Their textual authority was located in that hidden presence. As textual confusion was not compatible with it, there would be very many attempts to
draw eclectically on the Folio, the quartos and the existing editorial tradition in order to establish an ideal text, called Shakespeare's, for each play.
An illusion of transparency was thus produced between the text and its
source of textual authority by eighteenth-century and later reading and
editorial practices.

In other words, according to de Grazia and Stallybrass, we have been living with a Shakespeare of our own creation. Again we see a parallel with the
case discussed in Chapter 2 about medievalism supplanting the medieval,
and, as discussed in Chapter 6, with the older tradition of connoisseurship
creating and essentialising its own bohemian Rembrandt. This is the argument that we are always at one remove from the real thing. De Grazia and
Stallybrass are aware that their argument begs some fundamental questions

about the nature of the literary work and also depends on some existing ones about authorship. But that is not to say that the questions are answered, nor that the implications of their dependence are fully acknowledged.

The next section of this chapter enforces this critique of their materialist position, which certainly ruffled feathers in the community of Shakespeare scholarship. Some scholars answered in print: their contributions are discussed below. Others feared that the barbarians were now at the gates of the city. For my purposes, the dispute localises the issues that this book has been pursuing. Hence I address the proposal seriously both for what it can teach us and for what, in its blindnesses, it reveals needs to be done to realign theory and practice in Shakespearean editing, now, after the end of the heyday of the postmodern movement.

Examining the materialist Shakespeare

Although editing is less heroic than art conservation in that it does not irreparably change or destroy the physical object, it shares with conservation the need for its working methods to be justified in relation to an argued conception of the work in question. Diminishing the importance of the link of authorship to the literary or artistic work involves linking it instead either to its historical audiences or to the material practices of its period of first production. These arguments, if they are to prevail, demand fundamental shifts in our normal conceptions of the work.

De Grazia and Stallybrass recognise that acceptance of the materialist approach involves 'a need to reconceptualize the fundamental category of a *work* by Shakespeare'.[22] But do they provide it? As part of their demonstration of the significant textual multiplicity they find in the Folio and quartos, they have to resort to the terms 'single texts' as opposed to 'different "versions" of the "same" play'.[23] But they enclose the latter terms self-consciously in inverted commas as if they are not going to indulge in the kind of stemmatic relationship and text-critical terminology that, traditionally, allows a text's identity to be plotted in terms of its textual antecedents and descendants. In a very 1990s way, they wish to celebrate and liberate textual difference, not confine it within editorial categories. I am not sure that a work by Shakespeare *is* a fundamental category. It might better be thought of historically, as de Grazia and Stallybrass themselves show. But the concept of the work is surely fundamental.

Michel Foucault once promised that he would deconstruct it, just as he did authorship in his famous essay 'What Is an Author'.[24] As far as I know, he did not do so. But his concept of discourse subsequently did it for him, essentially by dissolving the work into a site of unstable discursive inscriptions. De Grazia and Stallybrass take post-structuralist thinking, including Foucauldian, for granted. But they bring bibliography to bear on it and find, as a result, that a rich lode of historical practices – to do with papermaking, typography and conceptions of character – may be revealed by close scrutiny of the Folio and quartos. They attempt to graft bibliographic evidence onto ideas of discursive practice. This is to the good. But the post-structuralist context also traps them into a binary for, on the one hand, they seek to discredit the 'solitary genius immanent in the text' as an 'impoverished, ghostly thing' in order, on the other, to privilege 'the complex social practices that shaped, and still shape, the absorbent surface of the Shakespearean text'.[25] The binary was perhaps necessary for the authors to draw attention to their argument. But it has more than a touch of iconoclasm about it and, though appearing to offer a brave new clarity, begs questions of its own.

The authors comment, for instance, on the variable spellings in the early printings. Spelling in English did not settle down properly till the eighteenth century, but signs of gradual regularisation can be seen from the mid-seventeenth century.[26] Speaking of the immediately prior period, de Grazia and Stallybrass comment:

Whether Holinshed [one of Shakespeare's sources] or Shakespeare or a given scribe or compositor of either author's work determined a given form is less significant than the capacity of a word in the language's preregulative or generative phase to take multiple forms. This is precisely what baffles the [editorial] project of retrieving the correct word, for it is a semantic field and not a single word that needs to be retrieved.[27]

But, we are entitled to ask, retrieved for what end? The answer is an abstraction: for multiplicity's sake, for the sake of exemplifying the complex discursive and material practices – the 'diversity of labors' that de Grazia and Stallybrass designate as the new materialist 'object of analysis'.[28] This is what is now to replace the figure of the immanent Author formerly believed to be legible beneath the Shakespearean text. Unfortunately, this new emphasis on the material 'surface' leaves the needs of the reader out of the equation even more than did editions based on the Authorial paradigm, which it explicitly sets out to replace.

Given de Grazia and Stallybrass's warning that the editorially constructed Shakespearean work can no longer be considered self-identical, the newly attuned reader is likely to be looking for a cause of the rich ambiguity of the original texts' orthography at this or that point. Such a reader might wish to imagine the text as a form of communication. In that case it *would* matter whether the editor could judge whether the spelling were Shakespeare's: the reader might want to appreciate his way of tracking across the then-available linguistic field. The reader might, alternatively, wish to imagine the text as something bearing passive witness to social, linguistic, stage or printing-house conditions contemporary with Shakespeare – to look *at* rather than *through* the pages of the early printings, as de Grazia and Stallybrass advise us to do.[29] In preparing for that interest, the editor would have much the same problem as before, given that the same ink traces on paper remained the primary evidence. Only now the reader needs to be sure that the ambiguity is *not* Shakespeare's, not author-intentional. To do that, the editor has to judge who *was* responsible, since someone was. To abrogate this responsibility would be to ignore human agency as a form of explanation in favour of a social-discursive paradigm. It would be to trade one abstraction (authorship, which, whatever its illusions, has at least spawned finely differentiating analytical methods) for another abstraction ('materiality', as de Grazia and Stallybrass call it, which so far has not).

Responses to the materialist Shakespeare

In their response to de Grazia and Stallybrass's article, Graham Holderness, Bryan Loughrey and Andrew Murphy contest the given definition of materialism.[30] They accept the major contention that 'the text [be] stripped of its mystery and spurious autonomy'.[31] But they object to de Grazia and Stallybrass's redefining of it as only 'an element in a process of cultural production' (and circulation) when it should, they argue, be read also 'as eloquent . . . of its own self-dispersal within the continuum of that process'.[32]

This is a difficult concept: it comes from their shared Marxist position. They see de Grazia and Stallybrass's position as a misreading of Marx: 'The object forming the commodity does not in Marx simply disappear into an undifferentiated process of production.'[33] They argue that a printed 'text's specific identity' comes from its 'exchange-value' being 'more manifestly marked than its use-value'.[34] In this, it differentiates itself from the manuscript or prompt book or script of a particular performance whose use-value is in each case identical with its exchange-value, used up either in the physical performance or, in the case of a manuscript, turned into scrap paper. We are told that 'we have (erroneously) been accustomed, by the theory and practice of modern editing, to identify [these] as analogous elements within a larger whole'[35] — by which I presume they mean the *work*, except that the respondents do not use the word.

Dispensing with the notion of the work is easier said than done. It is certainly a brave idea but not altogether consistent with the fact that the respondents cite various works in their footnotes, including works written by themselves. However, some revolutions happen more slowly than others, so it is probably fairer simply to observe that it is not clear how the Marxist notions of value secure the 'text's specific identity'. The respondents insist on the text's functioning as a commodity and therefore of its use to people or for a purpose. They thereby incorporate into their terminology the purchaser of the book or theatre ticket.[36] But that is not quite the same thing as incorporating a readership (which, if only by virtue of the new reading practice they are advocating, de Grazia and Stallybrass have begun to do). In other words, 'value' seems to confer objecthood on the text at the expense of its living effects on its readers. Furthermore, reliance on differentials in use-value and exchange-value might well separate prompt book from foul papers from printed book, but they do not obviously separate the prompt books or sets of foul papers or printings of two different works (as traditionally defined).

In addition, Holderness, Loughrey and Murphy tend to run together the textual and documentary dimensions of works (e.g. they refer to 'The text that was printed, sold and preserved').[37] This means that little allowance can be made for the categorical difference between unique objects (autographs) and printed texts as exact or variant copies of a state of a work (allographs). (This distinction, from aesthetic philosophy, is further described in Chapter 10.) The authors see both categories as 'various discrete and to some degree incommensurable textualizations produced by historical contingency' that have been 'coloniz[ed] by the modern edition', and that 'pass under such generic titles as "*King Lear*" or "*Hamlet*"'.[38] No theory of the literary work can get very far without taking account of the autographic–allographic distinction: 'textualization' is little more than gestural. It signals defeat.

The need to keep *text* separate from the notion of printed book or, more generally, from *document* can be seen here. In reaction against the traditional belief that the ideal text of the work is secured by the authorial presence, the Marxist materialists transfer all the phenomenological weight onto the idea of the text as physical commodity, in other words, onto the documentary dimension. Stressing one dimension at the expense of the other is, I believe, inevitably to produce a flawed and partial account.

Having in many ways discredited the illusion (as they see it) of the work's 'uncontaminated origin' in Shakespeare-as-Author, de Grazia and Stallybrass do not in fact start again from scratch. Rather their substitution of materiality (and sometimes performance) seems to keep them in a state of sharp reaction to authorship. Perhaps this goes with the patch. Shakespeare studies lack the documentary, and to some extent the contextual and biographical, riches that later periods have in abundance. Thus the materialists are able to mock at the 'purely imaginary and idealized status' of Shakespearean foul papers,[39] but they only need to look ahead chronologically to see the folly of this move. If they nourished their editorial thinking in, say, the literature of the nineteenth and twentieth centuries where autograph manuscripts are plentiful and not at all imaginary, different conclusions might emerge.

De Grazia and Stallybrass's argument is being hindered, I believe, by a conflation of basic terms, just as it is for Holderness, Loughrey and Murphy. I would have thought that proposals about a materialist Shakespeare ought consistently to distinguish the physical dimension from the mental: that is, the prints and the hypothesised foul papers and promptbooks from the engagement of producers and readers with them in raising textual meaning. In another response, Edward Pechter's objection to de Grazia and Stallybrass's essay is that 'They demonstrate merely that Shakespeare's texts *may* be studied as an aspect of the history of printing.'[40] But his term 'texts' (which repeats theirs) confusingly incorporates mentalised meaning (whether of today's readers or of Shakespeare's contemporaries), when what Pechter actually means is 'books' or 'printings'. This becomes clear when he immediately nominates printing history as the appropriate discipline for de Grazia and Stallybrass's interest – an interest that he then seeks to reduce in importance by differentiating it from literary criticism.

It is not surprising when literary critics sometimes get bibliographic terminology wrong. Strangely however, the materialists are equally at fault. Peter Stallybrass, in his reply to Pechter, says: 'writers do not necessarily *control* the pointing of literary texts – or, to put it more strongly, do not control the literary object itself'.[41] This formulation seems either to swallow up the manuscript or printing as a physical object within the notion of text, or conversely to reify the literary text as an object, thus doing away with its documentary foundation altogether. Again, de Grazia and Stallybrass in their joint article state: 'The Shakespearean text is thus, like any Renaissance book, a provisional state in the circulation of matter.'[42] What is 'provisional' here: physical document or mentalised text? Or both?

Running the two together allows the term 'text' to free-float and allows explanations involving personal agency (in the acts of writing, copying, revising, typesetting and printing that enabled and embodied the circulation) to be indefinitely deferred.

This is a post-structuralist reflex at work, and one wonders what has happened to the materialism at this point. Notions of text as fluid, decentred, unoriginated, in discursive circulation have been around for so long now that one scarcely notices the bibliographic black hole into which such thinking usually slips. Holderness, Loughrey and Murphy refer tellingly to the 'striking penetration of bibliographical preoccupations into theoretical and critical debate'.[43] But if materialism is to have a future then its practitioners will have to keep a closer eye on the implications of the documentary dimension for their understanding of the textual, particularly for the questions of personal agency that the documentary dimension so imperatively raises – just as we saw it did with forgery (in Chapter 4).

Materialist arguments expose editors' bibliographic selectivity and the danger of failing to see past the reading practices of one's own period. Their point is taken when they emphasise the likelihood of our falling under the spell of an authorial creature of our own culture's (inherited) imagining. Even when authorship is stripped of its aura (as de Grazia and Stallybrass, like Walter Benjamin before them,[44] argue powerfully it should be), the need for explanations remain not so much of textual origination as of textual transmission and reshaping. Why did the linguistic text as written or as printed take such and such a shape and no other?

Personal agency as an explanatory mode will not go away. It is powerful and familiar, even if it can and does create ideological illusions when it is puffed up into the unitary self believed to lie behind the text or the artwork: the real Shakespeare, the true Leonardo or Rembrandt the bohemian genius. When removed from the cultural pressure-cooker, however, personal agency offers less abstract explanations than materialist invocations of 'a productive and reproductive network' are ever likely to do.[45]

AUTHORSHIP'S SURVIVAL

If authorship is only a historical distortion gradually created by the marketplace in the era of the printing press, then the concept of the work would also seem to be in trouble since its ontology is conventionally secured by authorship. The free-floating term *text* as a metonym for a work or a book, was until fairly recent times a booksellers' and students' convenience (as in the term *textbook*). It was given a new and looser currency by the post-structuralist movement. Discourses came to be seen as inscribing both texts and people, who could then be imagined as the provisional sites of discursive traces rather than as unified or stable.

The post-structuralist carriage of de Grazia and Stallybrass's argument will, I think, finally force them to abandon the term *work*. How they will then show (what they presently assume, by dint of tradition) that the Folio and the two quarto *Hamlet*s have *any* relation to one another is not clear. Bibliography can restore the concept via its interest in the physical traces of textual activity – the documentary dimension. These traces reflect postulated intentions to mean (i.e. in what I am calling the textual dimension) on the part of the people responsible for them. The *work* as a concept can make sense as a regulative principle. The name of the particular work is an umbrella term that stakes out the ground upon which we can distinguish and interpret the activity of those personal agencies who were active in creating meaning and left behind their documentary traces.

This claim, which will be further developed in Chapter 10, requires demonstration. Any two copies of a single printing are usually physically variant in minute and sometimes in larger ways, even in nineteenth- and twentieth-century printings. They can be optically collated on a machine that uses mirrors to bring images of the same page in two copies of the same or different impressions up to the eyes of the operator simultaneously. The two images overlap in the brain and any physical difference between them seems, to the operator, to step up from the level of the page or to shimmer. This process often reveals minor corrections or the making good of damage to plates before the later of the two copies was printed. A new typesetting (i.e. a new edition), on the other hand, can introduce thousands of variations in styling and wording, and, especially in later centuries, usually involves a changed typeface, page-design and binding.

So well is bibliography able to describe and analyse variation both within and between editions that the concept of the work seems to arise naturally from these empirical methods. That it does not arise harmlessly is the burden of the materialist case. However, the decision of the scholarly editor that a particular work can tolerate a certain amount of variation before its variant texts and presentations constitute a different one is an interpretative act. The *work* emerges as a principle allowing the editor and reader to regulate that variation. The (abductive) decision also has to do with the physical capacity of the scholarly edition to contain and document it, and the willingness of a publisher to risk the resulting financial outlay.

The editor normally feels a duty to make the interpretation with some regard to the aim that the author (or other textual authority) had in mind. The original writing may have been done under the commercial pressure to get a novel ready for a certain Christmas market, say, or the need to revise the playscript for tomorrow night's performance at a new venue for a changed cast of actors, or the need to adapt an existing poem for a special occasion. The editor's use of the regulative principle will usually respect the original commercial pressures under which the work took shape. There are, of course, notable exceptions; such editions are usually controversial, as we will see in Chapters 8 and 9.

How is the reader to engage with the thousands of newly recovered details that editions reveal? Take away the personal agencies and intention, and the *work* is in danger of becoming too bloated to have any meaning, or, stripped of its apparatus of variant readings, will retain only its popular meaning in the marketplace of *book* or *title* or *text*. The documentary and textual dimensions will blur harmlessly but unenlighteningly in whatever experience the reader has. But if the reader wishes to examine that experience and starts asking the harder questions about textual identity and authority, then the problem of definition arises.

Unless those letterforms and features are imagined as having come into physical being in a miraculous way, questions arise as to the agencies and intentions involved in their genesis and transmission. Objects *point*. They ask sometimes complex questions of us. Bibliography shows us that the answering of them can be intriguing. However, only to recognise the bibliographic multiplicity – to gaze *at* the pages as the materialists enjoin us to do – seems to have no editorial outcome of a kind that might assist readers in answering their questions. The materialist pursuit offers a newly sensitised way of looking at the early printings, and for this it is valuable. But it explicitly denies readers an agented focus by which they might better understand why they react as they do to what they read.

Comprehensiveness needs to be attended by explanation and interpretation, if it is not, like Alfred Tennyson's undersea monster the Kraken (in his poem of the same name), to come to the surface only to die. The sharpening tool, I believe, remains what it has been: personal agency. An editorial policy may yet emerge from the materialist case. It may take a capacious electronic form. But if it ignores personal agency as an explanatory paradigm for dealing with variation, it will, I predict, have dumped upon us another big clean-up job. Semiotic flow is one thing, but we continue to need boundaries to make sense of it. For editors, this is the way of all text.

SHAKESPEARE FOR READING

Lukas Erne's book of 2003, mentioned above, has brought the economics of the Elizabethan and seventeenth-century bookselling marketplace, as well as bibliography, to bear on the question of the performance Shakespeare. His study has bearings also on the materialist case and, although he does not go so far, upon what directions Shakespearean editing might take in future. In his deliberate conjunction of a book-historical attentiveness with a bibliographic one he may be pointing towards a new phase in Shakespeare studies.

In his important essay of 1997 'The Publication of Playbooks', Peter Blayney demolished the longstanding belief, deriving ultimately from Alfred Pollard, that publishing playbooks was a lucrative business in Shakespeare's time. Such publishing had supposedly explained the appearance of his so-called bad quartos whose inferior texts must have been procured furtively from sources associated with the playhouses. Surveying the registration and subsequent printing of plays during the period 1583–1642, Blayney concluded that 'A demand for printed plays certainly existed' but that the small number of new plays printed, and the even smaller number (about half, during 1583–1622) that went into subsequent editions (the only ones likely to yield the publisher a substantial profit), show that they 'never accounted for a very significant fraction of the trade in English books'.[46]

Concentrating more narrowly on the years in which Shakespeare was involved with the Lord Chamberlain's and King's acting companies (1594–1613), Erne essentially confirms Blayney's result: playbooks accounted for only one title in thirty. But, if non-literary genres are excluded from the count, he found that 'printed playbooks accounted for approximately one-seventh of all literary titles', a fraction that, whatever it may mean for the time, is 'much larger . . . than it is today'.[47] Erne lists figures for three stationer-publishers for whom playbooks must have been commercially significant and observes (after Blayney) that the gradual abandonment of black-letter in favour of roman typography for playbooks earlier than for most other literary genres suggests 'that the market for printed plays was catering to an educated and progressive readership'. Erne also points to the fact of playbooks being part of private collections, in defiance of Sir Thomas Bodley's injunction not to collect such 'riff raff Books'.[48]

All of this evidence, while suggestive, is by itself inconclusive. But it opens the door to Erne's wider argument. The logic of it goes this way. Although modern copyright did not exist before 1709, authors were demanding and receiving patents in Shakespeare's time. Literacy was spreading, in part affected by the printed book. The idea that a writer might be immortalised in his writings was a theme of the period, as Shakespeare's sonnets show (compare the epigraph to this chapter); and *Troilus and Cressida* would address itself in 1609 to the 'Eternall reader'. A similar indication is that the provision of authors' names on play title-pages began to occur regularly from 1594 and by 1598 three-quarters of plays were attributed. Thus the rise of dramatic (capital *A*) Authorship of plays from the public stage did not wait till Ben Jonson's *Works* in 1616, as has been thought.[49] The social stigma of the playhouse was lessening.

In 1598 the marketability of Shakespeare's name changed from poet to playwright. Erne's evidence comes from the anthology *Palladis Tamia* chosen by Francis Meres. He chose ninety-five passages by Shakespeare, putting them alongside Spenser and other poets esteemed at the time. And from 1598 Shakespeare's name started to appear on the title-pages of his plays. In 1600 Robert Allott's *England's Parnassus* and A.M.'s (probably Anthony Munday's) *Belvedere, or the Garden of the Muses* excerpted passages from plays side by side with passages from poems by the respectable poets of the day. They were equally claimed to be 'The choysest Flowers of our Moderne Poets'.[50] Play-texts were, in other words, coming to be seen as worthy of entering the canon. Erne's conclusion is that this evidence, taken as a whole, questions the longstanding assumption that Shakespeare wrote only for the stage and would have been careless of his literary reputation.

The equally persistent assumption, mentioned earlier in this chapter, that acting companies considered publication to be against their best interest is also quite unfounded, Erne argues, in this following and extending Blayney's arguments. Only about two years intervene between the likely date of Shakespeare's composition of his plays of the 1590s and their being entered on the Stationers' register. Of his plays written for the Lord Chamberlain's Men that could legally have been printed none remained unprinted by 1602.

In the 1590s and afterwards, printed plays that did not enjoy reprintings were not especially profitable for their printers. After 1600, with growing competition and with much stock in hand, the number of printings of Shakespeare's plays slowed down. Of the plays written in this later period only *Hamlet* and *Pericles* were reprinted. Throughout both periods, the income from sale of rights cannot have been unwelcome and Shakespeare must have experienced a sense of his growing literary reputation. Thus, concludes Erne, quoting W. W. Greg: 'It is foolish to suppose that Shakespeare was indifferent to the fate of his own works.'[51] The use of revised or improved texts for the Folio (rather than existing 'good' quarto editions), and also the descriptive stage directions aimed at readers rather than players in *Antony and Cleopatra*, suggest Shakespeare's earlier involvement in their preparation, though without proving it.

In this context the varying lengths of the plays is a telling factor. Erne compares likely maximum play-lengths. The Royal Shakespeare Company can nowadays fit 1,700–1,800 lines into 'two hours traffique of the stage'. Alfred Hart in the 1930s estimated that Elizabethans could manage 2,300 lines. Even taking the famous two hours as merely indicative, Erne nominates 2,800 lines as the maximum stageable amount in Shakespeare's time. The comedies do not have long texts and are 'compatible with the constraints of the stage'.[52] The tragedies and histories are on average far longer and in conflict with the constraints.[53] Therefore Shakespeare must have written at least some of his plays knowing that they would be cut for performance. The simplest explanation is that he had or developed a sense that they would also function for the purpose of reading. This is the *literary* dramatist of the title of Erne's book.

Although the evidence is far from overwhelming because of their sparse survival rate, the likelihood that there was at least a modest demand for manuscript copies of plays suggests that some people wanted to read them.[54] If so, then it is very unlikely that Shakespeare would not have known of this practice. Erne concludes that the 'wide range of linguistic and dramatic textures among the Shakespearean "bad" quartos' means that 'any single narrative that claims to explain the origins of the entire group [e.g. memorial reconstruction] . . . is likely to be wrong'.[55] Their preparation is likely to have been 'more improvised' than they would typically become by the 1640s. Therefore 'the relationship of performances to the actual material witnesses that have come down to us can never be more than well-informed conjecture'. Thus it is 'simplistic' to affirm without qualification that the bad quartos present the plays as they were performed in Shakespeare's time.[56]

EDITORIAL CONSEQUENCES

To editors (such as myself) outside Shakespeare studies the conflation of quarto and Folio texts by editors seemed oddly inconsistent with the mainstream of copy-text final-intentions editing and too undifferentiated. It suggested nothing so much as a radical failure of bibliographical reasoning to yield convincing results, or to lead to real clarification of the line of textual transmission. So that when the exposé by Grace Ioppolo, Margreta de Grazia and others came in the early 1990s that this editorial attachment to genius was an illusion inherited from the eighteenth century, the dumping of it seemed at first like good advice.

But babies can get thrown out with the bath water. As we have seen, a brave or at least determined new world of performance criticism and editing took centre-stage, claiming to base itself on the plays as performed, preferring a firm historical grounding. But, as Dillon, Erne and others argue, its appeal to an ideal of performance is anything but firm. Does the earlier idea of the revising Shakespeare help? I have to say that I doubt it. Not every reader, and almost certainly not editors of works from later centuries, will agree that the two *Lears* (as in the 1986 Oxford Shakespeare), whether or not authorial revision is proven, are two works. Editors of works from later periods deal with far more radical forms of undoubted authorial revision and normally treat them as versions of the one work. That interpretative move of Wells and Taylor was perhaps too precious. I do not think it will retain lasting adherence.

What editorial implications flow from Erne's arguments? He himself does not pursue the matter. Doubtless, he had enough to do as it was. He was treading a minefield of scholarship and was proposing to remake the jealously held terrain. Nevertheless, the outsider can ask the question.

What we can say for sure of Shakespeare's printed play-texts is that all the plays were written. The migration of text backwards and forwards between private and public spaces in the act of writing makes all documentary texts inherently unstable. The migration is particularly important for dramatic texts where the public space gains the added scariness of exposure from memorisation of roles, and upon the stage in rehearsal and in performance. And further instability flows from whatever exigencies of scribal copying may have preceded or followed performance.

The doctrine of final authorial intention was not designed to respect such instability. Aided and abetted in Shakespeare editing by the practice of conflation, the approach offered an achievable way of establishing, as best the editor could, the ideal text of a work, and thus of keeping it singular. This text cannot respect the fluidity of agented textual production. In fact, it seeks to eliminate the work of all of the agents except the predictable one. With the Shakespearean text, those agencies crucially included playwrights with whom he collaborated on a number of plays, the compositors, the author and his fellow workers in the Lord Chamberlain's and then the King's company, as well as material written by other playwrights for incorporation into stage versions, and probably the agencies of editors or collaborators working on copy for the Folio.

The obvious way out of this impasse, it seems to me, is that, wherever possible, separate texts for reading and for playing should be aimed at. In other words, one should, in future, edit versions of the works not in relation to suspected authorial revision but rather in relation to their intended function. This does not change the nature of the documentary evidence one iota, but it does change the questions that an editor will have to ask of every piece of textual evidence, every textual variant and every piece of historical information.

The textual principles of the two editorial orientations might well be different, and indeed a more speculative form of editing than what we are used to might be justified, working from the relatively firm basis of facsimile editions of the early printings and from existing collations. An electronic environment might facilitate such editorial experiments. An edition that aimed to recover the playscript of performance would be historically orientated. It would have its existential anchor in the company's repertoire rather than the authorial canon. As far as possible the editor would differentiate the likely contributions of the different categories of people involved. But the editor would bear in mind Philip Brockbank's cautionary note of 1991: 'Since we may be confident that there was more than one performance, we cannot from the evidence have high hopes of preparing the performed text.'[57] Given that performance texts are inherently changeable according to the needs of the occasion and to the available facilities and actors, there can be no way, Brockbank argued, to capture *the* performance text of a play, only (given sufficient evidence) *a* particular one. Will even that be possible?

A performance text can be aimed at, but it may end up still bearing the collaborative and fragmentary imprint of many performances. We cannot therefore consider performance as anything more than an orientation for editorial endeavour. Certainly, after Erne's book, we should not think of it as the only one. Nevertheless, it would be a legitimate form of versional editing whose aims Erne's book helps us to clarify. Confusions of function can be lessened now.

In editing, performance cannot operate as an editorial criterion in the absence of intention, or rather of postulated intention, of all kinds: authorial, theatrical, publishing. This is because, at the level of editorial decision-making when dealing with a nonsense, an apparent lacuna or repeated material, the question of whether the reading was or was not intended is inescapable. Textual agency cannot be ignored, since someone had to do the intending. If we take the stage to be a corporate endeavour then it would *not* make sense to eliminate non-authorial text in an edition aimed at respecting the ideal of performance. But it would make a great deal of sense to attribute responsibility wherever that were possible. Every act of copying or of typesetting *licenses* speculation about the matter. The precise moments of documentary production are always crisis points in the transmission of text. They afford leverage on it.

Strangely enough with performance editions, the question that the analytical bibliographers of yesteryear struggled so mightily to address – of who typeset what, exactly? – may re-emerge, but under a different dispensation than before. The re-emergence will not be with the aim of stripping away the compositors' habits of spelling and pointing to reveal the features of the lost authorial manuscript. Rather the aim will be to differentiate, so far as possible, the collaborative textual agencies: of compositor, from abridger, from author, from that of copyholder recording stage business. We could not rule out sourcing emendations from say a Folio or 'good' quarto version (likely to be the basis of a reading edition) if that printing seemed to transmit aspects of the performed play more reliably than the 'bad' quarto closest to the performances itself did. Editorial experiments are needed, not editions produced to tight deadlines imposed by a publisher. There has been too much of that in the past.

The other area in which experiments would be needed is in the editorial establishment of the longer texts intended for reading. Erne argues for them as texts intended by Shakespeare. Here we seem to be back into old, familiar territory. But once one separates the two editorial orientations from one another, the aim is not the same as of old. For a start, reading editions may be quite impossible for some works, other than as reconstructed fragments, although even this would perhaps be worth aiming at. *Macbeth* would be an example. It is a short play; its longer version (assuming it had one) is lost.

But for plays such as *1 Henry IV*, *King Lear* and *Romeo and Juliet* the realisation of a reading edition *may* be possible. It would be based on the differentiation of the textual agencies apparent in the early printed witnesses. Material deemed to have been introduced for the stage only would not be incorporated nor deletions for the stage respected. Emendation from the bad quartos, and even conflation, *might* be justifiable if it was aimed at recovering a lost text intended by Shakespeare for reading. Such an edition would materialise in textual form an editorial argument about the transmission of the relevant documents, both extant and inferred.

That is what most scholarly editions do – *argue* – some more intelligently and cogently than others. They restore what may have existed, or may have been intended to exist, and provide all the evidence to challenge the editor's interpretation.

Sometimes very early painted reproductions transmit the colours of the original painting more accurately than it does itself because the reproduction happened to use more stable pigments. To edit Shakespeare is no doubt to grow used to living with such paradoxes. To edit with the double remit I have proposed will only multiply them. But that would merely underline the fact that mediation is inevitable. Any pretension or illusion that the work of the Bard is unproblematically captured in the edition is immediately replaced by the editorial self-consciousness, now turned upon the reader, that the edition is only the informed materialisation of an argument about the documentary sources.

Editions can be read against the grain as well as with it because they both establish reading texts and unravel them back into the contexts of their production. Restoration, if that is how we are prepared to describe the editorial act, takes on a different form from that of artworks and historic buildings. The argument I have been developing with all three, however, is that all parts of the production–consumption spectrum need to be respected. All deal with documentary objects that beg textual questions. All are intersected by time and by agency of one kind or another. Authorship, no longer puffed up with Romantic illusions, remains of crucial relevance because of its explanatory potential, as a form of agency. The significance of this approach lies in the philosophical grounding, around the notion of the work, that it puts in place. If it is useful for the purpose of restoration, then that is a pragmatic good.

CHAPTER 8

Modes of editing literary works: conflicts in theory and practice

> My object is . . . to submit this demonstration of Christianity to the
> verdict and decision of *Reason*.
>
> In executing this, I have not scrupled to make use of the thoughts
> and words of any man, when I found they could be pressed into the
> service of God; and I have often done this, without acknowledging,
> or perhaps knowing, or even being able now to discover, the sources
> from whence I took them. But for this I make no apology; because I
> have no vain desire of being thought an author, but merely wish to
> be useful in my day and generation.
>
> (Stephen Drew, 1828)[1]

> now . . . I am an *author*
>
> (Rolf Boldrewood, 1879)[2]

This book is about securing the past. It is a commentary on recent
approaches to restoring tangible and intangible forms of it, whether in
two- or three-dimensional forms. This chapter continues from Chapter 7
in dealing with the intangible: literary works from the past and the professional practices of their scholarly editing.

In the development of these practices in recent decades the literary
theory movement has been both a blessing and a curse. The critique of the
subject–object relationship inherited from Kant and the Enlightenment
project has been a blessing, but not an unqualified one. The heady rush
of the post-'68 theory movement in the anglophone countries in the 1980s
and 1990s repeated a pattern from the past. Successive cultural or aesthetic
theories tend to spin out of the one before, there is a jostling for competitive
position, the opposing group is seen off the premises, the theory that
has emerged triumphant gets more and more sophisticated and (to its
exponents) all-encompassing, a great deal of effort is spent in recolonising
the cultural terrain, and finally the exponents' papers and essays get bound
up in rehearsal of the now-influential theory. The inward-looking dynamic

means that practical outcomes are staved off and finally come to seem irrelevant.

But by the end of the 1990s the movement seemed nearly to have run out of steam. The official policy of multiculturalism had become, in a number of Western countries, a mainstream expression of the culture-bound relativity of values, an idea that the theory movement had introduced. But the policy was about to suffer the shock of 9/11 and its aftermath. It would be put officially into reverse in Britain in 2006, but only after having made many gains – for tolerance and fair play – for minority and ethnic groups.[3] Similarly, in the minds of the young, feminism was now only a movement their mothers had gone in for. Young women enjoy but mostly take for granted the gains that were made. And artists and architects were searching out post-postmodern directions.

During the theory decades, however, practitioners in the editing–restoration professions received little or no direct assistance from literary and cultural theory. This was the curse. Editing was usually cast as a lingering example of discredited nineteenth-century philology. The latter's diachronic, author-centred and filial principles of explanation had been superseded, so the account usually goes, by Saussurean structuralism. New principles, from 1968, were the synchronic, decentred models of textuality that showed how meanings are inscribed and circulated. (The material Shakespeare proposal, discussed in the preceding chapter, is a late expression of it.) Post-structuralist discursivity left no place of honour for authorship, which was cast as a historical creation of the printing press and copyright law, a mere mark of social cachet in the nineteenth century (as witnessed by the two epigraphs to this chapter). This was an inheritance from Romantic poetry, and it continued into the twentieth.

With the *work*, as I explain in Chapter 10, things were little better. Especially after World War II, the work as aesthetic object assumed a sort of iconicity. Literary critics praised works for their concreteness or organic wholeness, their self-sufficiency. But this would, in due course, render the work (routinely reduced to *text*) a favourite target for post-structuralist undoing. A new critical vocabulary found the primary interest of texts to be their ideological or discursive 'inscription', or their recirculation of dominant power-relations – or, as in the 1990s, their resistance to or hybridising of them.

Editors, who had typically understood literary works to be the creative expression of an individual, stood mutely by. They had been designing their editions to rest upon a concept of textual authority flowing from authorship. The ideal text aimed at would be the one that best approximated the text the author wanted published. Such editors were now – suddenly – dinosaurs, serving an outmoded model of the work. This outcome ought not to be surprising. For their part, editors looked in vain to the theoretical movement for any recognition, in the new models of inscription and discourse, of the documentary evidence of textual change that they, as editors, dealt with on a daily basis. Their understanding of inscription – physical markings on the page – raised questions of agency, of chronology, of the exercise of textual authority, of textual ownership. Who made this change in the first sentence here? When? Did it have the author's authority? Or was it the typesetter, or perhaps a bowdlerising or improving editor?

The two perspectives on text were in stalemate. They did not communicate. David Greetham's *Theories of the Text*, a monumental survey of the applicability of the complete range of theoretical positions to editing, appeared in 1999 and gathered his thinking from the previous ten or fifteen years. In its marvellously acrobatic self-consciousness, it is the last word on the subject. Yet it had no practical proposals whatsoever to offer.[4]

It is not surprising, then, that editors themselves during the 1980s and 1990s underwent one of their periodic reinspections of their methodology and assumptions. New approaches were tried, and there was some tentative cross-fertilising of the two main editorial traditions: the German and the Anglo-American. (This is dealt with in the next chapter.) Nor should it be surprising that the period also saw a number of rearguard actions from more traditional literary critics, fearful that the texts of their beloved works were being tampered with by innovating editors who, through their mediation, seemed to them to control the keys to the textual kingdom. This chapter covers a number of these disputes and looks for the enduring light that the heat produced. It discusses the pre-1980s editorial methodology and what gods it served, and looks at the alternatives that next presented themselves.

WHAT AN EDITOR DOES

A fundamental definition first: an editor mediates, according to defined or undefined standards or conventions, between the text or texts of documents made or orally transmitted by another and the audience of the anticipated publication. This definition includes the editors employed by publishing houses who adjust, abridge, embellish, correct or criticise an author's manuscript in the stages preceding its publication. The definition also includes translators whose mediation is aimed at remaking a work for a new audience: the rendering of biblical texts into gender-sensitive language is a subset of this activity. Newspaper and magazine editors select, and subeditors rewrite or correct, the articles of others with a view to satisfying the tastes of their audience (and, sometimes, of their proprietor). At another level, collectors of oral literatures are editors: this would include the editing of children's playground rhymes and of nursery rhymes, ethnographic transcriptions by linguist-anthropologists, and the transcriptions of interviews done from tape by oral historians. The blending or alteration of takes in filming and sound-recording is another editorial mediation; and so, in a different way, is the Laban or other notation of performed dance. All of these activities involve the taking of attitudes towards presentation of an existing text, whether the material form of that text is physical or intangible. Some of these editorial tasks might be deemed scholarly because of the rigour and intelligence with which they are carried out. But none necessarily presupposes the taking of a critical attitude to the *transmission* of the text or texts being prepared for presentation.

Yet a critical attitude to the transmission of a text that comes to us from the past can be an essential part of our understanding it. To know what changes it has undergone, what versions and packagings have been created over the decades or centuries, and by whom, is to be in a position to appreciate more precisely what the theory movement was highlighting. It is to understand the text's successive discursive inscriptions, its ideological absorbency. But to follow this track means keeping the documentary in touch with the textual. It means treating the material dimension of works – their historical witness – seriously. The material document was beneath the notice of most theorists and philosophers. Scholarly editors, by virtue of their trade, have always battened onto it as the primary site of the textual transaction.

Editions that restore missing or altered material are perhaps the most readily defensible. The journal of the pioneering diarist from early Melbourne, Georgiana McCrae, was edited by her grandson, the poet Hugh McCrae, and published in 1934. Many historians and literary scholars have quoted or anthologised from this version, treating it either as a historical document or as a piece of authentic life-writing, unaware that they were quoting a text that had been continuously filtered through the writing style of the grandson, and further misrepresented by his hundreds of deletions, additions and rearrangements. There is scarcely a paragraph left unchanged.[5] The 1934 publication amounted to a rewriting of the early colonial period in Melbourne during a decade in which the strivings of the early pioneers were being resuscitated and hailed.

In an article on another piece of interventionist editing, this one from the 1940s, of the nineteenth-century *Letters of Rachel Henning*, Anne Allingham has commented: 'That such [silent] truncation of this classic text of Australian colonial literature could stand unchallenged for forty years raises serious questions on standards prevailing in this country in the discipline of publish[ing] edited manuscripts.'[6] In the 1940s and 1950s there was a new interest in regaining contact and celebrating the still-living connection with the colonial period.[7] The hardiness and adaptability of the pioneers and bushmen had just been reinforced by the struggles of Australian soldiers during World War II in northern Africa, the Far East and New Guinea. Publishers recognised the appetite for the connection and so they fed it, in this case in a distorted form tailored for their present. Both the McCrae and Henning cases represent the sort of situation that begs for new editorial action. Whether done well or ill, it will depend upon taking a critical attitude to the transmission of the text such as historical documents do not normally require. (This form of scholarly editing is covered in this chapter's Coda, below.)

WHY CRITICAL EDITIONS ARE RESISTED: AN AUSTRALIAN CASE

Is a critical attitude to textual transmission always necessary with *literature* from the past? It has to be acknowledged that this is a contested issue. It erupts from time to time in reviews of editions that have been preceded by a full-scale bibliographical analysis. The reviews are usually written by literary critics. The first three titles of the Academy Editions of Australian Literature series, of which I had the carriage from its inception in the early 1990s until its final volume in 2007, received a composite review in 1999 in which the issue came bubbling up. Because of my own involvement I cannot pretend to be impartial. What follows, nevertheless, is how I have come to think of it, and what it may mean more generally.

The reviewer, Brian Kiernan, was especially forceful in his display of a no-nonsense practicality. He complained of the editions' unavailability for classroom use due to their high price (a fair point), which he took to reflect the costs of the underlying scholarship. (In fact, the price was directly related to the number of pages, usually around 800, and the number of copies likely to be sold.) 'The basic issue', he concluded, 'is not the unreliability of previous editions of earlier Australian texts, but how reliable texts can practically (meaning, yes, commercially) be made available to the largest potential market.'[8]

The curious logic of this position is that reliable texts can somehow be wished into existence without the hard work of ascertaining their textual features having been carried out. At the inception of the series, the novel that its editorial board was least concerned would involve tricky textual problems was Henry Kingsley's *The Recollections of Geoffry Hamlyn* of 1859. (Kingsley, brother of the more celebrated Charles Kingsley, was in the Australian colonies during the 1850s, and the novel is set there.) Problems unexpectedly encountered in the first English edition included stop-press correction of a section of the novel at proof stage. This is supposedly a pre-machine-age phenomenon only, but in this case it was probably caused by the collapse of a whole forme of type during the printing. Another section of the novel corresponding to one folded sheet of sixteen pages was found to exist in two states. The earlier one had been quoted extensively by a reviewer who had evidently been supplied with an advance copy, but in the meantime the author revised it significantly. Kingsley would return for more comprehensive revision at his next opportunity: when the first, three-volume edition was typeset for a one-volume cheap edition.[9] Nevertheless, the novel remained (editorially) a far simpler problem than others in the series such as Henry Handel Richardson's *Maurice Guest* (1907) or Marcus Clarke's *His Natural Life* (1874).

As a demonstration of his belief that the textual research behind the series was not worth the candle, Kiernan recommended two other fairly recent printings of *Geoffry Hamlyn*. One of them has, indeed, something to recommend it. It is the University of Queensland Press Australian Authors volume *Henry Kingsley* (1982), which, Kiernan states, 'includes a facsimile of the (now suddenly disreputable?) 1877 edition of *Geoffrey Hamlyn*'.[10] The ironic touch is Kiernan's, but otherwise he is repeating faithfully – except for the misspelled *Geoffry* – the account in that useful collection's Note on the Text. However, as the Academy Edition's introduction points out, the '1877 edition' does not represent an *edition* (in the bibliographic sense of a new typesetting). It is, rather, a stereotyped reprint – dating, in fact, from 1879 – of the English second edition of 1860 (which we call '*E2*').[11] It was chosen for the Australian Authors volume because, as the editor puts it, it was 'the earliest one volume edition available' (i.e. for disbinding, so that it could be photographed) and because it was 'substantially' close to the first edition of 1859.[12]

The latter statement turned out to be true, although not primarily because of the evidence cited in the volume's Note on the Text. (It refers to changes in chapter-titles in *E2*'s Contents pages.) Textual collation for the Academy Edition revealed about 950 divergences in *E2* from the first edition, for some proportion of which Kingsley was certainly responsible. He changed some wordings, he added whimsical footnotes, and he may have been responsible for a percentage of the very many changes in punctuation.

Kiernan dismisses the latter as being 'unlikely to worry any reader'.[13] This is a hasty judgement. The critical edition points out that the spoken-voice freshness of Kingsley's often loose-limbed sentences was impaired in *E2* and increasingly threatened thereafter by the regularising of successive typesetters. Attention to his sentence rhythms is important if we are to appreciate the tricksy, sometimes mercurial nature of the narrating position, and the freedom to move that it gave Kingsley.

He had of necessity to doff the cap to the expectations of his publisher – the high-minded firm of Macmillan – as well as to those of his clerical family. A scapegrace, he had cut himself adrift from them in going out to the Australian colonies. Upon returning home some years later, he was determined to make his way as a novelist. He was content to recirculate the enthusiasm for the warrior spirit that he must have encountered in the colonies – a hangover from the Peninsular War – as well as the squatters' (i.e. wealthy ranchers') view of local politics and of Aborigines. But he avoids a centred truthtelling. He figures the writing as an elaborate and collaborative editing; he interposes contrary voices. And he self-consciously implicates his reading audience in the cultural business literally in hand – that is, in the fact of the physical book itself and the wider negotiations it embodies. In the absence of the manuscript, the best chance one has to *hear* this happening is in the first edition, where Kingsley's rhetorical punctuation is at its greatest remove from the syntactical system that we have inherited for the purposes of silent reading. Kingsley's pointing is well adapted to reading out loud, with frequent comic effect. Partly because of this, the critical edition's reading text is based on the first edition. The changes in *E2* are given at the foot of the page.

Kiernan's alternative contender that he commends to readers of *Geoffry Hamlyn* is the 1993 Angus & Robertson (A&R) 'facsimile of what looks like (but is not identified as) the second English edition'.[14] This would be handy if it were true; but, unfortunately for his argument, Kiernan has got the facts wrong, despite their being spelled out with some care in the introduction to the volume he was reviewing. The A&R has only a distant connection to *E2*. It is a photographic reproduction of a typesetting prepared for the Home Entertainment Library in 1935. This edition appears to have been typeset from a Collins edition of a little earlier that was in turn set from either the third English edition of 1894 or *E2*. It has been reprinted in Australia a number of times since 1935.

Reflecting a principle of editorial theory that has been continually con-firmed in Anglo-American editorial projects since the 1950s, the foreword to the Academy Editions volumes points out that there are dangers in accepting as reliable the texts of reprints distantly related to a first edition, let alone to the second or later. Wording becomes scrambled, typos appear, footnotes if present get deleted or truncated, and the pacing and rhythm of an author's phrasing is gradually misrepresented as each successive type-setter consciously or unconsciously imposes the prevailing conventions of the day. In a novel that incorporates much geological and other scientific description it is as well to know that, for instance, the 1935 edition's 'sheer scraps of grey rock' is not an idiosyncratic phrasing but is, rather, a typo for ' . . . scarps . . .' and that Kingsley meant 'a grey faint cloud' rather than 'a grey afint' one, as 1935 has it.[15]

The literary-critical introduction to the A&R reprint was a challenging one when it first appeared, drawing attention to the novel's only half-suppressed anxieties about its complicity in the projects of Empire. At one point, it relies upon a footnote of Kingsley's translating an Aboriginal woman's short speech to make an interpretative point about seeing. In fact, the 1935 edition had truncated the footnote, the original wording of which invalidates the local interpretation being offered.[16] Intelligent literary criticism needs reliable texts upon which to work, but textual reliability does not (unfortunately for Kiernan's case and all cases like it) drop from the clouds ready for our use.

Again, it might have refined this same argument about the novel's being a piece of imperial fiction to know that in a late serialisation of the novel in the *Australian Town and Country Journal* published in Sydney during 1870–71, the novel's Colonial Secretary refers to the 'nomadic savages' who have been 'justly displaced' by the small landholders, whereas in its setting copy (*E2*) they were 'unjustly displaced'. While the Sydney serialisation elsewhere intentionally omits sections of the novel's account of the politics of land selection in the neighbouring colony of Victoria, compositorial error is a more likely explanation here. '[I]f so', the Academy Edition points out, 'the replacement of the *E2* wording with the expected one is itself revealing.'[17] But of course, until the bibliographic work is done, the fine-grained ways in which a literary text can be shown to duplicate or resist or reformulate the ideological cross-currents of its period are not reliably available for close inspection, although ungrounded generalisations may always be entertained.[18]

EDMUND WILSON AND BARBED-WIRE EDITIONS

Edmund Wilson's famous attack in the late 1960s on the editions of the Center for the Editing of American Literature (CEAA), run by the Modern Language Association (MLA), in the United States glimmers proleptically in the background of Kiernan's review (and in others like it in other countries). There is, as we shall see, a pattern.

The story starts a little earlier than Wilson, in fact with Lewis Mumford, primarily a sociologist and social commentator but also a literary critic. In early 1968 Mumford wrote for the *New York Review of Books* (*NYRB*) a review of the first six volumes of an edition of Emerson's Journals. The review was entitled 'Emerson behind Barbed Wire'. A critic of what he saw as the mismatch in the modern world between personal development and technology, Mumford diagnosed the editorial method in the Emerson edition as a radical departure from 'literary values and humanistic aims':

> the editors committed two monumental errors of judgment . . . The first one was to print all the available material *seriatim*, mingling the important with the inconsequential, the living and maturing mind of Emerson with the debris of his daily existence; and the other was to magnify this original error by transcribing their accurate notations [using an array of diacritical marks to indicate deletions and additions] to the very pages that the potential readers of Emerson might wish to read freely, without stumbling over scholarly roadblocks and barricades.[19]

Anyone who has used a modern edition in the form of a diplomatic transcription (a method sometimes used for previously unpublished matter) knows that it is not a general-reader's edition. It is meant for study rather than ease of reading. Yet at the crucial moment, when this (minority) form of modern editing was under attack in the influential *NYRB*, the then-emerging American editing establishment fell back from the barricades and failed to insist firmly on this (obvious) distinction. The reason was, I suspect, twofold.

First, many readers, and even editors at heart, doubtless agreed with Mumford's New Critical desire for a clear text that would represent the Journals as an integral work ('a consecutive, readable journal'[20]). Such a text would also, Mumford believed in an old-critical belles-lettristic way, afford 'intimate intercourse with Emerson's mind'.[21] The irony is that this desire would have depended for its fulfilment upon a selective and textually burnished presentation. It was one that would have inevitably created an Emerson of the editor's own making: a *desired* Emerson that juggled rather than respected the documentary evidence. But the more important reason for the falling back from the barricades was another attack, later the same year and also in the *NYRB*, this time upon the wider MLA editorial enterprise. It was written by Edmund Wilson and voiced sentiments of the same generation: like Mumford (and, incidentally, F. R. Leavis), he was born in 1895.

Wilson's two-part broadside, 'The Fruits of the MLA', put the scholarly editing fraternity in America onto the back foot. Various letters to the editor contested or supported Wilson's arguments, and in due course the MLA published a selection of the letters in a booklet together with some new essays putting its side of the case. Contributors stated that the format of the Emerson edition was not one that the CEAA encouraged new editors to adopt. The clear text was the desired format:[22] at least Mumford and those who shared his point of view could have no argument with that. The textual apparatus, however hard to read, was to be placed modestly at the end of the volume and could readily be removed to allow a cheap reprinting of the reading text alone.

Wilson, nothing mollified, turned his attention to the apparatus in order to highlight the waste of energy and money that its preparation for the editions would have involved. Because his own proposal for a series of editions of American classics had not been funded (but the MLA's had been), and because Wilson was much surer about the physical appearance and desirable weight of the volumes in his proposed series than he was about the editorial principles they would adopt, his challenge was relatively easy to shake off. But it was at the cost of removing from the agenda for some decades any challenge to Mumford's 'standpoint of humane letters'.[23] The MLA scholarly edition should be two things at once: an error-free, authorial, clear-text edition for the general reader and a repository of textual information for the specialist scholar.[24] Wilson later admitted that he had felt 'a curious interest' in the kind of textual recording that would unearth superseded phrasings and censored passages in edited works. But in his 1968 essays in *NYRB*, he stuck to an easier purism: 'we do not', he decreed, 'want served up to us the writer's rejected garbage'.[25] The contradiction was and is scarcely sustainable: it begged the question of what a work is, but Wilson was not inclined to push that question hard.

When innovative editions came along during the 1980s and 1990s they encountered similarly confused flak from critics. Despite the theory movement that had intervened, the later reviewers were still trying to hang on to a lost past, an unproblematic sense of what a work is. They hung on by attacking the editions. There was a history to it, of course. It amounted to a revival of a very longstanding suspicion dating from the early days of the New Criticism, if not before. The basic disagreement was between, on the one hand, literary scholars who insisted on the role of historical and biographical context in interpretation and, on the other, literary critics for whom the encounter with the text was more immediate, personal and, in the reader's respect for the object, aesthetic.[26] For the latter group, the isolation and enshrining for canonical analysis of the finished state of classic works of art and literature was the only defensible goal of editing. What was more, it ought to be possible with relatively little effort. It ought to be straightforward.

GABLER'S *ULYSSES*

This is the same lost innocence that some commentators on Hans Walter Gabler's 'critical and synoptic' edition of James Joyce's *Ulysses* (1984) seemed to be hankering after. Not far below the surface of a second wave of review-articles that appeared in and after 1988 a basic intolerance can be detected, a resentment at having the sacred turf encroached upon. Only it was not being done by aggressive literary theorists this time, but by editors who could in the past have been trusted to tend the playing field properly and let critics get on with the main game. Now the editors were wanting to expose the textual subsoil as well, to reveal the instabilities of textual process rather than establishing or confirming a textual product suitable for reprinting in student and general-reader editions.

Some explanation of the causes of this reaction is necessary. At first blush, it appeared that Gabler had provided, as is traditional, a clear reading text based on a fresh inspection of the documents and a new analysis of the textual evidence. This reading text appears on the right-hand pages of the edition. Here is an example from the Lestrygonians chapter at the point where Leopold Bloom, who has a professional interest in advertisements, decides, after some hesitation, to purchase a cheese sandwich for his lunch. He has earlier in the day attended Paddy Dignam's funeral, and we follow his wayward thoughts as he makes his decision:

Sardines on the shelves. Almost taste them by looking. Sandwich?
   Ham and his descendants musterred and bred there. Potted meats. What is home without Plumtree's potted meat? Incomplete. What a stupid ad! Under the obituary notices they stuck it. All up a plumtree. Dignam's potted meat. Cannibals would with lemon and rice. White missionary too salty. Like pickled pork. Expect the chief consumes the parts of honour. Ought to be tough from exercise. His wives in a row to watch the effect. *There was a right royal old nigger. Who ate or something the somethings of the reverend Mr MacTrigger.* With it an abode of bliss. Lord knows what concoction. Cauls mouldy tripes windpipes faked and

Sardines on the shelves. ⌐^Almost taste them by looking.^ Sandwich? Ham and his descendants musterred and bred there.⌐ Potted meats. What‹ is home without Plumtree's potted meat?› Incomplete. What a stupid ⌐(ᴮ)[ad.] ad!(ᴮ) ^⌐(ᴮ)[Right under] Under(ᴮ) the obituary notices ⌐(ᴮ)[too.] they stuck it.(ᴮ) ⌐All up a plumtree.⌐ ›Dignam's potted meat.‹^ ⌐(ᴮ)Cannibals would with lemon and rice. White ⌐[men] missionary⌐ too salty. Like pickled pork.(ᴮ) ⌐Expect the chief consumes the parts of honour. Ought to be tough from exercise. His wives in a row to watch the effect.⌐ ⌐*There was a right royal old nigger. Who ate or something the somethings of the reverend Mr MacTrigger.*⌐ With‹ it ⌐(ᴮ)an(ᴮ) abode of bliss.› Lord knows what concoction. ⌐(ᴮ)Cauls mouldy tripes windpipes faked ⌐and minced⌐ up. ⌐Puzzle find the meat.⌐ Kosher. ⌐No meat and milk together.⌐ Hygiene that was what they call now.(ᴮ) ⌐^Yom Kippur fast spring cleaning of inside. Peace and war depend on some fellow's digestion. Religions. Christmas turkeys and geese. Slaughter of innocents. Eat drink and be merry. Then casual wards full after.^ ⌐Heads bandaged.°⌐ Cheese digests all but itself. Mity cheese.⌐ —Have you a cheese sandwich?

Figure 8.1 Section of left-hand page from the synoptic and critical edition of James Joyce's *Ulysses* (1984), vol. 1, p. 362.

minced up. Puzzle find the meat. Kosher. No meat and milk together. Hygiene that was what they call now. Yom Kippur fast spring cleaning of inside. Peace and war depend on some fellow's digestion. Religions. Christmas turkeys and geese. Slaughter of innocents. Eat drink and be merry. Then casual wards full after. Heads bandaged. Cheese digests all but itself. Mity cheese.
—Have you a cheese sandwich?

The presentation of the equivalent passage of text on the left-hand page is very different: see Figure 8.1. Gabler's aim was to show there what he called the continuous manuscript text of *Ulysses*. He plots the relationship between invariant text – passages that remained the same throughout – and the emerging variant readings, as the text developed at Joyce's hands from manuscript working drafts and fair copying, through typescript versions and successive sets of proofs to early printed forms. On the left-hand pages each revisional level within a chapter is designated by a symbol so that one can follow Joyce's working on that level through the chapter in question, and then from document to document. He was intensively involved at nearly every stage.

The gradual elaboration of Bloom's playful thought-processes from one level of revision to the next is mapped by the symbolic notation. Half-square brackets around words indicate that they are revisions made between one document and another. Square brackets enclose deleted material. Pairs of carets pointed upwards (^ ^) indicate a first revision *within* a document, and, if pointed inwards, a second revision. The alphabetic symbols (in this paragraph, B and D only) refer to levels of revision witnessed by the extant typescript of this chapter, which copied the lost final working draft. B is the 1918 typing itself; D is a stage of revision from 1921 (dealt with below).[27]

The lost final working draft was not the famous (and extant) Rosenbach manuscript. *It* was earlier copied from that final draft at the point when Joyce fancied he was finished revising. But the act of fair-copying elicited further revisions and, rather than spoil his chances of being able to sell it later as *the* fair-copy manuscript, Joyce went back to the working draft to complete the revisional process there. The typescript was then copied from it (professionally, not by Joyce) in triplicate.[28] One copy of the three is extant. It therefore witnesses textual revisions actually first inscribed by Joyce on the lost final draft; and Joyce's inscriptions are what the synoptic display is primarily aiming to record. Alterations by others (e.g. typists) in the reported documents are emended so that the display represents his unhindered creative process. Gabler's way of identifying and eliminating such textual corruption, as it is called, is discussed below.

Comparing the extant typescript copy with the Rosenbach manuscript makes this process plain. Joyce squeezed in between lines of the Rosenbach the following words: 'Right under the obituary notices too. Dignam's potted meat.' But the typescript reads, in what is clearly a development: 'Under the obituary notices they stuck it. Dignam's potted meat.'[29] Joyce had presumably entered this reading back into the final working draft.

The *sticking* of the meat would later spark off in Joyce's mind, when he returned to it, the association with cannibalism, which we then see developed through the successive stages of revision of proofs (picked out by numerals: here, 1, 4 and 6) with a touch of fantasising ribaldry thrown in. The Jewish culinary anxiety was at first only a note in the Rosenbach ('Kosher.'). But in 1921, the typescript (which would shortly serve as this chapter's printer's copy for the novel's first edition of 1922) received a further overlay of revision (D): 'Yom Kippur fast spring cleaning of inside . . . casual wards full after.' Thus was Bloom's stream of consciousness when purchasing his cheese sandwich gradually arrived at.

After a little practice, one can witness the text's fluid formation and be in a position to appreciate its emerging directions and energies anew. And one begins to see how the newly introduced notes interact with motifs elsewhere in the novel. One wants then to know at what stage or stages *they* were introduced.[30] The novel gains dimensions one did not know it had.

The unmarked text is text that did not change during the processes of composition and revision. It happens to report the readings of (and suitably notated, the revisions within) the Rosenbach manuscript. But it also represents, as best it can be known, the text of the lost final working draft (and its final revisions, as we have seen). The function of the unmarked text is to serve as the basis, first, for editorially assembling the development of the text. So the Rosenbach manuscript is not the *copy-text* in the Anglo-American sense; it is rather a source text that is reported for the purpose of study. The ultimate purpose of the synoptic assembly is to enable the editor to capture on the right-hand pages, in a clear reading format, the *final* stage of authorial development of the text of *Ulysses*. Privileging this stage dislodges the authority of the text of the first edition: a move that, as we shall see, would have repercussions of an extraordinary kind.

The display on the left-hand pages was, however, the initial cause of offence. It *is* off-putting at first. One loses one's way in the forest of symbols, trying to follow the editor's path through a multitude of layered features – through the textual topography, so to speak. One heard mutterings at the time about Germanic scholarly overkill and the edition's suspect reliance on computer programs. This prompted more sceptical questioning. Was the new edition a disguised way, perhaps, of establishing a new copyright for the Joyce estate given that the copyright on the work would otherwise run out at the beginning of 1992? And why this newfangled German editorial methodology? (The edition is not, in fact, an example of German historical-critical editing as some commentators assumed it to be, although it is an adaptation of it. The two traditions, as we will see in the next chapter, had had almost no communication up until then.) In the shades of Lewis Mumford, the foreignness of the presentation was once again a cause of affront, and this sometimes surfaced, disgracefully and anti-intellectually, in what became in 1988 a sort of scholarly fracas.

By chance, I had recently put the novel on a new course I was going to teach, this being the only way to force myself to finish a work that had defeated me two or three times previously. Grains of sand still fall from among the leaves of the two volumes that I read on the beach on holidays that summer, firstly on the right-hand pages for fifty pages or so, and then, curious about what I was missing, on the left-hand side for a much slower but far more rewarding experience. I learned to appreciate Joyce's verbal ingenuity by seeing how he worked: how he would stumble about for a while, then hit upon a phrase fortuitously, which itself would unlock a dazzling play of wit. One could see it grow from level to level, and one wanted to know what other ideas at that level of revision linked to it. In the end, with time foreclosing, I had to revert to the right-hand pages for volume 3, regretting the fact all the while.

Jerome McGann remarked in his review of Gabler's *Ulysses* that one has to learn a new 'grammar' of presentation to read this edition.[31] I think of it more as a textual algebra or computer coding. As one reads, one performs operations on the display of invariant text using the imbedded variants, reconstituting the recorded versions on the fly. I found one has to persevere. After a while, the foreignness of it wears off. But one does need time. While one is reading a linear display of mainly invariant text one reads it in the ordinary way, but one repeatedly engages with what the German editorial theorist Gunter Martens (not having Joyce in mind) calls the 'paradigm of variants'. This is the phenomenon, not peculiar to Joyce, of an author's giving repeated attention to the same place in the text at each successive level of revision.[32] The textual energy flares in such places, and then goes quiet as the revisionary impulse falters. The recommencement of invariant or little-variant text then enables one to reorient oneself with ease.

Editorial forensics

Doing a scholarly editorial job entails subjecting every word, every mark of punctuation in the text to scrutiny. In collating the extant documents prior to original publication and also the printed editions subsequent to it, the editor learns to attribute responsibility for each change revealed by the collation. Archival evidence and published correspondence usually assist in this. This is why Gabler could rightly claim that his edition was the *first*: that is, the first where 'not just Joyce's novel, but the *text* of Joyce's novel *Ulysses* stands forth as an object of philological . . . analysis and presentation'.[33] A personal example will clarify this claim.

When I began editing *The Boy in the Bush* for the Cambridge Works of D. H. Lawrence series in 1981 I employed four postgraduate students, only one of them from my discipline, English. We worked for three or four hours every morning, making our way gradually through the novel. I read aloud from a photocopy of the manuscript, in Lawrence's hand.[34] The two differently revised copies of the typescript that had served as printer's copy for the first British and American editions of 1924, and the editions themselves, were assigned to my readers, one version each. Neither set of proofs was extant, so we could not deal with them directly. Lawrence had corrected one of them, and some of these corrections also made their way into the other edition.

Every time one of my readers detected a difference from what I had just read aloud, whether in wording or punctuation, and whenever we struck a homonym or a word whose spelling could vary, one or more of the readers stopped me. Each reader then reported how his version read, and any variant reading thus uncovered was recorded on paper and tape for later processing. By the end we had recorded about 5,000 variants.

Within a couple of weeks of starting this slow process none of the readers was content merely to do the allotted job. All wanted to attribute responsibility for the variants we encountered. In this way they could understand what had happened at the moments of copying. The act of copying is, as I have already remarked, the moment of crisis for a text since it presupposes an act of reading and, therefore at a basic level, an act of interpretation. Copyists make sense of their copy, often unconsciously. The author's sense may have been recorded accurately (or not) on the initiating document. The copyist's sense may or may not reproduce it. The logical gap – the textual abyss – between reading and copying is where the editorial lever is inserted to prise open and inspect the transmissional history.

As my readers quickly realised, most variants fall into categories. House-styling by typesetters of text layout, word-division, capitalisation, spelling, and occasionally grammar, typically explains the bulk of the smaller changes. Mechanical problems such as eyeskip can lead a typist or typesetter to miss a line or lines in copying, because two of them happen to start with the same word. And bowdlerising by the press's reader of religious or sexual references, of blaspheming and foul language, are also common enough. Usually, but not always however, the most interesting category of change will be the revisions made by the author. See Figures 8.2 and 8.3 for the same page in the two typescript copies revised by Lawrence. Their different handwritten readings are explained by his near simultaneous revision of them. He improved the wordings as he copied from one to the other copy, and then back again.[35]

Sometimes these categories of change are not easy to distinguish. There can be legitimate alternative explanations of them, but each case needs to be tested against every other case in the same category. Because a very large number of cases may be involved, a self-checking mechanism of considerable detail gradually sets itself up as the work proceeds and as the editor later reconsiders the cases at leisure. By these methods, the transmission of the text from document to document, or between parts of one and parts of another, becomes clearer. The clarification of how the text was revised and transmitted is the crucial matter, since the editorial policy will flow from it.

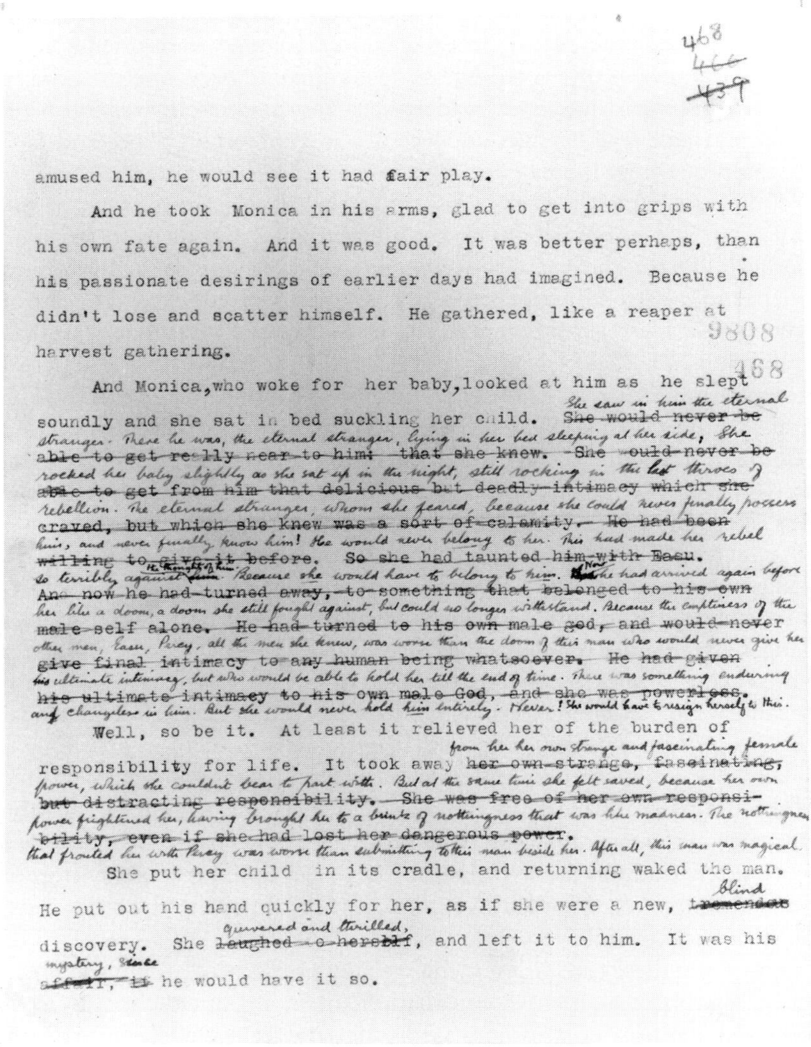

468
466
439

9808
468

amused him, he would see it had fair play.

And he took Monica in his arms, glad to get into grips with his own fate again. And it was good. It was better perhaps, than his passionate desirings of earlier days had imagined. Because he didn't lose and scatter himself. He gathered, like a reaper at harvest gathering.

And Monica, who woke for her baby, looked at him as he slept soundly and she sat in bed suckling her child. ~~She would never be~~ *She saw in him the eternal* ~~able to get really near to him:~~ *stranger. There he was, the eternal stranger, lying in her bed sleeping at her side. She* ~~that she knew. She could never be~~ *rocked her baby slightly as she sat up in the night, still rocking in the last throes of* ~~able to get from him that delicious but deadly intimacy which she~~ *rebellion. The eternal stranger, whom she feared, because she could never finally possess* ~~craved, but which she knew was a sort of calamity.~~ *He had been him, and never finally know him! He would never belong to her. This had made her rebel* ~~willing to give it before. So she had taunted him with Easu.~~ *so terribly against him. Because she would have to belong to him. The* ~~An now he had turned away,—to something that belonged to his own~~ *Now he had arrived again before her like a doom, a doom she still fought against, but could no longer withstand. Because the emptiness of the* ~~male self alone.~~ *other men, Easu, Percy, all the men she knew, was worse than the doom of this man who would never give her* ~~give final intimacy to any human being whatsoever.~~ ~~He had given~~ *his ultimate intimacy, but who would be able to hold her till the end of time. There was something enduring* ~~his ultimate intimacy to his own male God, and she was powerless.~~ *and changeless in him. But she would never hold him entirely. Never! She would have to resign herself to this.*

Well, so be it. At least it relieved her of the burden of *from her her own strange and fascinating female* responsibility for life. It took away ~~her own strange, fascinating,~~ *power, which she couldn't bear to part with. But at the same time she felt saved, because her own* ~~but distracting responsibility. She was free of her own responsi-~~ *power frightened her, having brought her to a brink of nothingness that was like madness. The nothingness* ~~bility, even if she had lost her dangerous power.~~ *that fronted her with Percy was worse than submitting to this man beside her. After all, this man was magical.*

She put her child in its cradle, and returning waked the man. *Blind* He put out his hand quickly for her, as if she were a new, ~~tremendous~~ *quivered and thrilled,* discovery. She ~~laughed to herself,~~ and left it to him. It was his *mystery, since* ~~affair, if~~ he would have it so.

Figure 8.2 *The Boy in the Bush*, revised typescript copy of page 468, from the setting copy for the first American edition.

Various scenarios have to be entertained whenever a pre-publication document is not extant. For instance, a typed or scribal copy of an earlier manuscript may be missing, yet later versions have survived. Often, proofs that intervene between the typescripts and the corresponding first editions

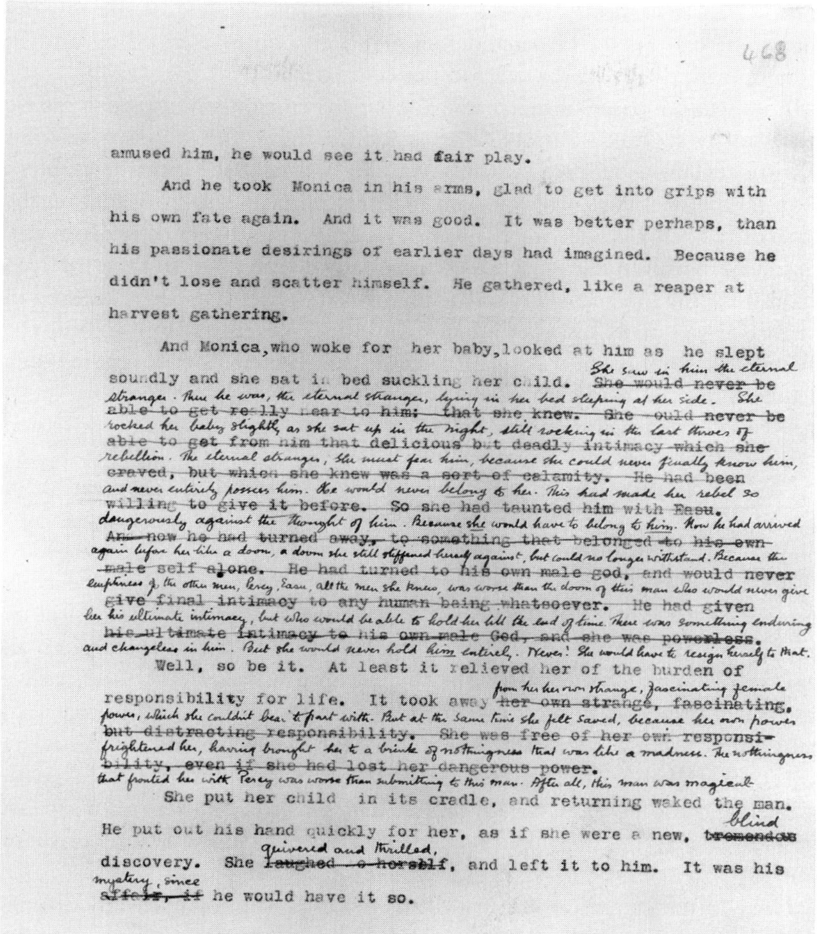

Figure 8.3 *The Boy in the Bush*, revised typescript copy of page 468, from the setting copy for the first English edition.

will have been discarded as worthless. But the readings of the missing document can usually be inferred with a high degree of accuracy, provided the preceding and succeeding documents exist. Further, it has been proven that, when an early document in the line of textual transmission is lost but two or more typesettings derive directly from it, and even though there are no other early versions extant to guide the editor, the text of the missing document can be reconstructed in its entirety, both in wording and in presentation, though not with 100 per cent reliability.[36]

In its second phase of reception, the *Ulysses* edition was attacked (as we shall shortly see) on a variety of grounds. Of them, the necessity to infer missing text is, I believe, the only actually vulnerable aspect of Gabler's editorial methodology. He was committed to a linear display of text on the left-hand pages. Because the display of later (extant) stages of revision and correction required the presence of the earlier, Gabler had to treat inferred readings in the linear display in the same way as ones actually witnessed in extant documents. This, they are not. But there was no attempt to hide the proceeding. On the contrary. The summary of the states of the text for each chapter puts the reader in possession of the relevant documentary facts, and symbols denote intended readings that have been editorially construed or whose intended position in the text has been inferred.

Gabler's defence – that editing has always required the application of critical judgement – is right insofar as emendations aimed at the establishment of a clear reading text is concerned. But his left-hand pages seemed to have a different aim. They seemed to constitute a synopsis of how exactly the text of the novel had developed, document by document, revision by revision, correction by correction, from one stage to the next, through all its developmental phases. In fact, the synoptic display embodies, as we have seen, analysis, interpretation and emendation: it is an edited text, rather than being a mere documentation of the textual evidence. Thus my objection scales back to this: that the recording is not quite as firmly based, as factually unobjectionable, as one at first assumes. There are bumps in the road that it takes a skilled reader to allow for, and even some of them were thrown at first.

The alternative method of recording, as far as Anglo-American editions are concerned, would have been what is called a *lemmatised* recording. In this system, at every point of variance, the reading in the clear text (the lemma) is given in a footnote or in a table at the end of the volume. A square bracket separates it from the variants in the other versions or states of the text; their readings are recorded after the bracket. This method of recording can become complicated to decipher if the situation gets complex, and especially when variants overlap one another. The reader has to reconstruct what happened, state by state. And if the reading text has been designed to capture the final intentions of the author for the text, then the user of the apparatus will often be working chronologically backwards, since the clear reading text is always the point of comparison.

Each such reconstruction is an interruption to one's reading, whereas, given time and a willingness to learn, one can read Gabler's left-hand pages.

His innovation was remarkable, and represented a significant break-through in accessibility. As things stand however, its influence on editorial procedure has been greatly delayed by some unfortunate aspects of its reception. As I explain more fully in the next chapter, I would have adopted it or, more likely, adapted it in the early 1990s if, in designing the Academy Editions of Australian Literature series, I had felt that readers could cope with it. This was the first major series of critical editions to be initiated with the benefit of the 1980s editorial theory movement behind it. But the reception Gabler's edition received suggested to me that anglophone readers would find it too far outside their tradition. As it is, some reviewers complain about ordinary lemmatised apparatus (or, as we have already seen, about the need for the scholarly editing at all), but at least they recognise the tradition behind it.

Gabler's right-hand pages: the critical text

Concern about the constitution of the reading text on Gabler's right-hand pages was the other main sticking point, especially when it became clear that it would also be published as the general-readers' text. It would in due course displace reprintings of the 1961 edition, deriving ultimately from the 1922 first edition, that a generation of critics had used for their commentaries on the novel. The Greg–Bowers tradition of copy-text editing had opened up for Gabler the option of essentially ignoring the first edition as the basis of the reading text that he was establishing in favour of earlier forms, especially manuscript. It is perhaps a register of how little postwar Anglo-American editorial thinking had infiltrated the literary-critical mind by the 1980s that Gabler's option of working chronologically forwards from a textual basis in the early documentary witnesses struck some commentators as an outrageous abuse of privilege. There was a sense of ownership usurped. But it was reactionary.

Gabler's reading text aimed to capture the novel, as he stated, at its highest point of compositional development. This was not the traditional way of expressing the idea of a text of final authorial intention, but in truth the aim was deeply traditional. The real innovation lay on the left-hand pages. On the right, because he was working chronologically forwards, Gabler was bound to change readings that had been corrupted in transmission (and thus made their way into the 1922 edition) and to reinstate readings that had been inadvertently omitted but that Joyce had failed to notice, whether or not he had in a general way approved them. The alternative – taking a firmer foundation from the text of the 1922 edition and proceeding to correct it for its errors – was held up as the obvious and logical procedure by Gabler's principal antagonist in the ensuing dispute, John Kidd, of whom more below.

Earlier in this chapter, for simplicity's sake, I gave the impression that the Greg–Bowers approach was the only postwar form of critical editing pursued within the Anglo-American editing community. But in fact it did not entirely sweep the literary field. In the 1970s James Thorpe in California and Philip Gaskell in Cambridge both argued that the literary work did not fully come into being until publication. This was what the author had aimed at. The author knew that the production was collaborative. Choosing an early *published* form of the work as copy-text, rather than an extant manuscript, therefore made sense.[37] But in doing so, this approach gave up the opportunity of making use of the author's own punctuation, spelling and other forms of presentation, since these were the things that copy-editors and typesetters would have felt free to supply (if missing), or correct (if deemed to be wrong) or otherwise to house-style.

It was nevertheless open to the editor to correct the first edition in matters of wording and detail. But because the first edition served as copy-text the onus was on the editor to prove that the author's intentions had been thwarted. When in doubt – under this method *or* under Bowers's – the copy-text's reading should prevail. That is why choosing one was necessary in the first place. In theory, as G. Thomas Tanselle has pointed out, if all the documentary witnesses were available and all the evidence of authorial revision and non-authorial change assembled then no copy-text would be necessary.[38] In the typical absence of this situation, both approaches sought to establish the text as the author wanted it published, but approached it from opposite ends of the production spectrum. The fact of the author's passing (i.e. reading and approving in a general way) readings in scribal copyings, typescripts and proofs tended to weigh more heavily with the Thorpe–Gaskell approach than it did with Bowers. The latter's approach was to select the holograph manuscript as copy-text, if it existed, and to emend it to incorporate what were judged to be the author's later revisions.

So, for Gabler's critical edition, wherever, say, Joyce was presented with a reading that was in fact a copyist's error of an unusual phrasing in the previous version, Joyce might, if he could remember it, reinstate it or, just as likely, try to retrieve the original reading but go wide of the mark. In such cases, Gabler treats the transmissional error as a corruption and overrules

Joyce's response to it as not an active revision. This is the approach, unless Joyce completely rewrote the passage and in this way reassumed creative control of it, thus effectively and in truth superseding what he had done previously. Interestingly, the Cambridge Works of D. H. Lawrence series came, independently, to exactly the same distinction between authorial correction of faulty transmission and revision of it. This series, which was conceived in the 1970s and began publishing from 1980, shifted from the Gaskell position to one closer to that of Bowers, but with some intelligent and more firmly historical adaptations of its own.[39]

Gabler was equally traditional in dealing with variants where critical judgement had to be applied to determine whether or not they are authorial. He did what many editors had done before him and what the Lawrence editors were also doing. He classified the suspect variants into groups and treated each member of the group alike, regardless of personal preference. Such avoidance of arbitrariness was a principal lesson of the New Bibliography of the early twentieth century. Editing decisions should not be based on the editor's taste. Except, that is, if the editor were absolutely sure that his or her aesthetic preferences would be of more use and interest to readers than what could be established of those of the author or of the author's collaborators. Not many scholarly editors will bend their heads to receive that self-deceiving accolade. Yet some commentators in the dispute, inexperienced in editorial thinking, expected Gabler to have done so.

Game on!

As a relatively junior research fellow at the University of Virginia John Kidd had, in 1985, publicly attacked the *Ulysses* edition in a paper given at the biennial conference of the Society for Textual Scholarship (STS) in New York. It had been leaked to the press, and there was a *New York Times* reporter present. Kidd was rebuffed by Gabler reading a reply from the floor – as he had been invited to do, but about which Kidd had been given no warning. Partly as a result of this interchange, some commentators would later – melodramatically – cast Kidd as an academic David to Gabler's Goliath God-Professor. As the sporting fraternity would put it, it was, thenceforth, 'game on!'

When three years later, on 30 June 1988, Kidd's article 'The Scandal of *Ulysses*' appeared in the *New York Review of Books* (*NYRB*), a James Joyce research centre was created for him by Boston University, thus benefiting from the publicity that the article and ensuing campaign generated. There were letters back and forth between various parties in the

NYRB and the *Times Literary Supplement* that year. Kidd promised to document fully his claims of the various categories of error and wrong-headedness of method that he believed he had detected in the edition. He had provided only a small number of examples in the *NYRB* article itself. As he showed little sympathy for the editorial goals of the edition it was difficult at the time to assess whether or not what he took to be errors were in fact so or whether they were consequences of the methodology adopted. For his part, Gabler refused to address the criticisms formally till Kidd had published them in the scholarly literature – as he had been undertaking to do for some time before the magazine piece appeared.

At length in June 1989 his 173-page article appeared in the *Papers of the Bibliographical Society of America*, though formally dated 1988. Although Kidd had evidently, in the meantime, read more widely in editorial theory and had realised that it was in that arena that he had to take Gabler on, his article only lost out by virtue of its extreme length. He had stuck to his belief that the 1922 first edition should have been the basis of Gabler's text. Now he had some authorities to back him up, though he tended to overlook the conflicting intellectual positions their quoted opinions were coming from. In any case, since an edition from either end of the production spectrum is possible (and indeed to have *both* would be very desirable) it was no criticism of Gabler's edition to fault it for having taken the opposite approach to the one Kidd favoured.[40] So Gabler's reply, when it came in 1993, could afford to be a short one in comparison (sixty-one pages), since he argued on underlying principles. There is a certain abstract formality, a heaviness, about his English expression, where Kidd is understandably more fluent and idiomatic in his native tongue. But Gabler's capacity to grasp and define textual principles is formidable. He closes off irrelevancies with the sharpness and finality of a steel trap. You don't want to leave your fingers there.[41]

It was not surprising then, that, when STS held a plenary session to discuss the dispute ten years on from its beginning in 1985, it was felt by many present that Gabler had won the day. Some errors of execution flowing from his methodology had been exposed and were admitted by all to need fixing. But those editors present probably shivered, as I did, at the prospect of their editions being subjected to the same level of scrutiny that Gabler's had. No scholarly edition is error-free. The evidence that has to be marshalled is typically too overwhelming to make that noble aim a realistic possibility. Having to work from reproductions of the unique documents, complemented by checks against the originals for visually ambiguous passages, is in practice inevitable, though some of the editorially inexperienced commentators said they were shocked at the thought. Kidd had been invited to speak at the STS plenary in 1995, and concessions to his requests about the format of debate were granted by the organisers. But in the event he withdrew.

The appearance in 1997 of a new, editorially unrelated Picador edition of the novel made matters worse.[42] The Joyce Estate had not authorised it, and took the publishers and editor to court. Further editorial scholarship on the author was effectively ended by this event. For any in-copyright works, it is foolhardy if not impossible, during the period of copyright, to carry out time-consuming editorial scholarship without the active agreement and cooperation of an author's estate. The extension of the copyright regime to seventy years in the 1990s meant that publication of such work may have to be put off till 1 January 2012 – and probably till 2030 in the USA. And even then, relevant unpublished materials will still be protected.

Other confusions

Commentators found other reasons to object to Gabler's edition. Charles Rossman uncovered from Richard Ellmann's papers at the University of Tulsa some disagreements among the distinguished members of the committee advising on the edition, of whom Ellmann had been one before his death. This article, which appeared in the *NYRB*, helped to keep the journalistic dispute bubbling along. But it was mainly an argument from reputation – of who would or would not vouch for the editorial methodology adopted – rather than about the methodology as such. It had its effect at the time, and the journalist Bruce Arnold, who published a book on the dispute in 1991, gave it a great deal of weight.[43] But it did not go to a matter of substance.

Like Ernst van der Wetering's conclusion that Rembrandt connoisseurship is a highly informed argument, but only an argument, about the scientific and other evidence, every scholarly edition has to be understood as an embodied argument about the textual transmission. It asks for engagement as an interpretation of the evidence by opening up for inspection the instabilities of composition and revision recorded in the textual apparatus. At the same time, it closes them down in the clear reading text. It *fixes* a text at the same time as its explanatory annotation opens it out into the discourses of its day. Editions can and need to be read with and against the grain.[44]

Sad to say, editions rarely receive such engagement. Gabler's attempt in his left-hand pages to present the textual genesis synoptically in an integral apparatus that corresponded to the dynamism of the text as it developed under Joyce's hand was, and remains, a striking experiment to which editors will return.[45] But its significance was occluded and the return delayed by the dispute. The responsibility for that avoidable outcome must be borne by those who attacked the edition and those who allowed themselves to be caught up in the wake of the attack. *That* was the so-called scandal of *Ulysses*.

Suspicions about the copyright motive for the editing were also raised by Rossman, Arnold and others. In fact, no court has so far decided that a new scholarly or critical edition creates a new copyright in the work itself (as opposed to a copyright in the typesetting or physical layout, which has long enjoyed a reduced form of protection). It is likely, though not certain, that a new scholarly edition would gain full copyright protection if recourse to a competent court were properly taken. But this would not affect the situation with the underlying work. Once *its* copyright protection has expired, the reprinting of any editions, including the first, that appeared in the author's lifetime could not be prevented, regardless of the appearance of any new scholarly edition in the meantime.

Some commentators professed to believe that because the Gabler edition and its popular reprintings would benefit the Joyce Estate, the whole editorial enterprise was somehow besmirched. Such persons fail to realise that we live, and have always lived, in a fallen world. It is much the same one that had put the 1961 edition of *Ulysses* into their hands in the first place and had paid their salaries in the interim.

The same consideration applies to art restorations. A Japanese television corporation paid for the Sistine Chapel repairs in return for rights to film the conservation work. Other corporations, as James Beck has pointed out, have put up money for the Brancacci Chapel restoration in Florence and for the restoration or repair of other very significant cultural monuments. Their boards evidently came to the conclusion that it makes business sense to have the corporation's name associated with the work. Nevertheless, this kind of support allows the work to take place at all, and that is when the substantive, professional questions that this book has been dealing with properly start. Similarly, as we saw in Chapters 2 and 3, in historic-house restorations the witness of the building's fabric has unfailingly to be respected. But conservators and curators have also to bear in mind the likely interests of visitors, who may or may not be willing to pay to see the result. Part of the reason that Uppark was restored after the disastrous fire was that the insurance would only be paid on that basis. The pressure that I have been putting on the professional practices dealt with in this book has been with the aim of clarifying their underlying assumptions and philosophies. *That* is what they must bring to the table and insist upon when preservation and conservation proposals are being negotiated.

Hopeful signs?

Other editors were copping flak in 1988. It was obvious in the language used by Roger Shattuck and Douglas Alden in their review in the *Times Literary Supplement* of some new editions of Proust's *A la recherche du temps perdu*. Their praise was of the begrudging kind. They refer to the 'impressive yet labyrinthine machine' offered by one edition, to another's system of notes as 'an imposing intellectual gadget', and to various kinds of 'scholarly paraphernalia'.[46] Praise offered with one hand is withdrawn by the other. But a complacency in Shattuck and Alden's point of view emerges in their comment that one edition of *Swann's Way* 'provides the ideal form in which to read Proust – large type, a comprehensive introduction, all the notes one needs, and two red ribbons. Every Proust-lover should have one such handsome volume.'[47]

The red ribbons give the game away. Despite the eminence of the two Proustians, one can detect here no real interest in or even tolerance for the new stimuli and information bibliography might offer. Although they profess marked interest in a 138-page deletion Proust made in *Albertine disparue* they will not allow it to alter their understanding of the boundaries of the text. They refer to the deletion as 'Proustian apocrypha' and declare that the function of good Proust editors should be 'to tell us how far the true text of [*A la recherche*] extends and where the ruins begin . . . Proust's most miraculous accomplishment was to create out of a confusing succession of abandoned and recuperated projects a single work.'[48] This endorsement of miracles strikes me as an act of faith. The reviewers' desire, apparently, is for the unambiguous transcendence of product – the 'single work' – out of process. They seem to yearn for the innocence of (in an older terminology) the Verbal Icon,[49] an innocence to which editors were, as late as 1988, *still* supposed to give their priestly blessing.

In the late 1980s, as anglophone editorial theory developed a new phase of interest in the literary processes of composition and revision, the certainties of the closed aesthetic object that Wilson and his ideological descendants clung to would be exposed as an illusion. In the later 1990s new centres for textual editing at the universities of Boston and Penn State, new graduate programmes in the area at the Universities of Washington, New Mexico and Toronto, and, more recently, new centres for textual and editorial studies at the universities of Birmingham and De Montfort in England, as well as a postgraduate degree in Textual Cultures at Stirling University in Scotland, have all signalled change at the institutional level. This proves only a minority interest, to be sure, but it is one that is no longer withering on the vine.

A new, text-critical understanding of the ontology and functioning of literary works may be filtering through to the general literary scene. The fourth edition of the *Norton Anthology of Poetry* in 1996 included for the first time 'significant textual variants' for some poems, explaining that this was '[i]n keeping with recent developments in editing'.[50] A review in 2000 in the *Times Literary Supplement* went further. The volume under review was by Harold Bloom who had instead, according to the reviewer, remained committed to 'the act of pure reading', to a 'self-enclosed aesthetic world'. The reviewer argues, however, that when

we pick up Byron's *Don Juan* or Spenser's *Faerie Queene*, we are no longer dealing with 'verbal icons' or 'well-wrought urns'; each work has its own bibliographical and sociological history, from which its potential and actual readings are derived. Immortal works have been reconfigured as volatile texts . . . Modern editions of classic titles, including paperbacks from Oxford, Penguin and Everyman, set each work firmly within a structure of scholarly apparatus, denying readers any easy opportunity to disentangle the work from its historical contexts. If the covers of a book used to be the doorway through which we entered into direct contact with literary works, they are now like a picture frame within which we can see a particular person, in a specific time and place, holding a distinct edition of the book in question. What's more, we can see ourselves looking at the picture.[51]

CODA: EDITIONS OF HISTORICAL DOCUMENTS

Back in the 1970s other negotiations were in progress, this time amongst the editors, occasioned by the fact that scholarly editing had also traditionally encompassed works of primarily historical significance – for example, the papers of early American presidents. Such documents would, in the main, never have been readied or intended for publication and might never have been considered to have an aesthetic dimension at all. As noted above, the determining of final intentions about variant wordings had been the pivot around which editions of literary works had been variously oriented for a long time. But here the issue was likely to be of less importance than preserving the historically laden nature of the document from which the text was taken. Drawing on a strong postwar tradition of historical editing in the USA, the establishment in 1978 of the Association for Documentary Editing helped to sharpen the distinction between the 'critical' editing of the literary kind and the non-critical editing of historical documents. The field of scholarly editing was now said to divide into these two areas.

Mary-Jo Kline's business in the Association's *A Guide to Documentary Editing* (1987) was to provide an account of the rationale and methodology of documentary editing, which up until then had been lacking. Critical editing in contrast had, since 1950, had the benefit of Sir Walter Greg's 'Rationale of Copy-Text' (outlined in Chapter 7) as a working basis and Fredson Bowers's notable elaborations and extensions of it. In the 1989 second edition of the MLA's *An Introduction to Bibliographical and Textual Studies*, William Proctor Williams and Craig S. Abbott, both editors of literary works, accepted Kline's division. Documentary editing, they comment, 'presents a text as it was available at a particular time in a particular document. Such editing is noncritical in that it does not emend the text, even a text that may not accurately reproduce an author's words.' On the other hand, 'Critical editing, the second major form of scholarly editing, does not reproduce the text of a particular document but produces an eclectic text based on several texts and on editorial emendations. It assumes that though multiple texts of a work may vary in authority, no one text is entirely authoritative.'[52] (The 1980s response to this position is discussed in Chapter 9.)

Scholarly but, in Bowers's sense, non-critical editing in the literary arena has also been much practised, as for instance in the old-spelling, type-facsimile editions of sixteenth- and seventeenth-century writings (where the need was to maintain the original orthography). A scholarly edition could also be a photo-facsimile edition, or a reset edition with specified emendations, of a historically important version of a literary work with the text surrounded with sufficient bibliographical analysis to render its significance plain. Another kind of scholarly edition has been the variorum edition of, for example, the work of major poets. A base text is selected and the apparatus records the variant readings in other historical printings.

In summary, the critical edition has been considered one which either: (1) for the classical or medieval periods, attempts to recover the text of a lost document, typically one as close as possible to the original text, but which is now represented by a range of much later scribal copies in various relationships of textual descent; or (2) for the modern period (which Williams and Abbott had in mind) where the documentary tradition may be more or less unbroken, attempts to establish a text according to some criterion of authorial intention – usually the text that the author would, under ideal circumstances, have wanted published.

One would go about critical editing in one of the following ways. In the *first* case a 'best text' is chosen and emended according to the editor's critical sense of its deficiencies, by reference to other documentary witnesses. Or, by means of what is known as Lachmannian analysis (after Karl Lachmann, the famous nineteenth-century German philologist), textual family-relationships, declared by the existence of shared errors, are plotted, and a systematic attempt is made to isolate and eliminate the errors, thus allowing the approximation of the original text. In the *second* case, a base- or copy-text is chosen and emended by readings from other extant states that the author is known to have revised: an eclectic text is thereby created. In both cases, the textual collation on which this work is based (the identification of variant readings in each version or document and within versions or documents) is conventionally published in whole or in part in some kind of tabular format. This textual apparatus may be divided into several kinds of recording.

Bear in mind that I am summarising the Anglo-American editing scene from the 1950s to the 1980s. In accepting the distinction between 'critical' and 'non-critical' scholarly editing, I am painting an apparently benign picture of peaceful co-existence amongst practitioners. But this was not the case, at least in the USA. Bowers, the energetic postwar leader of the critical-editing movement, was apt to see variorum editions as timorous because they only *displayed* textual variation rather than deciding on critical grounds what variant readings needed to be incorporated into the copy-text. One either established a reading text of the work, or one shrank from the responsibility and merely recorded the textual possibilities: the literary work was thus assumed to have in its ideal form (except in rare cases) *one* text, which it ought to be the editor's business to try to establish by critical means. In pointedly not claiming the mantle of 'definitive editing', Bowers had realised, before the Rembrandt Research Project team members were to do in 1969, that scientific certainty in editing or restoring works from the past was unobtainable. After all the bibliographic analysis had been done, the exercise of the editor's critical judgement was still necessary. The rejected term's datedness is nicely indicated by the fact that the MLA committee which preceded the CEAA (established in 1966, and succeeded by the Committee for Scholarly Editions in 1976) had been called the Committee on Definitive Editions. It was set up in 1947, but its attempts to secure funding for editions of American works had failed.

Bowers also hoped to educate the documentary editors into his point of view, and in this he was ably assisted by G. Thomas Tanselle's devastating essay in the 1978 issue of *Studies in Bibliography*, 'The Editing of Historical Documents'. Tanselle revealed illogicalities in documentary editing practice. His essay exposes example after example of documentary editors making emendations for readers' convenience (expanding some abbreviations, not recording deletions, removing repeated words and other slips of the pen) in contradiction of their central aim of respecting the historicity of the document. He further criticised such editors for failing to take advantage of analytical bibliography when dealing with published works (as critical editors routinely would). And he concluded remarkably that US critical editors, who had to provide a record of all deviations from the copy-text if they were to secure the CEAA seal of approval, showed thereby more respect for that text's historicity than historical-documentary editors themselves did. The essay, according to Kline, changed historical editing in America: since Tanselle wrote, there has been a swing back to a more conservative, less interventionist, form of historical editing.

Tanselle's victory was not, however, complete – as W. Speed Hill's review-article of Tanselle's 1993 biography of Bowers points out:

the general response of historical editors to Tanselle's strictures was one of immuno-logical rejection. Although the Association [for Documentary Editing] awarded Bowers its Julian P. Boyd Award in 1986, he confided to friends that he would have preferred that its members had paid more attention to his editorial principles, and he was memorably dismissive in his speech of acceptance.[53]

Immunological rejection takes place in hidden ways, under the surface. It is not inconsistent with Kline's stating and repeating in her *Guide* that many documentary editors were themselves having difficulties with the tradition in which they worked, and found Tanselle's essay an answer to their prayers. It gave them the opportunity to adjust their methodologies by questioning the assumptions of the old ones.

But they were not converted to Tanselle's larger intellectual agenda. The first chapter of the *Guide* offers a detailed and careful history of the relationships between critical and documentary editors. Kline is at pains to stress the achieved nature of the two forms of editing. On the surface, the chapter calmly and confidently articulates the outcome of the dispute. In contrast, the energy of its conclusion suggests the vigour of rejection, mixed with a note of continuing defensiveness:

Documentary editing, although noncritical in terms of classical textual scholarship, is not an *uncritical* endeavor. It demands quite as much intelligence, insight, and hard work as its critical counterpart, combined with a passionate determination to preserve for modern readers the nuances of evidence that exist in the sources on which the printed documentary editions are based.[54]

Kline's *Guide* must, I believe, be read as a manifesto of intellectual independence from the Greg–Bowers school and a claim of methodological and theoretical coherence. What has been essentially an American controversy pushed the issue to a clarification, but one complicated by inherently unstable academic-political imperatives.

CHAPTER 9

Readers and editors: new directions in scholarly editing

[E]ven an imaginative work like a novel, does not fall from the heavens a complete, crystallised object . . . the existence of a literary work may be precarious and complicated.

(Royal Gettmann, 1960)[1]

Fundamentally, the issue is whether, critically, the process of the writing is, or is not, integral to the product of the writing.

(Hans Walter Gabler, 1999)[2]

We normally separate the acts of writing a document and reading it. Yet a writer will repeatedly return to the document in the process of composition. Thus the document figures in the process, not just as its record but as a stimulation to further writing. The Stuttgart edition of the German poet Hölderlin (most of whose works were known only in manuscript) recognises this when, as a matter of editorial policy, it treats deletions made by the author not as 'outright annulments, but as provisional deletions. Invalidated [i.e. cancelled] wordings within a manuscript must be considered *potentially valid* if still legible to the author. Conversely, all wordings left valid should be considered *potentially invalid*.'[3]

For the writer, the writing and the already written feed off one another. A similar scenario applies for production of meaning at the reader's end, as Wolfgang Iser's reception theory (outlined in Chapter 4) shows. Since these textual dynamics characterise the functioning of works, the literary work cannot be ideal in and of itself. The notion of the ideal must be a reader's or editor's construction, a convenience for some purpose but one that does not correspond to ordinary textual practice.

A non-ideal understanding of the work emerged in the 1980s. The work came to be seen as something open at every point to its informing contexts, always in a process of formation and deformation, and textually never stable because of the dynamics of its production. What textual stability is said to exist – as in the common phrase 'the text of the work' – will have been imposed. It will have come about by virtue of agreements among groups of publishers, editors or readers. The dilemma of scholarly editors, if they are truly to secure the past, is that they must somehow bridge both positions.

This chapter explores that dilemma by taking seriously the role of the reader and of the editor *in* the literary work. The former is not explored from the basis of Iser's reception theory but from the documentary records of their reading that a special class of readers leaves behind. This sets the scene for an account of a powerful adaptation, during and after the 1980s, of the Thorpe–Gaskell position (described in Chapter 8). The new emphasis was now on the meaning-laden materiality of the public form of texts. Balancing this emphasis, the more recent Anglo-American encounter with the methods and assumptions of German historical-critical editing is described and analysed. Both emphases have set the stage for an adaptive future for scholarly editing that we still await.

DEFORMATION AND FORMATION

Reviewers as 'writers' of the work

Literary documents are usually written and printed *for* a readership, so that rigidly to separate work from reception can only be a convention sanctioned by tradition. But is it sanctioned by common sense? A reviewer's reading a book and then writing a review (which involves the writing of another, and different, document) are separable but not fully separate acts. The review is a report *on* the reading and normally follows hard on its heels. Reviews themselves (and any later critical essays) are also records of the literary work. They unfold it over time, influencing subsequent readings. Thus the work does its work in people's lives. It is hard to predict and it is chameleon.

A good illustration of this may be found in the reception of *The Boy in the Bush* (1924), the editing of which was described in Chapter 8. The novel is set in Western Australia, both in Perth and in the remote outback. The first version was written by an Australian bush-nurse and minor novelist Mollie Skinner but it was radically rewritten by D. H. Lawrence. Because she paid a press-cuttings agency to send her reviews, the novel's reception can be readily studied. The novel received the bulk of its reviews, notices and discussions in Britain (47), USA (19) and Australia (49). There were also five in Canada, four in New Zealand, three in France, two in Argentina, and one each in India, South Africa, Italy, Cuba and the Netherlands.[4]

In England it was praised for its account of outback life. The young hero of the novel, Jack Grant, a scapegrace, is sent to the colony of Western Australia in 1880. Gradually he resigns the civilised life of the principal town, Perth, for a wilder life in the outback. He wants to get in touch with his dark gods, the country and his own sexuality. Polygamy is on his rather earnest agenda. This touched a raw nerve in Australia. The Englishness of the country was a topic that was being hotly disputed in the pages of the Sydney *Bulletin* at the time.

Accordingly, many Australian reviewers were far less ready than their English counterparts to grant the novel the verisimilitude of its account of Australian outback life. But the most painful aspect of the alleged inaccuracy for many reviewers was the impression the novel was apt to give that the morality of colonials was 'simply farmyard morality'.[5] This apprehension at what the mother country, which had published it, would *think* is quite near the surface in the Perth *Onlooker*, a review that went to some trouble to fault the novel's historical accuracy. The anxiety was, I suspect, widely shared; it may help explain the virulence of some of the reviews.

Another facet of the novel's reception was the vexed question of its authorship, particularly the extent of the Australian co-author's share in it. Oddly perhaps, the question was not as generally taken up by Australian reviewers as by British, who fell into what may have been a trap cagily set by Lawrence's London publisher Martin Secker. In his advertising leaflet for the novel, he had carefully not disclosed any details of Lawrence's collaborator other than the nationality and giving her name on the book's title-page as simply 'M. L. Skinner'. Unlike his American counterpart Seltzer, Secker had thereby created a mystery, and the British reviewers did not fail to rise to it.

A second wave of commentary can then be distinguished as columnists or reviewers either directly responded to the initial reviews or made passing comments on the understanding that the novel was now an established thing and that knowledge of it could be assumed. This conversation crossed national borders. The Brisbane *Sun* reprinted a New York review. The Auckland *Star* in New Zealand ran a second item on the novel on 29 November 1924 referring to a disparaging review entitled 'Unclean Realism' by T.B.C. [T. B. Clegg] in the Sydney *Bulletin*: 'We are interested to find the "Bulletin" reviewer objecting to [the novel] on the grounds that we took – its descent into the bogs of sexualism.'[6] The anxiety had evidently crossed the Tasman Sea. The 'work' was picking up steam.

In even more patrician mode, Vance Palmer the Australian novelist and critic writing for the Boston *Independent*, also lectured Lawrence:

He is one of the few men of genius writing the English language today, and yet he flings off the intellectual control that would impose structure and balance on his books. Released from all restraint, his talent goes rioting along, losing itself in a maze of Freudian bogs and speculations about the solar system.[7]

The objection to a 'neurotic' or 'neurasthenic' obsessiveness in the novel appears in other reviews. An American doctor, Joseph Collins, had given licence to such remarks in his recently published psychoanalytic study of a number of writers including Lawrence, *The Doctor Looks at Literature* (1923).[8] A left-wing Australian reviewer R. S. Ross directed his discussion (in 1924) of Lawrence's earlier Australian novel *Kangaroo* against this trend. He felt it smacked of Nonconformist impeachment, remarking that '"Kangaroo" burst like a bomb among his would-be silencers.'[9]

For Palmer, *The Boy in the Bush* marked 'a stage in the disintegration of his powers',[10] whereas structure and balance had characterised the home-life sections of the earlier *Sons and Lovers*, Lawrence's high point. These qualities, which Lawrence was said to have abandoned in his recent novels, were qualities Palmer himself pursued in his own fiction: an artless-seeming realism in a controlled, unpretentious prose style. For Palmer, then, *The Boy in the Bush* was an instructive lesson about the danger of possessing genius without discipline; and it may, perhaps, have served as a consolation for lacking the former himself. Thus was another appropriation of the meanings of *The Boy in the Bush* effected, while the literary work went on circulating in and out of Australia, gathering significances.

An anonymous three-page attack on *The Boy in the Bush*, which appeared in the Melbourne monthly *Life*, reached the apogee of international currency. The reviewer cited the review in the *Times Literary Supplement* (which had commended the novel for allowing us 'to know the very spirit of the place'[11]) to demonstrate the danger that the view of Australia offered in the novel

may be accepted by multitudes as an accurate account both of Australia and of Australians . . . There is hardly a sane man or a pure woman amongst the personages Mr. Lawrence describes . . . What Mr. Lawrence leaves out of clean and happy households from his picture of Australia and Australians would make up many volumes . . . [On] the sex question . . . [Lawrence] has . . . no more respect for . . . his victims than a country butcher has for the carcases . . . that hang in his shop . . . The plain fact is that Mr. Lawrence's book is neither history, nor art, nor literature. It is a form of disease, and with some of the infective qualities a disease possesses.[12]

The reviewer goes on (predictably) to quote Joseph Collins as justification for 'the uncomfortable sense of perversion . . . [or] disgust' that Lawrence's books usually occasion in the reader.

Four months after the appearance of this review came a reply, not from Australia but from the English *Liverpool Courier*; the columnist's pseudonym was 'Panurge'. The *Courier* had not run a review of the novel, but the *Liverpool Post* had printed one criticising Lawrence's 'preoccupation with instincts rather than conduct'.[13] Whether or not he was influenced by that review, Panurge attacked the one in *Life* because of what it represented:

This attitude of regarding [Lawrence] as some sort of literary freak or curiosity, these foolish attacks, [which] are so many admissions of unreceptiveness, of mental sterility and lack of courage in the critic, whose job, above all, is to welcome genius wherever and in what strange form it may happen to appear.[14]

Lawrentians might take heart from this defence were it not for the inevitability that this too was an appropriation of the novel. Attempting to refute the *Life* reviewer's contrasting of Lawrence's work to that of a gifted artist whose drawings one 'wishes . . . might be fit to take home and hang upon the wall', Panurge claims this is to confuse Lawrence with 'the brilliant contributors of "passion serials" to the twopenny weeklies that circulate below stairs'.[15] The implication is that the below-stairs servants are not interested in genius, that genius is a preserve for those above-stairs and that, therefore, the *Life* reviewer's (implicit) sin has been to betray his class by not performing its special duty. This further significance the novel was doomed to bear. Lawrence hated being told he had genius; one sees why.

The novel as published, the material book, was acquiring an ultra-bibliographic life of its own from the very fact of its entering the force-fields of existing personal, moral, institutional and national affiliations and sympathies. It could not but be interpreted in the light of them. It could not resist being appropriated *by* them. The novel was rapidly becoming a multitude of recreated versions. The literary work had become, inevitably and cumulatively, a multifarious thing. The printed document was successively interpreted and reinterpreted, appropriated and reappropriated, till one might wonder how the participating readers could have imagined they were all talking about the same thing. This is no doubt the fate – the condition of existence – of all Lawrence's works and, with appropriate adjustment for different circumstances, of all published literary works in general.

In summary, the term *work* has a lot of work to do. Its vectors, picking up a theme from earlier chapters, are, once again, time and agency. The work extends from production to consumption. Both evolve, both unfold over time in response to bibliographic documents (for the author and producers, the manuscript, typescript(s) and proofs; for the reader, the packaged editions) and because of differently positioned agents. We need a theory of the work partly so that editors, not unlike restorers of artworks and historic buildings, know what it is that they are dealing with when they go about their business of restoration. To do this without entertaining illusions would be a good thing.

Editors as readers of the work

Editors, we can say, are at the production end of the spectrum. But is it so simple? Editors are far less likely than art restorers to entertain the illusion that they do not enter into the constitution of the work. The situation we saw in Chapter 5 in relation to the *Last Supper* can never obtain. Scholarly editing involves participation in the text of the work, by definition. Although it only comes after the most intensively historical preparation, emending the text is a matter of judgement, of interpreting intention.

Editors cannot but act as readers if they are to recover authorial intention and to distinguish it from non-authorial intention. But of course editors have no more direct access to the psychic state of the author as he or she wrote than do any other readers. When editors postulate authorial intention to mean – that is, semantic intention – they engage in what is (strictly) a quixotic activity. But they do so, sensitised and informed by their knowledge of the author's habits elsewhere. Their reading is only a means to an end. They are actually trying to recover a more material level of intention, with which they can far less vulnerably deal: the author's intention to *do*, to write this sequence of linguistic signs or that, as evidenced most obviously in altered readings in the documents. Of course the author did not intend to write mere sequences of signs, but their actual or inferred presence as ink on paper, as graphic substance, is the only thing to which the editor has reliable access.

The material realisation of intention is evidence of there having been an agent and a moment of inscription. These conditions of textuality are what gives editing its remit. Inscription, of course, is a contested metaphor. Reviewers and later readers of a text may, as we have seen, imbibe or seek to contest or adapt to their own ends a work's political, moral or other ideological inscription. But editors are only interested to follow suit while it allows them access to the level of physical inscription, of graphic substance. To pick up terminology from earlier chapters, their proper realm of activity is the documentary; but they must approach it via the textual.

This editorial focus admittedly involves a narrowing of attention. But it lends editing a forensic power, a textual leverage that can unlock with precision how works came to their published states; it can recreate versions of works that no longer exist in any documentary form and it can give versions the most densely biographical location.[16] But if the editor's role is formative of the text (and not only deformative, as is every reader's), how best may the editor present the work so that the ensuing deformations may be better *in*formed ones?

CHANGE IN THE 1980s

In Chapter 8, I contrasted the Greg–Bowers and the Thorpe–Gaskell approaches to copy-text editing. The one typically chose an early version as copy-text and worked forward, gathering up into the reading text revisions adjudged to be authorial. The other worked backwards from the ontological security of the first edition as the moment when the work had first come into public existence.

In the latter case, the public life of the work, once admitted as a moment, even if not a source, of textual authority, necessarily affected the editing procedure. Pre-publication forms of the work had to be treated as superseded and might or might not be systematically recorded. But they would certainly serve, wherever needed, to correct errors that had crept unnoticed into the published form. Post-publication variants (as for instance in second and subsequent editions during the author's lifetime) might be admitted into the reading text. The aim of both orientations was the same: to establish the text that the author had wanted published. The disagreement was about how one might best go about doing this.

Jerome McGann reinserted the legitimacy of the public-life orientation into the debate in the early 1980s. If works 'lived', as it were, a public life then that fact itself might well alter the editorial aim.[17] Textual authority in an edition would flow from the work's social existence. In this, McGann was tilting at a then-entrenched editorial tradition.

For instance, the Cambridge edition of *Sons and Lovers* by D. H. Lawrence, which had been in preparation since the late 1970s and would not be published until 1992, adopted the Bowers approach, working forward from a manuscript copy-text. But the socialised form of the work that,

until then, all readers of it had encountered was in fact an abridgement
carried out by a publisher's editor, Edward Garnett. Lawrence, who had
to earn a living and had no other real choice, effectively sanctioned the
abridging when he went on to correct the resulting proofs. Which version,
then, has the higher authority: the authorial text or the socialised one?
The latter version falls more squarely into the realm of a realist novel, at
least in the much-praised early chapters when Paul Morel is a boy. But the
account of the hero's brother William was pared down by Garnett, much
reducing the force of the novel's title. This socialised version is nevertheless
more stylistically unified than the manuscript's longer version. Arguably,
Garnett's abridgement makes for more satisfying reading. But it misrepresents the flux of Lawrence's extraordinary development as a novelist,
especially in the years 1912–13 when the novel moved through its final versions and when he was about to turn his hand to writing what became *The
Rainbow* (1915).

The authorial text and nothing but the authorial text

James L. W. West III had faced a similar problem with his 1981 Pennsylvania
Edition of Theodore Dreiser's novel *Sister Carrie* (1900). Dreiser's wife
Sara (known as Jug) and his friend Arthur Henry made suggestions on
the manuscript as he wrote it, and then again on the typescript. As an
ex-journalist 'used to working with copy editors and rewrite men from
his newspaper days', Dreiser mainly accepted their suggestions without
demur.[18] Jug became more confident and enterprising in her revising as
she proceeded, removing profanities and toning down immodesties – even
though Carrie runs off with a man of the world without yet being married
to him, and even though the sexual predation and callousness towards
chorus girls of male characters sets the tone for the novel.

In the typescript, which Dreiser worked on intently, Jug applied much
stylistic and grammatical polish, despite the working-class coarseness that
the dialogue had deliberately conveyed. Henry also undertook the job, and
did some heavy revising and minor deleting. They both encouraged Dreiser
to rewrite the ending, Jug provided some notes to help him with it, and
she later revised what he wrote in making a fair copy of it for the typist.
It was probably (although not certainly) when Harper declined to publish
the novel, and when the reader's report implied that cuts would benefit the
novel, that Henry went through the typescript, marking over 36,000 words
for removal. Dreiser implemented nearly all of the cuts. Subsequently, Doubleday, Page accepted the novel but required the substitution of fictional

names for real ones and marked some passages in the typescript for toning down; and in proofs various parties got to work on the text once again. It was only when Dreiser had the Doubleday, Page contract in hand that he could afford to resist demands to delete questionable passages. The result was a distinctly collaborative production whose text became the received one as the novel gradually became recognised as one of the realist classics of American literature.

What should a scholarly editor do in such a situation? There are at least two points of view here. One is that of those readers who are used to reading the familiar text and only want it cleared of errors. For them, a critical edition gives an imprimatur to the newly established text. A conservative impulse in them wants it to stay much the same. Although they will read about the novel's chequered history of production happily enough, it will not affect their sense of it as a work. They will most likely pass over the edition's recording of superseded readings.

Another point of view is that of the editor. As we have already seen in Chapter 8 with Hans Walter Gabler's edition of Joyce's *Ulysses*, the editor who has pored over the pre-publication documents is acutely aware of the mixed authority (i.e. the multiple sources) of the text of the first edition. So it was here. West concludes:

> In the strictest sense, [Dreiser's] authorial function ceased after he inscribed the holograph draft of *Sister Carrie*. Thereafter he acted as an editor and revised his own prose and decided what non-authorial alterations . . . to adopt . . . Dreiser undoubtedly agreed to make these excisions because he felt that they would make his novel more saleable.[19]

Springing from this awareness, the decision to implement a Greg–Bowers approach, in a peculiarly pure form, proved irresistible. The text of the Pennsylvania Edition is based on the novel's original manuscript, ruling out the deletions and additions (including the new ending) suggested by Jug and Henry. In this way, about 36,000 words are restored in the edition. Textual authority reverts, so far as possible, to the author alone. West thus effectively distinguished between textual authority (i.e. the textual agency of the author) and textual ownership. He based his edition on the former.

The first group of readers mentioned above is usually content with the imprecision of the latter notion, whether in the form of the text that the author is known to have authorised (here, a collaborative one) or the text that has been read for generations. Such readers usually have not thought their way past the question of whether the newly edited form of a text is or is not an aesthetic improvement. Some reviewers of the new *Sister*

Carrie edition saw no reason to doubt that there was improvement. They were happy to go along with the publicity claims that had preceded the edition's release and assume that this newly purified form of the novel now replaced the old: 'like art historians cleaning a Da Vinci fresco, [the editors] have uncovered the original glowing with an ancient newness'.[20] Others were more thoughtful but nevertheless allowed themselves to be confused by the aesthetic assumption, half the time assuming that the editorial method necessarily hung off it and should be judged by it, and the other half admiring the exhaustive application of text-analytical principles to the novel's versions. These principles allowed the text versions in effect to be disassembled and their merits assessed – word by word, comma by comma – and then reassembled as a new, clear reading text. So, Richard H. Brodhead's comment that 'Restoring Dreiser to his original form involves restoring him, among other things, to his original ineptitudes' can go along with his acknowledgement of 'this edition's superb historical commentary [which] makes us recognize . . . the extent to which the production of *Sister Carrie* was a collaborative affair'.[21]

Donald Pizer had prepared the Norton *Sister Carrie*, based on the first edition of 1900. In his review he draws a tougher conclusion. He criticised West's distinguishing between Dreiser's two roles (authorial *and* editorial) as 'extraordinary' because the distinction licensed West to overrule the author's final intentions (i.e. to overrule the textual results of the collaboration). For Pizer, 'The 1900 *Sister Carrie* is a historical artifact . . . in which the tensions, motives, and complexities which contributed to its revision are . . . a condition of the historical reality of the work', a 'historical validity' that the Pennsylvania Edition 'lacks'.[22] There is confusion here. A scholarly edition aims for a *critical* validity, as measured against an argued criterion of (usually) authorial intention. The moment an editor makes a single emendation, the *historical* integrity of the chosen copy-text is necessarily compromised. When, elsewhere in his long review, Pizer recommends that those emendations that the author had expressed a wish for ought to be accepted, the non sequitur of his case becomes plain.

In his review of West's edition, Hershel Parker replied to Pizer arguing that the latter evidently preferred 'to read what got published rather than what Dreiser wrote'.[23] If Sir Walter Greg's methodology for editing led to the conclusion that all changes that an author allows to be made after completing the manuscript must be treated as being of equal authority with what the author initially wrote then, Parker argues, the problem lies with the theory. The persistence of the problem ought to be no surprise:

The 1970s [he observes] were years when critics who had never really believed the truism that criticism depends upon textual scholarship happily abandoned any attempt to bring the author back from wherever the New Critics had exiled him; indeed, the cleverer critics of the decade killed the author off and exalted themselves in his place. And editors, to tell the truth, were often trying to do-it-by-the-dots, following a formula rather than bringing biographical, historical, and textual evidence to bear on the study of real authors creating real works of art. That was no time for clarifying textual issues.[24]

In 1981 it was still early days for digesting the sort of distinction between Dreiser as creative author and Dreiser as pragmatic editor that West was proposing. Later editors would feel the need to distinguish, in a related way, between an author genuinely in revision and the same author acting only as his or her own scribe, copying or miscopying wordings from one document to another. Understanding how such textual instabilities changed or should change our sense of what a work *is* was the implicit challenge that some editors were demanding of their readers in the 1980s. But this decade – dominated by the energetic emergence of post-structuralist literary theory – was a peculiarly unfavourable one to be requiring this of readers. It was, however, the decade in which the Society for Textual Scholarship (est. 1979) fully emerged and played a notable part, as we have seen, in the Gabler dispute: and the Society's first volume of *TEXT* appeared in 1984. There was, in the making, a gradual shift in the textual terrain to which all of the factors I have been describing in the last few chapters were contributing.

So: was West brave in respecting the authorial source of the work? Or foolhardy in intervening too far into the collaborative nature of its early production? The answer would seem to be: it depends on what you want to have and what you want to know. West did, in a real and practical sense, secure this novel's otherwise lost past. Because of its point of comparison, his textual apparatus allows a more readily comprehensible study of the changes made to the text of the manuscript draft by Dreiser and by his collaborators than if his edition had merely accepted the results of the collaboration as unchangeable. The latter of course is perfectly possible. West's scholarly edition of this novel may well not be the last.

But then, why should it be? There can be no definitive edition of any work, just as there can be no final connoisseurial judgement about a painting's authenticity. The information about workshop practice and the underlying versions and *pentimenti* revealed by scientific imaging, comparative analysis and archival research has its counterpart here in what is revealed about the history of the published text by the careful application of bibliographic forensics. This is, perhaps, the real achievement of scholarly editions. The text that they newly establish expertly embodies the editor's historical-textual discoveries and, in doing so, *tests* the editorial argument. But the historical and bibliographical analysis is what the whole edition depends on.

The publicity that preceded the publication of West's *Sister Carrie* is frequently referred to in the reviews and seems to have been a large part of the stimulus for the dispute. The claim that the new edition superseded all earlier ones, including that of 1900, suited the publisher – as it suits all publishers of scholarly editions, who are usually anxious to recoup their considerable investment. When an author's estate is another party to the publishing contract, the commercial fortunes of the scholarly edition only become more critical. Editors (and West is no exception) do not claim definitive status for their editions, but publishers are rarely so scrupulous. To be fair, they themselves had not yet adjusted to the new editorial insights into the textual condition of works that the 1980s projects were uncovering. What else, they must have thought, could an edition *be* that had been undertaken so scrupulously, at such length and at such cost *except* definitive? What was more, works had to be single-text, not multiple: for how else could these scholarly editions be produced? The publishers were in much the same mindset as those who were funding or reviewing the first volumes of the Rembrandt Research Project in the 1980s. So it was that, when Gabler's edition of *Ulysses* was published in 1984, much the same scenario played itself out but in a very much more heated way, for the reasons I explained in Chapter 8.

Anyone interested in a non-professional way in the texts of literary works would at first have been baffled by these events, and then perhaps become anxious. But at least, as J. C. C. Mays notes wryly, 'Purchasers of bad texts now apologise: "I know it contains harmful ingredients but it's all I can afford".'[25] The anxiety can only be a good thing if it sheds light on the truth of the textual condition of those works that we profess to admire and wish to discuss. That is why I cannot agree with Peter Shillingburg's suggestion that West's edition of *Sister Carrie* should 'probably' have carried another less 'potentially confusing' title.[26] When West edited an early version of *The Great Gatsby* in 2000 he entitled it *Trimalchio: An Early Version of The Great Gatsby*, after its name on the surviving galley proofs of the novel. It encountered none of the opposition that *Sister Carrie* provoked. But he has written recently that if he had the editing of the latter again he would make the same decisions about the text, only 'I would not be as insistent about the virtue of what I was doing.'[27]

When early versions are completely or very extensively rewritten into the form that went on to achieve publication – and when this supersession is clear and was intentional – treating the text of a long work in a scholarly edition as multiple rather than single will usually be the only feasible proceeding. One could cite many cases.[28] The book as a form can only take so many pages, publishers can only charge so much for the editions and must cover costs, readers have a limited appetite for textual matters, and, perhaps most importantly, editorial projects that become too ambitious may never get completed. So dividing up the work (in every sense) may simply be unavoidable. But where a scholarly edition establishes a text that is then in competition with the received text it should in general, I believe, bear the same title. Otherwise the textual issue, on which the edition was prepared in order to throw light, is likely to be defused rather than clarified. One way or another, through dispute if necessary, it is better that readers be able to, or be provoked to, understand the editorial premises of what text it is that they are reading.

Ten years after the publication of the Pennsylvania Edition of *Sister Carrie*, Jack Stillinger had no difficulty in making up *his* mind about it: this is 'Dreiser in his underwear', he declared. In his book *Multiple Authorship and the Myth of Solitary Genius* (1991), Stillinger ranges over a number of famous cases where authors have actively collaborated with editors or friends. He diagnoses the underlying problem and suggests 'that we drop the concept of an ideal single text fulfilling an author's intentions and put our money instead on some theory of versions' where 'the text of a version' would be understood as including 'all the words of that version, regardless of how many authors contributed to the writing . . . [E]ach contributor to the collaboration . . . [would have] an intrinsic rather than an extrinsic place in the text.'[29] The attractiveness of presenting multiple versions is obvious. It removes much of the burden of responsibility from the editor's shoulders, and it seems to take the heat out of the dispute. But, in book form at least, it is rarely practical except with large printing subsidies.

There is a theoretical problem too, and it is similar to the one we saw with the materialist Shakespeare proposal in Chapter 7. Stillinger's 'versional editing' melds the textual contributions of different parties. Thus it removes the possibility of literary or biographical criticism linked to the textual agent. In effect, it removes agency and its contexts from the equation. Or, more accurately, it looks at the question only to dismiss it. It throws the work back into the old, undifferentiated status of an aesthetic (or historical) object – or, rather, objects, since each version now has to be treated separately. The dangers of obscuring agency have been highlighted throughout this book in relation to various kinds of restoration.[30] The situation is no different here.

Material texts

In his *Bibliography and the Sociology of Texts* (1986), D. F. McKenzie sought to extend the range of bibliography. To do so meant emphasising the material forms that texts took on and in which, historically, they were read – in which they enjoyed a public 'life'. As mentioned above, Jerome McGann further developed this proposal, which has since become very influential. The basic argument is that the physical carriers of verbal text are themselves meaningful. McGann believes these meanings may be expressed as what he calls bibliographic codes. They affect the reading experience and should therefore properly come under the bibliographical gaze, rather than being ignored.[31]

Poets typically concern themselves with the ordering of poems in their published collections. They try to anticipate and guide the experience of their readers, often by ensuring thematic clusterings. Ignoring the orderings when later anthologies are prepared tends to eliminate this evidence. In recent scholarship, W. B. Yeats has emerged as the classic case. He 'regularly spent considerable time ordering his poems', George Bornstein has commented, 'virtually never printing them in chronological order of composition'. The 'customary role of the opening poem of a Yeats volume' is to present 'a parable of escape from this world . . . which ensuing poems will react against in various ways'. Material meanings can go further, he argues. The symbolism of T. Sturge Moore's striking cover design for Yeats's collection *The Tower* in 1928 was lost when the cover was not used for later editions of Yeats's poetry, which of course had their own, different production requirements. Again, the generous page design of Yeats's earlier limited-edition Cuala Press volumes conveyed meanings that were subsequently overlooked:

Cuala's deliberate imitation of William Morris's books, with their gesture towards late medieval or early Renaissance modes of production antithetical to those of late Victorian capitalism, encodes a critique of contemporary industrial production, and resistance to it, which consorts well with the conflict between spirit and material world in the poem itself and which disappears once the words of the poem are transplanted to a different display.[32]

Decisions about page-divisions when poetry is being typeset can have meaningful effects on reading since the pagination can be adjusted either to accentuate the importance of stanza divisions or to downplay them for the sake of economy. The poet may have been consciously counter-pointing voices or themes in successive stanzas, placing them carefully on the manuscript or typescript page or allotting each one a fresh page. This feature may or may not be respected in print.

Again, if poets write notes for their poems the decision about whether the text of a poem that is to be reprinted for a new collection embraces its authorial notes will have effects on interpretation, whatever the editor's decision. When, for instance, *Selected Verse* by the very long-lived Mary Gilmore was published in 1948 her by-then-unfashionable Scots dialect and colloquial forms from poems first published in the 1910s and 1920s (deriving from her Celtic heritage of the 1870s in colonial New South Wales) were modernised or formalised. Her notes were also eliminated, thereby stripping away the autobiographical and political contexts that they invoked. Readers were implicitly invited to read the poems as self-sufficient objects only, and they had little choice but to go on doing this until the completion in 2007 of a scholarly edition of Gilmore's collected verse.[33]

Scholarly editions in the past have not been immune from these problems. As we saw in Chapter 7, scholarly editors have usually defined as non-textual the original documentary formats: the headers, paper-stock and binding, the page- and line-breaks in the case of prose, the styling of chapter-titles, etc. And it is also true, as we can now see, that this stripping away eliminates some evidence of the historical moments of production and reading. But it *has* made critical editions possible, confined in their own presentation as they have been to the medium of the physical book with their own modern-day necessities of paper-stock, binding choice and typography. They cannot duplicate the physical particularities of the original editions and cannot inhabit their contexts; but then facsimiles, as books (if that is the alternative), do not and cannot either, except visually. Practical demands, then, do remove some of the argument's bite.

Nor is the breadth of application of the truism that the material medium signifies straightforwardly assessable. For one thing it probably varies with genre and according to the influence of the author over the production process. Many authors show little interest in it, assuming that their job has essentially ended once the manuscript has been written, or written and edited. Again, in a three-volume Victorian novel, how significant is the physical difference of every page from every other going to be in comparison to the difference in their verbal text? McGann's dividing line between the bibliographic and linguistic 'codes' turns out to be permeable in practice. He used the term *codes* metaphorically in 1991 in *The Textual Condition* but more literally in 2001 in *Radiant Textuality*. His chapters in the earlier book on D. G. Rossetti, Ezra Pound and William Blake make their best mileage from the interlinking of the two 'codings' for the imagined, original readers as McGann demonstrates the conscious concern with the look of the printed document that each poet showed.

While the broader applicability of what has become an energetic debate is still unclear, the existence of the debate has usefully focussed attention on the place of the reader-decoder *in* the text – that is, in its realisation in practice. This acknowledgement introduces an inherent, potentially unmanageable instability for editors. Nevertheless their job needs to be done in light of the empirical realities, to take its orientation from them, even if the assumed wholeness of the work as a result cannot be captured. The theoretical notion of the work advanced in Chapter 10 attempts to respond to these realities.

COPYRIGHT, CRITICAL EDITING AND THE IMPORTANCE OF TEXTUAL PROCESS

Chapters 7 and 8 adverted to the gradual loss of belief amongst editors in the ideal text of a work, which the edition's reading text would try to establish. The causes have been varied. Although the belief has by no means entirely abated, the change was of course related to the successive waves of post-structuralist theory. But it was more importantly a discovery of evidence from the editorial projects themselves. The evidence often did not sit comfortably with the single-reading-text approach. A final-intentions edition would usually be possible, but was it desirable? Did it serve readers well? Whatever the truth of the nutritionists' slogan 'You are what you eat', the librarians' one was closer to home for editors: 'You are what you read.' But editors were all too aware that there was a rider to this. They were deciding, for classic works, what form their presentation would take and the information about the functioning of these works that readers would be exposed to. The evidence they were finding was often at odds with their audience's expectations.

Editors of modernist works found this a particular problem as they began to realise the importance for their editing of the changed copyright regime following the passing of the Chace Act in the USA in the 1890s. This marked the end of US publishers being able to publish without licence works first published in other countries. But the Act imposed conditions. Whenever the same title was now to appear by arrangement in both London and New York, the only way that an American publisher could secure the full benefits of copyright protection was to set up their own edition in type so that it would appear at the same time as the counterpart British one. Since this meant that the author needed to provide two setting copies, the problem emerged of how to keep the two copies identical.

The author would typically have written a holograph manuscript and have sent it for typing in sections or all at once. If in sections and if the typings were immediately returned for further correction and revision before the author resumed work on the next section of manuscript, then manuscript and typescript were no longer discrete chronologically. One did not *succeed* the other since later sections in manuscript might well assume earlier revisions made in the already corrected sections of typescript. In any case, the two typescript copies became the revision and correction site for the author. But would the author find a way of improving the newly revised wording as he or she transcribed it to the other copy? The illustrations from the typescripts of *The Boy in the Bush* in Chapter 8 (Figures 8.2 and 8.3) showed how easily this could happen. The two copies gradually lost their identicalness: but how common a problem was this? There are scholarly editorial implications here because, if the typescripts as revised were dissimilar and the manuscript had been chosen as copy-text, the modern editor would have to decide which typescript copy had higher authority. That is, *which* typescript should be preferred to emend the copy-text, since there was a fair chance that *both* would contain later readings, but different ones in some cases.

In trying to come to grips with the phenomenon of the author-in-revision, further questions arise. At what stage was the copying of revisions from one typescript to the other done: page by page, or chapter by chapter? If the latter, did the author actually notice all the smaller changes that he or she had already made in the revision copy as the transferring of revisions was taking place? Writers are not clerks. Mechanical copying-out may start off as the aim but the process virtually guarantees it will fail. In other words, the chances are close to 100 per cent of non-identical setting copy being supplied to publishers and thus of the author authorising non-identical texts for the public appearance of the work. Spare a thought for the editor who is commissioned to establish a single reading text respecting the author's final intentions and who has to devise a cogent way of dealing with this creative instability.

Now let us give the screw one more turn. What if the New York and London simultaneous first editions were both preceded by serialisations in a magazine or newspaper? This arrangement, whenever it could be achieved, was definitely in the author's financial interest. But the revised typescript copies now had to go to the magazine editors rather than the book publishers because, again for copyright safety, the serialisations needed to finish at the same time as the book forms appeared. But, in this case, where was the copy for the book typesetters to come from, for they needed to get to work well before the serialisations ended?

There are various possible answers – and this was in fact the situation that Joseph Conrad faced with his novel *Under Western Eyes* (1911). The simpler case was faced by D. H. Lawrence on several occasions, also by Virginia Woolf, and doubtless by others. As the critical editions of modernist authors began appearing in the 1980s and 1990s, and as their editors were, during the course of their projects, reporting their disturbing findings at conferences, the assumption that a single reading text could adequately represent the work began to look shaky.

Because the established reading text typically drew on more than one version for its readings, it was necessarily an eclectic assembly of textual elements from various (historical) documents. It was a synchronic, static representation of a textual process that had been in fact diachronic, likely to span in composition and revision a couple of years but in some rare cases as many as thirty or forty years. Furthermore, the newly established text had not been read by the author's contemporary audience or seen by the author.

Such realisations began to worry sections of the anglophone editing community. A new understanding of their own enterprise was necessary. Editors had been aiming to capture the final intentions of the author for the work. But the obverse of this was that the edition's reading text could then *only* be a collaboration of dead author and live editor. Editors literally inscribed themselves into the reading text. The American habit of making the list of editor's emendations the primary apparatus at the end of the volume implicitly confirmed this. The list of variant wordings ('substantives') came next, but they were not so much variant readings as rejected ones. Variant formal matters such as punctuation, spelling and word separation ('accidentals') were not usually provided at all since the provision of a full *historical* record was not the aim.

It was in this situation that attempts to reconceptualise the aims of editions that would respect and record more aspects of the life of works began to be made and that Gabler's *Ulysses* edition, coming as it did out of another tradition, helped to stimulate.[34] The *process* of textual development began to be valued as against the so-called *product* that the single-reading text edition formalised and made central to the editing effort. It was argued that such attention would, in prospect at least, give literary criticism an extra dimension, since an author's works need not be treated as totally separate from one another if their underlying versions overlapped chronologically or intermingled textually. Versions of different works might have been in communication with one another all along in a sort of *authorial* intertextuality – except we had not properly registered it because of the design of our editions. Chronology, accordingly, began to assume a more important place, as did the question of distinguishing the agency of the variant readings rather than simply listing them as rejected.

Although it would not appear until 2001, John Bryant's *The Fluid Text* has underlined the significance of this breakthrough in thinking about textual process, a breakthrough upon which we have yet to capitalise fully. He paints a picture of a future editorial dispensation where effectively neutral electronic archives and frankly interpretative printed editions will supplement one another. His exploration of what he names textual fluidity is open to some objection[35] and his prophesying of the future is no laydown misère. But the potential interplay that he envisages between textual criticism and editions on the one hand, and literary criticism on the other, points towards a coming together in the present post-Theory moment of forms of literary scholarship that have traditionally gone their own, separate, and therefore mutually impoverished, ways.

THE GERMAN ENCOUNTER

The appearance of Gabler's edition of *Ulysses* in 1984 whetted many appetites for better access to the German tradition from which its left-hand pages had arisen. But it was not until 2001 that the first thorough-going adaptation of German methods to English poetry was published: J. C. C. Mays's edition of Coleridge's *Poetical Works*.[36] Reactions against the apparent foreignness of its presentation have been, in the reviews at least, surprisingly muted. Had the edition appeared when it was actually completed at the end of the 1980s, reviewers may have been lining up to take positions.[37] But in the interim the Gabler dispute had settled down, as we have seen, and the long delayed encounter with the German tradition had begun to happen. Before Gabler's edition, anglophone readers were largely restricted to Hans Zeller's account of the German tradition, published in the 1975 issue of *Studies in Bibliography*.[38] Finally, in 1995, a collection of translated essays, *Contemporary German Editorial Theory*, appeared. It was an important volume, and allowed many aspects of both traditions to fall into place in relation to one another.

What became plain was that, during the twentieth century, the German and Anglo-American editorial traditions had become, in some ways, the inverse of one another. In the 1930s and 1940s, the New Bibliographer and Shakespeare editor R. B. McKerrow attempted half-heartedly, and then Sir Walter Greg more completely, to shake themselves free of a doctrine of copy-text that forbade the eclectic combination of wordings from different authoritative texts of a work. This doctrine had itself been a reaction against an earlier more subjective editorial tradition. The New Bibliography was behind the reaction, offering as it did a sophistication of analysis of printed books not matched on the Continent, particularly not in France amongst literary scholars.[39]

Meanwhile German editors of modern secular literature were practising what Hans Zeller calls a 'philology of divination',[40] claiming the special editorial insight that long and sensitive attention to a poet's works afforded the emending editor. The overreaching of such claims to such sensitised attunement to the author's wishes gradually induced its own reaction, signalled by the eight-volume edition of the complete works of Hölderlin that began to appear from 1943, edited by Friedrich Beissner.

The pendulum in German editing thereafter swung towards the genetic tracing of the development of works, many of which were of the last 200 years and were witnessed by a plenitude of extant manuscripts. The German scholarly edition characterised itself as *historisch-kritisch*, not just 'critical', thus emphasising the archival dimension – the edition's historical gathering-together of textual materials. An edited text would be chosen, emended only for its indubitable *Textfehler* (textual faults that could not possibly make sense in context). A complex form of apparatus was developed to record the variant readings in printings and (especially) in manuscripts. Beissner's apparatus, laid out beneath each line of text in a stair-step form whenever a revision or correction occurred, clarified the temporal development of the text. Zeller's (from 1958) aimed additionally to capture the spatial layout of the manuscript alterations. The synoptic recording was sensitive to the internal relationships of levels and layers of revision and correction; and the media in which they had been carried out could be recorded. This was a remarkable achievement. It was an intelligent response to the textual documents that German editors were typically facing.

Postwar Anglo-American editing, on the other hand, coming out of Shakespeare and seventeenth-century literature where manuscripts were relatively few, was, as already remarked, necessarily book-based (i.e. bibliographic). Important exceptions emerged in Romantic and modern poetry in English, and not only in modernist prose such as we have seen. The Cornell Yeats series, for instance, was initially designed to resolve questions of compositional genesis by revealing the creative process by which W. B. Yeats's poems reached their authorially sanctioned final forms. High-quality facsimile images of manuscripts and typescripts, accompanied by transcriptions and text-critical analysis of how the successive versions superseded one another, provide an excellent basis for study in this series. Yeats's posthumous volume *Last Poems and Two Plays* (1939) created, however, a different order of problem. He did not live to finish it and so his wife, at first alone and then in collaboration with Yeats's editor at Macmillan, Thomas Mark, intervened wherever they felt it necessary, both in the arrangement of the poems and in the establishment of their texts for the posthumous editions: the Cuala Press *Last Poems and Two Plays* (1939), the Macmillan *Last Poems and Plays* (1940), and the so-called definitive edition of 1949, *The Poems of W. B. Yeats*.

James Pethica's *Last Poems* volume in the Cornell Yeats has further dismantled that claim of definitiveness, and his careful scholarship lends authority to a notable conclusion:

> In the case of Yeats – an inveterate and almost obsessive reviser, for whom authorial intention was ever shifting in his search for new perfection, and a man for whom the self and the self represented in the text were always in complex dialogue – the traditional notion of intentionality is one that should always be applied warily . . . the drafts do not always allow us to make easy decisions as to how the texts should be presented in future . . . the collection seems certain to remain less than "definitive" in various respects, and a continuing collaborative interplay of posthumous hands in its construction is unavoidable.[41]

With the publication of Pethica's transcription and analysis of the manuscript materials, and his collation and assessment of the later typescripts, proofs and early printed editions, any new editorial collaboration must be significantly better informed than before.

In using Pethica's volume, however, a curious thing strikes one: it provides no final text of each poem to use as a point of orientation against the preceding versions. Earlier volumes in the series had offered this consolation in a de facto sense by tracing the process up to and including the point where Yeats arrived at the final form of each poem. Pethica's volume cannot do so because Yeats died before he finished. As a result, the volume offers what might be called the ultimate in textual criticism (i.e. analysis of the versions' textual relationships to one another) but it leaves the provision of reading texts to future editors. Strictly speaking, it is not an edition at all, but rather a systematic recording and analysis of a complex textual process. In the Anglo-American tradition, text-critical analysis – even of this extraordinarily detailed kind – has always been thought of as preliminary to the critical editing. In Germany, as we shall see in the next section, the situation was different. The two activities were conceptualised in such a way that they could be folded seamlessly into the one edition.

Texte und Varianten

The thinking behind the developing German approach was laid out in a seminal volume of essays in 1971, *Texte und Varianten*, edited by Gunter Martens and Zeller. These two scholars, together with Siegfried Scheibe, have been the most influential figures in the movement. The position that emerged and would be further developed in the 1980s and 1990s can be summarised as follows.

Editors were to see themselves as historians of the text, not executors of the author's wishes. All versions produced or authorised by the author were to be treated as of 'equal standing'.[42] There is sense in this. As Scheibe remarks, the author, while alive, is likely to favour only one version of a work at a time: 'The work is . . . always in the present' for authors because it changes with and through them.'[43] But for the editor who comes later the prospect is of a series of versions. As the authorised ones all temporarily enjoyed authorial preference or acknowledgement, Scheibe argues that it is not up to editors, historically positioned as they are, to act as if they are the author by preferring a single one or creating a new one by emending one of the existing ones.

Rather, according to Scheibe, the editor is obliged to accept the consequences of the author's understanding that others would revise or produce his or her text. As a result, documents are authorised 'not only globally, but also in their parts and details'.[44] Authorisation is not for all time but only for the period of the author's instigation of production. When he dies, it ends. Scheibe defines *Textfehler* conservatively and wants as little intervention in the edited text as possible so as to preserve its historical authenticity: the editor 'is not an "over-author"'.[45] The editor's effort must go into deciphering and preserving intact the historical record because the text of the work is 'the sum' of the extant (historical) versions.[46]

In Zeller's 'Record and Interpretation' (originally in the 1971 collection), what is 'sought-after' is assumed to be the 'objectification of editing'.[47] He explains: 'A principle such as authorial intention cannot serve as a central criterion for the constitution of text' because it 'remains a mere idea of the author on the part of the editor, and as such cannot be established reliably.'[48] Zeller remarks: 'We cannot even easily determine our own "actual wills," still less our former intentions.'[49] While it is 'inevitable' that the editor will cast a 'shadow' over the text,[50] it is far better to rely on the *Befund* (the material record) rather than the *Deutung* (interpretation of it – that is, text). Thus it becomes the editor's duty 'to determine and reproduce authorized versions'.[51]

This archival aim has rigour and consistency but it does not help decide the criterion according to which the edited text ought to be chosen and to which the textual apparatus will thus be anchored. Because of the fixed boundaries of the physical book, this act of choice establishes a hierarchy of presentation between the text that we can read linearly and those texts available only synoptically. In Anglo-American editions, answering the empirical question of what text ought to become more widely available to the reading public through the editor's efforts is the aim from the very start. Therefore the question for the editor becomes, what is the most defensible way of establishing it? This is the inspiration for the whole endeavour, though with what consequences in extreme cases we have seen in the present and previous chapters. In comparison, relatively little thought amongst German editors seems to have been devoted to the question of the choice of reading text – as J. C. C. Mays found when he came to edit his variorum edition of Coleridge's *Poetical Works* in a German way.[52] Another way of pointing the contrast is to acknowledge that most Anglo-American editors work on the assumption that a reading text will ultimately be required by the publisher. But commercial necessities of this kind have no place in the strict line of reasoning in Scheibe's essays.

The historical impulse has always been a fundamental one in German philology, so it was no surprise to find, when the 1995 collection appeared, that the new editorial consensus had both rigorously and ingeniously expressed it. Less predictable for anglophone editors was the revealing of the other major impulse behind German editing: a Prague-structuralist basis for the accepted definition of *text*. This is represented in the volume by an essay of 1971 by Miroslav Cervenka. It is written from the standpoint, not of a practising editor, but of a structural analyst of literary phenomena.[53]

Cervenka is interested in all stages of the life-cycle of a literary work. His fundamental assumption is that the aesthetic object, in its workings, must be susceptible of analysis. He emphasises the semiotic significance of the act of publication. It marks the point when the 'genetic' dimension (the writer's willing the work forward in drafts) gives way to the 'intentional'. This is the intention of the work – not of the author – to invite the readership to participate in it, specifically to interpret it by inferring the author's personality. (This is as against the 'psychophysical *person* of the author':[54] he appears to mean something like Foucault's author-function invoked as a principle of thrift to limit available interpretations.) For Cervenka, the completeness of the text at publication is crucial; until that point it is only 'fragmentary'.[55] From that point onwards it has the quality of being semiotic, a 'social-cultural fact'.[56] It attains this quality in the advancing discourse, firstly – partially – in the revisions but then more importantly in the readings of it upon publication.

A completed literary work can be assumed to embody internal relationships between its textual elements. Under the gaze of structuralist analysis, these relationships articulate it as a semiotic object. Authorial intention becomes irrelevant once the text is granted this objective status, Cervenka argues. The corollary for textual critics and editors is to understand structural relationships within a version as constituting its existence. It gives the sense in which, as Gabler observes in his introduction to the 1995 collection, German editors edit the text rather than the author.

Scheibe, Zeller and Martens have been able to think their way through the life-cycle of literary works and have had (along with their compatriot editors) the determination to evolve very sophisticated ways of documenting it. This was partly because the structuralist approach liberated them from a dependence on the ideality of authorial intention. This is something to admire. But there is a cost here too that I will try to identify.

Being empirical versus being systematic

The first rule of thumb in editing is that every editing situation is different and therefore no rule will be universally applicable. I have noticed over the years that this is the only editorial tenet on which agreement is infallibly forthcoming amongst editors. Sir Walter Greg's 'Rationale of Copy-Text' only caught on amongst anglophone editors because of its irresistible appeal, not to a general theory, but to ordinary experience. It was a proposal based on a distinction between what fallible compositors were more likely to miscopy (punctuation, spelling etc.) and what less likely (wordings). Why should the editor be bound to accept the miscopyings in order to have a later text that embodied the author's revisions in wording? Editing history had, prior to his essay, backed editors like Greg into a corner. There was the enduring suspicion of the excesses of eclecticism on the one hand and, on the other, a new climate of confidence that analytical bibliography now gave editors a greater chance than ever of distinguishing corruptions from authorial revisions in the various printings of a work. His was a pragmatic attempt to try to give some very provisional order to a messy situation.[57]

Zeller counsels against what he calls the 'contamination' of correcting one authorised text from another. The ideal text that Greg's approach would thus establish misrepresents history: this objection is always at the back of the German thinking. But Zeller's other reason is structural:

> Such a 'corrected' version would be an unverifiable whole that even the editor as its producer could not vouch for either on the understanding of the whole as a concatenation of signs referring to one another, or in consideration of the notion that this structure changes with each variant.[58]

He gives Cervenka as his authority for that last notion. Given this redefinition of text as 'a system of signs characterized by the functional interrelation of its components',[59] there can only be one upshot for Zeller: 'The eclectic editor contaminatingly synchronizes that which occurred diachronically ... In principle [therefore], one must edit versions.'[60]

Given the empirical disposition on which it was founded, the Anglo-American endeavour was never going to rival the German as a firmly grounded general theory. Bowers frowned on the timidity of variorum (non-critical) editions: and here were the Germans putting an exemplary effort into the preparations for the (editorial) marriage but, after all that hard work, denying readers the much desired consummation – the critically established reading text. How to adjudicate this fundamental disagreement in what editors ought to do?

Most of Zeller's examples are of poetry, where a single change can indeed alter the run of a line and potentially the meaning of the whole poem. Also it is possible for both author and reader to hold a complete poem, if short enough, in the mind at once. The notion of a version as a system of signs makes some intuitive sense in this case. But in the case of long prose works – Conrad's *Under Western Eyes*, Joyce's *Ulysses*, or any of Dickens's serialised novels, for instance – it does not. Wherever, as in these cases, the author is revising a typescript or proofs of part of the work before the whole work exists in a finished version of *any* kind, the messiness of literary and professional life reasserts itself, undermining reliance on a clean, structuralist rationale. Obviously, only when the manuscript is *finished* can version-wide 'systems' be imagined.

Before that point is reached, one could, perhaps, peel back the structuralist claim and restate it in terms of the local relations within a chapter or section and so in effect treat each one as a text in its own right. But, if that defensive move were admitted, there is no logical reason to stop there. Why not go back to the paragraph or sentence or phrase, or, in the extreme, a single word and its accompanying punctuation? Relations between text elements exist at a micro-level as well as at a macro. Indeed local ones often exist more vividly, less abstractly. Furthermore, if other readers find as I do, that, in the use of a synoptic display of textual variants, one's attention is energised by the author's flare-ups of revisional energy at particular points, so that one is directed chronologically forwards at those points rather than structurally sideways, then one has the beginnings of a reasoned rejection of Zeller's reliance on a structural principle.[61]

The recognition of empirical realities sooner or later compromises systematic thinking. As Anglo-American editing has shown, flexibility and rigour *can* be antagonists. The former can more readily absorb unanticipated situations and does not rule out in advance presently unknown horizons. One of the central insights of Anglo-American editing has been that the textual authority of a document is usually mixed. The document (e.g. proofs) may have been read, corrected and approved by the author. But a lengthy published text will contain a great many wordings and textual features of presentation (for a long novel, certainly hundreds, possibly thousands) that did not derive from the author's manuscript but are the responsibility of an editor, typist or typesetter – or of all three. Under the German system, however, once a version is deemed to have been authorised it must be recorded. Authorisation operates only at the macro-level of the version.

Textual authority, on the other hand – a concept unknown in the postwar (especially post-1960s) German tradition – operates down to the level of the word or even the punctuation mark.[62] To sort out the question of authority, the Anglo-American editor must determine the agent responsible or probably responsible for the variant reading and only, in the absence of evidence, fall back upon the reading of the nominated copy-text. When German editors reject the eclectic mixing of readings taken from different historical versions to which this procedure leads, they believe they are on firm ground. They rightly pride themselves on the theoretical coherence that underpins their editions. But the question of the reading text, which is the central one for ordinary readers, is – as I have remarked – usually adjudicated on merely pragmatic grounds.[63]

If pragmatism be admitted here, then why not elsewhere? When German editors emend their chosen reading text for any *Textfehler* that may be present, they attribute the necessity, in theory at least, to a structural failure of the text. Seen from an Anglo-American point of view, what they are doing is (pragmatically and rightly) giving textual authority to their own trained judgement. Why is it necessary to invoke the doctrine of *Textfehler* when it is abundantly clear that someone wrote a wrong sign, as we all do, whenever we are writing too fast or with our attention wandering? Lurking in the background here for German editors when they *do* emend *Textfehler* is, I strongly suspect, an interpretation of intention, of what the writer probably *meant* to write. If so, then individual agency creeps back onto the editorial stage just when it seemed to have been dispensed with. That is because, at bottom, documentary texts are not self-identical. To be actualised – as Martens argues – texts need readers. They are inert documents otherwise. The writer, in the case of a manuscript, is continuously his or her own first reader. Copyists, typesetters, editors and readers of the first and later editions participate in the actualisation of text. This is an empirical fact. To pass over it out of loyalty to a belief that text is (exclusively) a semiotic system, is, I believe, unwise.[64]

Anglo-American editing, in contrast, is built around authorial agency, and therefore around the interpretation of intention. Its operative criterion, when assessing versions of works, is textual authority. As we have seen, it is normally a mixed one because of the various agents responsible for elements of a version's text. And, as we have also seen in assessing Zeller's arguments, text relations exist not only at the macro-level of the version but at a micro-level as well. An eclectic method of establishing a reading text allows the editor to identify these latter relations and to express them editorially. Witness the (pragmatic) method, described in Chapter 8, that has been developed for treating authorial correction of faulty copying differently from genuine, unhindered authorial revision.

Eclectic reading texts seem to me to be defensible whenever they allow the editor to capture the author's concentrated dealings with the work over the period it takes to write the manuscript, through whatever versions it proceeds to a first semblance of finality, then to revise and correct its copying(s), and subsequently to check proofs. Only copy-text editions can capture the final results of this process in a reading text, while dispensing with the non-authorial dross. Whether the non-authorial elements *are* dross has been one of the reassessments in which editors have been engaged for the last quarter-century. One of the upshots is that *authorship* as ordinarily understood need not be the source of textual authority that the edition primarily respects. (Witness the discussion of *Sons and Lovers*, above.) We are still awaiting the practical results of this shift in theoretical alignment. But no editor in the Anglo-American tradition would now insist that only one form of edition could be valid for any particular work. Editions embody arguments about the textual transmission, and all such reasoned arguments are, by nature, non-definitive – though they may be, and preferably *are*, persuasive.

Anglo-American editing never went through a structuralist phase: the Greg–Bowers homegrown methodology had been initially developed, then institutionally reinforced by the Center for the Editing of American Authors and Committee for Scholarly Editions (as described in Chapter 8); and its idealist concepts met the spirit of the times. But in the 1980s editors were finally catapulted into a post-structuralist crisis whose implications were still being addressed during the 1990s.[65]

It was an accident of chronology that led to my own general-editing role being exercised during this period. From the early 1990s it became my job to initiate, design and organise the editorial approach for the successive titles of the Academy Editions of Australian Literature. In this, I was assisted by an editorial board made up of scholars prepared to experiment, none of whom wore badges of allegiance to the Greg–Bowers or Thorpe–Gaskell approaches.[66] That is not to say that the Australian editions did not benefit from Anglo-American methodologies: they did. But the editorial theory movement of the 1980s and 1990s gave us, as I saw it, some freedom and reason to innovate. And the history of the book movement (and to a lesser extent postcolonialist theory) had its effect, as we began to realise the significance of recent findings for our authors.

To edit in a country that has been at the periphery of a print culture centred in London is to be forced to recognise that literary works, produced under such conditions, cannot be treated editorially as if they existed in an ideal realm of their own as aesthetic objects. Just as editors of modernist works have, as discussed above, gradually been realising the effect of the copyright regime on their methodology, we could not, with the Australian series, responsibly ignore the textually distorting effects of the imperial marketplace.

In only two cases have we established the reading texts eclectically, and even then very conservatively.[67] Copy-texts are nearly always taken from an existing document whether printed or manuscript or typescript, and emendation is kept to a minimum. The laying out for the reader of the record of revision and correction, whether by the author or, if it is interesting, by an editor or publisher, has been the goal. In principle one should edit versions:

that call, differently inflected by various commentators such as Zeller and Stillinger, is one that we have developed, but accommodated in such a way that the imperatives of agency, authorial and otherwise, have not been lost sight of. Wherever practical, we present what the first Australian audiences read, and then record in foot-of-page apparatus what changes were made to the text as it was taken up, usually by London publishers, and then distributed back to Australian readers in a new, often abridged or edited form. We have wanted to dismantle as far as possible the textual distortions caused by the British domination of the colonial book trade.[68]

Reluctantly, as noted in Chapter 8, I came to the conclusion that Gabler's synoptic display was not for us; and when I became more familiar with the apparatus volumes in German editions in the mid-1990s I felt that my decision was vindicated. The method requires more space than we were likely to be allowed. Most of our volumes are around 800 pages as it is. The luxury of multiple volumes per title was not available, and a lemmatised apparatus is far more economical of space than a synoptic one. In any case, given the kind of resistance that radically innovative editions have encountered, I could not convince myself that the bulk of our readers would welcome it.

The present book's final chapter is a venture into aesthetic theory. It takes into account the arguments in this book about the tension between the aesthetic and historical dimensions that restoration projects of all kinds have to bridge, and also the recognition of the role of readers in the work at every stage of its life-cycle. The operation, at a more fundamental level, of agency and chronology in the production–consumption spectrum has repeatedly been exposed by the crises in the restoration projects discussed in this book. The problems involved in securing the past, both the tangible and the intangible, argue that they need to be brought together into a model of the work that might help thinking whenever restorations of any kind are being proposed. Chapter 10 offers such a model for consideration. Eclectically based, it is thus inevitably provisional, and I am aware that it is far from the last word on the matter. Nevertheless, it points a fresh way forward, which, suitably adapted for the medium, may bring clarity to conservation philosophies. Otherwise, as this book has shown, they continually run up to the brink of crisis.

The editorial gaze and the nature of the work

I should choose my writing to be judged as a chiselled block, uncon-
nected with my hand entirely.

(Virginia Woolf, 1908)[1]

A theory of the work does not exist, and the empirical task of those
who naively undertake the editing of works often suffers in the absence
of such a theory.

(Michel Foucault, 1969)[2]

Work: only four letters, satisfyingly brief, apparently simple. In English,
the verb and the noun are the same, so that the concept of the work retains
its direct connection to the hand of its maker. The concept loses it in most
other European languages: so we have German *Werk* (as opposed to *Arbeit*),
French *œuvre* (versus *travail*), Italian *opera* (versus *lavoro*), Spanish *obra*
(versus *trabajo*), Russian *proizvedenie* (versus *rabota*), and so on. Getting
a grip on the concept is notoriously difficult in whatever language.[3] And,
by and large, editors and conservators who want to get things done avoid
taking the trouble. Yet, if the nature of the work undergoing expert treatment during cultural heritage conservation or scholarly editing is assumed
to be self-evident, then the danger looms that practitioners will, despite
the best of intentions, misrepresent works or just flounder about with
self-contradicting solutions when faced with difficult cases.

Aesthetic philosophers, theorising literary critics and editors, and reflec-
tive commentators on the restoration of paintings, buildings and monuments have repeatedly shown that the concept is anything but self-evident.
The present chapter examines some attempts to conceptualise this problematic area since the 1930s, before proposing a provisional solution that
may help to clarify thinking when practices of preservation and conservation are being determined. The language and thinking employed here
come ultimately from scholarly editorial activity. The working assumption
is that, with suitable adjustments for the medium, it will apply to other

historically or aesthetically oriented forms of cultural conservation that seek, in one way or another, to secure past achievement.

The first step is to characterise what can loosely be called the traditional understanding. Whether the work in question is *allographic* (as in the case of a literary work, where any copy is an instance of it) or *autographic* (as in the case of a painting, where the physical object is identical with it), we have traditionally come to the question of the work with a series of assumptions. The first is that the work is in some sense objective, standing over and apart from its maker and its perceivers, and that, conversely, its histories of making and reception stand over and apart from its essential nature as a work. The second is that the work has the potential to persist over time; and the third is that it has an identity that, amongst other things, sustains true descriptions of it (e.g. that the *Iliad* is in hexameter). Performance-works, it has long been recognised, raise their own problems of definition because of the gap between script and performance. Is an unsung song, for example, that exists only in written form truly a song? But other seeming paradoxes – such as, if the *Mona Lisa* is in the Louvre, where is *Hamlet*? – are readily dealt with by the allographic/autographic distinction.[4] This was the general understanding into the late 1960s when some memorable accounts of the literary work were put forward.

The granting of objectivity to the work placed conservation, editing and interpretation in a position essentially external to it. The argument of this book, on the other hand, has been that this 1960s position was and is basically wrong; that the post-structuralist strands of thought that succeeded this position got it wrong but in another way; and that, counterintuitively, preservation, conservation and interpretation are always and unavoidably *in*trinsic to the work. Fundamental philosophical positions undergird each of these arguments. They are examined here in turn. A solution is proposed and then applied to the problematics of historic-building conservation. But first, some examples of art conservation and editing that expose the inadequacy of the traditional understanding and that beg the questions that this chapter seeks to answer are briefly described.

WORKS IN DISTRESS

July 2006 was a time of celebration in Holland: it was the four hundredth anniversary of the birth of Rembrandt. Numerous public events marked the occasion, including important exhibitions of his recently restored paintings. In the Mauritshuis art museum in The Hague, for instance, several

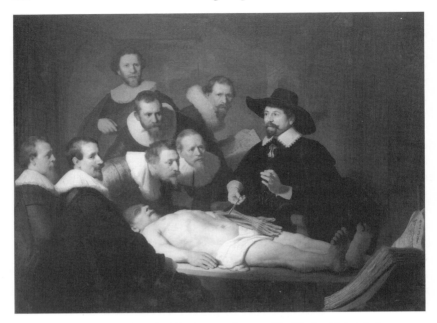

Figure 10.1 Rembrandt, *The Anatomy Lesson of Dr Nicolaes Tulp* (1632).

thoroughly restored Rembrandts were proudly on show, together with reports on, and a video of, the cleaning processes that the paintings had undergone. This sort of exhibit makes for a different kind of response from the traditional one of simple admiration. But it is a response that we have been gradually getting used to. As we saw in Chapter 6, this has been happening with Rembrandt in a concerted way since the late 1980s through a series of exhibitions around the world, which have been curated with scholarly care and extensive research. We are regularly invited to absorb and thus to naturalise the conservatorial gaze. We are slowly learning to see paintings differently.

This shift in attention comes at some cost to our preconceptions. X-radiographs on display at the Mauritshuis showed for instance that, in the famous *Anatomy Lesson of Dr Nicolaes Tulp* (1632), the corpse being dissected (based on an executed criminal whose right hand had earlier been cut off for some other malfeasance) acquired a well-proportioned hand even though Rembrandt had originally painted him in his non-entire condition. It was not a botched job by some later perfecter. It is authorial.[5] (See Figure 10.1.)

The *Anatomy Lesson* had previously been restored in 1951, when an eighteenth-century addition was deliberately obscured. The addition was a numbered list of the names of the doctors watching the dissection; it was placed in a drawing held by one of them, and corresponding numbers were added next to each portrait. The latest restoration (done in 1997–98) partially removed the obscuring medium so that now the information is just legible.

Sometimes restoration is justified by rhetorical appeal to the mastery of the artist, or alternatively to the aesthetic values of the painting as an object. (The two are not the same thing but are often elided.) Sometimes the ground of appeal is the painting's historical witness: here, the fact of the interpretation being felt desirable in the eighteenth century and its taking the form it did. The late 1990s restoration wanted, then, to have it both ways: to be, now with a wonderful new clarity, *of* Rembrandt but also (with a little less clarity) *of* the eighteenth century. It appeals to two different standards of textual authority (as a scholarly editor would put it) simultaneously. What *is* it, then, that we are seeing? What effect does such intervention have upon our notion of the work?

My account in Chapter 5 of Pinin Brambilla Barcilon's restoration of the *Last Supper* of Leonardo da Vinci, completed in 1999, raised much the same questions. In that discussion, I quoted Martin Kemp's observation:

Any programme of restoration of a badly damaged and extensively repaired artefact which aims to reinstate some measure of the original experience has to make an implicit choice as to which of the artist's intentions or groups of intentions and which of the various spectators' criteria are to be satisfied.[6]

Our 'conception of what is essential in a work of art', Kemp concludes, 'determines what demands we make on visual images'.[7]

Compare Kemp's conclusion with a startling reflection made in 1995 on another form of cultural preservation. Alois Pichler participated in the international text-encoding community's efforts during the 1990s to find satisfactory methods of transcribing manuscript and print documents of historical importance and of marking them up for electronic storage. The change in medium means that mark-up is unavoidably interpretative. 'Our aim in transcription', Pichler reasoned, 'is not to represent as correctly as possible the originals, but rather to prepare from the original text another text so as to serve as accurately as possible certain interests in the text.' And he added: 'what we are actually going to represent, and how, is determined by our research interests . . . and not by a text, which exists independently and which we are going to depict.'[8] In 1997 Allen Renear, a prominent member of the same community, objected to what he called this antirealist view of text, but his arguments seem finally to rest on the unproblematised notion that texts are or must be objective realities, which encoders would do well to represent faithfully.[9]

These cases point towards a conclusion with consequences. When it comes to the abstract question of the identity of the work that is being transcribed, Renear seems to deny the inevitability of the encoder's mediation. Similarly, Barcilon's reliance on scientific testing and naturalised reading practices (the seductive authorial fragment that the movie camera can linger on in close up) also allows the hand of the conservator to disappear as a constitutive part of the object we look at. That this consolation is an illusion is exposed by the conflicting conservatorial appeals in the 1997–98 *Anatomy Lesson*.

Although Barcilon's position is a very defensible one, although Renear's might seem like common sense and although the new *Anatomy Lesson* seems to be able to eat its cake and still have it, none can give us access to what does not exist: the true or real Leonardo, the essential Rembrandt painting or the printed or manuscript text in itself as an essence outside of the conservator's re-presentation. The conserved painting or the transcribed text do not, then, exist unproblematically, whether on the wall or in the computer file. In an important sense, each is completed by its readership both during conservation and after. This unsettling conclusion is one that this book has been repeatedly pointing to. It suggests that we need to know more about what works are. A closer examination of the 1960s consensus is therefore necessary.

THEORY OF THE WORK IN THE LATE 1960S

In 1966 René Wellek and Austin Warren added an important chapter to the third revised edition of their influential *Theory of Literature* (1942), called 'The Mode of Existence of a Literary Work of Art'. It brought together and crystallised many of the insights and working assumptions of the New Criticism. That movement had emerged in the 1930s, displaced belles-lettristic and literary-historical approaches during the 1940s and 1950s, and was itself, by 1966 when it was at its very peak, on the verge of being superseded by the coming post-structuralist movement.

In their essay, Wellek and Warren run through the various conceptions on which the idea of the literary work could be thought to be founded. It could not be identical with the physical medium that bears its inscription since every copy would then be a different work. It could not consist of someone's reading it aloud since that would ignore the physical inscription and the stability of that inscription, in comparison with the evanescence of performance. It could not be merely the experience or response of the reader since then the work would have no independent identity to discuss. This 'affective fallacy' had been famously paralleled by W. K. Wimsatt and Monroe C. Beardsley in 1946 with the 'intentional fallacy'. With the latter in mind, Wellek and Warren confirmed that the work could not be the same thing as the experience of the author. This was so both for the period of the writing (since we can have no part in that experience) and for the author's later articulations of what was meant to be conveyed in the writing. (The writer may have lost touch with the original experience and be acting now only as an interpreting reader.) Rather, poems, for instance, have an independent public existence: the poem is, as Wimsatt and Beardsley had put it, 'detached from the author at birth and [it] goes about the world beyond his power to intend about it or control it'.[10] But there was a further possible grounding. Could the work, Wellek and Warren asked, be regarded as the sum of all experiences of it, its existence granted only as a potential cause of the experiences? This ingenious explanation was however, they pointed out, thwarted by its ignoring the 'structure of determination' intrinsic to the work's meaning.[11] None of these groundings, then, underwrites the necessary conditions of the work's identity over time or its capacity to be known.

This compelling diagnosis of failed definitions was unfortunately not matched by an equally clear proposal that would underpin the requisite independence from document, author and readers. If none of the work's manifestations in the world did the job, then invocation of an ideal identity seemed unavoidable. But how to incorporate its manifestations at the same time? The first thing was to concede that works are not ideal in the perfect way that, say, a triangle is, because they change in their readings and thus in a sense enjoy a 'life'. Wellek and Warren argued that works, nevertheless, must somehow have a 'substantial identity of "structure"' and be comprehensible in relation to 'a system of norms[,] of ideal concepts which are intersubjective. They must be assumed to exist in collective ideology, changing with it, accessible only through individual mental experiences, based on the sound-structure of its sentences.'[12] This attempt to bring together several of the dimensions in which the work undoubtedly participates in fact bows, as we shall see, to the epistemology of Edmund Husserl and more directly to the 1930s aesthetic philosophy of his student Roman Ingarden, whose work was only very belatedly available in English.

The Wellek and Warren essay hovers uneasily between this broadening and the strong underlying assumption visible in their characteristic phrase, the 'concrete work of art'.[13]

The latter phrase had already become a byword in literary criticism, which should therefore primarily concern itself with the aesthetic dimension, not with the psychological, historical or sociological. The term *verbal icon*, as Wimsatt and Beardsley had famously called it in 1954 – in other words, the aesthetic object – announced an orientation that would also, as we saw in Chapters 8 and 9, condition the pursuit of scholarly editing in its Anglo-American forms. Behind the concrete work of art lay, in some sense, an ideal text: *this* was to be the editor's quarry. The ideal text, typically seen as the author's intended one, had, for one reason or another, not achieved publication, whereas inferior presentations of it had done so.

G. Thomas Tanselle brought this pursuit to an increasingly sophisticated level of definition in essays written from the 1970s to the 1990s.[14] His conjoining of intention with the ideal required the invocation, whether at first or second hand, of the work of Husserl. E. D. Hirsch's influential *Validity in Interpretation* of 1967 had shown the way. In relation to the definition of the work, Hirsch's argument crystallised the American literary-critical *Zeitgeist*. In a summary of Husserl's position (which he largely endorses), he observes that the textual meaning of a literary work must be unchanging ('determinate')[15] since only such a thing can act as a true object of study. 'Verbal meaning', he argues, 'is that aspect of a speaker's "intention" which, under linguistic conventions, may be shared by others.'[16] It is 'unchanging and inter-personal' and 'determined once and for all by the character of the speaker's intention'.[17] For published works, the author's meaning is the publicly accessible part of it – communicated intention, not what was going on in the head of the 'biographical' author as such.[18] This communicated meaning is, as we shall see, like one of Husserl's intentional objects.

For the scholarly editor this argument amounted to an underwriting of the ideal of the intended text of the work, which only the accidents and contrarieties of production had prevented from being realised. It would be the Anglo-American editor's job, by means of comparison of the multiple versions of the work, to identify which variant readings were the impediments to that realisation and to remove them, by eclectic combination of readings from different versions if necessary, thus establishing the text of final authorial intention. The rejected readings would be recorded, but only in the subsidiary position of the textual apparatus. The foundation of this conservatorial approach in Husserl's philosophy – of which most practising editors were blissfully unaware – needs next to be considered.

THE IDEAL TEXT: HUSSERL AND INGARDEN

The founder of phenomenology, Edmund Husserl (1859–1938), refused to entertain conceptual presuppositions. Like other epistemologists he was looking for a basis for absolute certainty in knowledge. His slogan was 'To the things themselves'. By 'the things' he meant acts of consciousness and the things that are constituted by them. He wanted to get clarity *there* before the traditional problems of philosophy were approached. His first business as a phenomenologist was therefore to describe the phenomena. He gave perceptual priority to the subject (i.e. the perceiver), postponing the question of the ontology of the object (Kant's 'things-in-themselves', which were not accessible to the mind). He came to the conclusion that mental acts are intentional in the sense of being of or about an object – or, more strictly speaking, of or about a would-be object, something supposed to be beyond those mental acts.

A much-discussed example of Husserl's intentionalism is how we come to know what a tree is: we can have many views of a tree but none of them fully presents the tree to us. Only the intended object as a whole (the tree itself) unifies all of the acts of perception. The 'object as a whole' exists for us as an entity only because the various sensory 'takes' we have of it postulate its existence as a way of ordering them. This is a separate question from *whether* the tree exists – which, within Husserl's orbit of thought, comes to seem a less important one.

Husserl's intentionalism appears to be the ultimate source of Tanselle's view of the text of the literary work, probably as inflected by Hirsch.[19] The existence of many documentary texts that read as if they are versions of one another show, according to Tanselle, that each represents but does not present the work. The documentary texts may be said to be somewhat like sense experience – what Husserl calls 'immanent', directly accessible to the mind. But the intended object (the tree, the work) is presented as transcendent, that is, outside the mind's direct experience. In both cases there is a unifying assumption that there is an object out there (the tree, the work) that is the unity behind the disparate appearances (or documentary texts). The assumption in both cases sustains the experienced variability, allowing it to seem to cohere. This, I believe, is the basic, normally unstated warrant of the idealist argument in editorial thought.

Roman Ingarden and the work

Husserl's gap between the material and intentional object created the space for an aesthetic theory. His student, Roman Ingarden (1893–1970), is important here as carrying on the phenomenological flame. Ingarden's ideas about the work would ultimately be taken up, as we have seen, by some Anglo-American aesthetic philosophers and New Critics in the 1960s, broadening their thinking in the process, and, somewhat later, by editors of the Anglo-American school, who by and large until then had been content to understand their activity empirically.

Given its complexity (such as I have outlined above in summarising the Wellek and Warren arguments), the literary work, Ingarden observes, 'is never *fully* grasped in *all* its strata and components but always only partially'.[20] Although, in reading, it can only be apprehended 'in the form of one of its possible concretizations',[21] when reading we are usually not conscious of this distinction. Being aware of the difference between the work and its concretisations, however, gives meaning to the term, the 'life of the literary work' – which is the name of one of his chapters. The fact that a work can be created, changed by revision or destroyed by its author before publication is further evidence of its having a 'life'. But it is also proof that, unlike a living being, it is not an *'ontically autonomous* object'.[22] It only 'lives' passively, dependent as it is on readers to concretise or change it.[23] Ingarden accepts the implications of his observation about the life of a literary work. He recognises that a history of readings, influencing one another over time, can change the literary work insofar as it lives in its concretisations. But those readings cannot change the identity of the literary work itself that he has already distinguished from them.

But what is this essence that is left over from the concretisations? Ingarden does not mean the physical document, since, for him, that is merely a founding stratum. He has already allowed that the work is not ontically autonomous. Being only therefore, as he says, ontically heteronomous, it cannot be an ideal object. But if it is to have the separate essence postulated by his argument, it has to be in some sense 'transcendent',[24] even as it always seems to dissolve in the manifold variety of its readings. At the level of sentences, he argues, the writer cannot create 'genuine realizations of ideal essences or ideal concepts' but only draw on their ideal forms. The writer can 'actualize' them but not – the stronger form – 'realize' them.[25] Ideal concepts must exist, according to Ingarden, since without them linguistic communication would be impossible 'in which both sides . . . apprehend an identical meaning content of the sentences exchanged'.[26] There are of course misunderstandings in real-life communication, but without ideal concepts the possibility of exchanging 'identical meaning content' cannot be envisaged.[27] So he staves off the 'danger of subjectivizing the literary work or of reducing it to a manifold of concretizations' but only 'by accepting the existence of ideal concepts'[28] even though he is convinced the work is not one of them, or at least not in the full sense. '[I]n terms of ontic autonomy', he concludes, the literary work 'is a "nothing" and yet a wonderful world in itself – even though it comes into being and exists only by our grace.'[29]

Later phenomenologists and literary theorists would further develop this insight about the heteronomy of texts. Wolfgang Iser's account of how, as we read, we continually project expectations, which reflect our beliefs and experience, of where the story is going, of what its world is like, only to be forced to adjust them as we read, suggests how we can open ourselves to the unexpected and the at-first unassimilable. Reading leaves us exposed to what we are not. As Paul Armstrong puts it: 'I act on the text (by projecting beliefs about it) only to have it act on me.'[30] The encounter makes us realise the contingency of our presuppositions. More subtly, 'we grant a text power over ourselves in various ways by lending it our powers'.[31] Again echoing Iser, Armstrong argues that reading is a form of play where the implicit rules, by which we agree to play as we open the book and open up *to* it, do not necessarily lead to a win-or-lose result. Reading can be, in fact is typically, reciprocal, not a rhetorical power-play. If so, then Ingarden's (and, later, Habermas's) requirement of the possibility of the inter-subjective exchange of 'identical meaning content' is unnecessary. We simply need a different model of reading.

If we focus on the *experience* of reading then we acknowledge, first, that a text's meanings do not or need not simply confirm the biases we bring to it, thus avoiding the vicious hermeneutical circle. Second, texts have a directedness towards new contexts unforeseeable at the time of their original publication. They reach over the horizon into unknown futures. Nothing is predictable there because a text's 'pastness . . . is not a stable, fixed quality but varies in relation to the present of interpretation'.[32]

The conclusion is one I find attractive, but a problem remains in this phenomenological debate. I find little or no appreciation of the importance of the distinction between *text* and *work*, for which my insertion of bibliography (and thus, agency) into the debate is gradually suggesting the need. *Texts* emerge, in this phenomenological argument, as essentially independent of their initiating agencies, as self-agented. They are cast, as we have seen, as providing resistances to our presuppositions as we read. The explanation only starts after they are in material existence. Their materiality is thus effectively overlooked.

Although Ingarden himself shows little bibliographic awareness, he is, as a phenomenologist, very open to empirical and structural evidence of a work's stages of existence and its functioning. But, at the end of the day and despite having substantially undermined it, he has to fall back on a belief in the transcendent condition of the literary work if his structure of thought is to hold. Husserl's method of bracketing the intentional object in order to study the subject's dealings with it had tended – given that the philosopher's attention was elsewhere – implicitly to grant the object a steady continuity of existence independent of its contexts. In relation to the work of art, this would have seemed an uncontroversial assumption during the first half of the twentieth century, given the overhang of aestheticism, and given the doctrines and methods of modernism, formalist criticism of art and New Criticism. (Compare the epigraph to this chapter by Virginia Woolf.) Seen in this general context, Ingarden's book is very much a reflection of its period. That it spoke so directly to Hirsch, and to Wellek and Warren, as late as the 1960s, and filtered through them to Tanselle even later, helps explain why change, when it came, would prove catastrophic.

WHAT CHANGED WITH THE WORK? HEIDEGGER AND POST-STRUCTURALISM

The changes came, of course, with the various forms of post-structuralist theory from 1968 as they made their way – gingerly at first, triumphantly at last – through the anglophone world in the 1970s and 1980s. The new theorists adapted the radically different phenomenology of Husserl's student Martin Heidegger (1889–1976), who, in addition to his major work *Sein und Zeit* (Being and Time, 1927), wrote 'Der Ursprung des Kunstwerkes' (The Origin of the Work of Art) in the mid-1930s.

Heidegger was deeply affected by the pre-Socratic philosophers. Their successors, Aristotle and Plato, eventually made possible the Enlightenment tradition of rational argumentation based upon the subject–object split. For Heidegger, this division into inner and outer was the root of the problem when what the early Greek philosophers had recognised as the primordial dimension of Being circulated through both and was the prerequisite for any recognition. On this assumption, no object can, strictly speaking, be bracketed for contemplation as Husserl's method required. The Kantian tradition, which Husserl extended, had sprung, in Heidegger's view 'not from a genuine perception of Being but from a *forgetting of Being*, from a taking-for-granted of the central existential mystery'.[33] As soon as the essence of an object is recognised as an idea or meaning, its Being is consumed by being given directedness, as it almost automatically is, within traditional Western processes of thought. Their idealism requires its essential being to be located elsewhere, whereas for Heidegger being is being-in-the-world, a living *of* time rather than living *in* it. Knowing is not a smash-and-grab raid on the object but what he calls a being-with, a concern, a not-having-power-over.

Accordingly, Heidegger was obliged to reinterpret all forms of knowledge as orientations towards Being. So he redefines truth not in terms, as analytical philosophers traditionally do, of the correspondence between subject and object but in terms of what he calls discoveredness:

> To say that a statement is *true* means that it discovers the beings in themselves. It asserts, it shows, it lets beings 'be seen' . . . in their discoveredness. The *being true (truth)* of the statement must be understood as *discovering*. Thus, truth by no means has the structure of an agreement between knowing and the object in the sense of a correspondence of one being (subject) to another (object).
>
> Being-true as discovering is in turn ontologically possible only on the basis of being-in-the-world. This phenomenon . . . is the *foundation* of the primordial phenomenon of truth.[34]

Heidegger and conservation, and the French existentialist legacy

What then is the nature of a work that lasts for centuries or is restored after damage or near destruction? In 'The Origin of the Work of Art', Heidegger argues that the work, upon its creation, discloses a previously unthought-of world by bringing its truth into being, but in doing so renders the awareness of it historical. As the centuries go by, the awareness fades even though the physical object may not: 'World-withdrawal and world-decay', he says, 'can never be undone. The works are no longer the same as they once were. It is they themselves, to be sure, that we encounter there, but they themselves are gone by.'[35]

His example, as we saw in Chapter 1, was the Aegina marbles, a ruined temple that King Ludwig I of Bavaria had bought in 1811 during a visit to the Greek island. The stones were restored speculatively into an integrated form (itself rearranged in the 1900s) and displayed in the Munich Glyptothek until the 1960s. At that time the elements that had been fabricated to complete it were removed and the fragments alone left on display. It turned out that they had been damaged by the restoration. Heidegger was of course unaware of this future fate and prepared, for the purposes of argument, to grant the restorers, Thorwaldsen, their interpretation. By doing this, Heidegger was able to raise the question of whether what he calls 'the work itself' can ever be encountered when it has been subjected to art-historical study – when it has been rendered the object of a science. For him, the very activity rendered the work inauthentic.

Heidegger's philosophy requires a leap of faith; finally the dimension of Being is mysterious. That does not make it untrue. But the challenge of going without the traditional tools of analytical thought, which normally presuppose a subject–object division, reveals the dilemma that Jacques Derrida, and other post-structuralists, struggled to bridge post-1968. They continued Heidegger's reaction against Enlightenment modes of thought and in particular against the metaphysics of self-presence implied, as they saw it, in Husserl's phenomenology. In it, the self-presence of the object as vouchsafed to the subject was the ground of meaning. It was an ideal meaning that reduced writing, according to Derrida, to a merely cognitive operation. Nor did it explain the iteration of meaning that allows it to be made present to readers over and over again. In Ferdinand de Saussure's structuralist account of language, meaning is always deferred. Signs refer to other signs, and meaning lies in the difference of their signification. This model allowed Derrida to free the workings of textuality from any anchor in intention or the writer. The ground of writing could henceforth be considered to be (other) writing, not authorship. This amounted to a new foundation for meaning, though always elusive, never achieved. If representation was the vehicle of meaning, then recourse to the subject–object binary would no longer be necessary. It did not however explain the work, as witness the epigraph to this chapter by Michel Foucault.

Editorial practitioners found this linguistic turn a hard pill to swallow, since they were encountering documentary traces of personal agency on a daily basis and were in the habit of inferring their intention. Nor did de Saussure's synchronic system assist with the analysis of textual processes of revision over time. Michel Foucault's account of socially circulating discourses changing with successive epistemes or periods, and therefore of works being expressions of discourses rather than of authors, only restated the problem in somewhat more historical ways. There was a stalemate. Scholarly editing meanwhile continued to take place, but during the 1980s and 1990s in mainly silent opposition to the dominant intellectual forces of the time. This was not a comfortable position to be in.

Although Derrida dealt with the Heideggerian inheritance directly, the route to the stalemated position actually went via French existentialist phenomenology: from Jean-Paul Sartre, through Maurice Blanchot, and then to Roland Barthes's 'The Death of the Author' of 1968. This essay became the *locus classicus* for the post-structuralist decentring of meaning from author to text. In *What Is Literature* (1947), Sartre saw writing as necessarily acting in the present as a form of commitment, political and personal, situated in and shared with the contemporary society or 'age' – and thus, somewhat akin to Heidegger's account of the Aegina marbles, losing its relevance upon the author's death.[36] Maurice Blanchot's *The Space of Literature* (1955) pushed the existentialist case further. For him,

> The work of art does not refer immediately back to the person who presumably made it. When we know nothing at all about the circumstances that contributed to its production, about the history of its creation – when we do not even know the name of the person who made it possible – it is then that the work comes closest to itself.[37]

The line from this isolation of the work from the author to Barthes's aim of liberating the reader from the authoritative shackles of writerly intention becomes apparent in Barthes's essay 'From Work to Text' (in French, 1971), especially in his catchphrase: 'the work can be held in the hand, the text is held in language'.[38] For Barthes, like Derrida, the author's life offered no point of origin for texts and therefore no hope of explanation for them. Existing only in language, texts could have neither origin nor closure. Given that their fate was to be traversed again and again by readers, texts could be experienced 'only in an activity of production', and were therefore irreducibly plural.[39] Participating in larger cultural flows of meaning, they were neither stable nor time-bound objects.

THE ANGLO-AMERICAN EDITORIAL SCENE

This became an influential position. It signally rejected the existing literary-critical understanding about works as aesthetic objects, and it left the editing of works and the study of their genesis out in the cold. And yet despite that, as we saw in Chapters 7–9, the last quarter century has seen a flowering of a new kind of editorial and textual theory. While borrowing terms and benefiting from some of the habits of thought that post-structuralism rapidly naturalised, these new forms of editorial theory have had essentially to work from the overlooked or neglected *empirical* realities of documents. In the Anglo-American scene, attention turned first to enunciating the importance of textual process (the genesis of versions of a work) rather than of finalising its text as an authoritative 'product'. Second, the importance of linking particular texts, regardless of their authority, to their historical audiences was recognised. Third, the peculiarities of the physical document itself, especially its *mise-en-page*, were seen by many as of such importance that their presentation could be considered a site and source of meaning, complicating that of the linguistic text with which earlier editors had been solely concerned. Last, there was theoretical and then practical exploration of opportunities in electronic editions that would be capacious enough to document these textual processes, now themselves seen as worthy of study.[40]

In these ways, liberation from the final-intentions school of postwar Anglo-American scholarly editing opened doors – but, ironically, to much the same dimensions of works that Wellek and Warren, and Hirsch, had been ushering into anglophone consideration in their essays of the late 1960s. Despite typically rejecting the ideal-text assumptions of editing – and thus, in effect, rejecting the Husserlian legacy – editorial practitioners have usually found little support in Heidegger. This is because the study of the processes of a literary work's genesis and development through successive versions is inauthentic in Heidegger's terms, as it tends to objectify the work.[41] A theory of the work that might ground what editors do still does not exist, and, as Foucault remarked, 'the empirical task of those who naively undertake the editing of works often suffers in the absence of such a theory'.[42] His warning is no less true today, despite the welcome broadening of attention to the workings of the work, if one may put it that way, that practitioners have more recently been engaged in.[43]

McLaverty and Shillingsburg

James McLaverty, for instance, took Nelson Goodman's (and also Richard Wollheim's) aesthetic theories of the work one step further in 1984 by pursuing the question of whether a literary work's notation is only the *score* of any number of more or less compliant performances over time, or whether the *script* of the work is the thing itself and thus independent of its productions over time. McLaverty examines Goodman's and Barbara Herrnstein Smith's debate in 1970 (discussed in Chapter 7, above) about whether readers perform texts as they read them. For simplicity's sake, he reduces this to the psychological question of whether or not we subvocalise as we read silently. (The answer is, we do and we don't.) But this move does not take into account the phenomenological developments out of which Wolfgang Iser and others were coming. Peter Shillingsburg, as we will see below, would argue in 1989 for the existence of the 'performance text' of a work that is read. This, and a general interest from the late 1980s in texts as being always in process, has displaced the score–script distinction from centre-stage in the ongoing debate. The lasting value of McLaverty's essay lies, rather, in his compelling argument that page-layout may be considered as part of the text (read visually) in cases where authors deliberately exploited it. He proves beyond doubt that Alexander Pope did. Pope's parodying, but also using to advantage, the established design of the variorum edition in the *Dunciad*'s first edition is McLaverty's brilliant example. The logic of the argument, although McLaverty does not go so far, would seem to be that such texts may be considered both script and score.[44]

Shillingsburg's argument, an even more ambitious one, absorbed and cogently re-expressed much of the new editorial theorising of the 1980s while retaining contact with traditional conceptions of the work. In his essay of 1989 he provides a conceptual map or modelling of the various ways in which text may be understood – whether as Matter, Concept or Action (to use the title words of his essay). So the 'Linguistic Text' may be considered, when physically inscribed, as the 'Material Text'. This 'union of Linguistic Text and Document'[45] encompasses the *mise-en-page* meanings that McLaverty (as well as D. F. McKenzie and Jerome McGann, in the interim) had been pointing to. The act of reading a Material Text is a 'Reception Performance'; it produces the 'Reception Text',[46] a notion which, for the literary work, runs score and script together. Shillingsburg deviates from McLaverty here but follows him (and also Tanselle) on another level when he argues that a work is only implied by physical manifestations of it; it is not identical with any or all of them. The reader infers the existence of the work and its text (*or* the versions of it and their texts), perhaps making allowances for any errors believed to be present. This text of the work is a 'Conceptual Text'[47] since it is not materially witnessed: hence the traditional need for editorial action to recover it.

There is a clarifying stability in this mapping of the work. As what Shillingsburg modestly calls an 'exercise in naming',[48] it provides usable handles for studying the production and consumption of works without neglecting either end of the spectrum. A problem I encounter with it, however, comes from the nominalising force of some of the terms he uses: from asking exactly what 'Text' means in each case. So, for instance, are Material Texts codifiable in anything like the way that linguistic ones are? It is true that meanings flow, as we read, from the material embodiments of linguistic texts. That is one possible meaning of *text*; and indeed it is one I take up in the next section of this chapter. But it is more a textual *experience* or (shifting the perspective slightly) a textual *dimension* than a textual code specifiable in the entirety of its manifestation. There is, in other words, no single 'Material Text' as such, available to all readers, that we can point to and discuss, although aspects of the experience of being influenced by paper-stock, luxury (or cheap) binding and sheet size, as well as page-layout certainly *can* be discussed with reference to the book's visual and tactile qualities, even to its smell.

Similarly with what Shillingsburg names the Performance Text. The idea makes sense as a placeholder within his taxonomy, but what is it in itself? We can describe our own or another reader's deviations from the printed text as we read, or we can describe (with less accuracy) what images, sounds, ideas and feelings we *experience* as we read: but in what sense is the subject of this attention – the performance itself – a 'text'? As for the Conceptual Text, although readers sometimes specify exactly where they believe a materially embodied linguistic text has gone wrong (as we are all tempted to do nearly every time we pick up a newspaper), this is not the same thing as saying that a Conceptual Text exists in anyone's head *in toto*, particularly if it is a long one. So in what sense is it a 'text'?

It may be objected that these queries of mine are impertinent: that one properly goes along for the ride, not necessarily committed to the conceptions of text on offer, but in the hope that the view on textuality that opens up will be pleasing and clear. This would be a fair comment. But one can equally take advantage of the light Shillingsburg's ambitious essay sheds to focus on a different order of thinking about texts. *This* is the direction of my own thinking here, which a statement in his own essay usefully focusses: 'These two fundamentals – the physical documents and the reading experience of decoding them – are the irreducible core of literary works. Without the reader, the physical documents are inert and inoperative; without the physical documents there is no reading.'[49] It seems to me that this is pointing to the need for a kind of commentary, different from the one upon which Shillingsburg goes on to concentrate. Rather than following his lead and remapping this truth about the life of works across to a stabilising taxonomy of texts, it may make more sense, and will at least yield different results, if we simply let the *work* take care of itself for a moment: that is, if we pull the 'two fundamentals' more firmly apart than his taxonomy permits him to do. In other words, rather than trying to locate on a conceptual map of the work its ostensibly complete Material or Conceptual or Performance Texts, let us instead tease out the fundamental dimensions of the work implicit in Shillingsburg's comment – even though this puts on hold the study of all the phases and manifestations of the life of a work, which he was implicitly trying to map in proposing his taxonomy. This shift in focus requires a digression to gather in some aesthetic philosophy before returning to the question.

WHITHER AWAY FOR THE WORK? PEIRCE AND ADORNO

What then is the way forward? I see two possibilities. The first would be to adopt or adapt as a basis for a definition of the work a text-defining semiotic that recognises agency and chronology, rather than the synchronic model of either Saussurean structuralism, upon which much post-structuralist thought rested, or of Prague structuralism, which was adopted by German editors, as we saw in Chapter 9. The American C. S. Peirce (1839–1914) philosophised in many areas, but at the centre was a mode of thinking that bypassed the subject–object binary. Peirce went back to the medieval scholastics, including St Augustine and Duns Scotus, to retrieve a missing third term – semiotic. Semiosis is the process of communication that mediates knowledge. The effect of inserting it into the subject–object relation is that it becomes triadic. The object cannot be directly available to knowledge if it can only be represented by the sign. The sign or representamen (e.g. 'the sky is blue') functions by creating ('determining') an interpretant (my or your interpretation of what 'the sky is blue' means) that may itself stand as a sign to a later interpretant, and so on. Peirce's semiotics is, as Leroy Searle observes, less a theory of language than a theory of the production of meaning.[50]

It can be difficult to appreciate the fundamentality of Peirce's semiotics at first. Peirce was trying to define the theory of the sign to stand as his logic and thereby as the basis of his metaphysics and epistemology. To humanise or psychologise the operation of the sign would compromise this fundamentality. Some commentators who have tried to adapt Peirce's semiotics have failed to acknowledge this, including Gunter Martens the German editorial theorist in 1989 and, more recently, the anthropologist Alfred Gell in *Art and Agency* (1998). Strictly, the interpretant is not a person but rather the counterpart of the representamen, and it stands in an equivalent or developed relation to the object. The sign as a whole is therefore a relation, in fact tri-relational; it is not a thing, although a thing may become a sign if it takes on that relational function.[51]

From this apparently severe semiotic Peirce developed a wide-ranging philosophical system usually referred to as Pragmatism.[52] His failure to publish an elaborated and complete form of it notoriously causes problems for those who would elucidate it from the basis of his occasional essays, reviews, letters and very extensive, often undated manuscripts. The failure also helps explain his comparatively meagre influence so far, as does the fact that the place that his semiotics might have occupied was taken by twentieth-century Saussurean structuralism. The latter is, in contrast to Peirce's, dyadic (two-termed: signifier versus signified), synchronic (the linguistic system is analysed at a chronological moment) and systematic (meaning is based on difference between terms in the system rather than, as for Peirce, on its practical outcomes or further development).

Peirce's incorporation of the interpretant into the definition of the sign means that semiosis is understood as ongoing and diachronic. Every sign, therefore, 'is essentially incomplete and . . . essentially developable'.[53] Development requires a notion of community; indeed, Peirce stressed continuity rather than arrival in what he called the path of inquiry. Insofar as the 'real' and the 'truth' could be said to exist at all, they were only the limiting conditions of this continuity. They committed the community of inquirers to the testing of the always provisional truth-claims – just as scientists do, routinely. Public truth or 'the real' is said to be 'the idea in which the community ultimately settles down'.[54]

Individuals and communities therefore may be said to participate in semiosis, but *it* does not originate in them.[55] Peirce commented in a late essay of 1905, 'What Pragmatism Is':

a person is not absolutely an individual. His thoughts are what he is 'saying to himself,' that is, is saying to that other self that is just coming into life in the flow of time. When one reasons, it is that critical self that one is trying to persuade; and all thought whatsoever is a sign, and is mostly of the nature of language.[56]

If even our private reflections function semiotically, then there can be no constitutive origin for meaning or knowledge outside semiosis, either in the self or in unmediated Heideggerian Being. There can, accepting this line of argument, be no capital A Author as pure source of the work. According to Peirce, there never is an 'I' thinking (or writing or reading) that is knowable independent of the signs that signal the activity. And just as there can be no knowable, originating, unitary presence or Author outside of semiosis, so there can be, we can conclude, no Work whose ontology is secured by that Author. Rather, textual agency is restricted to those who are involved in the ongoing semiosis. If Peirce is right then process is of the nature of the work, which presumably now takes on the lower case *w* and functions only as a regulative idea, not an ideal. In addition, the activity of each reader in creating the interpretant is part of the work.

'Textual agency' is not a Peircean term. In his system, the operation of the sign, though infinitely regressive, is nevertheless transactional. Therefore, if one extrapolates from his austerely logical starting point where semiosis is conceived as a purely functional relation, the production of both the representamen and the interpretant can be seen in practice to require agency. Nowhere is this more evident than when the production takes physical form in a document. In other words, a bibliographical extension of Peirce's account of semiosis might form the ground of a new conception of the work.[57]

The importance of the physical object – the documentary dimension of textual communication – is something that philosophers are apt to overlook or treat as trivial. This is despite the fact that the document is the pathway into the past. But it is only a pathway: the act of reading, of reviving the represented idea, reinvokes the unpredictabilities and flux that are always part of semiosis. Meanwhile, the document itself remains unaffected, stable and open to contrary readings. This documentary dimension would give Peirce's idea of the community of inquirers a force it presently lacks. It would generate the need for an account of the slowly changing linguistic conventions that allow communities to make sense of documents from the past. In the moment of reading, the document is inevitably a record of and from the past and lies at the cross-section of other histories: of the book trade, generic conventions, readerships, and political, social and other discourses. For readers it is the point of departure and return. Its stability provides the point of focus enabling profitable disputation (in the present) about the representamen, which may be differently inflected by every reader.

Adorno and negative dialectic

This proposed convergence of semiosis and bibliography may seem a strange one at first. It requires recourse to the only other possible way forward that I can presently see: namely, to adopt a diachronic model of the continually unfolding relationship between document and text, or between cultural object and interpretation.

The writings of the Frankfurt School philosopher Theodor Adorno (1903–69) offer such a model. It is not Adorno's aesthetic theory that I find helpful[58] but rather his central concept of negative dialectics. Giving the Kantian notion of the subject–object binary an epistemological twist, Adorno argued that subjects, situated in history as they are, are not identical with themselves over time. Nor therefore can the object stay still, or be self-identical, since it can only be known, over time, as it 'entwines with subjectivity'.[59] As a result, non-identity as between subject and object has to be taken as the basis of knowledge. The subject does not, after Kant, passively measure the object against a repository of categories that it holds in mind. Rather, through a process of reaching out towards the object, the subject seeks to approximate it mimetically in all its concrete particularity (to use a Frankfurt School term). Adorno refers to this process as 'exact fantasy': the subject transforms the object 'into a new modality'; it is not a replication but a translation.[60]

Peirce had rejected the subject–object binary at its base and replaced it with a tri-relational semiotic. Adorno locks subject and object together in an experiential embrace. Each requires the other's difference in order to secure its own identity. Each is, as it were, a constituting principle of the other. This rules out any appeal to an ontological ideal imagined as standing outside the process. Semiosis had a similar result for Peirce.

Take the relationship between nature and history. When beliefs that were once resisted become accepted over time, they are granted what Adorno calls a second-nature status – they are naturalised – only in turn to have their naturalness challenged by awareness of their history of becoming. The process is dialectical. But it does not lead to a higher synthesis, to a transcendental reconciliation of subject and object – as with Hegelian dialectic, at least as it is popularly known. Rather, the dialectic is negative in that it is based on awareness of the historicity in nature and of the naturalness in history. The one mediates the other.[61] In short, a negative dialectic describes an ongoing, antithetical but interdependent identity-relationship that unfolds over time.

There are possibilities here, which Adorno himself did not pursue, for conceptualising the ways in which authors, editors and readers 'perform' literary works – or concretise them, to use Ingarden's term. Adorno's favourite example is the way in which a translation transforms its original text into something new. Similarly, we might think that, in the act of reading, the text with which we engage and which we seek mimetically to approximate or perform is the literary work itself. But a little bibliographic attunement shows that it is a document of paper and ink that bears a text that we raise in the act of reading. While in Adorno's sense the document is a natural object, it is also a socially produced one that anticipates the observance of accepted conventions of raising meaning. The document, whether handwritten or printed, is the textual site where the agents of textuality meet: author, copyist, editor, typesetter and reader. In the acts of writing, copying or reading, the work's documentary and textual dimensions dynamically interrelate: they can be seen as a translation or performance of one another.

They are, in this sense, one another's negative constituting principle. Document, taken as the material basis of text, has a continuing history in relation to its productions and its readings. Any new manifestation of the negative dialectic necessarily generates new sets of meanings.

A consequence is that, if the documentary and textual dimensions are one another's negative constituting principle, then neither has a secure identity in itself. In other words, we need potentially readable text before paper and ink can constitute a document.[62] To have text, we need a material document (in any medium, whether printed, a computer-screen visualisation, or sound waves in an act of vocalisation). The two dimensions are conceptually separable but linked in practice. As they work off one another, they populate the production–consumption spectrum discussed in previous chapters. The *work* emerges only as a regulative idea, the name or container, as it were, of the continuing dialectic. The ongoing or recorded existence of the document is enough to link all the textual processes that are carried out under the name of the work. And bibliography is a technology for describing and relating its allied documents. By what Peirce calls abductive reasoning, all of them can be seen to be indexical of (i.e. to point at) agency.[63]

Following Ingarden, we can say that the continuing dialectic is the 'life' of the literary work – but without accepting the idealist belief that, for him, goes with it. Peirce's account of semiosis allows us to dispense with that; and its capacity, when applied as I have suggested, to incorporate agency and chronology sits happily enough with Adorno's unfolding dialectic. From Adorno we can define a concept of the work that does not sublate or supersede the empirical workings of textuality. The 'work' can be seen as a phenomenological concept, but not in the full, Husserlian sense of an intentional object. Rather, it can be understood in the weak sense that it operates as a regulative idea that immediately dissolves, in reading, into the negative dialectic of document and text. Seen as a regulative idea, the 'work' retains its function as a pragmatic agreement for organising our remembered experiences of reading documents that are closely related bibliographically. Similarly, as we saw in Chapter 7 in relation to the materialist Shakespeare proposal, the regulative idea is needed to delimit the relevance of documents being investigated for an editing project: for an edition of the 'work'.

Seen in action the work unravels, in every moment of its being, into a relationship between its documentary and textual dimensions. Their continuous interdependence shows that Tanselle's view of the text of a work, as existing through time but never perfectly represented in physical form, is the extrapolation of an ideal. The account is intended to be used as a basis for justifying editorial intervention to recover the ideal form, but it loses touch with how anyone experiences text. If the work can, then, no longer be imagined as a historical object, then the idealist position that seeks to secure its self-identity must be abandoned. The dynamic principle I am proposing is offered as an alternative that answers to the richly various lives of the work to which editorial commentators have been drawing attention since the 1980s. Similarly, once we accept the *work* as only a regulative idea, we are no longer constrained to nominalise *text* as an integral *utterance*, which basing his theory of text on speech-act theory pushes Shillingsburg to do in his mapping of the work, despite his awareness of the richness and disorderliness of those lives.[64]

In other words, this line of thinking leads us to pull back to a more fundamental dynamic that can clarify our confusions, especially when faced with crises of the kind treated in this book. So forgery and authenticity look differently, as we have seen in earlier chapters, when the documentary dimension is (conceptually) distinguished from the textual, and when questions about time and agency are directed to the document – as they fairly can be once the lure of synchronic modes of analysis are put to one side.

The unavoidable dynamic of the documentary and textual dimensions makes us realise that whenever we nominalise texts (Performance Texts, Material Texts, etc.) as representations of the work we are necessarily abstracting from the messy processes that all agents of textuality actually undergo throughout the production–consumption spectrum. When we so nominalise, we are erecting our own methodologies for productive ends rather than pointing to an actual ontology of texts. This is a significant matter. It is only on this basis and at this point that Shillingsburg's mapping of the textual terrain, with its helpful distinctions, can come usefully and justifiably into play. It is a basis upon which we can, now with newly clarified justification, analyse printed documents bibliographically, differentiate versions of works text-critically, and dispute meanings profitably in a literary-critical way.[65]

If such is the basis of the textual condition, then the editor (like every other reader) can never get outside it: the work can never be an object on which he or she *works*. Instead the editor must have – can only have – a participatory role in the life of the work. The editor's main work is textual; it leaves a documentary testament. Editions (as documents) represent the work by extending its life, by making further textual encounters possible: there can be no definite closure to a negative dialectic. We can conclude that the work is not an aesthetic object, if only because that traditional formulation collapses these interdependent dimensions.

Ambitious maps, models and taxonomies hack usable paths through the forest of textuality. But to the extent that they install a subject–object relationship, they obscure the editor-conservator's role *in* the work. This book has been about finding a different basis for editorial and conservatorial intervention, one that recognises the fundamental dynamic. It is always in danger of being absorbed and rendered invisible by the idealist or nominalist or ideological or discursive regimes into which we transform it – in order (as we anxiously hope) to secure the past.

BUILDINGS AND MONUMENTS AS WORKS: THE OBLIGATION
OF THEIR CARERS

But can this conclusion be extended to include artistic works, historic buildings and monuments? Potential complications of the different media should not shut down the attempt to map the conclusion across. Some remarks of Gary Taylor suggest a pathway. He is the general editor of a project to edit the works of Thomas Middleton (1580–1627), a playwright whose achievement has always been occluded by that of his great contemporary, Shakespeare. 'How can you love a work, if you don't know it?', Taylor asks. 'How can you know it, if you can't get near it? How can you get near it, without editors?'[66] This simple, rhetorical argument could equally be applied to the conservation of historic buildings or the restoration of damaged paintings. You can't love them if you can't see them or touch them: if you can't, in Heidegger's sense, be-with-them. But this still leaves unresolved exactly what the 'it', which Taylor speaks of, consists in.

To envisage the work as I am proposing, as constantly involved in a negative dialectic of material medium (the documentary dimension) and meaningful experience (the textual), and as being constituted by an unrolling semiosis across time, necessarily interwoven in the lives of all who create it, gaze at it or read it, is to acknowledge the central roles of agency and time. Depending on the perspective in play, the agency of authorship broadly considered (whether of playwright, architect, sculptor or editor) may be foregrounded: some intending person or persons had to create the 'document', which, from this point of view, will be forever embedded in the moment of creation. Equally the latter experience, the unrolling semiosis, may be focused on: the role (or, as an editor would say of a readership, the textual authority) of the people, say, who lived around the historic building may gain significance. It certainly did for Ruskin in

1849 as he considered the plight of fourteenth-century English churches subject to the new, religiously inspired craze for restoration. He was clear where authority lay: '[the churches] are not ours. They belong partly to those who built them, and partly to all the generations of mankind who are to follow us. The dead have still their right in them.'[67]

From this point of view, to detach the work from its idealist grounding in the absent architect-author does not necessarily remove the basis of its identity. To think of a building or monument as a work rather than merely a three-dimensional (documentary) object is to recognise that its meanings are not fully determined in advance by builder or architect. They are also assigned (in the textual dimension) by those who come into contact with it. Semiotic appeals to meaning will be embedded in conventions of reading architecture, in the functions of buildings within broader circulating discourses, and they will be assigned variously, and change over time. Thus, adapting Adorno, we can say that the building as work does not stay identical with itself.

This stands to reason. The historic building, *any* historic building, will always have been in a process involving, in varying degrees, conscious alteration, accidental change and natural decay. As argued in Chapter 2, the building does not and cannot have a stable constitution. Thus a historic house *cannot* be reliably returned in every detail to its original condition, even if this were desirable. And yet most visitors to heritage buildings believe this is what they are seeing. They want to believe that the neoplatonic ideal of the house-as-it-originally-was is here embodied.

For their part, conservators and curators necessarily participate in the building's unrolling semiosis, in the life of it as a *work* (in the sense that I am giving the term). They need to accept the responsibility that this awareness entails and not cater to illusions. Nor should they pretend to stand outside it as if it were only a (documentary) object to which they apply their science and taste. Management plans for historic buildings that appeal in a 1960s way to the famous architect as guarantor of the building-as-work's aesthetic integrity – almost as if it were a poem or painting, a 'concrete work of art' – need to beware of appealing in the next sentence to the necessity of preserving the historical witness of the building's original fabric. Both appeals falsely objectify the building. Appeals that flip-flop between aesthetic and historical groundings for the work are not likely to lead to coherent editorial solutions.

Historic buildings exist and persist, if they are suffered to do so, as 'document', stolidly awaiting their fate. Most continue to undergo physical change in response to people's needs. Meanwhile their further semiosis unrolls in the lives of their inhabitants and of passers-by. In this situation, the preservation of the documentary fabric must obviously be the primary aim and ethic of conservators. It is what conservation must conserve since, without it, the life of the building as a work would be impossible to capture or curate. We would not be able, in Taylor's phrase, to get 'near it'.

But, again in this formulation, what is the 'it'? It is not an object pure and simple, since, under the conservatorial gaze, the building's documentary fabric cannot be left alone. Some attitude towards its preservation must be arrived at, some standard appealed to. This involves making choices about what aspect of the building's life, what source of authority for its presentation as a work, the conservator will decide to respect. And what alterations or partial destruction will be deemed necessary so that the general public can be 'near' it.

The documentary dimension of the building only functions under the conservatorial gaze *as* fabric insofar as it is part of a negative dialectic with its interpretations. There is no innocent, no inevitable policy available, even though the simple, common-sense language of such heritage-policy documents as the Venice Charter of 1964 and the Australia ICOMOS Burra Charter of 1992 give rise to the hope that there is. We have to accept that the conservation and the curation will inevitably alter the nature, by shifting the grounds, of the building's continuing semiosis.

Honest curation will declare the compromise, will acknowledge its interpreting hand. Whether, say, the building and contents have been preserved and curated so far as possible to represent some point in their history, or perhaps as an inevitably partial and selective three-dimensional diary of the lives of the generations of families that have lived in it. Usually, with historic buildings, curation performs something of the function that annotation does in a scholarly edition, selectively pointing the reader-viewer towards what to look for in the fabric, giving advice as to how to read its historical testimony, and therefore by implication how to understand the conservatorial orientation and policy that have been applied.

The expansion since the 1980s of the possible, legitimate grounds of textual authority for the editing of literary works, described in Chapter 9, has been paralleled by more flexible policies of curation, such as those I have just described. In both pursuits, the avoidance of ad hoc or self-contradictory policies could be avoided, and aims clarified, by a more conscious understanding of the nature of the work. This book is offered as a stimulus to that debate, not as its final word.

As we have seen throughout, securing tangible and intangible works from the past, whether historic buildings, paintings or literary works, means facing up to (and often differentiating) their intertwined documentary and textual dimensions. Whenever conservation projects come under pressure, at points of crisis such as I have dealt with in this book, closely related themes emerge. Those I have stressed are agency and chronology, especially as they inflect and determine the production–consumption spectrum. Together they point towards the need for a broader understanding of the *work* than the 1960s bequeathed us. This book calls for a revival, both in theory and in newly clarified practice.

Notes

1 INTRODUCTION

1 Lowenthal, *Past*, p. 4.

2 Heidegger, 'Origin of the Work', p. 167.

3 Anon., 'Mawson's Huts', p. 14.

4 The term may originate with William Morris in 1877 ('[Letter, 10 March 1877]', p. 81): 'the newly-invented study of living history is the chief joy of so many of our lives'. He was proposing an association 'to keep a watch on old monuments, to protest against all "restoration"'.

5 Goodwin, *True Report*. The clergyman who restored the Bruton Parish church during 1905–7 was Goodwin's father.

6 See also Wright, *Old Country*; Inglis, *Sacred Places*; and the earlier studies: Burrow, 'Sense of the Past'; Chamberlin, *Preserving the Past*; and Clanchy, *From Memory*.

7 E.g. White, *Content of the Form*.

8 Practitioners no longer favour the term *restoration*, for reasons we shall see. But the term's popular recognition and its capacity to extend metaphorically to literary works have counselled its adoption here.

9 In this respect, it develops from a differently focussed and provocative study of 1995: Grigely, *Textualterity*; its chapter 2 contains useful commentary on the paradoxes of restoration approaches. Tanselle's *Rationale*, especially chapter 1, was helpful in a different way.

10 Pater, 'Marbles of Aegina', p. 257.

11 E.g., when I visited it in April 2007 the South African Museum in Cape Town still had on display an early 1970s exhibit of the material culture of various native peoples of the country. Although the static, timeless rendering of the cultures was given something of a historical dimension after the 1970s, a curator's recent notice invites visitors to think critically of the exhibition, including the effect their own position has upon them as they look down on the displays of implements, and ornamented mannequin-natives, usually seated on the floor in glass cases. Evidently, this exhibition has not got long to go.

12 Preziosi, 'Earth's Body', pp. 103, 102.

13 E.g. Said, *Orientalism*; Pratt, *Imperial Eyes*; and continued with adaptations and extensions by others. For an overview, see *The Post-Colonial Studies Reader*, ed. Ashcroft, Griffiths and Tiffin.

14 Kant, *Critique*, p. 110.

15 Derrida, 'Parergon', pp. 15–147.

16 Ernst, 'Framing the Fragment', p. 125. The claim that works of art may be defined as what art museums collect is a widespread simplification of Arthur Danto's subtler argument that what, say, distinguishes Marcel Duchamp's toilet from an ordinary toilet is that Duchamp's is situated within a history of the development of Western art. See Danto, *Transfiguration*.

17 See Ernst, 'Framing the Fragment', pp. 116–20. Cf. Forster, 'Monument/ Memory'.

18 Foucault, 'What Is an Author' (1969; 1979 in English).

19 Gadamer, *Truth and Method*, p. 479.

20 Ruskin, 'Lamp of Memory', p. 340.

2 THE WITNESS OF HISTORIC BUILDINGS

1 Woolf, *Orlando*, pp. 318–19. The description is based on Knole.

2 Ruskin, 'Lamp of Memory', pp. 353–5.

3 Brand, *How Buildings Learn*, p. 167.

4 See further Glassie, *Pattern*, pp. 26–117.

5 Brand, *How Buildings Learn*, p. 71.

6 Dellheim, *Face of the Past*, p. 83.

7 In *Ecclesiologist* (1858), quoted in Lowenthal, *Past*, p. 97.

8 Quoted in Dellheim, *Face of the Past*, p. 82.

9 Quoted in Tschudi-Madsen, *Restoration*, p. 33. Cf. Harvey, *Cathedrals of England* (1950, 1956): 'The destruction of a number of fine Perpendicular windows in the interests of sham Early English purity at St. Albans and elsewhere was the merest vandalism. And the effects of even well-meant surface reconstruction at Chester, Lichfield and Worcester are appalling . . . things might be much worse. Had not extensive works been done, some cathedrals would have become heaped ruins . . . With the possible exception of St. Albans . . . no English cathedral was so severely wrecked as to lose its character. It is unwise to trust to detail for historical purposes without the most careful investigation' (p. 200).

10 William Morris's letter to the editor of *The Times* in 1890 gave the objection its *locus classicus*: 'Will not every fresh piece of modern work make "the old place" (the church, I mean) look less old and more like a nineteenth-century mediaeval furniture-dealer's warehouse?': '[Letter, 15 August 1890]', p. 83.

11 See Tschudi-Madsen, *Restoration*, p. 16, n. 11.

12 Ruskin, 'Lamp of Memory', p. 355; see Tschudi-Madsen, *Restoration*, p. 16 and p. 38, n. 1.

13 Quoted in *ibid.*, p. 97.

14 Lowenthal, *Past*, p. 179.

15 From Kurt W. Forster's discussion of Riegl (1858–1905), 'Monument/Memory', p. 15. Riegl insisted that, with historic monuments, the 'wear and tear' should be allowed to show in order to preserve 'the signs of natural decay'. He diagnosed 'the new appreciation of monuments as the recognition of age-value'; he saw this as a reflection of a general acceptance of 'the steadily advancing death of culture' (*ibid.*, pp. 8, 9). See also Riegl, 'Modern Cult'.

16 Ruskin, 'Lamp of Memory', p. 358.

17 *Ibid.*, p. 339.

18 *Ibid.*, pp. 324–8, 330, 339–40.

19 *Ibid.*, pp. 353–4.

20 Pevsner, 'Foreword', p. 8, quoting his essay of 1973–74 in *Victorian Society Annual*.

21 Summerson, *Georgian London*, p. 132.

22 Trigg, 'Walking through Cathedrals', p. 33.

23 *Ibid.*, p. 30. There is a similar example in Barcelona where the National Art Museum of Catalonia now houses reconstructed apses and their frescoes from Romanesque chapels in the mountains of Catalonia. They had long ago fallen into disuse and were in danger of collapse.

24 Barnet and Wu, *Cloisters*, pp. 15, 19, 18–19.

25 Trigg, 'Walking through Cathedrals', p. 32.

26 This was James Broadbent at Elizabeth Bay House, a fine Greek-revival Georgian villa (built 1835–39, designed by John Verge 1782–1861), overlooking Sydney Harbour; it was built by Alexander Macleay (1767–1848), colonial secretary of NSW and a Linnaean collector of note. The next several pages of this chapter have been adapted from my 'The Golden Stain'.

27 *Hyde Park Barracks Museum Plan*, p. 40.

28 See further the brochure, *Hyde Park Barracks*, ed. Collins.

29 The curator of the Barracks, Peter Emmett, was part of a team whose members were, I was told, equally strong-minded. He went on to curate – with a free hand – the Museum of Sydney. His successor at the Barracks, Lynn Collins, is said to have softened Emmett's arty and pristine interpretation.

30 The Statement of Cultural Significance in the *Hyde Park Barracks Museum Plan* claims the Barracks is 'one of the finest works of the accomplished *colonial architect Francis Greenway*. The essence of his design has persisted through adaptations by government architects up to the present time' (p. 5).

31 Quoted in *Hyde Park Barracks Museum Plan*, p. 33.

32 See Marquis-Kyle and Walker, *Illustrated Burra Charter*.

33 Similar principles are encoded in the 1980s–90s US Secretary of the Interior's Standards for Rehabilitation prepared to guide applicants for taxation relief: 1992 version reproduced in Brand, *How Buildings Learn*, pp. 97–100.

3   THE NEW RUSKINIANS AND THE NEW AESTHETES

1 Quoted in Brand, *How Buildings Learn*, p. 94; originally in French from *Bulletin Archéologique*, vol. 1, 1839.

2 Broadbent, 'Past Imperfect', p. 152. See also Broadbent, *Australian Colonial House*.

3 Carr-Whitworth, 'Remembrance of Things Past', p. 4. See also the booklets *Brodsworth Hall* and *Brodsworth Hall and Gardens*.

4 Carr-Whitworth, 'Remembrance of Things Past'. The presentation of this bedroom as documented in the house booklet *Brodsworth Hall* has changed a little from its pre-conservation state (as in Figure 3.2: said to be before conservation but apparently after cleaning and some arranging). There were different coverings on the same bed by the time I visited in 2006.

5 Carr-Whitworth, 'Remembrance of Things Past', pp. 3–4.

6 Cf. Stillinger, *Multiple Authorship*, p. 197. For a commentary, see Eggert, 'Making Sense'.

7 Carr-Whitworth, 'Remembrance of Things Past', p. 4.

8 Marquis-Kyle and Walker, *Illustrated Burra Charter*, pp. 50, 52.

9 Rowell and Robinson, *Uppark Restored*, pp. 56, 107.

10 *Ibid.*, p. 107.

11 Ruskin, 'Lamp of Memory', p. 356.

12 Ruskin, 'Crystal Palace', pp. 117, 119.

13 '. . . *Reconstructed*' would be correct: 'restoration' is a flexible term in ordinary usage, but not so in curatorship and conservation: see the definitions above.

14 Rowell and Robinson, *Uppark Restored*, p. 89. Cf. Cruikshank, 'Rebuilding Uppark', p. 56: 'Demolition of the shell, or its maintenance as a controlled ruin, were quickly rejected, which left the Trust with a fine point to resolve. How should the building be reconstructed[?]'.

15 Deyan Sudjic in *Sunday Correspondent*, 17 September 1989, quoted in Rowell and Robinson, *Uppark Restored*, p. 34.

16 Rowell and Robinson, *Uppark Restored*, p. 38.

17 In comparison, the Ruskin–Morris position would have led, they contend, to 'peculiar visual results' (*ibid.*, p. 35).

18 *Ibid.*, p. 45

19 Sell (Vice-Chairman, SPAB), 'Effects of Uppark's Fire'.

20 Rowell and Robinson, *Uppark Restored*, pp. 47, 100.

21 *Ibid.*, pp. 175–6.

22 *Ibid.*, p. 44.

23 *Ibid.*, p. 46.

24 Pevsner, *Ruskin and Viollet-le-Duc*, p. 15.

25 Viollet-le-Duc, *Architectural Theory*, ed. Hearn, p. 91: from Viollet-le-Duc's *Entretiens sur l'architecture* [Discourses on Architecture], 2 vols., 1863, 1872.

26 Viollet-le-Duc, *Architectural Theory*, ed. Hearn, p. 274: from the entry 'On Restoration', in Viollet-le-Duc's *Dictionnaire raisonné*, vol. 8.

27 *Ibid.*, p. 269.

28 *Ibid.*, p. 277. Barry Bergdoll points to the parallel between Viollet-le-Duc's organicist belief and the anatomist Georges Cuvier's influential argument (in *Leçons d'anatomie comparée*, 1800–5) that each part of a skeleton was so perfectly adapted to its role that reconstruction of the whole skeleton from a

single part of a fragment of a fossil would in theory be possible: 'Introduction', pp. 18–19.

29 Viollet-le-Duc, *Architectural Theory*, ed. Hearn, p. 278.

30 Rowell and Robinson, *Uppark Restored*, p. 35.

31 Viollet-le-Duc, *Architectural Theory*, ed. Hearn, p. 281: from Viollet-le-Duc's 'Rapport adressé à M. le Ministre de la Justice et des Cultes' (1843), a report laying down the principles he intended to follow in restoring Notre-Dame.

32 *Ibid.*, p. 284.

33 Cf.: 'Viollet-le-Duc changed the form of the flying buttresses [in his restoration of Notre-Dame] along the nave, the earliest universally acknowledged buttresses in Gothic architecture, the original form of which was therefore historically important.' He also 'decided to "restore" the original wall configuration [of windows] in the bays adjacent to the [transept] crossing. He was, of course, removing genuine thirteenth-century work in order to make manifest the elevation he thought had been there at the outset': see further, Hearn's introduction to Viollet-le-Duc, *Architectural Theory*, pp. 1–19.

34 Rowell and Robinson, *Uppark Restored*, p. 87.

35 *Ibid.*, p. 73.

36 *Ibid.*, p. 98.

37 Interestingly, I was told that the Trust plans to give the display in the temporary Nissen hut a permanent, new stone building, thus confirming the new locus of significance of Uppark as a house.

38 Ruskin, 'Lamp of Memory', p. 357.

39 See Chapter 2, n. 9: Harvey, *Cathedrals of England*, p. 200.

40 Prøsch, *The Uthusprosjekt*, p. 14.

41 *Ibid.*, p. 18.

42 *Ibid.*, p. 18. The quoted statement by Jukka Jokilehto dates from a 1994 conference on authenticity, in Bergen.

4 FORGERY AND AUTHENTICITY

1 E.g. the collection of Impressionist paintings of Albert Coombs Barnes (1872–1951) in the collector's house, now a museum, in Merion, Pennsylvania.

2 Haywood, *Faking It*, p. 6.

3 *Ibid.*, p. 134. For a related position about Shakespeare manuscripts, see de Grazia, 'Essential Shakespeare'.

4 Haywood, *Faking It*, p. 77.

5 Another reading *is* possible: that Paul is merely referring to his first epistle, which has confused the Thessalonians.

6 See also the quotation at the end of Chapter 6 from Pliny the Elder in AD 77.

7 (John of Fidanza, 1221–74), quoted in Haywood, *Faking It*, p. 16.

8 Chartier, 'The Text'. A fuller account would also refer to St Jerome's four criteria of authenticity, which Foucault discusses ('What Is an Author?', pp. 110–11) and to the sixteenth-century Roman Catholic index of prohibited books,

Index librorum prohibitorum, published in various forms from 1529, with Pius IV's Tridentine Index (1564) being the most influential.

9 See Clanchy, *From Memory*, pp. 248–9.

10 See Ramsay, 'Forgery'.

11 Individual patentees (with grants usually from the Crown), and the two universities (Oxford and Cambridge), as well as the King's or Queen's Printers were not subject to the Company.

12 Haywood, *Faking It*, p. 30.

13 Saunders and Hunter, 'Lessons', pp. 498–9.

14 'The Booksellers are the Master Manufacturers or Employers. The several Writers, Authors, Copyers, Sub-writers, and all other Operators with pen and Ink are the workmen employed by the said Master Manufacturers': *Applebee's Journal* (1725), quoted by Haywood, *Faking It*, p. 30.

15 Quoted in Golvan and McDonald, *Writers and the Law*, p. 99.

16 Levine, '"Et Tu Brute?"', p. 71.

17 *Ibid.*, p. 73.

18 Bentley, *A Dissertation upon the Epistles of Phalaris* (1699): this was an extension of an essay published in 1697. Jean Mabillon had published *De re diplomatica* in 1681 specifying means of determining authenticity of documents by examining the style of the language and the writing itself. Palaeography would continue and extend this means of dating documents.

19 Levine, '"Et Tu Brute?"', p. 82.

20 *Ibid.*, p. 83. Bentley had written in 1697: 'it be the chief Province of a Critick to detect Forgeries' (quoted in Haywood, *Faking It*, p. 45).

21 Quoted by Levine, '"Et Tu Brute?"', p. 87 and see p. 88, n. 83.

22 Quoted by Haywood, *Faking It*, p. 41.

23 From D. H. Lawrence's poem, 'Song of a Man Who Has Come Through'.

24 Haywood, *Faking It*, p. 73.

25 *Ibid.*, p. 78.

26 *Ibid.*, p. 79.

27 Quoted in Rosenblum, *Prince of Forgers*, p. 178: a translation of and commentary on *Une Fabrique de faux autographes* (1870), by Henri Bordier and Emile Mabille.

28 Haywood, *Faking It*, p. 80. The exposure of Wise's forgeries in 1934 (in Carter and Pollard, *An Enquiry*) led to the discovery of Forman's involvement. He was a distinguished editor and Wise was a bibliographer of international renown. See further Collins, *Two Forgers*. As a triumph of bibliographic method, *An Enquiry* opened the way for the bibliographic forensics of such scholars as Nicolas Barker (see below).

29 Haywood, *Faking It*, p. 80.

30 Goodwin, *True Report*, pp. 119–20.

31 Haywood, *Faking It*, p. 83.

32 Barker, 'Forgery', pp. 13–14.

33 *Ibid.*, p. 9.

34 *Ibid.*, p. 10.

35 Iser, 'Reading Process', pp. 224, 223, 227, 225. Robert Scholes went further down the track of reader-centred phenomenology: 'Reading', he says, 'is always, at once, the effort to comprehend and the effort to incorporate. I must invent the author, invent his or her intentions, using the evidence I can find to stimulate my creative process (a stimulation achieved in part by offering restrictions on that process, to be sure). I must also incorporate the text I am reading in my own textual repertory . . . Reading consists of bringing texts together. It is a constructive activity, a kind of writing . . . Such construction is pleasurable in itself, because it is that fundamental human action of making the world intelligible': *Protocols of Reading*, pp. 9–11.

36 Discussed by Bodkin, 'Johannes Vermeer of Delft', pp. 4–5.

37 *Ibid.*, p. 8. The painting had sold to the Boymans-van Beuningen Museum in Rotterdam for £75,000.

38 *Ibid.*, p. 6.

39 Respectively: 1654, National Gallery of Scotland, Edinburgh; 1937, Museum Boymans-van Beuningen, Rotterdam. Reproductions of most of van Meegeren's paintings appear in Kraaijpoel and van Wijnen, *Han van Meegeren*. Some appear in *The Forger's Art*, ed. Dutton, pp. 26, 22.

40 Werness, 'Han van Meegeren *fecit*', p. 25.

41 Rijksmuseum, Amsterdam; cf. Werness, 'Han van Meegeren *fecit*', pp. 50–1.

42 The two paintings were, respectively, *The Woman Taken in Adultery* and *Jesus amongst the Doctors*. See further, Koningsberger, 'A Forger's Postscript', pp. 174–85.

43 Dutton, 'Editor's Preface', pp. vii–viii.

44 Alfred Lessing's term; see his 'What Is Wrong', p. 58.

45 Quoted by Meyer, 'Anthropology of Art', p. 79.

46 Barker, 'Forgery', p. 9.

47 Cf. Meyer, 'Anthropology of Art', p. 84.

48 See entry 'Ern Malley Hoax', in *Oxford Companion to Australian Literature*, ed. Wilde, Hooton and Andrews, p. 238; and Heyward, *Ern Malley Affair*.

49 For a discussion, see Eggert, 'Where Are We Now'.

50 At www.ozpages.com/eddieburrup accessed in 1999 but since removed. Elizabeth Durack died in 2000.

51 Aboriginal art is big business: 'It is estimated that approximately 6000 to 7000 Aboriginal people throughout Australia . . . are regularly engaged in the making of art and artefacts . . . [and] that sales of their art (including tourist art) is around [AUD] $200 million to $300 million annually. This is far in excess of Australia's other art sales and yet produced by those whose population is only a small percentage of Australia's total': *The New McCulloch's*, ed. McCulloch, McCulloch and McCulloch Childs, p. 2.

52 The saddest case is that of Emily Kngwarreye: see Greer, 'Selling Off the Dreaming'.

53 After that, the art dealers closed ranks, but the dealer in question, John Douglas O'Loughlin, became the first Australian to be sentenced for indigenous art fraud in 2001. (The artist was Clifford Possum Tjapaltjarri, 1932–2002.) An

authenticity labelling scheme was proposed but collapsed in 2003. In October 2006 the Australian government announced a Senate enquiry linked to the preparation of an Indigenous Art Commercial Code of Conduct. The report was tabled in Parliament in June 2007 but an official response was delayed by Federal elections in November, the same month in which Ivan and Pamela Liberto were gaoled in Victoria for producing fake Rover Thomas paintings – the first such conviction in that state.

54 *The Painters*, ed. Caruana and Lendon, p. 22. Information from Lendon's essay, 'Narrative in Paint' (pp. 20–37) is used here.

55 At any one time, more than one person in a clan can have the right to paint aspects of the story, and the individual's right to paint more of it can grow over time.

5 CONSERVATORS AND AGENCY

1 Hogarth, *Analysis of Beauty*, pp. 118–19.

2 Francisco Goya y Lucientes, quoted in Beck, *Art Restoration*, p. 142.

3 Beck, *Art Restoration*, p. 129.

4 For the introduction of Humboldtian science and the later turn to laboratory science, see Home, 'Humboldtian Science Revisited'; and 'Ferdinand von Mueller'. Mulhaus is partly based on von Mueller, who introduced Humboldtian science into the Australian colonies.

5 Kingsley, *Geoffry Hamlyn*, ed. Mellick, Morgan and Eggert, pp. 33–4. Edward Sabine (1788–1883) was a renowned ornithologist. These decaying nineteenth-century taxidermical collections are common in England's great houses. Calke's in Derbyshire is very extensive.

6 See further, McDonell, 'Exhibit'.

7 E.g. Dennis, *Cemeteries of Etruria*.

8 McGirk, 'Ghosts Who Talk'. The death mask is probably the Kesselstadt death mask. Now in Darmstadt, it was actually discovered in 1849 but its connection to Shakespeare is tenuous.

9 Colalucci, 'Sistine Ceiling Frescoes', p. 26.

10 Eggert, 'Editing Paintings', p. 65; originally given as a paper at the A. E. Housman Centenary Seminar, Melbourne, October 1992. Some of the present chapter has been adapted from the article. The quotation from Colalucci is from personal notes made at his lecture at the National Gallery of Australia, Canberra, 3 May 1992.

11 Bowers's words are from his *Textual and Literary Criticism*, p. 81 (see also p. 18) and are repeated with slight variation in 'Textual Criticism', p. 865.

12 Beck cites Paolo Giovio and Condivi who wrote biographies of Michelangelo during his lifetime, and Vasari and Armenino in the sixteenth century (Beck, *Art Restoration*, pp. 88–99).

13 *Ibid.*, pp. 96, 99–100. Wilson noted that 'the size colour [i.e. the colour added to the glue-size] has cracked as the plaster has cracked', showing that it was contemporary with the original plaster and not applied later (as required by

Colalucci's case). If it had been a later addition, it would have run into and filled the cracks (quoted p. 100).

14 *Ibid.*, pp. 87–8.
15 See Colalucci, 'Sistine Ceiling Frescoes', p. 26.
16 See Beck, *Art Restoration*, pp. 74–5. It had been believed that another had taken place in 1625 but has only been proven to have been to the walls (p. 77).
17 *Ibid.*, pp. 100–1.
18 *Ibid.*, pp. 67–9, 105–6.
19 The conferences were: Ottawa, October 1989 (see its proceedings *Shared Responsibility*, ed. Ramsay-Jolicoeur and Wainwright); London, June 1990 (*Appearance, Opinion, Change*, ed. Peter Booth *et al.*); and Canberra, May 1992 (*The Articulate Surface*, ed. Wallace).
20 Quoting a report of Mirella Simonetti: Beck, *Art Restoration*, p. 115.
21 *Ibid.*, p. 116.
22 Colalucci lecture: see n. 10 above.
23 Beck, *Art Restoration*, pp. 176, 180, 177. Beck's Ruskinite approach is confirmed by his requirement that, '*In principle, later transformations, adjustments and reformations added to the original statement should be left intact as marks of its history*' (p. 181).
24 The official account is given in Barcilon, 'The Restoration'. The volume in which this essay appears has magnificent, progressively nearer, close-up photography of all parts of the painting, and reproductions of various stages of the restoration.
25 Phillips, 'Long Last Supper'.
26 Kemp, 'Leonardo's *Last Supper*', p. 18.
27 *Ibid.*
28 See Neville, 'Facelift', p. 232.
29 Quoted in Hedley, 'Long Lost Relations', p. 163.
30 *Ibid.*, pp. 163, 164, 163.
31 *Ibid.*, p. 164.
32 Michalski, 'Time's Effects on Paintings', p. 40.
33 Magor, 'An Artist's Thoughts', p. 6.
34 *Ibid.*, p. 11.
35 *Ibid.*, p. 10.
36 See Parker's discussion of authors confusing the plots of their own novels (*Flawed Texts and Verbal Icons*, especially chapter 5 for his discussion of Mark Twain's *Pudd'nhead Wilson*).
37 Hardy, *Tess of the D'Urbervilles*, ed. Grindle and Gattrell.
38 See Smith, 'Shared Responsibility'.
39 Eagle, 'Sightings', p. 31.

6 SUBTILISING AUTHORSHIP

1 William Blake, MS Note-book, no. 55: in Blake, *Complete Writings*, p. 548.
2 Byron, *Childe Harold's Pilgrimage*, Canto IV (1818), stanza 53, in *Complete Poetical Works*, ed. McGann, vol. 2, pp. 141–2.

3 Berthoud, *Life of Henry Moore*, p. 385.

4 *Ibid.*, p. 417.

5 Quoted in McMullen, *Mona Lisa*, pp. 52–3.

6 *Ibid.*, p. 50.

7 Manuth, 'Rembrandt', p. 41.

8 McMullen, *Mona Lisa*, p. 66.

9 See Blankert, 'Looking at Rembrandt', p. 53. Other information in Blankert's essay has been drawn upon in this chapter.

10 Schwartz, 'Rembrandt in 1650'.

11 See *Corpus*, ed. Bruyn *et al.*, vol. 1, p. xviii col. 1.

12 The categories are, in full: 'Paintings by Rembrandt', 'Paintings Rembrandt's authorship of which cannot be positively either accepted or rejected', and 'Paintings Rembrandt's authorship of which cannot be accepted'.

13 A media fracas developed over *The Polish Rider* from a footnote in an early volume of the *Corpus*, questioning its status. At the Melbourne Rembrandt conference (see below in text), Ernst van der Wetering, by then sole director of the RRP, announced that it will be designated in a future volume as an unfinished Rembrandt, perhaps finished by someone else.

14 Bomford, Brown and Roy, *Art in the Making*, p. 72.

15 Thematisation is an idea drawn from phenomenology; Danto is developing an idea of Richard Wollheim. See Danto, 'Gettysburg', p. 242.

16 Von Sonnenburg, Liedtke *et al.*, *Rembrandt/Not Rembrandt*.

17 In Bruyn, Haak, Levie and van Thiel, 'Rembrandt Research Project'.

18 Announced in van der Wetering, '[Letter]'.

19 Formerly known as *Head of an Old Man*, no. 1 C22 in *Corpus*, ed. Bruyn *et al.*, vol. 1, p. 579. For the reattribution, see *ibid.*, vol. 4, p. 628 cols. 1–2.

20 Blankert, 'Looking at Rembrandt', p. 194.

21 *Ibid.*, p. 54.

22 For a survey of the effects of literary and cultural theory on the practice of connoisseurship and formalist analysis, and for a prognosis for their future, see Plant, 'Residual Connoisseurship'.

23 See Blokhuis, 'Life of Rembrandt'.

24 I use this term in C. S. Peirce's sense: see Chapter 10, n. 63.

25 Connoisseurship does not have to refer to individuals: one can talk of the connoisseurship of Greek vases. Stylistic integrity is what is sought.

26 See Schwartz, 'Rembrandt in 1650'.

27 Bomford, 'Rembrandt and Pentimenti'.

28 *Corpus*, ed. Bruyn *et al.*, vol. 1, p. xii col. 2.

29 *Ibid.*, vol. 1, p. xiii col. 2.

30 *Ibid.*, vol. 1, p. xx cols. 1–2.

31 *Ibid.*, vol. 1, p. xiv col. 1.

32 *Ibid.*, vol. 1, p. xvi col. 2.

33 *Ibid.*, vol. 1, p. xvi col. 2.

34 *Ibid.*, vol. 4, p. x col. 2.

35 *Ibid.*, vol. 4, p. x cols. 1–2.

36 *Ibid.*, vol. 4, p. xi col. 1.

37 *Ibid.*, vol. 4, p. xii col. 1.

38 *Ibid.*, vol. 4, p. xiii col. 1.

39 *Ibid.*, vol. 4, p. xvi col. 2.

40 *Ibid.*, vol. 4, p. xviii col. 1.

41 *Ibid.*, vol. 4, p. xviii cols. 1–2.

42 *Ibid.*, vol. 4, p. ix col. 1. This shift meant that the RRP could not restrict itself to Gerson's 420 works (as announced as a time-saving method in vol. 2) instead of Bredius's 611.

43 See *Corpus*, ed. Bruyn *et al.*, vol. 4, pp. 609–15. Cf. Gary Schwartz's prior scepticism (of 1997), now refuted, about the reattribution: 'After I Win'.

44 Pliny, *Naturalis historia*, XXXV. XL. 143–6, quoted by van der Wetering, 'Multiple Functions', p. 34.

7 MATERIALIST, PERFORMANCE OR LITERARY SHAKESPEARE?

1 William Shakespeare, Sonnet 18: in *Complete Works*, ed. Wells and Taylor, p. 753.

2 Smith, 'Literature, as Performance' and Goodman's '[Reply]'.

3 Iser, *Act of Reading*; Mailloux, *Reader*; and Fish, *Is There a Text*.

4 E.g., at the World Shakespeare Congress in Brisbane in 2006, a session was given over to the book.

5 Howard-Hill, '"Nor Stage . . ."', p. 38 and n. 31.

6 The fair copy and prompt copy may well often have been the same document. The Elizabethans simply called it 'the Booke'. It was not as detailed a document as modern promptbooks.

7 Greg, 'Rationale of Copy-Text' (delivered in 1949 to the English Institute).

8 *Corpus*, ed. Bruyn *et al.*, vol. 1, p. xx col. 2.

9 *Ibid.*, vol. 1, p. xvii col. 2.

10 Shakespeare, *Complete Works*, ed. Wells and Taylor. The editorial approach was preceded and underpinned by a decade of fresh argument on the matter, notably: *The Division*, ed. Taylor and Warren. See also n. 17, below.

11 See Dillon, 'Is There a Performance'.

12 Shakespeare, *Complete Works*, ed. Wells and Taylor, p. xxxix.

13 Quoted in Dillon, 'Is There a Performance', p. 74 from *The Hamlet First Published (Q1, 1603): Origins, Form, Intertextualities*, ed. Thomas Clayton (1992).

14 Dillon, 'Is There a Performance', p. 77.

15 With *Hamlet* it seems that only a severe rupture in the line of transmission (and not just cutting and reorganisation of material for the stage) could explain the printed results in the first Quarto. (I thank John Jowett for clarifying this matter: personal communication.) The Folio *Hamlet* probably derives from the company's playbook. If so, it may represent a theatrical text assembling as much material as possible to afford players some choice when cutting for

performance, but not playable as it stands. See further, Gurr, 'Maximal and Minimal Texts'.

16 The role of Shakespeare as a (non-Bardic) member of a company of players trying to earn their livings becomes an issue here too.

17 De Grazia and Stallybrass, 'Materiality'. In mainly non-Shakespearean areas, Randall McCleod was already the presiding genius of this bibliographically attuned but anti-editorial approach. For de Grazia's earlier work along similar lines, see her 'Essential Shakespeare' and *Shakespeare Verbatim*; on the former, see Eggert, 'Textual Product or Textual Process', pp. 67–9.

18 Amory, '[Review]', pp. 470, 469. See Chapter 5, n. 11, above.

19 For my own experience of this shrinking and how I dealt with it, see Eggert, 'Way of All Text', pp. 162–4. Some of the present chapter has been adapted from this essay.

20 See Wells and Taylor, *Textual Companion*, and n. 10 above. For an overview, see Ioppolo, *Revising Shakespeare*.

21 Shakespeare: *Complete King Lear*, ed. Warren; *Three-Text Hamlet*, ed. Bertram and Kliman; and *Hamlet*, ed. Thompson and Taylor (a three-text edition).

22 De Grazia and Stallybrass, 'Materiality', p. 255.

23 *Ibid.*, p. 268.

24 Foucault, 'What Is an Author?'.

25 De Grazia and Stallybrass, 'Materiality', p. 283.

26 See Howard-Hill, 'Early Modern Printers'.

27 De Grazia and Stallybrass, 'Materiality', p. 266.

28 *Ibid.*, p. 280.

29 See *ibid.*, p. 257.

30 Holderness, Loughrey and Murphy, '"What's the matter?"'.

31 *Ibid.*, p. 104.

32 *Ibid.*

33 *Ibid.*

34 *Ibid.*, pp. 104–5.

35 *Ibid.*, p. 105.

36 In Shakespeare's time, though, there probably were no theatre tickets as such.

37 Holderness, Loughrey and Murphy, '"What's the matter?"', pp. 104–5.

38 *Ibid.*, p. 117.

39 De Grazia and Stallybrass, 'Materiality', pp. 276–7.

40 Pechter, 'Making Love', p. 54.

41 Stallybrass, 'Love among the Ruins', p. 74.

42 De Grazia and Stallybrass, 'Materiality', p. 280.

43 Holderness, Loughrey and Murphy, '"What's the matter?"', p. 94.

44 Cf. Benjamin's remark: 'The presence of the original is the prerequisite to the concept of authenticity' – now superseded in an age of mechanical duplication: 'Age of Mechanical Reproduction', p. 214.

45 De Grazia and Stallybrass, 'Materiality', p. 276.

46 Blayney, 'Publication of Playbooks', pp. 389, 385.

47 Erne, *Shakespeare as Literary Dramatist*, p. 16.

48 *Ibid.*, p. 16, n. 50 (Thomas Creede, Edward Allde and Valentine Simmes published, respectively, thirty-five playbooks during 1594–1616; thirty-six, 1584–1624; and twenty-five, 1597–1611), pp. 17 and 11 (quoted).

49 Privately performed plays were a different matter. There was a well-established tradition of acting classical and religious drama in the schools, universities and court. There were fewer than thirty plays printed in English prior to Elizabeth I's accession in 1558. The first blank-verse tragedy in English, *Gorboduc*, written on the model of a Senecan tragedy by Thomas Sackville and Thomas Norton, was performed at the Inner Temple in 1561 and was printed twice in the next ten years.

50 Quoted in Erne, *Shakespeare as Literary Dramatist*, p. 71.

51 *Ibid.*, p. 112: from Greg, *First Folio*, p. 2.

52 *Ibid.*, p. 142.

53 The table of play lengths Erne gives on page 141 is particularly revealing when compared with lengths of plays from the so-called Beaumont and Fletcher Folio (table on *ibid.*, p. 151). The following plays exceed 2,800 lines: *1 and 2 Henry IV*, *Henry V*, *2 and 3 Henry VI*, *Richard III*, *Henry VIII* (only just longer), *Troilus and Cressida*, *Romeo and Juliet*, *Hamlet*, *King Lear*, *Othello*, *Antony and Cleopatra* and *Cymbeline*.

54 Actors making copies for sale or gift based on abridged performances seem to be encompassed by Moseley's statement in the prefatory material to the 1647 Beaumont and Fletcher Folio. He provides superior texts, he states. Although Howard-Hill finds Moseley's statement 'troubling' (partly because behind most of his printed texts 'theatrical copy is clearly predominant'), the 'consensual view' remains that Moseley probably gathered 'transcripts in private hands' to add to those given him by the King's Men ('"Nor Stage . . ."', pp. 36–7). Howard-Hill observes that 'No transcript of a play identified as the product of a bookseller's scribe has been located thus far. Yet analysis of the texts of printed plays may provide the basis of conjecture about the status of the text from which the edition was set in type, whether it was authorial or scribal, whether it was closely associated with the playhouse or more distinctively literary in character' (pp. 31–2). On balance, he is far more sceptical than Erne on the existence of scribal publication of plays.

55 Erne, *Shakespeare as Literary Dramatist*, p. 205.

56 *Ibid.*, pp. 205, 195, 195.

57 Brockbank, 'Towards a Mobile Text', p. 96.

8 MODES OF EDITING LITERARY WORKS

1 Drew (died *c.* 1826), *Principles of Self-Knowledge*, vol. 1, pp. xiv–xv.

2 Rolf Boldrewood [Thomas A. Browne], (Diary for 1879, entry for 6 September), when already a colonial author of several serialised novels and upon receiving reviews of his first novel to be published in book form in London, *Ups and Downs*.

3 See Button, 'Struggle', p. 31: 'This year [in the UK] the term multiculturalism began to disappear from its [the Government's] discourse. The new buzzwords can be found in the name of the Commission on Integration and Cohesion, established in June to look at how to mend, or end, multiculturalism.' In January 2007 the Australian government's Department of Immigration and Multicultural Affairs was renamed Immigration and Citizenship.

4 Greetham, *Theories of the Text*. For an extended commentary, see Eggert, 'These Post-philological Days'. For Greetham's reply, see his 'Philology Redux?'.

5 It was edited (as a photofacsimile and an annotated diplomatic transcription) in a PhD thesis: Weber, 'Port Phillip Papers'.

6 Allingham, 'Rachel Henning Letters', p. 262. This project still awaits an edition.

7 The colonial period ended in 1901 with the federation of the colonies into the Commonwealth of Australia.

8 Kiernan, '[Review]', p. 107.

9 See further, the introduction to the Academy Edition, ed. Mellick, Morgan and Eggert; and Eggert, 'A Cautionary Tale'.

10 Kiernan, '[Review]', p. 106.

11 The 1879 date is given in the printer's date-stamp on its last page: see the Academy Edition, ed. Mellick, Morgan and Eggert, p. lxii, n. 121.

12 Kingsley, *Henry Kingsley*, ed. Mellick, p. xxvii.

13 Kiernan, '[Review]', p. 106.

14 *Ibid.*

15 Kingsley, *Geoffry Hamlyn* (1935, 1993), pp. 243, 242.

16 Susan Martin writes: 'The only words that the old [Aboriginal] woman, Sally, will address to Sam are "Make a light", translated in the foot-note as "See". Sam manages not to see' (Introduction, in *ibid.* [1993], pp. xviii–xix). In the first edition and *E2* the footnote reads: '"Make a light," in blackfellow's gibberish, means simply "See." Here it means, "I'm only come to see how you are getting on," or something of that sort.' (Academy Edition, ed. Mellick, Morgan and Eggert, p. 313). The 1935 edition, which Martin is depending upon, has only: '"Make a light" means simply "See."' (p. 249).

17 Academy Edition, ed. Mellick, Morgan and Eggert, p. 680.

18 For an example of this function ('the fine-grained ways') of critical editions, see the Appendix '*Robbery Under Arms* in Montreal', in Boldrewood, *Robbery Under Arms*, ed. Eggert and Webby. For further discussion of the reviewing of the Australian series in 1999, see Eggert, 'Why Critical Editing Matters', from which some of this chapter has been adapted.

19 Mumford, 'Emerson behind Barbed Wire', p. 4.

20 *Ibid.*

21 *Ibid.*, p. 5.

22 Modern Language Association, *Professional Standards*, e.g. Fisher, 'The MLA Editions': 'The MLA Center for Editions has, since its inception in 1962, set as its objective the creation of a clear reading text, ready for popular publication,

alongside the collection of variant readings and textual history that will show what lies behind the clear text' (p. 22).

23 Mumford, 'Emerson behind Barbed Wire', p. 4.

24 Debate continued in several opinion-pieces in the *Bulletin of the New York Public Library* (see Freehafer, 'How Not To Edit') and elsewhere, e.g. Bruccoli, 'A Few Missing Words'. Criticising mistakes in execution rather than the essential aim (the 'purging of non-authorial features from copy-texts', p. 423), Freehafer charged that the 'excessively bibliographical style' of the MLA editions prevents 'their appreciation as works of literature' (p. 421).

25 Wilson, 'Fruits', in *Canon Barham*, p. 173.

26 The *locus classicus* for the disagreement was the exchange in 1953 between the editors of competing literary journals in Oxford and Cambridge, respectively: Bateson, 'Function of Criticism at the Present Time'; and Leavis, 'Responsible Critic' (reprinted together, with final remarks by both parties, in Leavis, *A Selection from Scrutiny*, vol. 2).

27 The symbols are assigned by individual chapter to accord with its surviving pre-publication materials. So, in reading this synoptic assembly, it is necessary to reorient oneself chapter by chapter.

28 In some other chapters Joyce did not take this route; the typescript was copied directly from the Rosenbach.

29 The parentheses around the symbol B are declaring that the document where the wording was originally entered – the final working draft – is lost.

30 See further, Gabler's analysis of this passage in 'Synchrony and Diachrony', pp. 320–4.

31 McGann, 'Gabler Edition', p. 291.

32 Martens, '(De)Constructing Texts', p. 138. Cf. Bryant, *Fluid Text*.

33 Gabler, 'Editor Reviews the Reviewers'.

34 Lawrence's MS is held by the Bancroft Library, University of California at Berkeley.

35 The typescript with the single pagination '468' served as setting copy for the English first edition; the other, with multiple paginations, for the American. For a discussion of this process, see Eggert, 'Document or Process'.

36 See Bowers, 'Multiple Authority'. For an Australian case that confirmed Bowers's argument, see Eggert, 'Version – Agency – Intention'.

37 Thorpe, 'Ideal of Textual Criticism'; and Gaskell, *From Writer to Reader*, p. 4. See also Gaskell, *A New Introduction*, pp. 336–60.

38 Tanselle, 'Editing without a Copy-Text'.

39 See further, Eggert, 'Reading a Critical Edition'.

40 Cf. Mahaffey, 'Intentional Error': 'many of the most widely publicized attacks are based on premises about textual editing that the general reading public takes for granted, so when a critic proves that Gabler has violated these guidelines, his editorial competence is implicitly or explicitly called into question. It takes a reasonably specialized reader to realize that the weakness of such arguments ... is at the level of the premise, since Gabler does not share many of the premises on which the critique is based' (p. 175). On page 176, Mahaffey quotes Gabler's

first 'Response' (p. 252) to Kidd: 'it makes little sense to hold against the edition that it does not do what it expressly sets out to avoid'. See also Mays, 'Gabler's *Ulysses*'.

41 Kidd, 'An Inquiry'; and Gabler, 'What *Ulysses* Requires'.

42 Edited (by Danis Rose) according to the 'curious criterion' of his own intuitive sense of '"the logic of the narrative"' – thus breaching, Lawrence Rainey argued, 'every principle and procedure of critical editing' ('Molly Bloom', p. 13).

43 Rossman, 'Hidden Controversy'; Arnold, *Scandal of Ulysses*, pp. 103, 196, 200–4. See also Rossman's later 'Gabler's *Ulysses* Kidd-Napped'.

44 Gabler's edition, as J. C. C. Mays points out, could have been more helpful in this latter respect. Because 'not underpinned by a theory of annotation', it denies the reader the needful contextual supplement for the text's locatedness at the level of general theme, schema and local detail as revisions of or precursors to Joyce's other writings ('Gabler's *Ulysses*', p. 6).

45 See further Gabler, 'Textual Criticism' and 'Genetic Texts'.

46 Shattuck and Alden, 'True Text', pp. 640, 641, 640.

47 *Ibid.*, p. 641.

48 *Ibid.*

49 See further, Chapter 10, for an account of this orientation in the New Criticism in and after the 1940s.

50 *Norton Anthology of Poetry*, p. lvii.

51 Jensen, 'Furnish a Self'.

52 Williams and Abbott, *An Introduction*, pp. 55–6.

53 Hill, 'Ironies of Paternity', p. 30.

54 Kline, *A Guide to Documentary Editing*, p. 24. For the second edition in 1998, 'quite', with its touch of acerbity, was deleted (p. 2).

9   READERS AND EDITORS

1 Gettmann, *A Victorian Publisher*, pp. 202–3, 230.

2 Gabler, 'Genetic Texts', p. 62.

3 Hurlebusch, 'Procedures of Authorship', p. 112.

4 Most are listed in the AustLit database (www.austlit.edu.au). The more important ones are listed in the critical edition, ed. Eggert, pp. liii–lvii. For a fuller account of the reception see Eggert, 'Work of a Readership', from which the next few pages are adapted.

5 Anon., '[Review]', *Onlooker*, p. 11.

6 Anon., '[Untitled comment]', *Star*, p. 18.

7 Palmer, 'Disintegration', p. 415.

8 Collins, 'Even Yet', pp. 256–88.

9 Ross, 'As Others See Us', p. 1.

10 Palmer, 'Disintegration', p. 415.

11 [Child], '[Anonymous review]', p. 523.

12 Anon., '"Y'Self is God!"', *Life*, pp. 22–3.

13 A.M.A., '[Review]'.

14 'Panurge', '[Review]', p. 4.

15 *Ibid.*

16 For a study of the biographical locatedness of texts, see further Eggert, 'Biographical Issue'.

17 The use of the term *life* as applied to literary works was an isolated and usually unknowing adaptation of the aesthetic philosophy of Roman Ingarden, via the influential writings of the American E. D. Hirsch in the 1970s: see further, Chapter 10.

18 West, *A Sister Carrie Portfolio*, p. 14: this volume illustrates in facsimile all stages of the novel's composition, revision, abridgement and production.

19 Dreiser, *Sister Carrie*, ed. West, pp. 580, 581–2.

20 Lingeman, 'Sister Carrie's Chaperones', p. 57.

21 Brodhead, '"New" *Sister Carrie*', pp. 599, 598.

22 Pizer, '[Review]', pp. 732, 737. See his further development of the argument in his 'Self-censorship' (a revised version of a conference paper given in 1982); and, for further commentary, Shillingsburg, 'Being Textually Aware', pp. 171–2.

23 Parker, '[Review]', p. 335.

24 *Ibid.*, p. 336. But it must be noted that the 1970s was the decade when G. Thomas Tanselle became productive as an (always acute) commentator on textual issues. His articles in *Studies in Bibliography* and elsewhere acted as reasoned antidotes to the enthusiasms of the day. He sought to extend and refine the logic of the Greg–Bowers approach to editing as new objections to it arose, sophisticating it to embrace aspects of textual scenarios that various editors were reporting and others were reflecting upon theoretically.

25 Mays, 'Gabler's *Ulysses*', p. 10.

26 Shillingsburg, 'Being Textually Aware', p. 171.

27 West, 'We've Come To Know', p. 39. To my question in personal correspondence with West: 'I take it that you were making a distinction between the *Trimalchio* vs *Great Gatsby* case (two scholarly editions needed in practice) and the Pennsylvania vs 1900 text of *Sister Carrie* case (one scholarly edition sufficient), yes?', West's reply was: 'Yes, exactly. If Dreiser had had an earlier title for *Sister Carrie*, I might have used it for my Pennsylvania Edition simply to make reference easier, but he always called it *Sister Carrie*' (2 July 2007).

28 In 1999 a critical edition, based on manuscripts in D. H. Lawrence's hand, called *The First and Second Lady Chatterley Novels* appeared (ed. Mehl and Jansohn) in which the novel first published in 1944 as *The First Lady Chatterley* and the rewritten version first published in 1972 as *John Thomas and Lady Jane* are presented as *Lady Chatterley's Lover Version 1* and *Lady Chatterley's Lover Version 2*.

 The forthcoming Cambridge University Press edition of Joseph Conrad's *Under Western Eyes* (ed. Keith Carabine, Paul Eggert and Roger Osborne) may in due course spawn an edition of the novel based on the form in which Conrad first finished it, *said* it was finished, and before he cut it radically. (He did the cutting while recovering from a nervous breakdown, brought on in significant part by the finishing of the manuscript.) This version may be given the title (on the manuscript and typescript) 'Razumov', the novel's main character.

29 Stillinger, *Multiple Authorship*, p. 200.

30 See further, Eggert, 'Making Sense'; Shillingsburg, *Resisting Texts*, chapter 6 (especially p. 154); and Bryant, who exposes the helplessness, especially when dealing with manuscripts, that Stillinger's identification of version with physical document entails (*Fluid Text*, pp. 76–9).

31 McKenzie, *Sociology of Texts*. See also Shillingsburg, 'Meanings' and his review 'Three *Moby-Dicks*'.

32 Bornstein, *Material Modernism*, p. 67. See further, Holdeman, 'Much Labouring'.

33 Gilmore, *Collected Verse*, ed. Strauss, see vol. 1, pp. xxxi–xxxii. E.g., in *Selected Verse*, 'The Brucedale Scandal' (poem G33 in *Collected Verse*), a conversation poem, loses its note and present tense indicators are altered from, e.g., 'says she' to 'she said': see its textual apparatus and cf. that for B1 ('Marri'd').

34 Such calls began to be formulated in papers from 1985 at the biennial meetings of the Society for Textual Scholarship and (with elaboration and growing confidence) at a conference in Canberra in 1989: see the paper by Gabler ('Textual Studies'), and more especially those by Eggert ('Textual Product') and Shillingsburg ('Autonomous Author').

35 See Chapter 10, n. 43.

36 See further, Mays, 'Reflections'.

37 The appearance of the six-volume edition was delayed by ten years by a variety of factors at the Press and the funding foundation, and by the death of the general editor Kathleen Coburn in 1991.

38 Zeller, 'A New Approach'.

39 See Kirsop, 'French Connection'; and cf. Willison, 'Editorial Theory': in contrast to 'the imperious historico-sociological *élan* of the *Annalistes*, such as Lucien Febvre, who launched the enterprise' that led to the *histoire du livre* movement, Anglo-American book historians 'see the bibliographical skull beneath the cultural skin' (pp. 111–12).

40 Zeller, 'Record and Interpretation', p. 23.

41 Yeats, *Last Poems*, ed. Pethica, pp. xxix–xxx.

42 Scheibe, 'Authorization and Constitution', p. 175.

43 Scheibe, 'Editorial Problem', p. 199.

44 Scheibe, 'Authorization and Constitution', p. 185.

45 Scheibe, 'Editorial Problem', p. 205.

46 *Ibid.*, p. 201. This definition is open to objection but, as we shall see below, Martens gives it a subtilising twist.

47 Zeller, 'Record and Interpretation', p. 54 n. 25.

48 *Ibid.*, pp. 24–5.

49 *Ibid.*, p. 24.

50 *Ibid.*, p. 22.

51 *Ibid.*, p. 25.

52 See Mays, 'Reflections', pp. 143–4, 148 and p. 152 n. 10. Mays's dry remark that 'A genetic or synoptic display does not of course answer the question of which version is to be recited on a school prize-day' (p. 148) only half-answers a criticism that the Cornell Wordsworth's exhaustive recording of textual genesis had also attracted. That edition's aim of presenting hitherto unknown early versions of Wordsworth's poems rather than the canonical later ones – an editorial trajectory that completes Ernst de Selincourt's printing in 1926 of the early (1805) version of *The Prelude* – means that the later versions are given only as variants in apparatus form. Jack Stillinger objects 'that for all practical purposes they have dropped out of sight', even though these are the versions that made Wordsworth's reputation ('Textual Primitivism', p. 17).

53 Cervenka, 'Textual Criticism and Semiotics'.

54 *Ibid.*, p. 61.

55 *Ibid.*, p. 64.

56 *Ibid.*, p. 60.

57 It need not apply in other cases, as Greg's edition, *Jonson's 'Masque of Gipsies'*, shows. See Howard-Hill, 'Dangers of Editing', especially p. 56.

58 Zeller, 'Record and Interpretation', p. 27.

59 Zeller, 'Structure and Genesis', p. 106.

60 *Ibid.*, pp. 106–7.

61 In 'What Is a Text' (originally 1989), Martens, responding to then-recent post-structuralist thinking, looks elsewhere for a structural principle – to the semiotics of the American late nineteenth-century Pragmatist, C. S. Peirce, who, according to Martens, promisingly incorporates the user of the sign (e.g. writer, reader) into the definition of the sign, and thus of the text-as-sign. (This is taken up in Chapter 10. Cf. also my commentary on Martens's proposal (in 'Shadow'), from which some of the present commentary has been adapted.)

62 See further Eggert, 'Autorität des Textes'.

63 For an enlightening but uncritical account of this pragmatism, see Plachta, '"Royal Way" of Philology', especially pp. 35–43.

64 I have not discussed French *critique génétique*. Even though it can be seen (from an Anglo-American point of view) as a practice of textual criticism or (from a German point of view) as a form of interpretation of the variant listings in editions, it does not aim at editing per se. See further, Hay, 'Genetic Editing'; Grésillon, *Eléments de critique génétique*; de Biasi, 'What Is a Literary Draft?'; and Ferrer, 'Production, Invention'.

65 For an early and prescient statement of this crisis at an Australian editing conference in 1984, see Ruthven, 'Textuality and Textual Editing'.

66 The other Editorial Board members were Virginia Blain, †Harold Love, Chris Tiffin and Elizabeth Webby. The first title appeared in 1996, the tenth and last in 2007. The experimentation reached a peak in the edition of a pantomime called *The House that Jack Built* in *Australian Plays*, ed. Fotheringham. The edition is an 'enfolded' text of the Sydney and Melbourne versions, both of which, the editor argues, are of equal authority in relation

to their own audiences. For a discussion, see Eggert, 'Version – Agency – Intention'.

67 They are two novels by Henry Handel Richardson, *Maurice Guest* (1908) and *The Getting of Wisdom* (1910), ed. Probyn and Steele.

68 The most striking examples are: Marcus Clarke, *His Natural Life*, ed. Stuart; and Rolf Boldrewood, *Robbery Under Arms*, ed. Eggert and Webby.

10　THE EDITORIAL GAZE AND THE NATURE OF THE WORK

1 Woolf, '[Letter]', p. 325.

2 Foucault, 'What Is an Author?', p. 104.

3 In *Fluid Text* (2001), John Bryant distinguished *œuvre* and *travaille* (*sic*; p. 61), extending earlier thinking about (1) the 'work' done by readers of texts as being construable, in some sense, as part of the *work* in its ordinary sense of *œuvre* (cf. my 'Literary Work of a Readership'); and (2) the revisional work of the author and co-producers that text-as-process insights of the same period engendered (see below, n. 43).

4 The distinction is Nelson Goodman's (*Languages of Art*, chapter 3). Other definitional problems lay in wait for it: silk-screen prints, conceptual art, as well as *arte povera*, found objects, installations, and protest art where commercially printed or manufactured objects deliberately replace hand-made or painted ones.

5 See Runia and van Suchtelen, *Rembrandt in the Mauritshuis*, pp. 40–7.

6 Kemp, 'Looking at Leonardo's *Last Supper*', p. 18.

7 *Ibid.*, p. 20.

8 Pichler, 'Transcriptions', pp. 691, 690.

9 Renear, 'Out of Praxis': discussed in Eggert, '"Work-site"'.

10 Wimsatt and Beardsley, 'Intentional Fallacy', p. 5.

11 Wellek and Warren, 'Mode of Existence', p. 152.

12 *Ibid.*, pp. 155, 156.

13 *Ibid.*, p. 147.

14 Tanselle made intelligent adjustments to the Greg–Bowers approach to allow for the editing of versions of works and for basing an edition upon sources of textual authority other than that of the author. He avoids talk of 'ideal' texts. But his argument that the intended text of the work is historical though unachieved implies ideality: see Eggert, 'Work Unravelled', part of which is adapted here.

15 Hirsch, *Validity in Interpretation*, p. 230.

16 *Ibid.*, p. 218.

17 *Ibid.*, p. 219.

18 *Ibid.*, p. 244.

19 See Tanselle, 'Editorial Problem' (1976), p. 171 and n. 9.

20 Ingarden, *Literary Work*, p. 334.

21 *Ibid.*, p. 336.

22 *Ibid.*, p. 346.

Notes to pages 222–8

23 *Ibid.*, p. 352.

24 *Ibid.*, p. 362.

25 *Ibid.*

26 *Ibid.*, p. 364.

27 Grabowicz (editor and translator of *The Literary Work*) reports that in the Polish revised translation of 1960 Ingarden 'warns that he now questions [the] existence' of ideal concepts; this reflects his 'later commitment to realism' ('Introduction', p. lix).

28 Ingarden, *Literary Work*, p. 364.

29 *Ibid.*, p. 373. Grabowicz – who is very sympathetic to Ingarden's thought – is less circumspect in his averrals that the work is a 'purely intentional formation, "transcendent to all conscious experiences, those of the author as well as those of the reader"' ('Introduction', p. lviii; the last is a quotation from Ingarden's *The Cognition of the Literary Work of Art*, orig. in Polish 1937). When Grabowicz tries to draw out the idea, he states that the work is 'finally an *intersubjective* intentional object [i.e. in relation to all readers] constituted . . . on the basis of a constant and faithful intentional reference to some given real object which is the work of art itself' (p. xxi). The definition is circular, and it leaves aside the question of the way in which the work may be said to be 'given'.

30 Armstrong, *Conflicting Readings*, p. 27.

31 Armstrong, *Politics of Reading*, p. ix.

32 Armstrong, *Conflicting Readings*, p. 38.

33 Steiner, *Heidegger*, p. 33.

34 Heidegger, *Being and Time*, p. 201.

35 Heidegger, 'Origin of the Work', p. 167.

36 Sartre defines as a 'new absolute . . . The age [which] is the intersubjectivity, the living absolute, the dialectical underside of history' ('*What Is Literature?*', p. 241). The link between Barthes and Sartre is made in Bushell, *Text as Process*. She comments that awareness of it 'should cause a re-definition of our understanding of what Barthes means by his title ["The Death of the Author"] and a reminder of the historicized nature of his statement' (chapter 2). I thank Sally Bushell for so kindly making this work available to me prior to its publication.

37 Blanchot, *Space of Literature*, p. 221.

38 Barthes, 'From Work to Text', p. 157.

39 *Ibid.*

40 For process, see Shillingsburg, 'Autonomous Author'; and Cohen and Jackson, 'Emerging Paradigms'. For the linking of texts to their audiences, see McKenzie, *Sociology of Texts*. For meanings in physical documents, see any of the writings of McLeod, e.g. writing as Random Cloud, 'Enter Reader'; and McGann, *Textual Condition*. For electronic editing, see *The Literary Text*, ed. Finneran; and McGann, *Radiant Textuality*.

41 In *Text as Process*, Bushell argues that there is room in Heidegger's thinking to allow such study despite its admitted inauthenticity (see her final chapter).

42 Foucault, 'What Is an Author?', p. 104.

43 E.g. Bryant's *Fluid Text*: his definition of *work* as 'a flow of energy' (p. 61) emerges from a lucid critique of intentionalist (e.g. Tanselle's) and materialist (e.g. McGann's) positions. In both, the work 'is essentially a product or set of products, not a process' (p. 61). The 'ontology of process' revealed by Bryant's notion of fluid text is a deeper principle, he argues, that encompasses the two positions and leaves the editor-critic free to interpret the 'psychological and cultural principles' manifested in acts of revision: these acts are his primary focus (p. 61). However, this promising move leaves unexplained how we shall differentiate one set of energies from another so as to know the boundaries of a work: the documentary principle (as perhaps the yoke required by textual energies?) is given too little weight. Bryant's preparedness to define what he calls revision sites as, in themselves, texts (when they are ordinarily considered only to be text-fragments, p. 103) would require a full-blown redefinition of *text*; and his acknowledgement that 'textual fluidity, paradoxically, does *not* flow' but only 'represents a place in the text where multiple alternative words vie for our attention' (p. 139) reveals as only rhetorical or metaphorical, not ontological, the principle for which he is arguing.

44 McLaverty, 'Mode of Existence' and 'Concept of Authorial Intention'.

45 Shillingsburg, 'Text as Matter', p. 54. In 1997, this essay appeared in slightly revised form in his *Resisting Texts*.

46 *Ibid.*, p. 60.

47 *Ibid.*, p. 51.

48 *Ibid.*, p. 75.

49 *Ibid.*, p. 42.

50 Searle, 'Peirce', p. 724.

51 Cf. Peirce's letter of 23 December 1908 to Lady Welby: a sign is 'anything which is so determined by something else, called its Object, and so determines an effect upon a person, which effect I call its Interpretant, that the latter is thereby mediately determined by the former'. He goes on to say 'My insertion of "upon a person" is a sop to Cerberus, because I despair of making my own broader conception understood': Hardwick, *Correspondence*, pp. 80–1. Gell's account of Peirce in *Art and Agency* appears to depend exclusively on Umberto Eco's account of him. (See further, n. 57, below.) Martens's source (in 'What Is a Text?', pp. 214–15) is given as Köller, 'Der sprachtheoretische Wert'. His invocation of Peirce is nevertheless important in the context of German editorial theory as signalling a possible shift away from reliance on Prague structuralism for a systematic definition of text. See further, Chapter 9.

52 See Peirce, *Collected Papers*, ed. Burks, Hartshorne and Weiss. A scholarly but not complete edition, *Writings of Charles S. Peirce: A Chronological Edition*, gen. ed. Max H. Fisch, is in progress (1982–). For commentaries on Peirce's philosophy, see: Gallie, *Peirce and Pragmatism*; Apel, *Charles S. Peirce*; Hookway, *Peirce*; Keeler and Kloesel, 'Communication, Semiotic Continuity'; and Keeler, 'Iconic Indeterminacy'.

53 Gallie, *Peirce and Pragmatism*, p. 129.

54 Peirce, *Collected Papers*, vol. 6, p. 620. Peirce himself had been a research chemist, and this was undoubtedly the source of his model.

55 Cf. Riddell, 'Hermeneutical Self', p. 86.

56 Peirce, *Collected Papers*, vol. 5, p. 421.

57 In *Art and Agency*, Gell offers suggestions. He specifically excludes written art-forms in his book in order to simplify the complexity of having to model the workings of agency in relation to art objects. According to Gell, idols, for instance, are not important because of what they represent and how the representation links to other representations (which is a view of art-as-text). Rather idols have importance because of what they *do*: that is, what social operations they perform: 'Whenever an event is believed to happen because of an "intention" lodged in the person or thing which initiates the causal sequence, that is an instance of "agency"' (p. 17). The art object is therefore, in Peirce's sense, an *index* of agency. It *points*, but not only at its maker. Artworks are like social agents: they have kinship to one another, can be positioned in a common genealogy and be considered, like persons, as the sum of their relations to one another and as existing in dynamic, unstable flux. 'We can only appreciate it [the artist's *œuvre*, Gell comments] by participating in its unfolding life' (p. 242).

58 *Aesthetic Theory* was collected only after Adorno's death: ed. G. Adorno and Tiedeman. It is partly caught up in Walter Benjamin's broad-brush Marxist rejection of 'the aesthetics of Genius' (p. 244) – the work seen as the reflection of the creative personality. Adorno saw it as a facile explanation of a complex process and Benjamin as a capitalist diversion from the real business of the artist's altering the relations of production. For Adorno, the 'artist's absolute act [of putting pen to paper, brush to canvas] is of minuscule importance' (p. 239). However 'the moment of making or fabrication' is of importance (p. 244) because the artist, at that moment, 'functions as the executor' of the relation between subject and object (p. 238). But Adorno's major interest in art is its potential to help us escape political ideology and social repression: the rise of fascism and the failure of Marxism deeply affected his thinking.

59 Adorno, *Negative Dialectics*, p. 186.

60 Buck-Morss, *Origin of Negative Dialectics*, p. 88.

61 As Adorno once famously said: 'History is in the truth; the truth is not in history': quoted in Buck-Morss, *Origin of Negative Dialectics*, p. 46. Adorno did not invent the notion of negative dialectic: it goes back to Socrates and early Plato.

62 Similarly, cultural objects, as objects, need the potential to be read meaningfully as such. Witness the misread gifts offered and received in early encounters between European sailors and native peoples in the Pacific islands: see further, Thomas, *Entangled Objects*.

63 As opposed to *deduction* (from, say, a law of nature) or *induction* (from a study of many similar examples), abduction is an empirical inference that

may lead to conclusions confirmed in practice. It is thrifty in that it constrains the production of an indefinitely large number of logically alternative explanations.

64 In 1991 ('Text as Matter') and in 1997 in a more developed way in *Resisting Texts*, Shillingsburg draws on J. L. Austin and later writings by John R. Searle. When speaker and listener are tethered to the same moment and place, the communicated meaning of a speech is not necessarily the same as the words would have on another occasion. But communication can happen successfully partly because of the shared contexts present to both parties. So, for Searle, *sentence* (the sequence of words) is iterable whereas *utterance* (the intended, shared meaning) is not. Shillingsburg adapts Searle's distinction to written works. Publication becomes a form of utterance: production of a book, say, 'always takes sentence, as originated by an author, and re-utters it in a new form' (*Resisting Texts*, p. 155). Hence the situation where 'One "sentence" stands as witness to multiple utterances' (*ibid.*, p. 157). But treating text as utterance (e.g. 'Material Texts are the production of Utterance': 'Text as Matter', p. 55) tends to reify it as something complete, despite the fact that the speech-act theory is an explanation of very short utterances, not extended ones. Cf. McKenzie: 'The ostensible unity of any one "contained" text . . . is an illusion': *Sociology of Texts*, p. 50.

65 So now we can say that the version as a conceptual entity (in Shillingsburg's taxonomy) cannot exist in the mind in complete form as such, but the *idea* of it certainly can: in fact, the idea of it needs to if we are to get very far with our editorial practice. Similarly, we can say that neither a Material Text nor a Conceptual Text exists as such, because both experiences weave in and around one another constantly as we read the document. But the terms themselves, as placeholders, may enable us to make useful distinctions about the meanings we experience and about what aspects of the life of the work our editions are aiming to capture or to ignore.

66 Taylor, 'End of Editing', p. 133.

67 Ruskin, 'Lamp of Memory', p. 358.

Bibliography

Scholarly editions of works are listed by author. Essays in collections are listed individually; but where it has been necessary to cite collections of essays as a whole, they appear alphabetically by title.

Adorno, Theodor, *Negative Dialectics*, tr. E. B. Ashton (1966; New York: Seabury Press, 1973)

    Aesthetic Theory, ed. Gretel Adorno and Rolf Tiedemann, tr. C. Lenhardt (1970; London: Routledge and Kegan Paul, 1984)

Allingham, Anne, 'Challenging the Editing of the Rachel Henning Letters', *Australian Literary Studies*, 16 (1994), 262–79

A.M.A., [Review of *The Boy in the Bush*], *Liverpool Post*, 1 October 1924

Amory, Hugh, [Review of *The Life and Work of Fredson Bowers* by G. Thomas Tanselle], *TEXT*, 9 (1996), 466–74

Anon., *Brodsworth Hall* (n.p.: English Heritage, 1995)

Anon., *Brodsworth Hall and Gardens* (1995; rev. edn: n.p.: English Heritage, 2000)

Anon., 'Mawson's Huts Rescue Team's Work Snowed Under', *Canberra Times*, 4 November 2006, p. 14

Anon., [Review of *The Boy in the Bush*], *Onlooker* (Perth), 15 January 1925, p. 11

Anon., [Untitled comment on *The Boy in the Bush*], *Star* (Auckland), 29 November 1924, p. 18

Anon., '"Y'Self is God!": A Literary Slander on Australia' [Review of *The Boy in the Bush*], *Life* (Melbourne), 1 January 1925, pp. 22–4

Apel, Karl-Otto, *Charles S. Peirce: From Pragmatism to Pragmaticism* (Amherst: University of Massachusetts Press, 1981)

Appearance, Opinion, Change: Evaluating the Look of Paintings, ed. Peter Booth *et al.* (London: United Kingdom Institute for Conservation, 1990)

Armstrong, Paul B., *Conflicting Readings: Variety and Validity in Interpretation* (Chapel Hill: University of North Carolina Press, 1990)

    Play and the Politics of Reading: The Social Uses of Modernist Form (Ithaca: Cornell University Press, 2005)

Arnold, Bruce, *The Scandal of Ulysses* (London: Sinclair-Stevenson, 1991)

Australian Plays for the Colonial Stage 1834–1899, ed. Richard Fotheringham. The Academy Editions of Australian Literature (St Lucia: University of Queensland Press, 2006)

Barcilon, Pinin Brambilla, 'The Restoration', in Barcilon and Pietro C. Marani, *Leonardo: The Last Supper*, tr. Harlow Tighe (Chicago: University of Chicago Press, 2001), pp. 327–430

Barker, Nicolas, 'The Forgery of Printed Documents', in *Forged Documents: Proceedings of the 1989 Houston Conference Organized by the University of Houston Libraries*, ed. Pat Bozeman (New Castle, Del.: Oak Knoll, 1990), pp. 7–18

Barnet, Peter, and Nancy Wu, *The Cloisters: Medieval Art and Architecture* (New York: Metropolitan Museum of Art; New Haven: Yale University Press, 2005)

Barthes, Roland, 'From Work to Text', in Roland Barthes, *Image Music Text*, tr. Stephen Heath (New York: Hill and Wang, 1977), pp. 155–64

Bateson, F. W., 'The Function of Criticism at the Present Time', *Essays in Criticism*, 3 (1953), 1–27

Beck, James, with Michael Daley, *Art Restoration: The Culture, the Business and the Scandal* (1993; enlarged edition New York: Norton, 1996)

Benjamin, Walter, 'The Work of Art in the Age of Mechanical Reproduction', in Walter Benjamin, *Illuminations*, ed. Hannah Arendt, tr. Harry Zohn (1970; London: Fontana, 1992), pp. 211–44

Bergdoll, Barry, 'Introduction', in Eugène-Emmanuel Viollet-le-Duc, *The Foundations of Architecture: Selections from the Dictionnaire raisonné*, ed. Bergdoll, tr. Kenneth D. Whitehead (New York: George Braziller, 1990), pp. 1–30

Berthoud, Roger, *The Life of Henry Moore* (London: Faber, 1987)

Blake, William, *Complete Writings with Variant Readings*, ed. Geoffrey Keynes (1966; London: Oxford University Press, 1972)

Blanchot, Maurice, *The Space of Literature*, tr. Ann Smock (1955; Lincoln: University of Nebraska Press, 1989)

Blankert, Albert, 'Looking at Rembrandt, Past and Present', in *Rembrandt: A Genius and his Impact*, ed. Blankert (Melbourne: National Gallery of Victoria, 1997), pp. 32–57

Blayney, Peter W. M., 'The Publication of Playbooks', in *A New History of Early English Drama*, ed. John D. Cox and David Scott Kastan (New York: Columbia University Press, 1997), pp. 383–422

Blokhuis, Marleen, 'On the Life of Rembrandt van Rijn 1606–1669', in *Rembrandt: A Genius and his Impact*, ed. Albert Blankert (Melbourne: National Gallery of Victoria, 1997), pp. 22–31

Bodkin, Thomas, 'Johannes Vermeer of Delft', in *The Paintings of Jan Vermeer* (New York: Oxford University Press, 1940), pp. 3–11

Boldrewood, Rolf [Thomas A. Browne], Diary for 1879. Mitchell Library, State Library of New South Wales, MSS 1444/2

   Robbery Under Arms (1882–83), ed. Paul Eggert and Elizabeth Webby. The Academy Editions of Australian Literature (St Lucia: University of Queensland Press, 2006)

Bomford, David, 'Rembrandt and Pentimenti', conf. paper, 'Rembrandt: A Genius and his Impact' conference, Melbourne, 1997

Bomford, David, Christopher Brown and Ashok Roy, *Art in the Making: Rembrandt* (London: National Gallery, 1988)

Bornstein, George, *Material Modernism: The Politics of the Page* (Cambridge: Cambridge University Press, 2001)

Bowers, Fredson, *Textual and Literary Criticism* (Cambridge: Cambridge University Press, 1966)

'Textual Criticism', in *A Shakespeare Encyclopaedia*, ed. Oscar James Campbell and Edward G. Quinn (London: Methuen, 1966), pp. 864–9

'Multiple Authority: New Problems and Concepts of Copy-Text', *The Library*, 5th ser., 27 (1972), 81–115

Brand, Stewart, *How Buildings Learn: What Happens after They're Built* (1994; rev. edn: London: Phoenix Illustrated, 1997)

Broadbent, James, 'Past Imperfect', *Vogue Living*, August 1986, p. 152

The Australian Colonial House: Architecture and Society in New South Wales 1788–1842 (Pott's Point, NSW: Hordern House in association with the Historic Houses Trust of New South Wales, 1997)

Brockbank, Philip, 'Towards a Mobile Text', in *The Theory and Practice of Text-Editing: Essays in Honour of James T. Boulton*, ed. Ian Small and Marcus Walsh (Cambridge: Cambridge University Press, 1991), pp. 90–106

Brodhead, Richard H., 'The "New" *Sister Carrie*' [Review of the Pennsylvania Edition of Theodore Dreiser's *Sister Carrie*], *Yale Review*, 71 (1982), 597–600

Bruccoli, Matthew, 'A Few Missing Words', *PMLA*, 86 (1971), 587–9

Bruyn, J., B. Haak, S. H. Levie and P. J. J. van Thiel, 'The Rembrandt Research Project' [Letter], *Burlington Magazine*, 135, no. 1081 (April 1993), p. 279

Bryant, John, *The Fluid Text: A Theory of Revision and Editing for Book and Screen* (Ann Arbor: University of Michigan Press, 2002)

Buck-Morss, Susan, *The Origin of Negative Dialectics* (Hassocks, Sussex: Harvester, 1977)

Burrow, J. W., 'The Sense of the Past', in *The Context of English Literature: The Victorians*, ed. Laurence Lerner (London: Methuen, 1978), pp. 120–38

Bushell, Sally, *Text as Process: Creative Composition in Wordsworth, Tennyson and Dickinson* (Charlottesville: University of Virginia Press, forthcoming)

Button, James, 'The Struggle for a United Kingdom', *Sydney Morning Herald*, 9–10 December 2006, p. 31

Byron, Lord, *Childe Harold's Pilgrimage*, in *Complete Poetical Works*, ed. Jerome J. McGann, vol. 2 (Oxford: Clarendon Press, 1980)

Carr-Whitworth, Caroline, 'Remembrance of Things Past', *Conservation Bulletin*, November 1995, 3–4

Carter, John, and Graham Pollard, *An Enquiry into the Nature of Certain Nineteenth Century Pamphlets* (London: Constable, 1934)

Cervenka, Miroslav, 'Textual Criticism and Semiotics', in *Contemporary German Editorial Theory*, ed. Hans Walter Gabler, George Bornstein and Gillian Borland Pierce (Ann Arbor: University of Michigan Press, 1995), pp. 59–77

Chamberlin, E. R., *Preserving the Past* (London: Dent, 1979)

Chartier, Roger, 'The Text between the Voice and the Book', in *Voice, Text, Hypertext: Emerging Practices in Textual Studies*, ed. Raimonda Modiano,

Leroy F. Searle and Peter Shillingsburg (Seattle: University of Washington Press, 2004), pp. 54–71

[Child, Harold], [Anonymous review of *The Boy in the Bush*], *Times Literary Supplement*, 28 August 1924, p. 523

Clanchy, M. T., *From Memory to Written Record: England 1066–1307* (Cambridge, Mass.: Harvard University Press, 1979)

Clarke, Marcus, *His Natural Life*, ed. Lurline Stuart. The Academy Editions of Australian Literature (St Lucia: University of Queensland Press, 2001)

'Cloud, Random' [McLeod, Randall], 'Enter Reader', in *The Editorial Gaze: Mediating Texts in Literature and the Arts*, ed. Paul Eggert and Margaret Sankey (New York: Garland, 1998), pp. 3–50

Cohen, Philip, and David H. Jackson, 'Notes on Emerging Paradigms in Editorial Theory', in *Devils and Angels: Textual Editing and Literary Theory*, ed. Philip G. Cohen (Charlottesville: University Press of Virginia, 1991), pp. 103–23

Colalucci, Gianluigi, 'The Technique of the Sistine Ceiling Frescoes', in *The Sistine Chapel: A Glorious Restoration*, ed. Pierluigi de Vecchi (1992; English-language edn New York: Harry N. Abrams, 1994), pp. 26–45

Coleridge, S. T., *Poetical Works*, 6 vols: *Poems (Reading Text)*, *Poems (Variorum Text)* and *Plays*, ed. J. C. C. Mays. The Collected Works of Samuel Taylor Coleridge (Princeton: Princeton University Press, 2001)

Collins, John, *The Two Forgers: A Biography of Harry Buxton Forman and Thomas James Wise* (New Castle, Del.: Oak Knoll, 1992)

Collins, Joseph, 'Even Yet It Can't Be Told: The Whole Truth about D. H. Lawrence', in *The Doctor Looks at Literature: Psychological Studies of Life and Letters* (New York: Doran, 1923), pp. 256–88

Contemporary German Editorial Theory, ed. Hans Walter Gabler, George Bornstein and Gillian Borland Pierce (Ann Arbor: University of Michigan Press, 1995)

Corpus of Rembrandt Paintings, A. Vols. 1–3, ed. J. Bruyn, B. Haak, S. H. Levie, P. J. J. van Thiel and Ernst van der Wetering, tr. D. Cook-Radmore (The Hague: Stichting Foundation Rembrandt Research Project, 1982–89). Vol. 4 (*The Self-Portraits*), ed. Ernst van der Wetering, tr. Jennifer Killian *et al.* (Dordrecht: Springer, 2005)

Cruikshank, Dan, 'Rebuilding Uppark', *Country Life*, 18 January 1990, pp. 56–7

Danto, Arthur C., *The Transfiguration of the Commonplace: A Philosophy of Art* (Cambridge, Mass.: Harvard University Press, 1981)

'Gettysburg', in *Philosophizing Art: Selected Essays* (Berkeley: University of California Press, 1999), pp. 233–50

de Biasi, Pierre-Marc, 'What Is a Literary Draft? Toward a Functional Typology of Genetic Documentation', *Yale French Studies 89: Drafts* (1996), 26–58

de Grazia, Margreta, 'The Essential Shakespeare and the Material Book', *Textual Practice*, 2 (1988), 69–86

Shakespeare Verbatim: The Reproduction of Authenticity and the 1790 Apparatus (Oxford: Clarendon Press, 1991) de Grazia, Margreta, and Peter Stallybrass, 'The Materiality of the Shakespearean Text', *Shakespeare Quarterly*, 44 (1993), 255–83

Dellheim, Charles, *The Face of the Past: The Preservation of the Medieval Inheritance in Victorian England* (Cambridge: Cambridge University Press, 1982)

Demidenko, Helen [Helen Darville], *The Hand that Signed the Paper* (St Leonards, NSW: Allen and Unwin, 1994)

Dennis, George, *Cities and Cemeteries of Etruria* (1848; 2nd edn London: J. Murray, 1878)

Derrida, Jacques, 'Parergon', in *The Truth in Painting*, tr. Geoff Bennington and Ian McLeod (Chicago: University of Chicago Press, 1987), pp. 15–147

Dillon, Janette, 'Is There a Performance in This Text?', *Shakespeare Quarterly*, 45 (1994), 74–86

Dreiser, Theodore, *Sister Carrie*, ed. James L. W. West III (Philadelphia: University of Pennsylvania Press, 1981)

Drew, Stephen, *Principles of Self-Knowledge: or, an Attempt to Demonstrate the Truth of Christianity, and the Efficacy of Experimental Religion, against the Cavils of the Infidel, and the Objections of the Formalist*, 2 vols. (London: Longman, 1828)

Dutton, Denis, 'Editor's Preface', in *The Forger's Art: Forgery and the Philosophy of Art* (Berkeley: University of California Press, 1983), pp. vii–x

Eagle, Mary, 'Sightings', in *The Articulate Surface: Dialogues on Paintings between Conservators, Curators and Art Historians*, ed. Sue-Anne Wallace (Canberra: Humanities Research Centre and National Gallery of Australia, 1996), pp. 31–7

Eggert, Paul, 'The Literary Work of a Readership: *The Boy in the Bush* in Australia 1924–1926', *Bibliographical Society of Australia and New Zealand Bulletin*, 12 (1988), 149–66. Rpt. in part in *The Reception of D. H. Lawrence around the World*, ed. Takeo Iida (Fukuoka: Kyushu University Press, 1999), pp. 209–32

'Textual Product or Textual Process: Procedures and Assumptions of Critical Editing', in *Editing in Australia*, ed. Paul Eggert (Canberra: English Department, University College ADFA, 1990), pp. 19–40. Rpt. in *Devils and Angels: Textual Editing and Literary Theory*, ed. Philip G. Cohen (Charlottesville: University Press of Virginia, 1991), pp. 57–77

'Authenticity and Forgery: "This Branch of Human Wickedness"', *Bibliographical Society of Australia and New Zealand Bulletin*, 15 (1991), 5–10

'Dealings with the Firm of Greg and Bowers: A Tribute to the Work of Fredson Bowers, 1905–1991', *Bibliographical Society of Australia and New Zealand Bulletin*, 15 (1991), 73–87

'Document or Process as the Site of Authority: Establishing Chronology of Revision in Competing Typescripts of Lawrence's *The Boy in the Bush*', *Studies in Bibliography*, 44 (1991), 364–76

'Document and Text: The "Life" of the Literary Work and the Capacities of Editing', *TEXT*, 7 (1994), 1–24

'Editing Paintings/Conserving Literature: The Nature of the "Work"', *Studies in Bibliography*, 47 (1994), 65–78

'A Cautionary Tale: Stop-Press Correction in *The Recollections of Geoffry Hamlyn* (1859)', *Bibliographical Society of Australia and New Zealand Bulletin*, 19 (1995), 267–70

(with Kym McCauley) 'Critical and Scholarly Editing in Australia and New Zealand in the Last Twenty-five Years: An Essay on the Nomenclature of Editions and a Representative Listing', *Bibliographical Society of Australia and New Zealand Bulletin*, 19 (1995), 241–55

'Making Sense of Multiple Authorship', *TEXT*, 8 (1995), 305–23

'Reading a Critical Edition with the Grain and Against: The Cambridge D. H. Lawrence', in *Editing D. H. Lawrence: New Versions of a Modern Author*, ed. Charles L. Ross and Dennis Jackson (Ann Arbor: University of Michigan Press, 1995), pp. 27–40

'The Shadow across the Text: New Bearings on German Editing', *TEXT*, 11 (1998), 311–24

'The Work Unravelled', *TEXT*, 11 (1998), 41–60

'Where Are We Now with Authorship and the Work?' *Yearbook of English Studies*, 29 (1999), 88–102

'The Biographical Issue: Lives of Lawrence', *The Cambridge Companion to D. H. Lawrence*, ed. Anne Fernihough (Cambridge: Cambridge University Press, 2001), pp. 157–77

'Why Critical Editing Matters: Responsible Texts and Australian Reviewers', *English Studies in Canada*, 27 (2001), 179–204

'The Golden Stain of Time: Editorial Theory and Historic Houses', *Books and Bibliography: Essays in Commemoration of Don McKenzie*, ed. John Thomson (Wellington: Victoria University Press, 2002), pp. 116–28

'These Post-philological Days . . .', *TEXT*, 15 (2003), 323–36; rpt. with 'Postscript (late 2005): Signs of the Times, Signs of the Future', *ecdotica*, 2 (2005), 80–98

'Autorität des Textes oder Autorisation: Die postkoloniale Adaptation herkömmlicher Editionsverfahren für *Robbery Under Arms*', *editio* special issue, 21 (2004), 315–24

'The Way of All Text: The Materialist Shakespeare', in *Voice, Text, Hypertext: Emerging Practices in Textual Studies*, ed. Raimonda Modiano, Leroy F. Searle and Peter Shillingsburg (Seattle: University of Washington Press, 2004), pp. 162–76

'Text-encoding, Theories of the Text and the "Work-site"', *Literary and Linguistic Computing*, 20 (2005), 425–35

'Version – Agency – Intention: The Cross-fertilising of German and Anglo-American Editorial Traditions', *Variants: Journal of the European Society for Textual Scholarship*, 4 (2005), 5–28

'The Conservator's Gaze and the Nature of the Work', *Library Trends*, 56 (2007), 80–106

Emerson, Ralph Waldo, *The Journals and Miscellaneous Notebooks of Ralph Waldo Emerson*, ed. William H. Gilman, Alfred R. Ferguson, Merrell R. Davis, Merton M. Sealts, Jr. and Harrison Hayford, 16 vols. (Cambridge, Mass.: Belknap Press of Harvard University Press, 1960–82)

Erne, Lukas, *Shakespeare as Literary Dramatist* (Cambridge: Cambridge University Press, 2003)

Ernst, Wolfgang, 'Framing the Fragment: Archaeology, Art, Museum', in *The Rhetoric of the Frame: Essays on the Boundaries of the Artwork*, ed. Paul Duro (Cambridge: Cambridge University Press, 1996), pp. 111–35

Ferrer, Daniel, 'Production, Invention, and Reproduction: Genetic vs. Textual Criticism', in *Reimagining Textuality: Textual Studies in the Late Age of Print*, ed. Elizabeth Bergmann Loizeaux and Neil Fraistat (Madison: University of Wisconsin Press, 2002), pp. 48–59

Fish, Stanley, *Is There a Text in This Class? The Authority of Interpretive Communities* (Cambridge, Mass.: Harvard University Press, 1980)

  Doing What Comes Naturally: Change, Rhetoric and the Practice of Theory in Literary and Legal Studies (Durham, NC: Duke University Press, 1989)

Fisher, John H., 'The MLA Editions of Major American Authors', in Modern Language Association, *Professional Standards and American Editions: A Response to Edmund Wilson* (New York: MLA, 1969), pp. 20–6

Fitzgerald, F. Scott, *Trimalchio: An Early Version of The Great Gatsby*, ed. James L. W. West III (Cambridge: Cambridge University Press, 2000)

Forster, Kurt W., 'Monument/Memory and the Mortality of Architecture', *Oppositions: A Journal for Ideas and Criticism in Architecture*, 25 (Fall 1982), 2–19

Foucault, Michel, 'What Is an Author?' (1969, in English 1979), and selections from *Discipline and Punish*, in *The Foucault Reader*, ed. Paul Rabinow (London: Penguin, 1986), pp. 101–20, 170–238

Freehafer, John, 'How Not To Edit American Authors: Some Shortcomings of the CEAA Editions', *Bulletin of the New York Public Library*, 75 (1971), 419–23

Gabler, Hans Walter, 'The Synchrony and Diachrony of Texts: Practice and Theory of the Critical Edition of James Joyce's *Ulysses*', *TEXT*, 1 (1984), 305–26

  'The Editor Reviews the Reviewers', conf. paper, 11th International James Joyce Symposium, Venice, 1988

  'A Response to: John Kidd, "Errors of Execution in the 1984 *Ulysses*"', *Studies in the Novel*, 22 (1990), 250–6

  'Textual Studies and Criticism', in *Editing in Australia*, ed. Paul Eggert (Canberra: English Department, University College ADFA, 1990), pp. 1–18

  'What *Ulysses* Requires', *Papers of the Bibliographical Society of America*, 87 (1993), 187–248

  'Genetic Texts – Genetic Editions – Genetic Criticism; or, Towards Discoursing the Genetics of Writing', in *editio*, 14, special issue *Problems of Editing*, ed. Christa Jansohn (Tübingen: Max Niemeyer, 1999), pp. 59–68

  'Textual Criticism', in *The Johns Hopkins Guide to Literary Theory and Criticism*, 2nd edn, ed. Michael Groden, Martin Kreiswirth and Imre Szeman (Baltimore: Johns Hopkins University Press, 2005), pp. 901–9

Gadamer, Hans-Georg, *Truth and Method* (1965; London: Sheed and Ward, 1979)

Gallie, W. B., *Peirce and Pragmatism* (Harmondsworth: Pelican, 1952)

Gaskell, Philip, *A New Introduction to Bibliography* (Oxford: Clarendon Press, 1972)

From Writer to Reader: Studies in Editorial Method (Oxford: Clarendon Press, 1978)

Gell, Alfred, *Art and Agency: An Anthropological Theory* (Oxford: Clarendon Press, 1998)

Gettmann, Royal A., *A Victorian Publisher: A Study of the Bentley Papers* (Cambridge: Cambridge University Press, 1960)

Gilmore, Mary, *The Collected Verse of Mary Gilmore*, 2 vols., ed. Jennifer Strauss. The Academy Editions of Australian Literature (St Lucia: University of Queensland Press): vol. 1 *1887–1929* (2004); vol. 2 *1930–1962* (2007)

Glassie, Henry, *Pattern in the Material Folk Culture of the Eastern United States* (1968; Philadelphia: University of Pennsylvania Press, 1980)

Golvan, Colin, and Michael McDonald, *Writers and the Law* (Sydney: Law Book Company, 1986)

Goodman, Nelson, *Languages of Art: An Approach to a Theory of Symbols* (Indianapolis: Bobbs-Merrill, 1968)

[Reply to Barbara Herrnstein Smith], *Journal of Philosophy*, 67 (1970), 570–3

Goodwin, Rutherfoord, *A Brief and True Report Concerning Williamsburg in Virginia: Being an Account of the Most Important Occurrences in that Place from its First Beginning to the Present Time . . .* (1941; 3rd edn Williamsburg: Colonial Williamsburg Foundation, 1972)

Grabowicz, George G., 'Translator's Introduction', in Roman Ingarden, *The Literary Work of Art: An Investigation on the Borderlines of Ontology, Logic and Theory of Literature*, tr. George G. Grabowicz (1931; Evanston, Ill.: Northwestern University Press, 1973), pp. xlv–lxx

Greer, Germaine, 'Selling Off the Dreaming', *Sydney Morning Herald*, 6 December 1997, Spectrum p. 5s

Greetham, D. C., *Theories of the Text* (Oxford: Oxford University Press, 1999)
'Philology Redux?', *ecdotica*, 3 (2006), 103–27

Greg, W. W., 'The Rationale of Copy-Text', *Studies in Bibliography*, 3 (1950), 19–36
The Shakespeare First Folio: Its Bibliographical and Textual History (Oxford: Clarendon Press, 1955)

Grésillon, Almuth, *Éléments de critique génétique: lire les manuscrits modernes* (Paris: Presses Universitaires de France, 1994)

Griffiths, Tom, *Hunters and Collectors: The Antiquarian Imagination in Australia* (Melbourne: Cambridge University Press, 1996)

Grigely, Joseph, *Textualterity: Art, Theory and Textual Criticism* (Ann Arbor: University of Michigan Press, 1995)

Gurr, Andrew, 'Maximal and Minimal Texts: Shakespeare v. the Globe', *Shakespeare Survey*, 52 (1999), 68–87

Handler, Richard, and Eric Gable, *The New History in an Old Museum: Creating the Past at Colonial Williamsburg* (Durham, NC: Duke University Press, 1997)

Hardwick, C. S., *Semiotic and Significs: The Correspondence between Charles S. Peirce and Victoria Lady Welby* (Bloomington: Indiana University Press, 1977)

Hardy, Thomas, *Tess of the D'Urbervilles*, ed. Juliet Grindle and Simon Gattrell (Oxford: Clarendon Press, 1983)

Harvey, John, *Cathedrals of England and Wales* (1950; 2nd edn London: Batsford, 1956)

Hay, Louis, 'Genetic Editing, Past and Future: A Few Reflections by a User', *TEXT*, 3 (1987), 117–33

Haywood, Ian, *Faking It: Art and the Politics of Forgery* (Brighton: Harvester, 1987)

Hedley, Gerry, 'Long Lost Relations and New Found Relativities: Issues in the Cleaning of Paintings', in *Shared Responsibility: Proceedings of a Seminar for Curators and Conservators*, ed. Barbara A. Ramsay-Jolicoeur and Ian N. M. Wainwright (Ottawa: National Gallery of Canada, 1990), pp. 159–69

Heidegger, Martin, 'The Origin of the Work of Art', in *Basic Writings: From Being and Time (1927) to The Task of Thinking (1964)*, ed. David Farrell Krell (San Francisco: Harper and Row, 1993), pp. 143–87

Being and Time: A Translation of Sein und Zeit, tr. Joan Stambaugh (Albany: State University of New York Press, 1996)

Heyward, Michael, *The Ern Malley Affair* (St Lucia: University of Queensland Press, 1993)

Hill, W. Speed, 'The Ironies of Paternity' [Review of G. Thomas Tanselle, *The Life and Works of Fredson Bowers*], *Documentary Editing*, 16 (1994), 29–33

Hirsch, E. D., *Validity in Interpretation* (New Haven: Yale University Press, 1967)

Hogarth, William, *The Analysis of Beauty: Written with a View of Fixing the Fluctuating Ideas of Taste* (London: J. Reeves for the Author, 1753)

Holdeman, David, *'Much Labouring': The Texts and Authors of Yeats's First Modernist Books* (Ann Arbor: University of Michigan Press, 1997)

Holderness, Graham, Bryan Loughrey and Andrew Murphy, '"What's the matter?" Shakespeare and Textual Theory', *Textual Practice*, 9 (1995), 93–119

Home, R. W., 'Humboldtian Science Revisited: An Australian Case Study', *History of Science*, 33 (1995), 1–22

'A Botanist for a Continent: Ferdinand von Mueller (1825–96)', *Endeavour*, 22 (1998), 72–5

Hookway, Christopher, *Peirce* (London: Routledge and Kegan Paul, 1985)

Howard-Hill, T. H., 'The Dangers of Editing, or, the Death of the Editor', in *The Editorial Gaze: Mediating Texts in Literature and the Arts*, ed. Paul Eggert and Margaret Sankey (New York: Garland, 1998), pp. 51–66

'"Nor Stage, nor Stationers Stall can Showe": The Circulation of Plays in Manuscript in the Early Seventeenth Century', *Book History*, 2 (1999), 28–41

'Early Modern Printers and the Standardization of English Spelling', *Modern Language Review*, 101 no. 1 (2006), 16–29

Hurlebusch, Klaus, 'Conceptualisations for Procedures of Authorship', *Studies in Bibliography*, 41 (1988), 100–35

Hyde Park Barracks, ed. Lynn Collins (Sydney: Historic Houses Trust, 1994)

Hyde Park Barracks Museum Plan: Incorporating Analysis and Guidelines on Conservation, Interpretation and Management (Sydney: Historic Houses Trust, 1990)

Ingarden, Roman, *The Literary Work of Art: An Investigation on the Borderlines of Ontology, Logic and Theory of Literature*, tr. George G. Grabowicz (1931; Evanston, Ill.: Northwestern University Press, 1973)

Inglis, K. S., *Sacred Places: War Memorials in the Australian Landscape* (Carlton South, Vic.: Melbourne University Press, 1998)

Ioppolo, Grace, *Revising Shakespeare* (Cambridge, Mass.: Harvard University Press, 1991)

Iser, Wolfgang, 'The Reading Process: A Phenomenological Approach', *New Literary History*, 3 (1972), rept. in *Modern Criticism and Theory: A Reader*, ed. David Lodge (London: Longman, 1988), pp. 212–28

    The Act of Reading: A Theory of Aesthetic Response (1976; Baltimore: Johns Hopkins University Press, 1978)

Jensen, Hal, 'Books Do Furnish a Self' [Review of Harold Bloom, *How To Read and Why*], *Times Literary Supplement*, 1 September 2000, pp. 5–6

Jonson, Ben, *Jonson's 'Masque of Gipsies' in the Burley, Belvoir and Windsor Versions: An Attempt at Reconstruction*, ed. W. W. Greg (London: Oxford University Press for the British Academy, 1952)

Joyce, James, *Ulysses: A Critical and Synoptic Edition*, ed. Hans Walter Gabler, 3 vols. (New York: Garland, 1984)

    Ulysses, ed. Danis Rose (London: Picador, 1997)

Kant, Immanuel, *Critique of the Power of Judgment* (1790), ed. Paul Guyer, tr. Paul Guyer and Eric Matthews (Cambridge: Cambridge University Press, 2000)

Keeler, Mary, 'Iconic Indeterminacy and Human Creativity in C. S. Peirce's Manuscripts', in *The Iconic Page in Manuscript, Print and Digital Culture*, ed. George Bornstein (Ann Arbor: University of Michigan Press, 1998), pp. 157–94

Keeler, Mary, and Christian Kloesel, 'Communication, Semiotic Continuity, and the Margins of the Peircean Text', in *Margins of the Text*, ed. D. C. Greetham (Ann Arbor: University of Michigan Press, 1996), pp. 269–322

Kemp, Martin, 'Looking at Leonardo's *Last Supper*', in *Appearance, Opinion, Change: Evaluating the Look of Paintings*, ed. Peter Booth *et al.* (London: United Kingdom Institute for Conservation, 1990), pp. 14–21

Kidd, John, 'An Inquiry into *Ulysses: The Corrected Text*', *Papers of the Bibliographical Society of America*, 82 (1988), 411–584

    'The Scandal of *Ulysses*', *New York Review of Books*, 30 June 1988, pp. 32–9

Kiernan, Brian, 'White Elephants' [Review of the Academy Editions of Henry Kingsley, *The Recollections of Geoffry Hamlyn*, Henry Handel Richardson, *Maurice Guest* and *The Journal of Annie Baxter Dawbin 1858–1868*], *Overland*, 155 (1999), 105–7

Kingsley, Henry, *Henry Kingsley*, ed. Stanton Mellick. Portable Australian Authors series (St Lucia: University of Queensland Press, 1982)

    The Recollections of Geoffry Hamlyn (1935); with introduction by Susan K. Martin (Sydney: Angus and Robertson, 1993)

The Recollections of Geoffry Hamlyn, ed. Stanton Mellick, Patrick Morgan and Paul Eggert. The Academy Editions of Australian Literature (St Lucia: University of Queensland Press, 1996)

Kirsop, Wallace, 'Fredson Bowers and the French Connection', *TEXT*, 8 (1996), 53–66

Kline, Mary-Jo, *A Guide to Documentary Editing* (Baltimore: Johns Hopkins University Press, 1987; 2nd edn 1998)

Köller, W., 'Der sprachtheoretische Wert des semiotischen Zeichenmodells', in *Zeichen, Text, Sinn: Zur Semiotik des literarischen Verstehens*, ed. K. H. Spinner (Göttingen: Vandenhoeck and Ruprecht, 1977), pp. 7–77

Koningsberger, Hans, 'A Forger's Postscript to Vermeer', in Koningsberger and the editors of Time-Life Books, *The World of Vermeer 1632–1675* (rev. edn; New York: Time Inc., 1968), pp. 174–85

Kraaijpoel, D., and H. van Wijnen, *Han van Meegeren 1889–1947* (Zwolle: Waanders Uitgevers, 1996)

Lawrence, D. H., 'Song of a Man Who Has Come Through', in *Look, We Have Come Through!* (London: Chatto and Windus, 1917)

Sons and Lovers, ed. Helen Baron and Carl Baron. The Works of D. H. Lawrence (Cambridge: Cambridge University Press, 1992)

The First and Second Lady Chatterley Novels, ed. Dieter Mehl and Christa Jansohn. The Works of D. H. Lawrence (Cambridge: Cambridge University Press, 1999)

Lawrence, D. H., and M. L. Skinner, *The Boy in the Bush*, ed. Paul Eggert. The Works of D. H. Lawrence (Cambridge: Cambridge University Press, 1990)

Leavis, F. R., 'The Responsible Critic: Or the Function of Criticism at Any Time', *Scrutiny*, 19 (1952–53), 162–83

A Selection from Scrutiny, 2 vols. (Cambridge: Cambridge University Press, 1968)

Lendon, Nigel, 'A Narrative in Paint', in *The Painters of the Wagilag Sisters Story 1937–1997*, ed. Wally Caruana and Nigel Lendon (Canberra: National Gallery of Australia, 1997), pp. 20–37

Lessing, Alfred, 'What Is Wrong with a Forgery?', in *The Forger's Art: Forgery and the Philosophy of Art*, ed. Denis Dutton (Berkeley: University of California Press, 1983), pp. 58–76

Levine, Joseph M., '"Et Tu Brute?": History and Forgery in 18th-century England', in *Fakes and Frauds: Varieties of Deception in Print and Manuscript*, ed. Robin Myers and Michael Harris (Winchester: St Paul's Bibliographies, 1989), pp. 71–97

Lingeman, Richard, 'Sister Carrie's Chaperones' [Review of the Pennsylvania Edition of Theodore Dreiser's *Sister Carrie*], *Nation*, 11–18 July 1981, pp. 53–7

Lowenthal, David, *The Past Is a Foreign Country* (Cambridge: Cambridge University Press, 1985)

McDonell, Jennifer A., 'The Exhibit: Robert Browning's *The Ring and the Book* and Nineteenth-Century Archaeology', *Australasian Historical Archaeology*, 11 (1993), 21–7

McGann, Jerome J., '*Ulysses* as a Postmodern Text: The Gabler Edition', *Criticism*, 27 (1985), 283–305

'Theory of Texts' [Review of D. F. McKenzie's, *Bibliography and the Sociology of Texts*], *London Review of Books*, 18 February 1988, pp. 20–1

The Textual Condition (Princeton: Princeton University Press, 1991)

Radiant Textuality: Literature after the World Wide Web (New York: Palgrave, 2001)

McGirk, Tim, 'Cult Looks Again at the Ghosts Who Talk', *Canberra Times*, 9 May 1995, p. 8

McKenzie, D. F., *Bibliography and the Sociology of Texts: The Panizzi Lectures 1985* (London: British Library, 1986)

McLaverty, James, 'The Concept of Authorial Intention in Textual Criticism', *Library*, 6th ser. 6 (1984), 121–38

'The Mode of Existence of Literary Works of Art: The Case of the *Dunciad Variorum*', *Studies in Bibliography*, 37 (1984), 82–105

McMullen, Roy, *Mona Lisa: The Picture and the Myth* (Boston: Houghton Mifflin, 1975)

Magor, Liz, 'An Artist's Thoughts on Conservation and Curatorial Issues', in *Shared Responsibility: Proceedings of a Seminar for Curators and Conservators*, ed. Barbara A. Ramsay-Jolicoeur and Ian N. M. Wainwright (Ottawa: National Gallery of Canada, 1990), pp. 6–11

Mahaffey, Vicki, 'Intentional Error: The Paradox of Editing Joyce's *Ulysses*', in *Representing Modernist Texts: Editing as Interpretation*, ed. George Bornstein (Ann Arbor: University of Michigan Press, 1991), pp. 171–91

Mailloux, Steven, *Interpretive Conventions: The Reader in the Study of American Fiction* (Ithaca: Cornell University Press, 1982)

Manne, Robert, *The Culture of Forgetting: Helen Demidenko and the Holocaust* (Melbourne: Text Publishing, 1996)

Manuth, Volker, 'Rembrandt and the Artist's Self Portrait: Tradition and Reception', in *Rembrandt by Himself*, ed. Christopher White and Quentin Buvelot (London: National Gallery and Royal Cabinet of Paintings Mauritshuis, 1999), pp. 38–57

Marquis-Kyle, Peter, and Meredith Walker, *The Illustrated Burra Charter: Making Good Decisions about the Care of Important Places* (1992; corrected edn Canberra: Australia ICOMOS, 1994)

Martens, Gunter, '(De)Constructing Texts by Editing: Reflections on the Receptional Significance of Textual Apparatuses', in *Contemporary German Editorial Theory*, ed. Hans Walter Gabler, George Bornstein and Gillian Borland Pierce (Ann Arbor: University of Michigan Press, 1995), pp. 125–51

'What Is a Text? Attempts at Defining a Central Concept in Editorial Theory', in *Contemporary German Editorial Theory*, ed. Hans Walter Gabler, George Bornstein and Gillian Borland Pierce (Ann Arbor: University of Michigan Press, 1995), pp. 209–31

Martin, Susan K., 'Introduction', in *The Recollections of Geoffry Hamlyn* by Henry Kingsley (Sydney: Angus and Robertson, 1993), pp. ix–xx

Mays, J. C. C., 'Reflections on Having Edited Coleridge's Poems', in *Romantic Revisions*, ed. Robert Brinkley and Keith Hanley (Cambridge: Cambridge University Press, 1992)

'Gabler's *Ulysses* as a Field of Force', *TEXT*, 10 (1997), 1–13

Meyer, Leonard B., 'Forgery and the Anthropology of Art', in *The Forger's Art: Forgery and the Philosophy of Art*, ed. Denis Dutton (Berkeley: University of California Press, 1983), pp. 77–92

Michalski, Stefan, 'Time's Effects on Paintings', in *Shared Responsibility: Proceedings of a Seminar for Curators and Conservators*, ed. Barbara A. Ramsay-Jolicoeur and Ian N. M. Wainwright (Ottawa: National Gallery of Canada, 1990), pp. 39–53

Modern Language Association, *Professional Standards and American Editions: A Response to Edmund Wilson* (New York: MLA, 1969)

Morris, William, [Letter to the editor, 10 March 1877], in *Selected Writings and Designs*, ed. Asa Briggs (Harmondsworth: Penguin, 1962), pp. 81–2

'Restoration' [Manifesto for the Society for the Protection of Ancient Buildings], *Athenaeum*, 2591 (23 June 1877), p. 807, reprinted in Stephan Tschudi-Madsen, *Restoration and Anti-restoration: A Study in English Restoration Philosophy* (Oslo: Universitetsforlaget, 1976), pp. 144–6

[Letter to the editor, 15 August 1890], in *Selected Writings and Designs*, ed. Asa Briggs (Harmondsworth: Penguin, 1962), p. 83

Mumford, Lewis, 'Emerson behind Barbed Wire' [Review of *The Journals and Miscellaneous Notebooks of Ralph Waldo Emerson*], *New York Review of Books*, 18 January 1968, pp. 3–5

Neville, Richard, with Allan Byrne, 'Facelift: Conserving Portraits at the State Library of NSW', in *The Articulate Surface: Dialogues on Paintings between Conservators, Curators and Art Historians*, ed. Sue-Anne Wallace (Canberra: Humanities Research Centre and National Gallery of Australia, 1996), pp. 231–40

Norton Anthology of Poetry, 4th edn, ed. Margaret Ferguson, Mary Jo Salter and Jon Stallworthy (New York: Norton, 1996)

Oxford Companion to Australian Literature, ed. William H. Wilde, Joy Hooton and Barry Andrews (Melbourne: Oxford University Press, 1985)

Palmer, Vance, 'Lawrence in Double Harness' [Review of *The Boy in the Bush*], *Triad* (Sydney), 1 December 1924, p. 36

'The Disintegration of D. H. Lawrence', *Independent* (Boston), 114 (11 April 1925), pp. 414–15

'Panurge', 'The Genius of D. H. Lawrence' [Review of *The Boy in the Bush*], *Liverpool Courier*, 30 April 1925, p. 4

Parent, Michael, 'Doctrine for the Conservation and Restoration of Monuments', in ICOMOS (International Council on Monuments and Sites), *Nessun futuro senza passata*, Acts of the 6th General Assembly (Rome: ICOMOS, 1981), pp. 37–70

Parker, Hershel, [Review of the Pennsylvania Edition of Theodore Dreiser's *Sister Carrie*], *Resources for American Literary Study*, 11 (1981), 332–6

Flawed Texts and Verbal Icons: Literary Authority in American Fiction (Evanston, Ill.: Northwestern University Press, 1984)

Partridge, Loren, Fabrizio Mancinelli and Gianluigi Colalucci, *Michelangelo: The Last Judgment: A Glorious Restoration*, tr. Lawrence Jenkens (New York: Harry N. Abrams, 2000)

Pater, Walter, 'The Marbles of Aegina', in *Greek Studies: A Series of Essays* (London: Macmillan, 1918), pp. 251–68

Pechter, Edward, 'Making Love to our Employment; Or, The Immateriality of Arguments about the Materiality of the Shakespearean Text', *Textual Practice*, 11 (1997), 51–67

Peirce, C. S., *Collected Papers of Charles Sanders Peirce*, ed. A. W. Burks, C. Hartshorne and P. Weiss., 8 vols. (Cambridge, Mass.: Harvard University Press, 1931–58)

Writings of Charles S. Peirce: A Chronological Edition, gen. ed. Max H. Fisch (Bloomington: Indiana University Press, 1982–)

Pevsner, Nikolaus, *Ruskin and Viollet-le-Duc: Englishness and Frenchness in the Appreciation of Gothic Architecture* (London: Thames and Hudson, 1969)

Foreword to Stephan Tschudi-Madsen, *Restoration and Anti-restoration: A Study in English Restoration Philosophy* (Oslo: Universitetsforlaget, 1976), pp. 7–8

Phillips, Ian, 'The Long Last Supper', *Sydney Morning Herald*, 30 August 1997, p. 15s col. 4, sourced from the *Guardian*

Pichler, Alois, 'Transcriptions, Texts and Interpretation', in *Culture and Value: Philosophy and the Cultural Sciences*, ed. K. Johannessen and T. Nordenstam (Kirchberg am Wechsel: The Austrian Ludwig Wittgenstein Society, 1995), pp. 690–5

Pizer, Donald, [Review of the Pennsylvania Edition of Theodore Dreiser's *Sister Carrie*], *American Literature*, 53 (1982), 731–7

'Self-censorship and Textual Editing', in *Textual Criticism and Literary Interpretation*, ed. Jerome J. McGann (Chicago: University of Chicago Press, 1985), pp. 144–61

Plachta, Bodo, 'In Between the "Royal Way" of Philology and "Occult Science": Some Remarks about German Discussion on Text Constitution in the Last Ten Years', *TEXT*, 12 (1999), 31–47

Plant, Margaret, 'Residual Connoisseurship and Formalism in Recent Art Writing: What Does the Articulate Surface Articulate?', in *The Articulate Surface: Dialogues on Paintings between Conservators, Curators and Art Historians*, ed. Sue-Anne Wallace (Canberra: Humanities Research Centre and National Gallery of Australia, 1996), pp. 19–30

Plumb, J. H., *The Death of the Past* (1969; London: Penguin, 1973)

Pratt, Mary Louise, *Imperial Eyes: Travel Writing and Transculturation* (London: Routledge, 1992)

Preziosi, Donald, 'Brain of the Earth's Body: Museums and the Framing of Modernity', in *The Rhetoric of the Frame: Essays on the Boundaries of the Artwork*, ed. Paul Duro (Cambridge: Cambridge University Press, 1996), pp. 96–110

Prøsch, Fredrik, *The Uthusprosjekt/Uthusprosjektet: Preservation of Wooden Build-ings in World Heritage Site Røros 1995–1999: Lessons Learned*, exhibition catalogue ([Seattle]: Uthusprosjekt and Center for Advanced Research Tech-nology in the Arts and Humanities, University of Washington, 1999)

Rainey, Lawrence, 'How Molly Bloom Got her Apostrophes', *London Review of Books*, 19 June 1997, pp. 12–14

Ramsay, Nigel, 'Forgery and the Rise of the London Scriveners' Company', in *Fakes and Frauds: Varieties of Deception in Print and Manuscript*, ed. Robin Myers and Michael Harris (Winchester: St Paul's Bibliographies, 1989), pp. 99–108

Randles, Sarah, 'Re-building the Middle Ages: Medievalism in Australian Archi-tecture', in *Medievalism and the Gothic in Australian Culture*, ed. Stephanie Trigg (Carlton, Vic.: Melbourne University Press, 2006), pp. 147–70

Renear, Allen, 'Out of Praxis: Three (Meta)theories of Textuality', in *Electronic Text: Investigations in Method and Theory*, ed. Kathryn Sutherland (Oxford: Clarendon Press, 1997), pp. 107–26

Richardson, Henry Handel, *Maurice Guest*, ed. Clive Probyn and Bruce Steele. The Academy Editions of Australian Literature (St Lucia: University of Queens-land Press, 1998)

   The Getting of Wisdom, ed. Clive Probyn and Bruce Steele. The Academy Editions of Australian Literature (St Lucia: University of Queensland Press, 2001)

Riddell, Joseph N., 'The Hermeneutical Self: Notes towards an "American" Prac-tice', in J. Riddell, *Purloined Letters: Originality and Repetition in American Literature*, ed. Mark Bauerlein (Baton Rouge: Louisiana State University Press, 1995), pp. 72–98

Riegl, Alois, 'The Modern Cult of Monuments: Its Character and its Origin' (1903), tr. Kurt W. Forster and Diane Ghirardo, *Oppositions: A Journal for Ideas and Criticism in Architecture*, 25 (fall 1982), 21–51

Riemer, Andrew, *The Demidenko Debate* (St Leonards, NSW: Allen and Unwin, 1996)

Rosenblum, Joseph, *Prince of Forgers* (New Castle, Del.: Oak Knoll, 1998), a translation of *Une Fabrique de faux autographes* by Henri Bordier and Emile Mabille (1870)

Ross, R. S., 'As Others See Us: Lawrence's Remarkable Book: All about Australia', *Daily Standard* (Brisbane), 14 July 1924, p. 1

Rossman, Charles, 'The New *Ulysses*: The Hidden Controversy', *New York Review of Books*, 8 December 1988, pp. 53–8

   'The Critical Reception of the "Gabler *Ulysses*": Or, Gabler's *Ulysses* Kidd-Napped', *Studies in the Novel*, 21 (1989), 154–81 (Part I); 22 (1990), 323–53 (Part II)

   'The "Gabler *Ulysses*": A Selectively Annotated Bibliography', *Studies in the Novel*, 22 (1990), 257–69

Rowell, Christopher, and John Martin Robinson, *Uppark Restored* (London: National Trust, 1996)

Runia, Epco, and Ariane van Suchtelen, *Rembrandt in the Mauritshuis* (Zwolle: Waanders, 2006)

Ruskin, John, 'The Lamp of Memory', in *Ruskin, The Seven Lamps of Architecture* (1849, 2nd edn 1880; London: Allen and Sons, 1910), pp. 320–60
'The Opening of the Crystal Palace Considered in Some of its Relations to the Prospects of Art', rpt. in Stephan Tschudi-Madsen, *Restoration and Anti-restoration: A Study in English Restoration Philosophy* (Oslo: Universitetsforlaget, 1976), pp. 110–19

Ruthven, K. K., 'Textuality and Textual Editing', *Meridian*, 4 (1985), 85–7

Said, Edward, *Orientalism: Western Conceptions of the Orient* (1978; London: Penguin, 1991)

Samuels, Raphael, *Theatres of Memory*: vol. 1 *Past and Present in Contemporary Culture* (London: Verso, 1994)

Sartre, Jean-Paul, *'What Is Literature?' and Other Essays* (1947; London: Routledge, 1988)

Saunders, David, and Ian Hunter, 'Lessons from the "Literary": How To Historicise Authorship', *Critical Inquiry*, 17 (1991), 479–509

Scheibe, Siegfried, 'On the Editorial Problem of the Text', in *Contemporary German Editorial Theory*, ed. Hans Walter Gabler, George Bornstein and Gillian Borland Pierce (Ann Arbor: University of Michigan Press, 1995), pp. 193–208
'Theoretical Problems of the Authorization and Constitution of Texts', in *Contemporary German Editorial Theory*, ed. Hans Walter Gabler, George Bornstein and Gillian Borland Pierce (Ann Arbor: University of Michigan Press, 1995), pp. 171–92

Scholes, Robert, *Protocols of Reading* (New Haven: Yale University Press, 1989)

Schwartz, Gary, 'Rembrandt in 1650: The Master and his Clones', unpubl. conf. paper at 'Rembrandt: A Genius and his Impact' conference, Melbourne, 1997
'After I Win the Game I'll Tell You What the Rules Were; or, A New Rembrandt from 1632', posted 8 October 2005 (revised version of a newspaper article published 1997), *The Schwartzlist*, www.garyschwartzarthistorian.nl, accessed 16 January 2007

Searle, Leroy, 'Peirce, Charles Sanders', in *The Johns Hopkins Guide to Literary Theory and Criticism*, ed. Michael Groden, Martin Kreiswirth and Imre Szeman, 2nd edn (Baltimore: Johns Hopkins University Press, 2005), pp. 722–6

Sell, John, 'The Effects of Uppark's Fire' [Letter to the Editor], *Country Life*, 5 April 1990, p. 167

Shakespeare, William, *The Complete Works*, ed. Stanley Wells and Gary Taylor (1986; compact edn Oxford: Oxford University Press, 1988)
The Complete King Lear 1608–1623, ed. Michael Warren (Berkeley: University of California Press, 1989)
The Three-Text Hamlet: Parallel Texts of the First and Second Quartos and First Folio, ed. Paul Bertram and Bernice W. Kliman (New York: AMS Press, 1991)
Hamlet, ed. Ann Thompson and Neil Taylor (London: Arden Shakespeare/Thomson Learning, 2006)

Shared Responsibility: Proceedings of a Seminar for Curators and Conservators, ed. Barbara A. Ramsay-Jolicoeur and Ian N. M. Wainwright (Ottawa: National Gallery of Canada, 1990)

Shattuck, Roger, and Douglas Alden, 'Searching for the True Text', *Times Literary Supplement*, 10–16 June 1988, pp. 640–1

Shillingsburg, Peter, 'The Meanings of a Scholarly Edition', *Bibliographical Society of Australia and New Zealand Bulletin*, 13 (1989), 41–50

'The Three *Moby-Dicks*', *American Literary History*, 2 (1990), 119–30

'The Autonomous Author, the Sociology of Texts and the Polemics of Textual Criticism', in *Editing in Australia*, ed. Paul Eggert (Canberra: English Department, University College ADFA, 1990), pp. 41–64. Rpt. in *Devils and Angels: Textual Editing and Literary Theory*, ed. Philip G. Cohen (Charlottesville: University Press of Virginia, 1991), pp. 22–43

'Text as Matter, Concept and Action', *Studies in Bibliography*, 44 (1991), 31–82

Resisting Texts: Authority and Submission in Constructions of Meaning (Ann Arbor: University of Michigan Press, 1997)

From Gutenberg to Google: Electronic Representations of Literary Texts (Cambridge: Cambridge University Press, 2006)

'On Being Textually Aware', *Studies in American Naturalism*, 1 (2006), 170–95

Smith, Barbara Herrnstein, 'Literature, as Performance, Fiction and Art', *Journal of Philosophy*, 67 (1970), 553–63

Smith, Brydon, 'Shared Responsibility: Welcome and Introduction', in *Shared Responsibility: Proceedings of a Seminar for Curators and Conservators*, ed. Barbara A. Ramsay-Jolicoeur and Ian N. M. Wainwright (Ottawa: National Gallery of Canada, 1990), pp. 1–5

Stallybrass, Peter, 'Love among the Ruins: Response to Pechter', *Textual Practice*, 11 (1997), 72–9

Steiner, George, *Heidegger*, 2nd edn (London: Fontana, 1992)

Stillinger, Jack, 'Textual Primitivism and the Editing of Wordsworth', *Studies in Romanticism*, 28 (1989), 3–28

Multiple Authorship and the Myth of Solitary Genius (New York: Oxford University Press, 1991)

Summerson, John, *Georgian London* (1945; 3rd edn Harmondsworth: Penguin, 1978)

Sutherland, Kathryn, 'Looking and Knowing: Textual Encounters of a Postponed Kind', in *Beyond the Book: Theory, Culture and the Politics of Cyberspace*, ed. Warren Chernaik, Marilyn Deegan and Andrew Gibson (Oxford: Office for Humanities Communication, 1996), pp. 11–22

Tanselle, G. Thomas, 'The Editorial Problem of Final Authorial Intention', *Studies in Bibliography*, 29 (1976), 167–211; rpt. in Tanselle, *Textual Criticism and Scholarly Editing* (Charlottesville: University Press of Virginia for the Bibliographical Society of the University of Virginia, 1990), pp. 27–71

'The Editing of Historical Documents', *Studies in Bibliography*, 31 (1978), 1–56; rpt. in Tanselle, *Textual Criticism and Scholarly Editing* (Charlottesville:

University Press of Virginia for the Bibliographical Society of the University of Virginia, 1990), pp. 218–73

A Rationale of Textual Criticism (Philadelphia: University of Pennsylvania Press, 1989)

'Editing without a Copy-Text', *Studies in Bibliography*, 47 (1994), 1–22; rpt. in Tanselle, *Literature and Artifacts* (Charlottesville: Bibliographical Society of the University of Virginia, 1998), pp. 236–57

Taylor, Gary, 'The Renaissance and the End of Editing', in *Palimpsest: Editorial Theory in the Humanities*, ed. George Bornstein and Ralph G. Williams (Ann Arbor: University of Michigan Press, 1993), pp. 121–50

T. B. C. [T. B. Clegg], 'Unclean Realism' [Review of *The Boy in the Bush*], *Bulletin* (Sydney), 13 November 1924, p. 3

Texte und Varianten: Probleme ihrer Edition und Interpretation, ed. Gunter Martens and Hans Zeller (Munich: C. H. Beck, 1971)

The Articulate Surface: Dialogues on Paintings between Conservators, Curators and Art Historians, ed. Sue-Anne Wallace (Canberra: Humanities Research Centre and National Gallery of Australia, 1996)

The Division of the Kingdoms: Shakespeare's Two Versions of King Lear, ed. Gary Taylor and Michael Warren (Oxford: Oxford University Press, 1983)

The Forger's Art: Forgery and the Philosophy of Art, ed. Denis Dutton (Berkeley: University of California Press, 1983)

The Literary Text in the Digital Age, ed. Richard J. Finneran (Ann Arbor: University of Michigan Press, 1996)

The New McCulloch's Encyclopedia of Australian Art, ed. Alan McCulloch, Susan McCulloch and Emily McCulloch Childs (Melbourne: Miegunyah Press, 2006)

The Painters of the Wagilag Sisters Story 1937–1997, ed. Wally Caruana and Nigel Lendon (Canberra: National Gallery of Australia, 1997)

The Post-Colonial Studies Reader, ed. Bill Ashcroft, Gareth Griffiths and Helen Tiffin (London: Routledge, 1995)

Thomas, Nicholas, *Entangled Objects: Exchange, Material Culture and Colonialism in the Pacific* (Cambridge, Mass.: Harvard University Press, 1991)

Thorpe, James, 'The Ideal of Textual Criticism', in *Principles of Textual Criticism* (1972; San Marino, Calif.: Huntington Library, 1985)

Trigg, Stephanie, 'Walking through Cathedrals: Scholars, Pilgrims and Medieval Tourists', *New Medieval Literatures*, 7 (2005), 9–33

Tschudi-Madsen, Stephan, *Restoration and Anti-restoration: A Study in English Restoration Philosophy* (Oslo: Universitetsforlaget, 1976)

van der Wetering, Ernst, 'The Rembrandt Research Project' [Letter], *Burlington Magazine*, 135, no. 1088 (November 1993), 764–5

'The Multiple Functions of Rembrandt's Self-Portraits', in *Rembrandt by Himself*, ed. Christopher White and Quentin Buvelot (London: National Gallery and Royal Cabinet of Paintings Mauritshuis, 1999), pp. 8–37

Viollet-le-Duc, Eugène-Emmanuel, *The Architectural Theory of Viollet-le-Duc: Readings and Commentary*, ed. M. F. Hearn (Boston: Massachusetts Institute of Technology, 1990)

Von Sonnenburg, Hubert, Walter Liedtke *et al.*, *Rembrandt/Not Rembrandt in the Metropolitan Museum of Art: Aspects of Connoisseurship*, 2 vols. (New York: Metropolitan Museum of Art, 1995)

Weber, Thérèse, 'Port Phillip Papers: The Australian Journal of Georgiana McCrae', PhD thesis, 2 vols. (University of New South Wales at ADFA, Canberra, 2001)

Wellek, René, and Austin Warren, 'The Mode of Existence of a Literary Work of Art', in *Theory of Literature* (London: Cape, 1966), pp. 142–57

Wells, Stanley, and Gary Taylor with John Jowett and William Montgomery, *William Shakespeare: A Textual Companion* (Oxford: Clarendon Press, 1987)

Werness, Hope B., 'Han van Meegeren *fecit*', in *The Forger's Art: Forgery and the Philosophy of Art*, ed. Denis Dutton (Berkeley: University of California Press, 1983), pp. 1–57

West III, James L. W., *A Sister Carrie Portfolio* (Charlottesville: University Press of Virginia, 1985)

'The *Sister Carrie* We've Come To Know', *Dreiser Studies*, 32 (fall 2001), 39–41

White, Hayden V., *The Content of the Form: Narrative Discourse and Historical Representation* (Baltimore: Johns Hopkins University Press, 1990)

Williams, William Proctor, and Craig S. Abbott, *An Introduction to Bibliographical and Textual Studies*, 2nd edn (New York: Modern Language Association, 1989)

Willison, Ian, 'Editorial Theory and Practice and the History of the Book', in *New Directions in Textual Studies*, ed. Dave Oliphant and Robin Bradford (Austin: Harry Ransom Humanities Research Center, University of Texas at Austin, 1990), pp. 110–25

Wilson, Edmund, 'The Fruits of the MLA: I. "Their Wedding Journey"', *New York Review of Books*, 26 September 1968, pp. 7–10; 'The Fruits of the MLA: II. Mark Twain', 10 October 1968, pp. 6–13. Reprinted, revised and with an addendum (pp. 194–202), as 'The Fruits of the MLA' in Wilson, *The Devils and Canon Barham* (London: Macmillan, 1973), pp. 154–202

Wimsatt, Jr., W. K., and Monroe C. Beardsley, 'The Intentional Fallacy', in Wimsatt and Beardsley, *The Verbal Icon: Studies in the Meaning of Poetry* (Lexington: University of Kentucky Press, 1954), pp. 3–18

Woolf, Virginia, [Letter to Clive Bell, 15 April 1908], in *The Flight of the Mind: The Letters of Virginia Woolf*, vol. I: *1888–1912*, ed. Nigel Nicolson (London: Hogarth Press, 1975), pp. 324–5

Orlando: A Biography (New York: Harcourt Brace, 1928)

Wright, Patrick, *On Living in an Old Country: The National Past in Contemporary Britain* (London: Verso, 1985)

Yeats, W. B., *Last Poems: Manuscript Materials*, ed. James Pethica. The Cornell Yeats (Ithaca: Cornell University Press, 1997)

Zeller, Hans, 'A New Approach to the Critical Constitution of Literary Texts', *Studies in Bibliography*, 28 (1975), 231–64

'Record and Interpretation: Analysis and Documentation as Goal and Method of Editing', in *Contemporary German Editorial Theory*, ed. Hans Walter Gabler, George Bornstein and Gillian Borland Pierce (Ann Arbor: University of Michigan Press, 1995), pp. 17–58

'Structure and Genesis in Editing: On German and Anglo-American Textual Criticism', in *Contemporary German Editorial Theory*, ed. Hans Walter Gabler, George Bornstein and Gillian Borland Pierce (Ann Arbor: University of Michigan Press, 1995), pp. 95–123

Index

Scholarly editions of works are listed as sub-entries under the original author of the work. Page numbers for illustrations are in *italics*.